𝔚orld's 𝔅est 𝔥istories

IRELAND

THE PEOPLE'S HISTORY
OF IRELAND

BY

JOHN F. FINERTY

Frederick

PRESIDENT OF THE UNITED IRISH LEAGUE OF AMERICA

Illustrated

IN TWO VOLUMES

VOLUME TWO

NEW YORK AND LONDON

THE CO-OPERATIVE PUBLICATION SOCIETY

Copyright 1904
By P. F. COLLIER & SON

HISTORY OF IRELAND

VOLUME TWO

CONTENTS

BOOK VIII

Contents

BOOK X

Contents

vii

BOOK XI

Contents

BOOK VIII

BEGINNING WITH THE STRUGGLE OF HENRY GRATTAN
AND HIS SUPPORTERS FOR THE INDEPENDENCE OF THE
IRISH PARLIAMENT, AND CONCLUDING WITH THE DE-
PARTURE OF THEOBALD WOLFE TONE, ORGANIZER OF
THE UNITED IRISH SOCIETY, FROM IRELAND TO AMERICA

CHAPTER I

The Struggle for Parliamentary Independence—Perpetual Mutiny Bill
—The Volunteer Convention—Declaration of Dungannon—
Grattan's Eloquence

SUCCESS, as is usual in such cases, served to embolden the Patriots. Poynings' Law, which compelled Ireland to submit the heads (provisions) of her bills to the English king and Privy Council before they could be acted on by the Irish Parliament, galled their pride. They also bitterly denounced the 6th of George I, which declared the dependency of the Irish on the English Parliament. Notices of a motion to repeal these enactments were placed by Grattan on the journal of the House of Commons. But he was resisted by the Castle party, and Flood, who, with some others, favored postponement, did not support him. Fitzgibbon, afterward Lord Clare, led the opposition to Grattan, and pointed out that there was already on record in the House a resolution which covered the points made by the latter. It was passed by the Irish Parliament of 1641 as a protest against Strafford's despotism. The House practically reaffirmed the resolution of '41, and thus Grattan was excluded from the privilege of carrying his own motion. But England received no comfort from his discomfiture—if such it was—because she recognized that the Irish Parliament, after recent victories, would not consent to be bound by English laws. The concluding portion of Grattan's speech, in moving that "the king's most excellent Majesty, and the Lords and Commons of Ireland are the only power competent to make laws to bind Ireland," affords a good illustration of his style of oratory. A few extracts from it will be at once instructive and interesting. He said: "And as anything less than liberty is inadequate to Ireland, so is it dangerous to Great Britain. We are too near the British nation, we are too conversant with her history, we are too much fired by her example, to be anything less than her equal; anything less, we should be her bitterest enemies—an enemy to that power which smote us with her mace, and to that constitution from whose blessings we are excluded: to be ground, as we have been, by the British nation, bound by her Parliament, plundered by her crown, threatened by her enemies, insulted with her protection, while we returned thanks for her condescension, is a system of meanness and misery which has expired in our determination, as I hope it has in her magnanimity. . . . Do not, then, tolerate a power—the power of the British Parliament over this land, which has no foundation in utility, or necessity, or empire, or the laws of England, or the laws of Ireland, or the laws of nature, or the laws of God—do not suffer it to have a duration in your mind. Do not tolerate that power which blasted you for a century, that power which shattered your loom, banished your manufactures, dishonored your peerage, and stopped the growth of your people; do not, I say, be bribed by an export of woolens, or an import of sugar, and permit that power which has thus withered the land to remain in your country and have an existence in your pusillanimity.

"I might, as a constituent, come to your bar and demand my liberty. I do call upon you, by the laws of the land and their violation, by the instruction of eighteen counties, by the arms, inspiration, and providence of the present moment, tell us the rule by which we shall go—assert the law of Ireland—declare the liberty of the land!"

But in that brilliant legislative assembly, even Grattan had a rival in picturesque eloquence. This was the Hon. Walter Hussey Burgh, who, although he held one of the highest judicial offices in the gift of the crown, rose in his place on the government bench and vehemently supported the policy of Grattan. He went further, and said: "It is not by temporary expedients, but by free trade [meaning free commerce] alone that this nation can be saved from impending ruin." This sentiment was adopted as an amendment to the address without a dissenting vote. Further along in his address this great orator exclaimed in a voice that made his hearers tremble with emotion, replying to a member who said Ireland was at peace: "The words penalty, punishment, and Ireland are synonymous—they are marked in blood on the margin of the English statutes, and, though time may have softened the calamities of the nation, the baneful and destructive influence of those laws [meaning the navigation laws which restricted Ireland's commerce with other nations] have borne her down to a state of Egyptian bondage. Talk not to me of peace! It is smothered war! England has sown her laws as dragons' teeth, and they have sprung up as armed men!"

This magnificent allusion to the rise and progress of the Irish volunteer movement is one of the finest passages in the oratory of ancient or modern times. He remained faithful to the cause of Irish independence throughout the remainder of the struggle and resigned the position of Prime Sergeant —the precursor of the Lord Chancellorship—so that he might be free to serve his country. He only survived a little more than a year the triumph of 1782, but attained the rank of Chief Baron of the Exchequer, under the Irish national régime. He died poor, and the Irish Parliament generously granted to his family, on the motion of the noble-hearted Henry Grattan, who almost wept while he was making it, a pension of £2,000 ($10,000) a year. Hussey Burgh was only forty-three years old when his brilliant career was ended by the unsparing hand of death. When he resigned his former office, Grattan said to him: "The gates of promotion are shut; the gates of glory are opened!" And Flood, when announcing his departure from this world, exclaimed: "He did not live to be ennobled by patent; he was ennobled by nature!"

The English ministers in this same year, with their customary fatuity, returned the Irish mutiny bill, which definitively limited the voting of supplies for the army from year to year, as in England since the Revolution of 1688, changed so as to make it perpetual. In spite of a most zealous opposition, the Castle party succeeded in having it carried, chiefly by the use of bribes among the "rotten borough" members of the House of Commons, who were generally for sale at a cash valuation, or else for office or title. It was this base conduct on their part that subsequently led Flood and other patriots to seek the reformation of this evil, by the abolition of the borough system. Following the example of Hussey Burgh, Flood had resigned his office under the crown, in the autumn of 1780, and entered eagerly into the battle for Irish independence in alliance with Henry Grattan. The latter, however, because of his courage, consistency, and, above all, his tongue of flame, was universally accepted as the leader of the Irish people. Unlike Flood, he was an ardent friend of Catholic emancipation and equality. He saw the folly of sectarian ascendency. "The question is now," said he, in

February, 1782, "whether we shall be a Protestant settlement or an Irish nation; whether we shall throw open the
gates of the temple of liberty to all our countrymen, or
whether we shall confine them in bondage by penal laws.
So long as the penal code remains, we can never be a great
nation. The penal code is the shell in which the Protestant
power has been hatched, and now it has become a bird, it
must burst the shell or perish in it. . . . Bigotry may survive persecution, but it never can survive toleration! . . . As
the mover of the Declaration of Rights, I would be ashamed
of giving freedom to but 600,000 of my fellow-countrymen,
when I could not extend it to two millions more!'"

The passage of the perpetual mutiny bill had the effect of
arousing the whole country to a full recognition of British
arrogance in regard to Ireland. When Parliament met, in
October, 1781, Grattan, Flood, and Yelverton, successively,
made vain attempts to have it repealed. A Catholic relief
bill, supported by the patriots named, but opposed by Flood
in the Commons and by Charlemont in the Lords, was also
beaten. On the national issue, however, Flood and Grattan
continued to act together. The convention of delegates
from the various volunteer corps was called to meet at Dungannon, County Tyrone, on February 15, 1782, and it was
held in the old Presbyterian Church, or meeting-house, of
that town—where stood the ruins of the ancient castle once
occupied by the brave O'Neills—on the appointed day. Two
hundred and forty-two delegates, the representatives of one
hundred and forty-three volunteer corps, mostly from the
province of Ulster, attended in full uniform. Previously
there had been a consultation at the country seat of Lord
Charlemont between that peer and Flood and Grattan.
They deliberated on the resolutions to be presented at the

Dungannon meeting-house, and agreed without dissent on the necessity for demanding the repeal of the Poynings Law, but Grattan had some difficulty in persuading his confrères to add a resolution favoring Catholic emancipation.

The principal resolutions, which embodied the pressing demands of Ireland at the period, were as follows:

"That a citizen by learning the use of arms does not abandon any of his civil rights.

"That a claim of any body of men other than the king, lords and commons of Ireland, to make the laws to bind this kingdom is unconstitutional, illegal, and a grievance.

"That—one voice dissenting—the powers exercised by the Privy Councils of both kingdoms, under, or under color or pretence of, the law of Poynings, are unconstitutional and a grievance.

"That the ports of Ireland are, by right, open to all foreign countries not at war with the king; and that any burden thereupon, or obstruction thereto, save only by the Parliament of Ireland, is unconstitutional, illegal, and a grievance.

"That—one voice only dissenting—a mutiny bill not limited in point of duration from session to session of Parliament, is unconstitutional and a grievance."

Then followed resolutions calling for the independency of the Irish judiciary; declaring the determination of the convention to seek the redress of the grievances complained of by all constitutional means; thanking the patriotic majority in the Irish Parliament for their exertions in the cause of Ireland and appointing a committee of four members from each Ulster county to act for the volunteers; and resolving that "as men and as Irishmen, as Christians and as Protestants, we rejoice in the relaxation of the penal code against our Roman Catholic fellow-subjects, and that we conceive the measure to be fraught with the happiest consequences to the union and prosperity of the inhabitants of Ireland."

There were only two voices against the resolution last quoted and another which preceded it, affirming that the convention held "the right of private judgment in matters of religion to be equally sacred to others as ourselves."

Before adjourning this memorable and illustrious convention adopted the following address to the patriot minorities in the Irish Houses of Lords and Commons:

"Lords and Gentlemen: We thank you for your noble and spirited, though hitherto ineffectual, efforts in defence of the great constitutional, as well as commercial, rights of your country. Go on! The almost unanimous voice of the people is with you, and, in a free country, the voice of the people must prevail. We know our duty to our sovereign, and are loyal. We know our duty to ourselves, and are resolved to be free. We seek for our rights, and no more than our rights; and, in so just a pursuit, we should doubt the being of a Providence if we doubted of success."

The foregoing was, in brief, Ireland's Declaration of Parliamentary Independence. Had it been adhered to, England would have been spared many a blot of shame on her escutcheon, and Ireland would have been one of the most prosperous among the smaller states of Europe.

The spirited action of the volunteers of Ulster was immediately supplemented by similar gatherings in the other three provinces. Connaught gathered under the presidency of Lord Clanricarde; Munster under that of Lord Kingsborough, and Leinster under Colonel Henry Flood. All the conventions passed resolutions in full accord with those adopted at Dungannon.

About this time, the Catholic Relief bills, introduced in

the Irish Commons by Mr. Luke Gardiner, were, after strenuous opposition by Fitzgibbon (afterward Lord Clare), Henry
Flood, and others; and after eloquent advocacy by Henry
Grattan, Hussey Burgh, and Yelverton, passed by Parliament. They were not broad in their scope, because their
author was afraid anything more radical might shock the
Protestant ascendency interest, and merely provided that
Catholics had equal privilege with Protestants in the purchase and disposition of lands; that the statutes against the
celebration of Mass and requiring the registration of priests
were repealed; that the law against the residence of bishops
and other clergy in Ireland was also repealed; that Catholic
teachers could instruct in schools and that Catholics could be
guardians of their own children, and of other children of
that faith.

The ridiculous and degrading statutes restricting Catholics from owning a horse over the value of five pounds;
mulcting them for robberies committed in their districts,
and forbidding residence in Limerick and Galway, were also
wiped out. Having gone so far in the way of reform, one
is surprised at finding this same Parliament defeating, by a
majority of eight votes, a bill permitting the marriage of
Protestants and Catholics! Flood, as usual, sided with the
bigots, while the noble-minded Grattan voted consistently
for every measure of Catholic relief.

CHAPTER II

Irish Independence Conceded by England—Grattan Addresses "a Free People"—Ireland's Reward to Her Patriot—Odious Acts Repealed

EDMUND BURKE, in a letter of great power, addressed to an Irish peer, bitterly reproaching Parliament for the paucity of rights extended to the Irish Catholics, who were taxed without representation and were still held subject to other burdens, said, "If a state should be so unhappy as to think it can not subsist without such a barbarous proscription, the persons so proscribed ought to be indemnified by the omission of a large part of their taxes, by an immunity from the offices of public burden, and by an exemption from being pressed into any military or naval service."

The time had come for the Irish Protestant minority to make lasting friends of the Catholic majority, and thus ensure the permanency of that parliamentary independence which both so much desired; but, unfortunately, the narrow prejudices of Flood in the Commons and of Charlemont in the Lords—both commanding a considerable following—prevented the passing of a radical emancipation bill, such as Grattan advocated, and to this fatal policy most of Ireland's subsequent misfortunes may be, with strict justice, attributed. The Catholics distrusted England, but they naturally felt bitter toward men who, while professing an ardent patriotism, would still keep their Catholic fellow-countrymen in penal bondage, as if they were of an inferior order of creation. This unfortunate condition of affairs paved the way for Catholic indifference at a later, and more

crucial period of Ireland's history, when, had Catholics
been permitted to sit in her Parliament, she would surely
have remained a nation.

Grattan made his first attempt to have passed an address to the king declaring the rights of Ireland toward
the end of February, but the corrupting influence of the
viceregal court overcame the spirit of the House of Commons, and his motion was defeated by a vote of 137 to 68.
Soon afterward followed the defeat of Lord North in England, and his retirement from public life. He was, to use
the language of Mitchel, "the worst Minister that England
ever had, whose obstinate perseverance in principles opposed to the theory of the British Constitution lost to England the noblest member of her great confederation. He
was obliged to relinquish, with disgrace, the post he had
held with dishonor."

The Irish Parliament, on motion of Grattan, was summoned to meet on Tuesday, April 16, to deliberate on the
question of Irish rights.

Lord Carlisle, who had been Lord North's principal agent
of corruption in Ireland, was recalled from the viceroyalty
by the administration of Lord Rockingham and Charles
James Fox; and Lord Portland was sent over in his stead.
He was well received by the Dubliners—especially by the
aristocratic and shop-keeping classes, who delighted in the
revels and patronage of the viceregal court.

The new Lord Lieutenant, pursuant to instructions from
the Rockingham ministry, sought to delay the progress of
the Irish nation toward constitutional liberty, but neither
Grattan nor Charlemont would halt in the march or recede
an inch from the Dungannon demand. Fox saw, at once,
that immediate concession was the only way out of the dif-

ficulty. He counseled the king to yield, and, on April 9, 1782, the following royal message was communicated to the English House of Commons:

"George R—His Majesty being concerned to find that discontent and jealousies are prevailing amongst his loyal subjects in Ireland upon matters of great weight and importance, earnestly recommends to this House to take the same into their most serious consideration, in order to such a final adjustment as may give mutual satisfaction to both kingdoms."

John Hely Hutchinson, principal Secretary of State for Ireland, made a similar communication to the Irish Parliament, and, in doing so, affirmed his own attachment to the principles put forth by the patriots.

When the 16th of April came, the Irish capital was ablaze with excitement, and its principal streets were lined by volunteer regiments, of varied uniforms, all in an excellent state of discipline, as became men who were commanded by general officers, many of whom had seen hard and bloody service on the Continent of Europe. Had the North Ministry remained in power, it would have still resisted the popular demand; an armed conflict would have been inevitable, and helpless as England was in that particular hour, the absolute independence of Ireland must have resulted from the struggle.

Grattan's motion, put before a crowded House of Commons, took the usual form of an amendment to the address; reiterated, practically, the demands of the Dungannon convention, and called for the repeal of Poynings' Law and the 6th of George I, which definitively declared the dependency of the Irish Parliament on that of England.

Grattan's speech in moving the amendment was superb.

The following passages from it are the very highest form of eloquence: "I am now to address a free people. Ages have passed away and this is the first moment in which you could be distinguished by that appellation. I have spoken on the subject of your liberty so often that I have nothing to add, and have only to admire by what Heaven-directed steps you have proceeded until the whole faculty of the nation is braced up to the act of her own deliverance. I found Ireland on her knees, I watched over her with a paternal solicitude; I have traced her progress from injuries to arms, and from arms to liberty. Spirit of Swift! spirit of Molyneux! your genius has prevailed! Ireland is now a nation! in that new character I hail her, and, bowing to her august presence, I say Esto perpetua!"

The address was carried without a dissenting voice in either House, and Parliament adjourned in order to give England sufficient time to swallow, with some degree of deliberation, the bitter pill presented to her by Ireland.

England took a month to decide. On May 17, Lord Shelburne in the Lords, and Mr. Fox in the Commons, having read to the respective bodies the address of the Irish Parliament, moved the repeal of the 6th of George I, entitled, "An act for the better securing the dependency of Ireland on the crown of Great Britain." The motions prevailed without much loss of time, and the fact was formally communicated to the Irish Houses by the Duke of Portland ten days afterward. As Poynings' Law was an Irish statute, it had to be repealed by the Irish Parliament, and this was accomplished on the motion of Mr. Yelverton, the House of Lords concurring. Thus was Ireland, at long run, freed from the British yoke, but there still lingered that ominous political cord umbilical, "the golden link of the crown," which was foreordained to finally develop into a mighty and almost unbreakable chain.

At this session of the Irish Houses, the perpetual mutiny bill was also repealed, and a law enacted by which it was supposed the appellate jurisdiction of the Irish House of Lords over the courts of Ireland was finally asserted—a supposition that was afterward found to be erroneous.

Henry Grattan, the real liberator of Ireland, was not a man of wealth. The Irish nation was grateful for the great services he had rendered, and resolved to purchase for him an estate. The original proposition fixed the sum at £100,000, but Grattan and his friends declined to accept more than half that amount, which was, accordingly, voted unanimously by the Irish Parliament. An offer made by the English Government, through Mr. Conolly, to place the Viceregal Lodge in the Phœnix Park at Grattan's disposal was politely, but peremptorily, declined. Ireland's greatest commoner could not afford to be under any compliment to the government of her rival.

CHAPTER III

Grattan and Flood Clash—England's Act of Renunciation—Parliamentary Reform—Second Dungannon Convention

ENGLAND, having given way to Ireland, because she could not help herself at the time, was filled with suppressed resentment against the nation that had outwitted her. An independent Irish Parliament meant a commercially unrestricted, and, therefore, a prosperous Ireland; and the English merchants and manufacturers of that period did not love to contemplate a progressive and prosperous Ireland any more than they do in our own day. It can be said, without stretching the truth, that of all classes of Englishmen, the mercantile class has always been the most hostile to the material interests of Ireland. We have already shown that, in the reign of William III, when the king himself was not desirous of crippling Irish industry, the English merchants forced him to destroy the Irish woolen trade because it competed with that of England! These are the cold, selfish acts that even more than warfare and physical persecution make bad blood permanent between peoples politically connected. Ireland had, finally, taught England a severe lesson. The worm had turned. From that moment all the resources of English statesmanship, and of the English treasury, were secretly directed toward the extinguishment of the Irish Parliament. The Irish triumph of May 17, 1782, begot the Irish catastrophe of January 1, 1801. The last day of the eighteenth century beheld her still a nation. The first sun of the nineteenth shone upon a province.

The condition of representation in the Irish Parliament was extremely bad. The Catholic four-fifths of the nation were utterly unrepresented in it, as we have shown; and of the 300 Protestant members only 72 were returned by the people—or such limited portion of the people as had the franchise; 123 were members for boroughs, which were the patronage of certain peers and others, mostly devoted to the English connection, in some form; and it is claimed by the historian Mitchel, as well as other chroniclers, that "fifty-three peers directly appointed these legislators [the borough members], and could also ensure by their influence the election of about ten others. Fifty commoners also nominated ninety-one members and controlled the election of four others. With such a condition of the 'popular' representa-

tion, the British ministry knew they could soon render it
manageable, and they only waited till their own foreign
troubles should be over to re-establish the supremacy 'where
[as they put it] nature has placed it.' "

Henry Flood, whatever his religious narrowness, was a
profound statesman, and saw much deeper into the English
character than did the franker and less suspicious Grattan;
and Flood took the ground that the renunciation by Ireland of England's claim to bind her by English laws was
not sufficient. England, herself, in order to make the matter eternally binding on both countries, should make a special act of renunciation. He was sustained in this view by
John Fitzgibbon and other able Irish lawyers, and they insisted that England should be called upon to pass such an
act. Grattan and his immediate followers, on the other
hand, would not accept the security of an English statute
covering Flood's proposition, and stood upon the theory that
Ireland had a charter of her own, which protected her independence as a distinct and separate nation connected with
the other kingdoms by an imperial crown. He professed
his belief in the good faith of England and lamented that
such a question had been raised in the Irish Parliament.
Grattan's voice prevailed in the latter body, but Flood had
convinced the volunteers that he was in the right and they
gave him their support. Thus opened the disastrous feud
between the two great Irishmen, which finally wrecked the
bright hopes of their unfortunate country. The Duke of
Portland, whose correspondence with Lord Shelburne exists, had already in his mind the carrying out of a legislative
union project, through the influencing of Parliament by
methods afterward found efficient for that purpose, and,
no doubt, the spectacle of Flood and Grattan eloquently

quibbling over the respective merits of "renunciation acts" and "simple repeal" gave him exceeding great joy. This joy was further intensified when the orators passed from argument to gross personality in speeches which, although of the highest order of forensic ability, reflect no credit on either orator. It is bad policy to stab your country by assailing the virtue of a defender of her rights—even if he is a rival leader. And this was the fault committed by both Flood and Grattan. Flood asked leave, on June 19, 1783, to bring in a Bill of Rights, but the Commons refused, influenced by Grattan, who, after withdrawing a stronger motion, declared that "the sole and exclusive right of legislation in the Irish Parliament in all cases, whether internally or externally, hath been already asserted by Ireland, and fully, finally, and irrevocably acknowledged by the British Parliament."

The Lawyers' Corps of the volunteers, siding with Flood, and considering that "repealing a declaration was not destroying a principle, and that a statute renouncing any preexisting right [in the British Parliament to bind Ireland] was an indispensable guarantee for future security," appointed a committee to make inquiry into the entire subject. This committee, after due deliberation, reported that they considered it necessary that "an express renunciation should accompany the repeal of the 6th of George I." Grattan's own corps of volunteers, of which he was colonel, presented him with an address in which the members urged him to support the policy of Flood. This offended him, for he was of a very sensitive nature, but he did not immediately resign his command, although he intimated that he expected the regiment to choose another colonel. He was, however, reelected and did not quit the command of the regiment until the October of 1784, when he supported the army budget in opposition to the wish of the volunteers. He was also addressed by other volunteer bodies, but no representation or argument could shape his opinion differently, and he adhered to his original position to the last. The Belfast volunteers, disgusted with his attitude, made overtures to Flood and received him into their ranks. The quarrel spread until the fate of that great military body, which had rescued Ireland from degrading provincialism, was already foreshadowed. But England brought about the solution of the problem in controversy toward the end of 1783, when an appealed Irish case was decided by Lord Mansfield in the English Court of King's Bench. This raised a storm in Ireland and gave force to the arguments of Flood. And so the English Parliament passed a renunciation act, by which it was decreed "that the exclusive rights of the Parliament and courts of Ireland in matters of legislation and judicature" were acknowledged, and that "no writ of error or appeal from any of the king's courts in Ireland could be received, heard, or adjusted in any of the king's courts in England." This seemed sufficiently conclusive, but there yet remained a deep doubt in many intelligent Irish minds regarding England's sincerity.

Reform of the Parliament now became the chief object of Henry Flood and his friends, and the volunteers, as an overwhelming majority, sided with them. Grattan, imbittered by his controversy with Flood, did not take kindly to this most necessary work, but the volunteers were not discouraged by his inaction. At Belfast, on June 9, 1783, delegates from thirty-eight corps met and passed a strong resolution, in which they demanded Parliamentary reform, as a measure for "checking venality, promoting public virtue,

and restoring the native spirit of the Constitution." Resolutions of the same purport were adopted by the volunteers throughout the island. On September 8, the new
movement gathered great force by the second Dungannon
convention, which was attended by five hundred volunteer
delegates. Among the distinguished men present were
Henry Flood and the Earl of Bristol, who was also the
Protestant Bishop of Derry. He was an Englishman by
birth, but a strong advocate of Irish independence. An
able man, his ability was marred by eccentricity and a love
of display that was truly Oriental. Nothing like the splendor of his equipage was ever seen in Ireland, up to that
time. His bodyguard was a troop of volunteer light
horse, magnificently uniformed and caparisoned, and their
commander, the bishop's Irish nephew, George Robert Fitzgerald, of Mayo, was the finest horseman, and subsequently
became the greatest ruffian, in Ireland. He terminated an
evil life by an ignominious death on the scaffold. But at
the period of which we are writing, he was a young man
not yet entirely contaminated by bad associations. Earl
Bristol conceived a violent affection for the cause of Irish
independence. He had no faith in the good intentions of
his English fellow-countrymen toward Ireland, and he became really a separatist in principle. He has been accused
of ambitious and generally unworthy motives, but all men
of extreme opinions have been so accused; mostly without
good reason. It is certain that had his advice been followed in 1783, Ireland would have been spared humiliation,
discrownment, and provincialism. One Bristol was worth
a hundred Charlemonts. Sir Jonah Barrington, in his "Rise
and Fall of the Irish Nation," presents a brilliant picture of
Bristol and also of the volunteers, of whom he had become

the hope and the idol. He says of the latter: "The regular forces paid them military honors; the Parliament repeatedly thanked them for supporting a constitution upon which their establishment had undoubtedly encroached. They were adored by the people, dreaded by the minister, honored by the king, and celebrated through Europe. . . . They had raised their country from slavery . . . and were loyal but determined to be free, and if their Parliament had been honest, Ireland would have kept her rank, and the nation preserved its tranquillity."

The second convention of Dungannon passed several resolutions favoring Parliamentary reform, and also resolved that a national convention be held in Dublin on November 10, to formulate a policy looking toward that object.

CHAPTER IV

The Rotunda Convention, 1783—Flood in the Ascendant—The Earl of Bristol—Treachery of Charlemont—Failure of Reform and Decline of Volunteer Movement

LORD TEMPLE succeeded the Duke of Portland as viceroy, but his régime was of brief duration, and is memorable only for the establishment of an order called "the Knights of St. Patrick," which came into existence March 17, 1784. It was an institution designed by the English ruler to turn the minds of Irishmen away from Parliamentary reform and other grave subjects. Lord Northington relieved Temple within a few months and dissolved Parliament. The general election did not materially change the personnel of the Commons, and the new body met in College Green on the same day that the national convention, having adjourned from the Royal Exchange, which was found too small, to the capacious Rotunda, began its proceedings. Dublin was crowded with spectators, and the volunteer uniforms were everywhere conspicuous.

The Bishop of Derry was the central figure of the occasion. He was a strong supporter of Flood, who, for the time, quite outshone Grattan as a popular leader. It is sad to have to confess that neither Grattan nor Charlemont came up to the expectations of Ireland while this fateful convention sat in the Rotunda. The design of the delegates was to make Earl Bristol permanent president of the convention, and this object the Earl of Charlemont, who was of a timid and distrustful nature, resolved to balk at any cost. He well knew that the courageous bishop would not hesitate for an instant, backed by the volunteers, to present an ultimatum to England which would inevitably provoke war and lead to the final separation of Ireland from Great Britain. Bristol, wearing an Irish mitre, conceived himself to be an Irishman by adoption, and, in fact, he proved himself to be more Irish than most of the Irish themselves. Thus did history repeat itself. Charlemont, who was still powerful, was elected president of the convention, and immediately fell in with the views of the alien executive at "the Castle." He departed from the path of exactitude and honor; prevaricated, manipulated, and trimmed, like any caucus politician. Above all, he was the narrow-minded enemy of the Catholics, and he and Flood absolutely neutralized the good words said for that persecuted class of Irishmen by the generous and liberal Earl of Bristol, who, Protestant prelate as he was, did all that in him lay to have the convention recognize the Catholic claims, as presented by Sir Patrick Bellew, in protest against a mean and cowardly surrender of Catholic right to representation made by the contemptible "Catholic" Earl of Kenmare, who, disgracefully for his creed, had many sympathizers in aristocratic and commercial circles. And these moral poltroons were ever a stumbling-block in the path of Catholic emancipation. Surely, "Christ never died" for such sycophants as they were.

The battle was now on between the Parliament and the convention. The former was controlled by placemen, and the latter, in a measure, by bigots. But the bigots were far less dangerous to the liberty of Ireland than the placemen, because, eventually, the Catholic majority could not fail to wrest their rights from the Protestant minority, and, as a choice of evils, religious ascendency is a trifle less odious than foreign domination. If many Irish Protestant leaders were bigots and tyrants, the Catholic Irish, like Byron's modern Greek, might console themselves by reflecting that

> "—Their tyrants, then,
> Were still, at least, their countrymen."

By the refusal of the convention to recognize the Catholics, it struck itself a death-blow. The sympathies of five-sixths of the Irish people were alienated from it, and when, after long deliberation, the reform bill, molded by the ripe experience of Flood, was presented by him as a member of the House of Commons, it was refused consideration by a vote of 77 for and 157 against. Grattan supported the measure, but not with his old-time vehemence, while Yelverton disgraced his record and gave notice of future desertion by hypocritically opposing it, although himself a volunteer, as "a bill introduced into Parliament on the point of a bayonet." The debate was marked by the grossest personalities. As if to put a finishing touch to the discomfiture of the volunteer convention, Yelverton moved and had carried a resolution which declared that "it has now become indispensably necessary that the House express its determination to maintain its just rights and privileges against all encroachments whatsoever."

When the news of the failure reached the convention hall, many of the members were absent, and there was an adjournment until the following Monday. But, on Sunday, a conference was held at Lord Charlemont's house, and there it was decided to advise the convention to accept the rebuff rather than come into open conflict with Parliament.

The convention reassembled on Monday, December 1, and a full delegation was present. Lord Charlemont peremptorily called Captain Moore to order, when that gentleman attempted to denounce the cavalier manner in which Parliament had treated the reform bill which had emanated from the convention. Then Henry Flood, in carefully worded sentences, related the action of the House of Commons and counseled a temperate course of action. Bristol, alone among the recognized leaders, was for resistance, but he was overruled by the weak hearts led by Charlemont. Flood moved a weak conciliatory address to the House of Commons, and the meeting adjourned until Tuesday morning. Charlemont had the indecency to proceed to the Rotunda before the hour fixed for meeting, accompanied by several of his partisans, and, after passing some unimportant resolutions, declared the convention adjourned sine die. He dreaded the influence of the Earl of Bristol, whose bold spirit was apt to communicate its fire to others, and descended to a caucus trick to baffle his policy. Verily some "noblemen" are made of a very inferior grade of clay.

The adjournment sounded the knell of the volunteers. They, for a time, continued to exist, rather than to act, and speedily lost their strength and influence. Flood, disgusted with the outcome, went over to England for a period. On his return he attempted to pass a new reform bill, but was unsuccessful, although it passed to a second reading. Grattan's support was not vigorous. Afterward Flood, supported by Napper Tandy, commander of the volunteer artillery, and some others, attempted to organize a national congress, but, with his old-time fatuity, again omitted the Catholics from consideration. This made the congress a failure. In the end, Flood, soured by defeat and foreseeing the doom of the Irish Parliament, retired from that body, settled in England, and became a member of the House of Commons in that country. He made no particular impression. When Grattan, who admired while he disliked him, heard of his comparative failure in England, he remarked in his figurative way: "He was an oak of the forest—too old to be transplanted at fifty!" Flood, in spite of his crass bigotry—the result of a narrow environment in his youth—was a good Irishman and loved his native country vehemently. As a statesman, he was ahead of Grattan, and, as an orator, was hardly his inferior. Had he possessed Grattan's tolerant spirit, he would have been the undisputed Irish leader of the era in which he lived. He died in the city of Kilkenny in 1791—happily, for him, before the "union" was accomplished—and bequeathed most of his private fortune to Trinity College, Dublin, "to enrich its MS. library and to found a permanent professorship of the Irish [Gaelic] language." McGee considers it doubtful whether he and Grattan ever became reconciled, but avers that the latter, who survived until 1820, when he felt his end approaching, said he wished it to be known that he "did not speak the vile abuse of Flood reported in the debates"—referring particu-

larly to the powerful philippic of 1783.   Ireland, while
lamenting Flood's unfortunate shortcomings, the result not
of natural harshness, but of miseducation, remembers his
services with gratitude.

The Earl of Bristol, after the dissolution of the Rotunda
Convention, attempted to reanimate the volunteers, and, replying to an address presented by the Bill of Rights Battalion, concluded by saying: "Tyranny is not government,
and allegiance is due only to protection!"   Fitzgibbon counseled the government to prosecute the bold bishop for this
"incendiary" language, but the viceroy and minister thought
it might be playing with fire and took no action.   The spirit
of the volunteers was now declining.   They were no longer
the men of 1782, who had labeled their cannon with the sig-
nificant demand: "Free Trade [commerce] or else—!"
When the Irish Parliament, now preparing to dig its own
grave, increased the regular army establishment to 15,000
men, Grattan weakly concurring; and when Luke Gardiner,
in 1785, introduced and had passed a bill for the clothing
of a militia force—for which there was no necessity—the
volunteers accepted these hostile measures as a virtual notice of disbandment, and, although some corps still continued to muster, made little or no sign of resistance.   Their
aristocratic officers had deserted them, and Grattan, fatally
for Ireland, no longer identified himself with their policy.
The Earl of Bristol, finding himself virtually unsupported,
abandoned the struggle in disgust and disappeared forever
from the stormy arena of Irish politics.

CHAPTER V

Anglo-Irish Commercial Propositions—John Philpot Curran, Orator
and Wit—Insanity of George III—The Regency Question
—Ireland Offends Pitt

THE period from 1784 to 1793 was chiefly consumed in
financial and general economic debate with England.
The latter, following out her traditional policy, wished
to sound Ireland's intentions in regard to commercial
relations between the two countries, and also with regard to the proportion and distribution of the public
revenues.   On the part of the English interest, represented by the Castle government, Chief Secretary Orde,
subsequently Lord Bolton, laid before Parliament eleven
propositions, which were supposed to provide for all con-
tingencies of commerce and taxation.   They were adopted
in the shape of resolutions, after having been modified by a
leading merchant of Dublin, Joshua Pim—a Quaker and a
patriot.   In this form they were transmitted to the English
Houses, and received the approbation of the younger Pitt,
then Chancellor of the Exchequer.   Subsequently he increased the propositions to twenty, and the added provisions sought to bind Ireland to acquiesce in any marine
measures passed by the English Parliament; would limit her
right of import and export, and, in the interest of the East
India Company, would debar her from trading with any
of the countries beyond the Cape of Good Hope to the
Straits of Magellan.   Thus England attempted to undo the
work of the volunteers, who were now virtually disorgan-
ized and, consequently, helpless.   But the Irish Parliament
received the additional proposals of Pitt so coldly that the

government feared a defeat and withdrew them. Some writers have held that their adoption would have saved the Irish Parliament from subsequent destruction. No attempt was again made by either Parliament to renew them. William Pitt did not forget the incident, and, from that hour, in his inmost heart, doomed the Irish Legislature to extinction.

An earnest attempt was made by the patriots in the succeeding session of Parliament to reduce the pension list, and among the foremost of the reformers was the celebrated orator and lawyer, John Philpot Curran, who had entered the Commons in 1783. He was of small stature, insignificant appearance, extremely ugly, and a sloven, but he had a soul of flame, and his speeches, particularly as an advocate in defence, are among the classics of the English tongue. An intense patriot, he was devoted to the national cause. During the debate on the pension bill he came in conflict with John Fitzgibbon, who had become a virulent Castle partisan, and both indulged in language eloquently vituperative. Fitzgibbon, a professional browbeater, could not browbeat the ugly little counselor, and a duel was finally resorted to. They met and exchanged three shots each, but neither happened to be hit, which caused amusement to the seconds and spectators. The courage of both men was undoubted. In after years, Curran fought a pistol duel with the famous "Bully Egan," a Dublin "character." Egan was a much larger man than his opponent, and Curran's friends remarked upon the fact. "Never mind," replied the wit. "Just chalk off my size on his carcass, and if I should hit him outside the mark, the shot will not count."

An attempt to reform the Protestant charter schools, and establish a better system of national education, failed, in

1787, although the resolutions favoring such action, introduced by Chief Secretary Orde, were adopted. Grattan's brave attempt at having the tithe system—that is, the paying of tribute in money or produce to the clergy of the Established Church—reformed also failed, although the evil was notoriously productive of sanguinary riots and general disorder in the poorer districts of the island. The great orator made a second attempt with equal ill-success, although his speeches on both occasions were altogether worthy of his early reputation. Had he gone heartily with Flood for Parliamentary reform, in 1783, he would not have been subjected to this mortification.

George III became temporarily insane in 1788, and this event brought up at once the question of a regency. George, Prince of Wales—afterward the notorious George IV—had the undisputed title to assume the duties of Regent, but there was a question as to whether his powers should be limited or not. Reduced to small compass, the problem to be solved was whether the prince should rule with as full authority as if the king were really dead, or whether he should be, in some measure, restricted. The Pitt party in England were for restriction, while the party led by Fox advocated giving Wales full regal privileges. Ireland sided with the party of Fox. Pitt's idea prevailed in England, but the Irish Parliament, somewhat too effusively, offered the Prince Regent the crown of Ireland as de facto sovereign. The Marquis of Buckingham, who was then viceroy, refused to forward the address of the Irish Houses, which greatly incensed both Lords and Commons. A joint deputation was appointed to convey the address to the Regent. When the delegates reached London, they were chagrined at learning that George III had regained his senses, such as they were, and was attending to business as usual. The prince, however, received the Irish Lords and Commoners cordially at Carlton House, "wined and dined" them, paid them sweet compliments, and seemed to be their very good friend. But he had, in reality, a false nature and a hollow heart, as he proved in his dealings with Irish matters when he finally became king. Pitt, indignant that his example should be set at naught, never forgave the Irish Parliament, and, no doubt, also prejudiced George III still more against that body. George III was a tyrant, but, at least, he meant to be honest. George, Prince of Wales, was also a tyrant, but he could not be honest if he tried. And the Irish members were very foolish to estrange the powerful Pitt in order that they might minister to the vanity of the worthless prince.

Grattan, during the interregnum, had brought in several reform bills, covering supplies, police, pensions, and elections; and seemed in a fair way toward having them passed when the restoration of the old king to such reason as he originally possessed nipped the prospective legislative blossoms in the bud. Parliament passed a vote of censure on the viceroy for having failed to transmit its message to the Prince of Wales, and the Castle faction, representing Pitt, and hounded on by Fitzgibbon, and other professional bullies, resolved to punish all who had voted censure, and who held offices of honor, trust, or emolument from the crown. In vain did a "Round Robin," signed by eighteen peers, headed by the Duke of Leinster and the Archbishop of Tuam, together with most of the leading commoners of Ireland, issue in strong protest against such an insulting attack on the independence of Parliament. Leinster himself was dismissed from the honorary office of Master of the Rolls, the Earl of Shannon from the vice-treasurership, and so on. About a dozen prominent members of the House of Commons lost place and pension through their unnecessary interference in a purely English quarrel—thus illustrating the wisdom of every nation attending stringently to its own business. John Fitzgibbon, who had been attorney-general for some time, was promoted to the Lord Chancellorship on the death of Lord Lifford, which occurred soon after the Castle took its revenge on the Regent's quixotic champions. He was destined, together with another anti-Irish Irishman, as yet unknown to infamy, to be the main instrument in destroying the independence of his country. The peers who had adhered to Pitt's policy were elevated in rank, and the Commons of the same class were variously promoted to peerages, or to judgeships, or other offices and "honors" which made them a power for evil in the land. It was the beginning of the end of Irish political liberty. Fitzgibbon was the great wire-puller, by whose manipulation all the traitor puppets danced. Grattan, always epigrammatic, if not always wise or practical, summed up the new situation by exclaiming in the Commons: "In a free country the path of public treachery leads to the block; but in a nation governed like a province, to the helm!" Unhappy man, with all his noble gifts and pure intention, his own irresolution, or jealousy, in 1783, had done most to produce this disastrous result!

The persecuted Regentites, if so we may term them, formed themselves into the Whig Club, in imitation of a similar body in England, and took considerable part in Irish politics so long as Ireland remained even nominally independent. But the popular indignation against the corrupt and corrupting Marquis of Buckingham became so strong that

Pitt was forced to recall him.   He left Ireland, almost like a hunted felon, under cover of darkness.   But he left behind him the hot sting of his corruption, to still further fester and make putrid the body politic of "the most unfortunate of nations."   The new Lord Chancellor and Speaker Foster were sworn in as Lords Justices, to await the coming of a new Lord Lieutenant from England.

We must here make a reference to the Duke of Rutland, who had preceded Buckingham in the government of Ireland, and whose rather uneventful reign had lasted three years.   He was young, handsome, and dissipated, and had an equally young, handsome, and dissipated wife.   His life was a short and eminently merry one, and, after more than a century has elapsed, his orgies are still remembered in Dublin—the account of them having been handed down from sire to son.   Rutland drank like a fish, and, while intoxicated, was capable of the most outlandish actions.   He is commemorated, although anachronistically, by Lever, in "Jack Hinton," as the viceroy who forgot to dismiss his hussar escort, and who knighted Corney Delaney, while he hobnobbed with Mr. and Mrs. Paul Rooney.   He was very popular with the convivial and easy-going Dubliners; but, although eminently liberal and good-natured, was too much of a rake not to be a demoralizer.   His foolish example paved the way for the moral and financial ruin of many a thoughtless Irish lord and squire.   His Dublin admirers wept at the news of his early death, for, among the aristocratic and mercantile classes, he was the most popular Lord Lieutenant who had ruled in Ireland since the days of Chesterfield.   He, undoubtedly, by his bad example, in which he had a cordial ally in his consort, undermined public virtue in the Irish capital, and thus rendered the task of conquest by bribery easier for the enemies of Irish independence. All the viceroys mentioned, as well as their successors down to 1800, with one honorable exception, did all that in them lay to prevent a reform of the Irish Parliament. Reform meant the abolition of rotten boroughs and the exclusion of placemen from Parliament. Had it carried, the legislative union could never have been accomplished, because Ireland's honestly elected representatives would have remained faithful to their trust.

CHAPTER VI

Famous Men Enter Irish Parliament—Wellington One of Them; Lord Castlereagh Another—Catholic and Protestant Reformers—Services of Irish Emigrants in the American War for Independence

THE Earl of Westmoreland, succeeding Lord Buckingham, landed in Dublin in January, 1790. Parliament was immediately dissolved and a new election ordered. Many of the old members were re-elected; Grattan, Curran, Ponsonby, and Lord Henry Fitzgerald being among them, while among the new members appeared Arthur Wellesley, for Trim—afterward the famous Duke of Wellington; Lord Edward Fitzgerald, for Athy; Arthur O'Connor, afterward an Irish revolutionist and French general; Sir Jonah Barrington, the noted writer, and Robert Stewart, subsequently Lord Castlereagh, then a vehement "reformer," but destined to become the virtual extinguisher of the independence of his country. The sessions of 1790-91 were barren of great results. Prosperity had come to the country with a free commerce, and a prosperous people rarely take pleasure in political agitation and are generally adverse to any radical change in legislation or government. Men's minds were, of course, more or less excited by the startling events of the French Revolution, and "French principles," as they were called in reproach by the conservatives, began to be well understood in Ireland, and particularly in the northern province.

Another factor in the formation of public opinion was that section of the Catholic population which had grown wealthy, either as landowners or merchants, since the mitigation of the penal laws, in the matter of property and commerce. A Catholic committee, composed of such men, was formed in 1790. The recognized leader was John Keogh, a rich business man, and his foremost lieutenants were, at the outset, Richard McCormick and Edward Byrne, also men of social and commercial prominence. Among the ardent Protestant sympathizers with these Catholic reformers were Lord Edward Fitzgerald, brother of the Duke of Leinster, who had served as an officer in the British army; Theobald Wolfe Tone, a native of Dublin and by profession a barrister; and Sir Simon Bellew, a representative of one of the ancient and wealthy Anglo-Irish families. These gentlemen were as ardent opponents of Catholic disabilities as if they had been Catholics themselves. Henry Grattan, faithful to his liberal principles, was their eloquent champion in Parliament; and in this same connection of Catholic sympathizers we first hear of Thomas A. Emmet, a rising lawyer, and elder brother of another Emmet foredoomed to immortality as an Irish martyr to liberty.

Many serious agrarian disturbances, mainly confined to Ulster, occurred at this period, and were chiefly a result of Protestant landlords accepting Catholic tenants in lieu of Dissenters who had emigrated by whole parishes to the American colonies, to escape the harsh exactions of the rapacious owners of the soil. The remaining "loyal" Protestants objected to the settlement of Catholics among them, and organized to drive them out.   Bloody combats ensued between the Peep o' Day Boys, composed of Church of England peasants, for the most part; and the Defenders, who were Catholic peasants, inflamed to ferocity by persecution. Mutual atrocities were committed, greatly to the detriment of Ireland's happiness at home and her good name abroad. Nor did that generation see the last of such disorders.   They were continued under other names, for long and bitter years, and are not wholly unknown in Ulster even now.

The Irish Presbyterians and Catholics who had emigrated to the American colonies, by the myriad in the case of the former, and by the thousand in that of the latter, bore a brave and conspicuous part in the American Revolution on the side of the patriots.   Many of the officers and rank and file of Washington's army were natives of Ireland, and a still larger number were sons of Irish immigrants.   This was particularly true of the celebrated regiments known as the Pennsylvania and Maryland Line.   They also came numerously from the New England colonies, from Virginia, and the Carolinas.   The presence of many Irish soldiers in the American ranks at Bunker Hill is attested by the fact, unearthed by the American-Irish Historical Society of Boston recently, that over two hundred men of the battalions that fought under Prescott and Stark bore the Christian name of "Patrick," and Patrick is an almost distinctively Irish Catholic designation.

Among the Protestant—generally Presbyterian—Irish, or Irish-Americans, who distinguished themselves on the patriot side during that long war may be mentioned Major-General Richard Montgomery, killed at Quebec, on the last day of 1775; General James Armstrong, General James Butler, General James Clinton, General William Davidson, General Edward Hand, General William Irvine, General Henry Knox, commander of Washington's artillery; General William Maxwell, General Andrew Pickens, General Andrew Porter, General John Stewart, General John Sullivan, General William Thompson, and General Anthony Wayne. Of Catholic Irish, or Irish-Americans, may be mentioned General Stephen Moylan, the dashing commander of the American cavalry; Colonel John Fitzgerald, Washington's aide-de-camp; Commodore John Barry, called "the Father of the American Navy," and Captain Jeremiah O'Brien, who won the first sea fight over England in Machias Bay.* This battle is known in American annals as "The Concord of the Seas." But this list, numerous as it is, does not by any means cover the number of Irish-Americans who distinguished themselves in the Revolutionary War. American historians have commented on the fact that the Irish Parliament, at the beginning, almost, of the struggle, voted 4,000 men to aid British aggression against the colonies. It must be borne in mind, as we have elsewhere remarked, that the Irish Parliament was not then a free agent, and merely followed the commands of England. Neither should it be forgotten that five-sixths of the Irish people, namely, the Catholics, had neither vote nor voice in that Parliament, and that many of the Protestant minority—notably the illustrious Grattan—voted against sending troops to coerce the Americans. In his terrible philippic against Flood in the Irish House of Commons, October 28, 1783, Grattan said: "With regard to the liberties of America, which are inseparable from ours, I will suppose this gentleman [Flood] to have been an enemy decided and unreserved; that he voted

---

* Some recent authorities claim that O'Brien was a Protestant.

against her liberty, and voted, moreover, for an address to send 4,000 Irish troops to cut the throats of Americans; that he called these butchers 'armed negotiators,' and stood with a metaphor in his mouth and a bribe in his pocket, a champion against the rights of America, the only hope of Ireland, and the only refuge of the liberties of mankind."

Nor were the services of Irish-Americans to the patriot cause exclusively military or naval. Among those who served America in civil capacities during that momentous period, we should remember the names of Charles Carroll, of Carrollton, one of the signers of the Declaration of Independence; Matthew Thornton and Thomas Lynch, who also signed that immortal document, together with several other gentlemen of Irish descent; Charles H. Thompson, a native of Derry, who was Secretary to the Continental Congress, and read the Declaration to the people from the steps of Independence Hall at Philadelphia; Governor James Sullivan, brother of the general, already mentioned; Governor Thomas Ford, Robert and William Patterson, Samuel Meredith, Right Rev. John Carroll, Catholic Bishop of Maryland — the first Catholic prelate consecrated in the United States; George Read, Edward Rutledge, and the long array of the membership of the Friendly Sons of St. Patrick, who so greatly aided the starving and shivering army of the American Fabius while he held the lines of Valley Forge, during the terrible winter of 1777-78. We may add, in this connection, that Washington was the only non-Irishman ever elected a member of the Friendly Sons, whose constitution demanded that all members should be of Irish birth or lineage. Washington could not claim this distinction. Therefore, the Friendly Sons suspended their constitution and made him "an adopted Irishman!" This measure settled the difficulty and the Father of his Country was admitted to membership, which he gracefully accepted, and retained until his death.

There can be no historical doubt that the great Irish immigration of the eighteenth century had much to do with the success of the American Revolution. The Presbyterians, who formed a majority of the immigrants of that day, were of a republican turn of mind, and hated England intensely because of her ingratitude for the services their forefathers rendered her at Derry and the Boyne, and, above all, because of her bad land laws and tyrannical industrial and commercial restrictions, which, they clearly saw, she intended practicing upon the colonies, when her Parliament passed laws which sought to prohibit American manufactures, lest they might conflict with the English colonial trade. Grattan predicted the inevitable result, when, speaking on the commercial restrictions in the Irish Parliament, he uttered the memorable prophecy, already quoted, about Irish resentment, banished across the seas, meeting English interests in America and battling against them. England's senseless attacks on American industry were really begun in Ireland, when she interfered with the woolen trade, and drove thousands on thousands of Irish settlers to the colonies.

CHAPTER VII

The "Place Bill"—Ulterior Results Thereof—The Catholics Bestir Themselves for Reform—Call on the King—Relief Promised and Given, After a Fashion—United Irish Society Founded

DURING the Westmoreland administration Grattan and his friends of the opposition brought in a bill to vacate the seats of members accepting offices under the government, and, strange to say, this was acquiesced in by the

Castle. Sir Jonah Barrington points out that the phrase "bona-fide offices" was omitted from the bill, "thereby leaving the minister the power of packing the Parliament," and the only opponents of its passage were Sir Jonah himself, Mr. Newenham, and Sir John McCartny. Barrington greatly admired Grattan, yet said of him, in discussing his support of the Place bill: "On this occasion, the ministers were too subtle for him, and he heeded not that fatal clause which made no distinction between real and nominal offices. . . . As the House was then constituted, the minister might almost form the Commons at his pleasure." The danger alluded to by Barrington was that any corrupt, but cowardly, member might accept a nominal office—akin to the Chiltern Hundreds in England, the acceptance of which enables a member of the Commons to resign—and thus vacate his seat, so that an open supporter of ministerial measures might be appointed by the patron, not chosen by the people, in his stead. And his fears were duly justified, for he says, in his "Rise and Fall": "The fatal operation of the Place bill can be no longer questionable. In one word—it carried the Union!"

Meanwhile, the Catholics continued to agitate for the removal of their grievances, but found a vast deal of timidity among the aristocratic leaders of their creed, who dreaded a union with the Protestant democracy, represented by such men as Wolfe Tone, because of their hatred and distrust of "French principles." Accordingly, John Keogh and his associates were disgusted, but not wholly surprised, when the slavish Lord Kenmore and sixty-seven other members, mainly of his class, withdrew from the Catholic committee. This made a final breach between the Catholic aristocrats and the Catholic democracy of that era, and unquestionably hastened the formation of that formidable organization of earnest patriots of all creeds known as the United Irishmen.

In 1792, a deputation, consisting of twelve members of the Catholic committee, proceeded with a memorial, explaining the claims of the Catholics to equality before the law, to the Castle, and were refused a hearing by the Chief Secretary. This churlishness angered the Catholic democrats, and Keogh, Byrne, and other chiefs determined on bolder measures. The first-named gentleman proceeded to London, and was there received and befriended by the illustrious Edmund Burke, who introduced him to Mr. Dundas, a leading member of the cabinet. He had some difficulty in convincing this gentleman of the necessity of granting further rights and privileges to the Irish Catholics. Mr. Keogh was not to be discouraged, and, after laboring for three months, succeeded in obtaining from the minister several important concessions, covering the magistracy, the grand juries, the sheriffs of counties, and admission to the bar. He then left for Ireland, accompanied by Richard Burke, son of the great orator, who was to act for the Catholics in Dublin. A great meeting, presided over by Byrne, marked Mr. Keogh's return from England. Dublin was wildly enthusiastic, and then it was decided that a national convention should be called to assemble in the capital immediately. In spite of opposition from many quarters, the convention met, as called, in January, 1793, and was attended by over 200 delegates. Many of the leading Catholics of the country attended, including Sir Patrick Bellew and Sir Thomas Ffrench, both of whom took strong ground in favor of demanding absolute emancipation. In this position they were ably supported by the democratic leaders, and their policy, after a debate of two days' duration, finally prevailed. A deputation, consisting of Ffrench, Bellew, Keogh, McDermott, Teeling, Devereux, and the Chairman and Secretary, was appointed to proceed to London and place the ultimatum of the Catholics of Ireland in the hands of King George. They went by way of Belfast, where they were enthusiastically received—the Presbyterians, outdoing even the Catholics in marks of approbation, unyoked the horses and drew Mr. Keogh's carriage in triumph through the streets. Belfast was then the very centre and hotbed of "French principles"—that is, republicanism—and so remained until after the unhappy outcome of the gallant but ill-ordered insurrection which broke out five years later.

The king received the Catholic deputation, as we are told, "very graciously," and the members were presented to him by the Home Secretary and Mr. Burke. The memorial was left with the monarch, who promised that the matter should receive attention in the next speech from the throne, at the meeting of Parliament. The result was that the delegates, on their return, were received by the viceroy, who was very plausible. The Chief Secretary soon afterward introduced in Parliament a modified bill, falling far short of public expectation. It received the support of a majority of the Patriot party, including Grattan, Curran, Ponsonby, and Hely Hutchinson; but it is regrettable to find on record that it was opposed by Speaker Foster and the Hon. George Ogle—supplemented by bigots who were not patriots—in the Commons; and that the Lord Chancellor, Fitzgibbon, the son of an apostate Catholic, made it an occasion for a virulent attack on his Catholic fellow-countrymen in the House of Peers. It was also fought there by a majority of the lords spiritual. However, the bill became a law. One of its most important provisions was the restoration of the franchise to the Catholic "forty-shilling freeholders"—men who had a life lease, and whose farms produced at least forty shillings' profit above the rent to be paid the landlords. There was a large number of such freeholders, and, of course, it gave the humbler class of Catholics more political power than they had possessed since the days of James II.

Wolfe Tone, who, although a Protestant, had been chosen secretary of the Catholic committee after Richard Burke's return to England, would seem to have been much pleased with the provisions of the bill, which, in his memoirs, he thus summarizes: "By one comprehensive clause all penalties, forfeitures, disabilities, and incapacities are removed; the property of Catholics is completely discharged from the restrictions and limitations of the penal laws, and their liberty is in a great measure restored by the right of elective franchise, so long withheld, so ardently pursued. The right of self-defence is established by the restoration of the privilege to carry arms, with a few reasonable restrictions. The unjust and unreasonable distinctions affecting Catholics as to service on grand and petty juries are done away with; the army and navy and all other offices and places of trust are opened to them, subject to restrictions hereafter to be mentioned. Catholics may be Masters, or Fellows, of any college hereafter to be founded, subject to two conditions: that the college be a member of the university, and that it be not founded for the education of Catholics exclusively. They may be members of any lay body corporate, except Trinity College . . . and they may obtain degrees in the University of Dublin. These, and some lesser immunities and privileges, constitute the grant of the bill." But the Catholics were still excluded from sitting in Parliament, and, although admitted to the bar, were refused the honors of the bench. Neither could any Catholic reach to a higher rank than that of line officer in the military establishment. And Catholics were, furthermore, excluded from the offices of Lord Lieutenant, Lord Deputy, and Lord Chancellor. Many other degrading restrictions were allowed to remain on the statute books for more than a generation thereafter, and, even yet, the office of Lord Lieutenant of Ireland can not be held by a Catholic.

The Catholic convention, which had led to partial emancipation, so alarmed "the Castle" that it called upon the Irish Parliament to pass a "Convention Act," which would prevent such assemblages in the future, and that tyrannical measure was enacted accordingly. It was, likewise, alarmed at a sort of revival of the volunteers, under the guise of a national guard, in Dublin and Belfast, and this led to the passage of the "gunpowder" and other disarming acts, which prohibited the sale of powder or firearms to the people at large, and gave magistrates the power to search for arms and ammunition in any house at their pleasure. These disarming acts were rigidly enforced and their enforcement explains why the disaffected Irish masses were so poorly provided with arms and ammunition when the day of trial came. After the extinction of the Irish Parliament, the British Parliament resorted to the same measures—making them even more stringent—so that for at least a century Ireland has been the most carefully disarmed country in the world. The assemblage of independent military bodies, such as the volunteers and national guards, was also prohibited, under severe penalties, and, in Ireland of to-day, no man may drill or bear arms, unless in the service of the British government or licensed to be armed by a resident magistrate.

The Catholic committee recorded its gratitude to the Irish Parliament for the act of partial emancipation, by passing resolutions of thanks at a general meeting held shortly after the bill became a law. It was deemed inexpedient to dissolve, while yet many grievances remained to be redressed, and among the latter the unreformed condition of Parliament was held to be the weightiest. There were also complaints of the interference of the English minister, through the machinery of Dublin Castle, with the will of the Irish people. The pension list had been, without good pretext, extravagantly enlarged during the administration of the Marquis of Buckingham, and public demoralization had actually reached the danger mark. The most intelligent members of the committee saw plainly that the influence of England was again becoming paramount, and that the independence of Parliament, if not its very existence, was again seriously threatened. Wolfe Tone, who had reached a commanding position as secretary of the Catholic committee—although himself a non-Catholic, as has been stated—was filled with French ideas of "liberty, equality, and fraternity." He clearly perceived that he could accomplish little in the way of political progress with such conservative Catholics as John Keogh, Sir Thomas Ffrench, and others of their kind, and, naturally, gravitated toward the more radical Catholics, such as Dr. W. J. MacNevin, and the republican Presbyterians, like Simms, McCracken, and Neilson of Belfast. He had become an able and expert pamphleteer, of the school of Molyneux, Swift, and Lucas, only much more radical, and his philippics against the Castle government were, in many instances, "Junius"-like in their keenness and force. His writings breathed a spirit of nationality utterly foreign to the careless squires,

cautious merchants, and timid churchmen who formed the
bulk of the old Catholic committee. The few "nobles"
who had belonged to that body were worse than an obstruction—they were a menace to the cause of reform,
owing to class pride and hereditary distrust of the "common people." Accordingly, although the committee still
held together, all that was progressive of its membership
flocked to the ranks of the newer and more vigorous organization of the United Irishmen. This organization, at
the outset, was open and not oath-bound. Its main objects
were the reform of Parliament and the redress of such
Catholic grievances as still remained. As time rolled on,
the spirit-stirring example of France—ere yet the Reign
of Terror had begun—fired the enthusiasm of the manhood of Ireland. "French principles" became popular, particularly among the Ulster Dissenters, whose hatred of
England, at that period, was hot and bitter. With these
men, and the Catholics who acted with them, Tone was an
idol. They fully sympathized with his idea of forming an
alliance, offensive and defensive, with the French republic,
for the purpose of utterly severing the English connection
and setting Ireland up as an independent commonwealth.
Soon this disposition became so diffused that the leaders
thought it prudent to change the association from an open
to a secret body, sworn to the accomplishment of Irish
national independence. Men of standing, such as Lord
Edward Fitzgerald, Thomas Addis Emmet, Richard Mc-
Cormick, Samuel Neilson, John and Henry Sheares, Oliver
Bond, Archibald Hamilton Rowan, and many others then,
and afterward, known to fame, became affiliated, and the
organization quickly spread, "like a prairie fire," throughout Ulster and Leinster. Munster and Connaught also

caught the flame, and the numbers sworn in were, as early as 1794, estimated at more than 100,000 men. By some historians it is asserted that the total membership, at one time, reached 300,000, mainly regimented and brigaded, but this is, no doubt, an exaggeration.

John Keogh showed the feeling of the more conservative Catholic element by dropping out when the society became oath-bound; and many of the timid ones followed his example. He was never afterward a leading factor in Irish politics. Much new blood, however, poured itself into the association. Its point of greatest power was Belfast—a city inhabited mainly by the close kinsmen of the brave and daring Ulster emigrants, who had aided the American colonies in throwing off the English yoke. These Belfast men ardently longed to emulate the actions of their American cousins. Most of the leaders of the United Irishmen had arrived at the conclusion that the time for moral suasion had passed away, with the virtual disbandment of the old volunteers, and they thought that if Ireland ever meant to be free, it must become so through the methods found so efficacious by the American patriots and French revolutionists. Yet, the Irish people had but a poor knowledge of arms—unless those who had served in the volunteers—and the officers of aristocratic blood, who had seen active service, were mostly in English pay. They had few cannon and no military stores to speak of—the government having laid its hands on all that was of value in that line in the country. But there were rumors of the manufacturing of pikes—a rude form of spear, with a hatchet for hacking helmets, and a sharp crook, for the cutting of bridle-reins or dragging a horseman from his saddle, on each side of the long, sharp blade. As the handle of the pike was from twelve to sixteen feet long, it was, at that period, when short-ranged old "Brown Bess," and the primitive bayonet, were still in use, a most formidable weapon, not alone against cavalry, but also infantry; and, at close quarters, even artillery. Under these circumstances, the leaders thought it rather imprudent to risk an insurrection without the co-operation of a regular force, backed by cannon. About 10,000 French soldiers, they considered, would, because of their great experience in war against all Europe, give the numerous native army strength, cohesion, and thorough mobility. This policy, in the light of after events, was not a wise one. The revolutionary iron, then at a white heat, was allowed to cool off, and the French, distracted by their own affairs, although entirely honest in their sympathy with the Irish revolutionists, were unable to fulfil their promises to the United Irishmen.

CHAPTER VIII

Principles of the United Irishmen Expounded by their Founder—Tragical Fate of Rev. William Jackson—Wolfe Tone's Narrow Escape—He Sails to America with his Family—His Eyes on France

THE principles which actuated the United Irishmen can not have better interpretation than in the words of Theobald Wolfe Tone himself, as expressed in his stirring memoirs: "To subvert the tyranny of our execrable [Anglo-Irish] government, to break the connection with England, the never-failing source of all our political evils, and to assert the independence of my country—these were my objects. To unite the whole people of Ireland, to abolish the memory of all past dissensions, and to substitute the common name Irishman in place of the denominations of Protestant, Catholic, and Dissenter—these were my means. To ef-

fectuate these great objects, I reviewed the three great sects.
The Protestants [Established Church Episcopalians] I de-
spaired of, from the outset, for obvious reasons. Already
in possession, by an unjust monopoly, of the whole power
and patronage of the country, it was not to be supposed they
would ever concur in measures the tendency of which must
be to lessen their influence as a party how much soever the
nation might gain. To the Catholics I thought it unnecessary to address myself, because as no change could make
their political situation worse, I reckoned upon their support to a certainty; besides, they had already begun to manifest a strong sense of their wrongs and oppressions; and,
finally, I well knew that, however it might be disguised or
suppressed, there existed in the breast of every Irish Catholic an inextirpable abhorrence of the English name and
power. There remained only the Dissenters, whom I knew
to be patriotic and enlightened. However, the recent events
at Belfast [Tone alluded to some opposition to the Catholic
claims which arose at a public meeting] showed me that all
prejudice was not yet removed from their minds." This
being the fact, Tone, aided by Thomas Russell—once a
captain in the British army, but a most intense Irish patriot
—proceeded to convert the Dissenters to his own liberal
way of thinking, and, in a great measure, succeeded. His
pamphlets were models of common-sense and political tact.
While Samuel Neilson, of Belfast, is generally credited with
having been the actual founder of the United Irishmen,
Theobald Wolfe Tone was, indisputably, their greatest organizer, and, on the whole, the ablest and boldest man their
movement produced. He had hardly a drop of Celtic blood
in his veins; in fact, he was of English extraction, on both
father's and mother's side, but his hatred of the English

governmental and commercial system was intense, and, in many respects, while having the military instincts of Washington, he closely resembled our own illustrious Thomas Jefferson. Had success finally crowned his efforts, Tone would have become one of the really great figures in modern history. When he began to breathe life into the flagging United Irish movement, he was less than thirty years old. His marriage was a very happy one; several lovely children were born to him—he had every inducement that could make a man selfish, and, had he taken the English side against his country, Theobald Wolfe Tone might have held one of the highest civic offices in the gift of the crown.

The government, as might have been anticipated, did not keep faith with the Catholics in the matter of the few privileges granted them by act of the Irish Parliament. In the matter of jury service, they were vilely discriminated against, as was shown in several "trials" of Defenders, in Leinster, where every Catholic was systematically excluded from the panel, because the prisoners to be tried were their co-religionists. This was the real beginning of the odious "packed jury" system of which the world has heard so much; and no governmental abuse has produced more bitterness in Ireland; no abuse, certainly, has done more to bring British "law" into disrepute in that country. The bugbear of "French principles" having frightened the Catholic aristocrats out of the national ranks, the democracy of that faith joined in ever increasing numbers — Leinster standing next to Ulster in point of strength. Four Catholic archbishops and five bishops, who dreaded a return of the penal laws in case of failure, denounced the United Irishmen and were quite unnecessarily complimentary to the British form of government in Ireland. They had suffered so long, and so much, that the mitigations of 1793 seemed to them a priceless boon; but, nathless their denunciations, the people went on with their work unshrinkingly, and soon became so formidable that the Castle government resolved to check the movement. Already, in 1792, Oliver Bond and Simon Butler, for insisting that Parliament needed to be reformed, and for condemning the sale of peerages for votes in the House of Commons, were accused of breach of privilege at the bar of the House of Lords, found culpable, and fined £500 each, together with being imprisoned for six months. In the following year, Archibald Hamilton Rowan—one of Tone's most trusted friends—was charged with sedition, said to have been uttered in an address delivered to a feeble remnant of the volunteers. The jury, as usual, was packed; Rowan was found guilty and sentenced to pay a fine of £500, together with being imprisoned for two years. He was also required to find security for his "good behavior" for seven years, himself in £2,000, and two sureties in £1,000 each. The United Irish Society of Dublin voted Mr. Rowan an address of sympathy, and declared their resolve to work for the good cause with "inflexible determination." Another public meeting of the same body, which was attempted to be held at Taylor's Hall, was broken up by the police, who seized upon the official papers. And, thus, an odious system of despotism was inaugurated in the Irish capital fully four years before the people, driven to desperation with malice prepense, finally rose in revolt.

Early in 1794, a clergyman of the Church of England, the Rev. William Jackson, arrived in Dublin, saying he had come from France by way of England. He claimed to be the bearer of a message from the French government to the leaders of the United Irishmen, inviting the latter to send a representative to France, there to settle with the Directory a plan for the invasion of Ireland. Jackson was accompanied by one Cockayne, a London attorney, and a "personal friend," in whom the confiding minister implicitly trusted. It was a fatal confidence, because Cockayne, to whom Jackson foolishly confided the object of his mission, had immediately sold the information to William Pitt, the English premier, who had him employed to act as a spy, under the guise of friendship, on Jackson in Dublin. The clergyman had letters of introduction to Lord Edward Fitzgerald, whose national sympathies were well known, and who, at the outbreak of the French Revolution, had gone to Paris and renounced his title. He also declared himself a republican. For this action he was summarily dismissed from the British army, in which he held the commission of major. Because of his persecution, he became an object of popular favor in Ireland. Although not noted for prudence, Lord Edward suspected Jackson and declined to receive him. Wolfe Tone, for some reason, was not so cautious. He held three meetings with the unhappy man, but, observing the latter's confidence in Cockayne, drew out, not, however, before he had, in a measure, compromised himself. In parting with Jackson, he said, referring to Cockayne: "This business is one thing for us Irishmen, but an Englishman who engages in it must be a traitor one way or the other." Poor Jackson retained his faith in the London attorney, and even had the hardihood to visit Hamilton Rowan in prison, with Cockayne as "guide, counselor, and friend." The impetuous Rowan, smarting under his wrongs, immediately committed himself beyond recall. Another of the patriots visited and implicated was a Dr. Reynolds, who was willing to act as Parisian agent. This dirty work hav-

ing proceeded sufficiently far for the purposes of "government," the Rev. Mr. Jackson was suddenly arrested on a
charge of high treason, and committed to jail. Fortunately,
Dr. Reynolds had time to escape to the United States, and
Archibald Hamilton Rowan, aided by friends in the service
of the enemy, got out of Newgate prison, sailed to France
in a fishing-smack, and, finally, landed on American soil.
Mr. Jackson lingered long in his cell, but was finally brought
to trial, and his chief accuser in the witness-box was his
quondam friend, Cockayne! Of course, he was found guilty
and sentenced to be "hanged, drawn, and quartered," according to the barbarous code of that epoch. But some
friend had provided him with a dose of arsenic, which he
swallowed while sentence was being passed upon him, and
fell dead in the dock at the feet of the cruel judge and the
false friend. Cockayne lived for years afterward, but all
decent Englishmen avoided him, as if he were a leper, and
his miserable existence must have been a well-merited "hell
on earth." He had sold his friend for cash, and, like Judas,
had his reward in a memory destined to be eternally infamous.

Wolfe Tone, through the friendship of Hon. Marcus Beresford, Chief Baron Wolfe, and other Irish Tories, some of
whom had been his college mates at Trinity, was allowed
to leave the country, no conditions as to his future political
conduct having been exacted from him. He labored under
the belief, until the moment of Jackson's suicide, that that
ill-fated person was nothing more or less than an English
secret service agent. "Before going away," says Mitchel,
"he wrote a narrative of the two conversations he had had
with Jackson." In this narrative he gave no names, and
he told his Tory friends that, as between being hanged and

going on the witness stand, he would, without hesitation, accept the first alternative. Tone's son, who edited his father's memoirs, has this to say in explanation: "When my father delivered this paper, the prevalent opinion, which he then shared, was that Jackson was an emissary of the British government. It required the unfortunate man's voluntary death to clear his character of such a foul imputation. What renders this transaction the more odious is that, before his arrival in Ireland, the life of Jackson was completely in the power of the government. His evil genius was already pinned upon him; his mission from France, his every thought, and his views were known. He was allowed to proceed, not in order to detect an existing conspiracy in Ireland, but to form one, and thus increase the number of victims. A more atrocious instance of perfidious and gratuitous cruelty is scarcely to be found in the history of any country but Ireland."

Theobald Wolfe Tone, always perfectly dauntless, both morally and physically, did not leave Dublin until after the self-execution of the sadly destined Jackson. On the day the latter died, Tone showed himself in his accustomed haunts, and was prepared for the worst his enemies might decide on doing, but they made no hostile movement. In May, 1795, accompanied by his wife, children, and faithful sister, he went to Belfast and there bade adieu to many old friends and associates. His destination was America, and he finally sailed from the northern seaport to Wilmington, Delaware, and proceeded from thence to the city of Philadelphia. Before sailing, he made pilgrimages to some well-remembered, historic spots in the neighborhood. What his determination, and that of his friends, was may be gathered from the following passage in his memoirs: "I remember particularly two days we passed on Cave Hill. On the first, Russell, Neilson, Simms, McCracken, and one or two more of us, on the summit of McArt's fort, took a solemn obligation, which I think I may say I have on my part endeavored to fulfil, never to desist from our efforts until we had subverted the authority of England over our country and asserted her independence."

It was known in higher revolutionary circles, both in Dublin and Belfast, that Tone was resolved, circumstances favoring him, to proceed from the United States to France, to urge upon the government of that country the importance of aiding Ireland by a naval and military expedition in her struggle to get rid of the English connection, but on terms precisely the same as those accorded by France to America, when she aided the latter against Great Britain during the Revolutionary War.

BOOK IX

TREATING OF AFFAIRS IN IRELAND FROM THE VICEROY-
ALTY OF EARL FITZWILLIAM AND HIS RECALL TO THE
DEFEAT OF THE UNITED IRISHMEN OF ULSTER, 1795-1798

CHAPTER I

LORD WESTMORELAND, owing to a political "deal" of the English ministers, who had formed with the Whigs what was called "a coalized administration," was recalled from the viceroyalty, and Earl Fitzwilliam, a liberal Whig, a friend of Burke, Sheridan, and other brilliant Irishmen resident in England, and a champion of complete Catholic emancipation, was sent over in his place. It was said that he accepted the Lord Lieutenancy solely on condition that emancipation of the Catholics would be made a government measure during his term in office. The impressionable Dublin people received the new viceroy with every mark of enthusiasm. The fact that he possessed large estates in Ireland and was a liberal landlord added to his popularity. The sincerity of Earl Fitzwilliam himself has not been called in question, but there has existed in Ireland, from his day to the present, a well-grounded belief that the English ministers made use of him to further delude the too trustful Irish nation—so much in the habit of acting on magnanimous impulse. The Irish Parliament voted £1,200,-000 to the English king, together with 20,000 men, to carry on the war with France—a quarrel in which Ireland had no real concern, unless, indeed, on the side of the French, who sympathized with the republican aspirations of the United Irishmen. One is sorry to find Henry Grattan

the successful mover of the warlike grant. Lord Fitzwilliam strengthened popular confidence in his good intentions
when he removed the obnoxious Under Secretary Cooke
from office and removed one of the rapacious Beresfords,
John of that ilk, from the remunerative office of customs
commissioner. We read, with intense pleasure, that petitions for complete emancipation of the Catholics came into
Parliament from many almost exclusively Protestant com-
munities and corporations. Among the latter, Londonderry,
so famous in the defence of the Protestant ascendency in the
days of the Revolution, was conspicuous. Grattan, who,
as usual, took the lead in behalf of the Catholics, introduced
a bill for their admission to Parliament, about the middle
of February. It was known to all concerned that the Lord
Lieutenant ardently favored the measure, but Lord Chancellor Fitzgibbon, greatly aided by Cooke, the Beresfords,
and their numerous and influential friends, made a vicious
campaign against it. John Beresford, who was both bold
and able, proceeded to London and procured an interview
with George III, whose feeble and narrow mind he succeeded in turning against the Catholic cause. He was led
to believe that the Protestant religion was assailed and that
to sign a bill admitting Catholics to Parliament would be a
direct violation of his coronation oath. Beresford's arguments were ably seconded by the wily Fitzgibbon, who sent
the king an elaborate statement of what the result of a liberal policy would be, from a purely anti-Catholic standpoint.
George III was always prepared to believe any charge that
might be urged against subjects of that persuasion. The
efforts of Beresford and his supporters did not terminate
with imbittering of King George against the Catholic claims.
They also labored sedulously with the ministers, who were

nothing loth to go back on their former liberal policy. Earl
Fitzwilliam, all unconscious of these dishonorable proceedings, was allowed to commit himself more deeply than ever
to the Catholic champions. His chagrin and indignation
may be imagined when the naked truth was revealed. Instructions were sent him by Pitt not to further advance the
pending bill, because the king would never consent to sign
it, and, without his signature, it could not become a law of
the land. The noble earl now remembered, with mortification, that the naval and military grant for the war with the
French Republic had all the appearance of a dirty political
trick, at which his lofty soul revolted. But his vehement
protests were written in vain. The king and his advisers
remained inexorable, and Lord Fitzwilliam was finally rescued from a position which he found insupportable, by being
recalled from the viceroyalty. The generous people understood and sympathized with this really great and good Englishman—one of the few real friends of the Irish people
that had occupied the position of Lord Lieutenant. When
he left Dublin for England, on March 25, 1795, all Dublin,
except the Castle clique, turned out to bid him farewell.
Old residents remembered a scene almost similar when the
Earl of Chesterfield was recalled half a century before. The
Irish capital closed its shops and went into mourning. Lord
Fitzwilliam's last hours in Ireland were, however, imbittered by the knowledge that John Beresford had been restored to office, and that the government was about to
degrade the Irish peerage by elevating thereto the odious
John Fitzgibbon under the title of Earl of Clare. The
Catholics of Ireland, in particular, recognized that the
viceroy's recall was a notice to them to hope for no further
reforms, as long as King George lived, or while William

Pitt remained Prime Minister. It also gave notice to the United Irishmen, and all who sympathized with their principles and objects, that government would yield nothing further to moral suasion, and that there remained for Ireland abject submission, with the alternative of a bloody and, probably, unsuccessful insurrection. Thoughtful people, guided by the signs of the times, felt that the patriot party would soon be forced into adopting the violent alternative. The English minister had made up his mind to goad the Irish nation into a premature revolt, and then fall upon it with all the weight and resources of the empire. There was, it is true, a strong possibility that, with France as an ally, Ireland might be successful in her rebellion. If she should succeed, England would be little worse off, because, while the Parliament of Ireland remained even partially independent, Great Britain could not control Irish commerce or finances, beyond a trifling extent. The loss would, therefore, be a purely territorial one. On the other hand, the chances were all, or nearly all, on the side of the stronger power, and Ireland, once subdued in the field, the destruction of her Parliament would be a comparatively easy matter. In a word, the recall of Lord Fitzwilliam was the first step in the direction of provincializing Ireland. John Mitchel, with his customary frankness and perspicuity— gifts in which he far excelled all other Irish writers, with the exception, perhaps, of Jonathan Swift—thus sums up the Anglo-Irish relations of this period:

"If the compact made with Lord Fitzwilliam had been observed, and all the remaining disabilities of the Catholics frankly removed, at once, the insurrection would never have taken place, and infinite misery and atrocity saved to the country. But Mr. Pitt knew very well that if there were no insurrection there would also be no 'union.' He had his plans already almost matured, and his chief adviser for Irish affairs was the thorough Lord Clare" (Chancellor John Fitzgibbon).

Lord Camden, a man of fierce Tory instincts, and a reactionist—quite as unscrupulous as the very worst of his predecessors—succeeded the popular Fitzwilliam as viceroy. His arrival in Dublin was signalized by a furious riot. The military were called out and two citizens were killed—an event not unlike the Boston massacre of 1772. Independently disposed Catholics thought it strange that St. Patrick's College, at Maynooth, should be endowed under this ferocious régime. It looked to them as if the British government wished to put the students for the Catholic priesthood at that institution under bond to be "loyal" to the English connection—something the Catholic priests, educated on the Continent, during the penal times, were not suspected of being, except in a few instances. Indeed the priests educated in exile were potent factors in keeping alive the patriotic spark that still defiantly smouldered in the hearts of the persecuted Irish Catholics—particularly those who belonged to the working classes. St. Patrick's College at Maynooth was, therefore, established in the end of this year (1795), and the first endowment voted by the Irish Parliament was the sum of $40,000, which was afterward increased. It was plainly a step toward denationalizing the Irish priesthood, and, unfortunately, in some instances, although not in general, it had the desired effect. In a similar spirit, the political bribe, known as the Regium Donum ("royal gift"), given for the support of Presbyterian ministers in Ireland, had been increased from $3,000 —out of the secret service fund—in the reign of Charles II, to $30,000, in 1792; and was made five times that amount after the events of the last lustra of the eighteenth century made it apparent that the Presbyterians of Ireland had not been sufficiently placed under obligations to the British crown. These annuities were paltry in amount, when contrasted with the munificent revenues of the Established (Episcopal) Church of Ireland, derived mainly from the confiscated estates of the Catholic "nobility and gentry," who had followed the fortunes of James II. No wonder that most of its members remained faithful to the English interest, because they had only one Irish interest—their fat livings, which remained to them and their successors down to 1870, when the "Irish" Church was finally disestablished under Mr. Gladstone's administration. The Regium Donum and Maynooth grant, both of which had been confirmed and enlarged by the English Parliament after "the Union," fell with the church—compensation being made to all the surviving interests in "bulk" sums. The Irish Catholics never took kindly to governmental support in any form, and, although "payment of the priests" had been a favorite suggestion of "advanced" English statesmen, the laity could not be brought to approve it, nor could the great body of the priests themselves, who have been, and are, as in the United States, supported by voluntary contributions.

September 21, 1795, was made sadly memorable by an affray between the Catholic "Defenders" and Episcopal "Orangemen," which occurred in the County Armagh, and was called "the battle of Diamond," from a village of that name in the neighborhood of the scene of conflict. The better armed Orangemen were victorious—several of the "Defenders" having been killed or wounded, and, thenceforth, the unhappy Catholics became objects of persecution in the Orange districts of Ulster. They were given the alternative of going "to hell or to Connaught," as in the time of Cromwell, and the bitter animosities engendered by the rabid bigotry of that period linger even yet in the hearts of some, at least, of the descendants of both factions. It is this bad spirit that Moore so nobly rebuked in the poem here quoted:

"As vanquished Erin wept beside
    The Boyne's ill-fated river,
She saw where Discord, in the tide,
    Had dropp'd his loaded quiver.
'Lie hid,' she cried, 'ye venomed darts,
    Where mortal eye may shun you;
Lie hid, for oh! the stain of hearts
    That bled for me is on you!'

"But vain her wish, her weeping vain,
    As time too well hath taught her,
Each year the Fiend returns again
    And dives into that water;
And brings, triumphant, from beneath
    His shafts of desolation,
And sends them, wing'd with worse than death,
    Through all the madd'ning nation.

"Alas, for her who sits and mourns
    Even now beside that river—
Unwearied still the Fiend returns
    And stored is still his quiver.
'When will this end, ye Powers of Good?'
    She weeping asks forever,
But only hears from out that flood
    The Demon answer 'Never!'"

CHAPTER II

Catholic Emancipation Bill Defeated—Patriot Members Leave Parliament in Disgust—An Atrocious Military Mob Let Loose on the People—Sir Ralph Abercrombie's Rebuke of Army

AN attempt made by Grattan and his colleagues to pass a complete Catholic Emancipation bill during the summer session of 1796 was defeated by a vote of 155 to 55, and the rejection was accompanied by a tempest of anti-Catholic bigotry, in which the voices of John Toler (afterward the notorious Lord Norbury) and Dr. Duigenan, who is "credited" with having been a renegade Catholic, rose loudest of all. In the sessions of 1796, the patriot party fared no better—Grattan being again defeated, on a purely commercial motion, by a vote of 14 to 126. Other of his motions suffered a like fate, but the miserable Parliament passed an Insurrection Act, which empowered magistrates to proclaim martial law in their several districts; an Indemnity Act to protect magistrates who went outside of the law in matters of coercion, and a Riot Act, which enabled the authorities to disperse any gathering of the people, whatsoever, by force of arms. In addition, the Habeas Corpus Act was suspended by a vote of 157 to 7. Only about a third of the members of the House of Commons attended, and these were, in the main, the supporters of the government. The last effort of the small band of patriots, in the Commons, was made in May, 1797, when George Ponsonby moved his usual resolution for the reform of Parliament and it was beaten—30 ayes to 117 noes. Grattan proclaimed the future course of himself and colleagues when he said, in the course of the debate : "We have offered you our measure—you will reject it. We deprecate yours —you will persevere. Having no hopes left to persuade or to dissuade, and having discharged our duty, we shall trouble you no more, and, after this day, shall not attend the House of Commons." In July, when the general election occurred, Grattan, Lord Henry Fitzgerald, Lord Edward Fitzgerald, John Philpot Curran, Arthur O'Connor, and other distinguished gentlemen, declined to stand for Parliament, so that, when the new body was elected, there remained only Plunket, Kendall Bushe, and Foster, with one or two less prominent members, to grapple with the arrogant government majority. And, meanwhile, under martial law and the suspension of Habeas Corpus, the country was being ridden over by a military despotism. "Soldiers of the king" were given "free quarters" in the houses of the innocent country people, and these ignorant and ferocious mercenaries committed crimes which revolt all decent human beings. The less said of these vile occurrences the better.

Before a shot was fired by Ireland, she was handed over by Camden to the tender mercies of English "fencibles," Welsh irregulars—notably the cavalry regiment known as "Ancient Britons"—Scotch Highlanders and the half-savage Orange yeomanry—recruited from the ranks of the murderous banditti, formerly called the Peep o' Day Boys, who were officered by the aristocratic, or semi-aristocratic, scions of the old Established Church "ascendency." The Scotchmen alone conducted themselves respectably, and few, if any, charges of blackguardism are laid at their doors, although they were always fierce in battle. Nor were such English regulars as were drafted into the country nearly as vile as the riff-raff English city militia who had preceded them. But the general ruffianism of the British soldiery, and their "Royal Irish" allies of that era, is best summed up in the words of their Scotch commander-in-chief, the brave Sir Ralph Abercrombie, who resigned his post in chivalrous protest against their misconduct, "They are formidable to everybody except the enemy!" Sir Ralph, the gallant and humane, is still remembered with gratitude by the progeny of the harassed generation he endeavored to protect from military outrage, and, in the midst of her sorrows and sufferings, Ireland mourned his premature fall on the bloody sands of an Egyptian battlefield. He was succeeded in the supreme command by General Lake, an Englishman of ferocious disposition, who regarded mercy to an "Irish rebel" as senile weakness. But another Scottish general, well known among the military immortals, Sir John Moore, the hero of Corunna, indorsed the opinion of his fellow-countryman, Abercrombie, by exclaiming in a moment of indignation, after witnessing some uncalled-for act of cruelty, "If I were an Irishman, I would be a rebel!"

Lake's chief lieutenants in the dragooning process were Generals Dundas, Duff, and Hutchinson, whose main object was to drive the people into premature revolt. Carhampton, who commanded before both Abercrombie and Lake, was, Mitchel claims, sincere in his desire to crush the United Irish Society, and so prevent the possibility of a rebellion. On discovering the motives of the government, which he could not indorse, he retired to private life. Carhampton was a lineal descendant of Henry Luttrell, his namesake, who "sold the pass," and gave the victory to England, at Aughrim. Complaints of the evil actions of the soldiery poured on the executive from all quarters of

Ireland, but no heed was given them. Lord Camden, although credited with personal amiability, which his acts went far to contradict, was but a weak instrument in the hands of such unscrupulous agents of the British minister as Fitzgibbon, Castlereagh, and John Claudius Beresford.

To add to the horror of the situation, the Orange society in the northern province became so fiercely intolerant that 1,400 Catholic families were driven from their homes in Ulster, and this meant the displacement, by violence, of 7,000 souls, in 1797-98. These figures are given on the authority of John Mitchel, himself, as already explained, an Ulster Protestant, and he also states that among the most merciless persecutors of the brave and virtuous peasantry of Leinster, at that period, were the Orange yeomanry of the North.

CHAPTER III

Literary Ireland in the Seventeenth and Eighteenth Centuries—Long Roll of Poets, Orators, Playwrights, Satirists, Philosophers, Scientists, and Leaders of Human Thought

IT may not be amiss to turn, for a period, from Irish politics and persecutions, to contemplate, however briefly, Ireland as a factor in the realm of science, art, and literature during the seventeenth and eighteenth centuries. Although vigorous efforts had been made by successive English rulers to drive the native Gaelic tongue from the field of letters, they were not entirely successful, and to the Gaelic writers of those centuries we are deeply indebted for a consecutive account of the Old Irish nation, its origin, rise, progress, and downfall. The Rev. Dr. Geoffrey Keating, born in Munster, but educated in Spain, made a profound study of the traditions and antiquities of his native country, and his "History of Ireland," translated into English from the Gaelic by the late John O'Mahony, of New York, is one of the most valuable contributions to the ancient lore of Ireland.   It is particularly interesting as a genealogical work, for in it are set down the names and pedigrees of all the principal, and most of the tributary, Irish septs, clans, or families.   It is also rich and rare in heroic legends of the Fenians, or native militia, of the olden Ireland, and their mighty chiefs, principal of whom was Fionn, or Finn, meaning "the Fair"; MacCool, mentioned elsewhere, who may be called the Irish Ajax.   Dr. Keating drifted occasionally into poetry, but, while the merit of his prose is undeniable, it can not be truthfully said that he wooed the muses with a soul of fire.   It may be that he suffered in the translation, for O'Mahony, although both a savant and a patriot, was nothing of a poet.   His name, however, is indissolubly linked with that of Keating, and his translation of the latter's annals was a most scholarly achievement.   No historical library would be complete lacking this learned and interesting volume.

The Gaelic society of Dublin, which "flourished" at the beginning of the last century, and whose valuable MSS., we are informed, passed into the possession of Trinity College library, published many translations of the ballads of Teige MacDaire, who wrote in the seventeenth century, but whose sweet warblings of Irish song never fell upon "Saxon" ears, in the days in which he lived and was stirred to melody by the charms of nature, and the even more alluring charms of nature's fairest offspring—woman.

By the lovely waters of the Bay of Donegal, under the shadow of the ruined Franciscan abbey, temporarily repaired for their convenience, Brother Michael O'Clery, and his kinsmen, Peregrine and Conary O'Clery, assisted by the learned O'Mulconrys, under the patronage of the generous Fergal O'Gara, Lord of Moy O'Gara and Coolavin, compiled, from the ancient Celtic chronicles, preserved intact from Danish and Norman and Saxon spoliation, throughout the tempestuous centuries of Irish resistance to successive swarms of invaders, by the fidelity of the monks, the immortal work known as "The Annals of the Four Masters," which gives the history of Ireland from the earliest period down to A.D. 1616. In their great task they often had the aid of another great Gaelic scholar, Brother Peregrine O'Duigenan, or O'Degnan, whose name is imperishably connected with theirs. The Annals were begun in 1632, and were completed, after prodigious toil, in 1636. A portion was translated by the scholarly Owen O'Connellan, and published in 1846; but it remained for Professor John O'Donovan, who collaborated with the equally distinguished Gaelic savant, Eugene O'Curry, to complete the translation.

Another representative of the intellectual glory of the Gael was Owen Roe, or Red Owen, MacWard, hereditary bard of the princely O'Donnells, whose "Lament for the Princes of Tyrowen and Tyrconnel," buried at Rome, has been translated into English by the gifted and unhappy James Clarence Mangan, who has been called the Edgar Allan Poe of Ireland. This really great poem, which can be found in Mangan's collected works, or in any of the numerous volumes of modern Irish poetry, ranks second to none as an emanation of elegiac genius. It breathes out all the love and sorrow of the vanquished Celtic nation, of the Elizabethan and first Stuart period.

Many other gifted men wrote also in Gaelic, and, by degrees, owing to the exertions of a few noble enthusiasts, their works are coming to light. The general revival of the Gaelic tongue in Ireland is lending a new impetus to Celtic translation, and, no doubt, the twentieth century will add many works of great merit to the already large catalogue of ancient and medieval Irish literature.

The first Irishmen of English derivation who attained to literary standing in Great Britain, as well as in his native country, was Richard Stainhurst, who was born in Dublin, and became a commoner of Oxford University, in England. He made a meritorious translation of Virgil (first four books) in the English hexameter, and was also a successful translator of several other classic works.

The Very Rev. James Ussher, D.D., a Protestant divine, who won enduring fame as a writer on ecclesiastical subjects, was also, by birth, an Irishman. He is generally referred to by historians as "the learned Dr. Ussher," and even those who radically dissent from his views pay deserved tribute to his talents.

Another seventeenth century Irish writer of high distinction was Sir James Ware, who devoted himself, mainly, to archæological subjects, such as "The Antiquities of Ireland" —a work held in high repute; "Works Ascribed to St. Patrick," and "The Lives of the Irish Bishops." McGee says of him: "Ware was a great, persevering book-worm, a sincere receiver and transmitter of truth."

The same century produced, in Ireland, the poet-scholar, Sir John Denham; the literary bishop, Right Rev. Dr. French, of Ferns; Maurice Dugan, poet, who wrote in Irish and was the composer of one of the earliest versions of that exquisite melody, "The Coolin"; Donald MacFirbis, the Gaelic chronologist, genealogist, and historian; Roger

Boyle, otherwise Lord Broghill—a merciless Cromwellian general, but a most gifted writer on many learned subjects; William Molyneux, author of "The Case of Ireland Stated"—which produced such a commotion in the reign of William III—and other political works; Wentworth Dillon, Earl of Roscommon, who wrote "Horace's Art of Poetry," "An Essay on Translated Poetry," and many charming verses; Hon. Robert Boyle, called "the Philosopher," brother of Lord Broghill, whose views on philosophy, science, and theology are, even in our day, a delight to the learned; Henry Dowdall, historian and scientist; Roderick O'Flaherty, antiquarian and historian; Anthony, Count Hamilton, author of the famous "Memoirs of Grammont," "Fairy Tales," and numerous brilliant fragments; Thomas Parnell, a distinguished poet, who wrote "An Allegory of Man" and "Edwin and Sir Topaz"—a story of fairy doings, which is still popular with the young; Robert, Count Molesworth, a polished writer, who has left behind him, as if to attest his versatility, two productions of a diametrically opposite tendency—"The Art of Love'" and "The Art of Cookery"; Sir Richard Steele, a sparkling literary genius, and one of the chief contributors to the celebrated "Spectator," conducted by Joseph Addison, who had the reputation of being the most correct writer of his day; William Congreve, the poet and playwright; Turlough O'Carolan, called "The Last of the Irish Harpers," although others, not as meritorious, came after him. O'Carolan was afflicted with blindness, through an attack of small-pox. Before his misfortune, although but a mere youth, he had seen and formed an attachment for a young lady named Bridget Cruise, who, at a later day, rejected him. To her he addressed some of the finest and most touching of his numerous ballads. He never played for money, being a man of comparative independence as to fortune. His contemporary poets all regarded him as a most gifted person, and posterity has awarded him some measure of fame. Oliver Goldsmith said of him: "He was, at once, a poet, a musician, and a composer, and sang his own songs to the accompaniment of his harp." Only a very few of his compositions have come down to us, but such as have, although merely translations from the original Gaelic, show that he was a man of fine feeling and powerful intellect.

Jonathan Swift, the celebrated "Dean of St. Patrick's," was born in Ireland of English parents, but, notwithstanding his alien blood and English training, was, in many respects, one of the most intense and effective of Irish patriots. Some of his political works have been alluded to elsewhere. His literary fecundity was marvelous, but his best-known works are "Gulliver's Travels," the "Tale of a Tub," and "The Battle of the Books." Sir Walter Scott was a great admirer of Swift, and says of him: "He was blessed in a higher degree than any of his contemporaries with the powers of a creative genius. The more we dwell on the character and writings of this great man, the more they improve upon us. His wit, his humor, his patriotism, his charity, and even his piety, were of a different cast from those of other men. He had in his virtues few equals and, in his talents, no superior. In that of humor, and especially irony, he ever was, and probably ever will be, unrivaled."

The virtual founder of the British Museum—one of the greatest of the world's institutions—was Sir Hans Sloane, the eminent physician and botanist. He left, when he died at the age of ninety-two, a collection valued at £80,000 to the state, for the benefit of science, and also richly endowed many London hospitals. He was so enthusiastic a scientist that he left to his family only a small portion of his rich estate. Sir Hans was of Irish birth.

But the litany of Irish celebrities of the two centuries under consideration is not, even yet, nearly recapitulated. Thomas Southerne, entitled "the great founder of the modern school of dramatic production," and the author of numerous successful plays, was born in the Irish capital, A.D. 1660, and died at a ripe age, leaving behind him a memory to be honored.

Matthew Corcoran, an "all-round" poet, is best remembered as the author of what may be termed a wholesome bacchanalian song, called "October Ale," which used to be sung at the dinner-tables of our great-grandfathers, and, perhaps, at the tables of a later generation.

What American—what reader of any nation—has not heard of that great Irishman, Right Rev. George Berkeley, theologian, philosopher, scientist, and poet? This brilliant author of the "Theory of Vision," "Inquiry Into the Human Mind," and "Principles of Human Knowledge," who, by his peculiar theories, impelled Lord Byron to write of him—

> "When Bishop Berkeley said there was no matter,
> And proved it—it made no matter what he said,"

is best known on this continent by his "Ode on America," in which he wrote—

> "Westward the course of Empire takes its way,
> The four first acts already past;
> A fifth will close the drama with the day—
> Time's noblest offspring is the last."

Another member of the prolific, martial, and literary family of Boyle was John, Earl of Cork and Orrery. He translated and compiled "Pliny's Letters" and wrote a brilliant criticism of Jonathan Swift's life and writings. About the same time lived and wrote a Gaelic poet named John Mc-Donnell, who has been given the title of "Ireland's Alexander Pope." Unfortunately, nothing of his work remains except a few doubtfully translated lyrics, mostly of a local character.

Laurence Sterne, author of "Tristram Shandy" and "A Sentimental Journey," was, like Swift, of English parentage, but would seem to have caught from the Irish soil on which he was born some of the sparkling genius of the native race.

A brilliant nebulæ of writers, of different schools, flashed around the larger orbs of this remarkable literary era, but their enumeration would be tedious, so we will pass on to Oliver Goldsmith, "the inspired idiot," as an English critic called him, because of his wasteful habits and unbusinesslike methods. He was born in Pallas, County Longford, which is said to be the exact geographical centre of Ireland, in 1728, but was brought up at Lissoy, in the same county. The son of a clergyman, he was carefully educated and developed great powers as an author of both prose and poetry. Of the former, the best example is "The Vicar of Wakefield," and of the latter "The Deserted Village," in which "Sweet Auburn" takes the place of Lissoy. He was also the author of that popular comedy, "She Stoops to Conquer," and of "The Good-Natured Man." Goldsmith was quite ugly, but had an amusing amount of vanity. It is related that, on one occasion, when his funds were high, he invested in a dashing costume, and wore, as was then the custom among those above the peasant class, a long sword, which contrasted ludicrously with his small, dumpy figure. Walking down the Strand in London, one fine day, he met that blunt scholar, Dr. Samuel Johnson, of learned but uncouth memory. "Well, Doctor," cried Goldsmith, looking at his sword with an oblique but admiring glance, "what do you think of me?" "Sir," replied Johnson, solemnly, "you remind me of a fly with a pin stuck through it!"

The Rev. Thomas Leland, born in 1722, wrote an impartial history of Ireland, which has been highly praised, and is, certainly, a conscientious work, although now rather out of date. Thomas Sheridan, father of a man destined to be much more widely known, produced the play of "Coriolanus," and made a great figure in both Dublin and London. Charles Macklin, playwright and actor, was justly considered the greatest artist of his time, in the histrionic sense, made and lost several fortunes, and finally died all but penniless at the extreme old age of a hundred years. Walter Hussey Burgh, the statesman and orator, has been already dealt with in relation to the Irish struggle for a free commerce.

Edmund Burke, born in Dublin, was, perhaps, the greatest intellect of his age. He was ponderous, but brilliant, like a mountain of gold. As an orator, he had no peer in language, although many surpassed him in manner. His delivery, although majestic, sometimes became monotonous. His most popular work is the well-known essay on "The Sublime and the Beautiful," and his ablest speech was that delivered against Warren Hastings, the spoiler of India, on the occasion of that individual's impeachment. His "Reflections on the French Revolution," although a grand piece of literary work, leaned too much to the side of monarchy to please the democracy of Europe. He designated, in this volume, the French revolutionary leaders "Architects of Ruin."

Charles Johnstone, a recognized satirist, was born in

Limerick, in 1735. Scott called him "the prose Juvenal," in recognition of his satirical gifts.

Isaac Bickerstaff, the dramatist, established a school of his own, but was not financially successful, although one of his plays, "Love in a Village," remained popular for many years. Thomas Dermody, a promising poet, known as "the Chatterton of Ireland," died in the flower of his youthful promise. A great pulpit orator of the period was the Rev. Walter Blake Kirwan, a native of Galway, who was ranked in eloquence second only to Grattan. Dr. Kirwan's popularity in Ireland was much diminished among the masses of the people by his apostasy from the Catholic faith, which was not considered a matter of conscience. Robert Jephson was an Irish dramatist of some renown, but his works are now almost forgotten.

Joseph Cooper Walker wrote the "Historical Memoirs of the Irish Bards," "A Historical Essay on the Dress of the Ancient Irish," and "A Memoir of the Weapons of the Irish"—all extremely valuable in public libraries as works of reference. Arthur Murphy, actor, lawyer, dramatist, and journalist, made quite a figure in the Irish capital about the end of the eighteenth century, as did also Edward Lysaght, "Pleasant Ned Lysaght," as his comrades called him, a rollicking poet and an incorruptible patriot, who refused to sell his country for either title, office, or money. He wrote "The Irish Volunteers" and many other stirring lyrics—some of them rather free and easy, but abounding in fun and good-fellowship.

Richard Brinsley Sheridan, probably the most versatile of Irish literary men, was born in Dublin in 1751, and was the son of Thomas Sheridan, the distinguished dramatist already alluded to. He went with his father to London in his early youth and received a finished education. He shone as a wit, an orator, a poet, a dramatist, and a statesman. He was the author of "The Rivals" and "A School for Scandal," which still hold the boards. The latter has been called "the most perfect of English comedies." His fame as an orator outshone even that of Burke and Chatham. Says Lord Macaulay, alluding to his speech in denunciation of Hastings, "It was so imperfectly reported that it may be said to be wholly lost, but it was, without doubt, the most elaborately brilliant of all the productions of his ingenious mind."

Among the literary stars of lesser magnitude, we may mention Mrs. Mary Tighe, poetess; Edmund Malone, the commentator on Shakespeare; Andrew Cherry, actor, dramatist, and song-writer, who composed "The Green Little Shamrock of Ireland," "The Bay of Biscay O," which has delighted thousands of sailor hearts, and "Tom Moody," the huntsman's dirge.

Richard Alfred Milliken, a native of Cork, made "The Groves of Blarney" immortal by his fine song of that title, which a later Cork poet ("Father Prout") has somewhat improved upon.

Sir Philip Francis, now generally acknowledged to have been the gifted author of "The Letters of Junius"—the fiercest philippics against corruption and misgovernment ever written—deserves to rank high among the really great men Ireland has produced. He had the vigor of Burke, without its ponderousness, and the irony of Swift, without its coarseness.

Dr. William Drennan was known as "The Poet Laureate of the United Irishmen," and is famous as having conferred in one of his fine ballads the title of "The Emerald Isle" on

Ireland. James Orr was another song-writer of the United Irish period, and his ballad of "The Irishman," written during his long exile from his beloved country, is one of the most touching lyrics in the English tongue.

John Philpot Curran, like Henry Flood, Henry Grattan, Hussey Burgh, Kendall Bushe, William Saurin, William Conyngham Plunkett, and other Irish Parliamentary contemporaries, belongs more to the school of orators and statesmen than of authors. The group just named, together with Burke and Brinsley Sheridan, constituted the grandest fellowship of human eloquence the world beheld since Cicero charmed the Roman Senate by the magic of his words, and Demosthenes stirred the Athenians to "march against Philip and conquer or die."

CHAPTER IV

Wolfe Tone in France—Friendship of General Hoche—French Assistance Promised Irish Revolutionists—Failure of Bantry Bay and Texel Expeditions—Death of Hoche—Ireland Bitterly Disappointed —Camperdown

WHILE the United Irish Society continued to extend itself throughout Ireland, and the repressive, or rather exasperating, measures of the government increased in rigor, Theobald Wolfe Tone was contemplating the life of a farmer in the United States. He actually purchased a small farm in the neighborhood of Princeton, New Jersey, and was beginning to think himself quite a Cincinnatus, when a communication from Ireland, sent by his intimate friends, the Simms, Russell, Neilson, McCracken, and others, changed his whole plans and threw him again into the vortex of Irish politics. They informed him that the revolutionary spirit was more ardent than ever in Ireland, and urged him to proceed to France and urge the government of that country to send an armed expedition, of formidable strength, to aid the Irish patriots in their contemplated uprising against the English power. Robert Simms empowered Tone to draw on him for such funds as might be needed in the furtherance of his mission. The wife and sister of Tone, women cast in the heroic mold, who were with him at Princeton, so far from attempting to dissuade him from going to France, did all they could to hasten his departure, because they, too, hated the English government and longed to see Ireland a republic. All his preparations were completed during the winter of 1795-96. He was provided by the French agent at Philadelphia with a letter of introduction to Charles de la Croix, French Minister of Foreign Affairs, and with another to James Monroe, afterward President and Father of the famous "Doctrine," who then represented the United States in Paris. He bade an affecting farewell to his wife, sister, and children, and, after a comparatively brief and uneventful voyage, reached the French capital on February 1, 1796. He was a total stranger to Paris, had but an imperfect knowledge of the French tongue, and, worse than all else, had a very meagre supply of money. He was, at one time, indebted to the generous Monroe for financial accommodation. That gentleman also instructed him in the routine necessary to obtain the ear of the French government. The many difficulties in his path would have daunted any spirit less resolute, but this most extraordinary young man soon succeeded in winning both the ear and confidence of De la Croix, Carnot, "the organizer of victory"; General Clarke, afterward Marshal Duke of Feltré; General Lazare Hoche, the able pacificator of the royalist province of La Vendee, and other men high in the councils of the French Republic. Even the envious machinations of certain Irish marplots in Paris, who were jealous of his influence, could not thwart his purpose. The brave and gifted Hoche regarded him so highly that, aided by Carnot and Clarke, he was admitted into the French service, where he soon rose to the rank of adjutant-general, and saw considerable service on the frontiers. His military *nom de guerre* was "Smith," so that his identity as Tone, the Irish revolutionist, remained for a long time unrecognized in England. But the French government, oppressed and distracted by a multitude of cares of state, moved slowly in the matter of fitting out the naval and military expedition for a descent in force on the shores of expectant Ireland. This delay, which might have been avoided, and which was destined to produce untoward results, drove the ardent Tone almost frantic. The diary, published in his Memoirs, teems with expressions of impatience and maledictions on the slowness of the French officials. At length, toward the end of autumn, and after a clandestine visit to Switzerland of Lord Edward Fitzgerald and Arthur O'Connor, who there conferred with General Hoche, General Clarke, and other representatives of the French government, Tone was rejoiced to learn that preparations for the great adventure were almost completed at Brest, where France had assembled a formidable fleet and an army of 15,000 men—all seasoned veterans — to be commanded by the illustrious Hoche in person.

By the middle of December, 1796, all was ready and the muster of the troops showed 13,975 men, with 45,000 stand of spare arms, plentiful cannon, and ammunition, for the armament of their expected allies; and to carry and de-

fend all, 17 sail of the line, 13 frigates, 5 corvettes, and 8
transports, making a total of 43 sail. Tone sailed on the
Indomptable, while, by some fatality, Admiral Morand de
Galles, General Hoche, General Debelle, and other officers
of high rank, embarked on the *Fraternite* frigate, which
met with a series of mishaps, and was not again seen by
the survivors of the expedition until after their return to
France. This accident deprived the troops of the services
of their favorite chief, and left General Grouchy—the same
who nearly twenty years afterward failed Napoleon at the
crisis of the battle of Waterloo—second in command. It
also placed Rear-Admiral Bouvet, who was well known to
be hostile to the expedition, second in command of the fleet.
There never sailed from any port a more unlucky expedition. In passing through the difficult channel of the Raz,
one ship of war capsized on a sunken rock and about a thousand men perished. The vessels became separated first in
a fog, and afterward in clear weather. In fact, the French
navy was as inefficient as the French army of that period
was admirable, and to the lukewarmness and incompetency
of the naval officers, more even than to the constitutional
irresolution of Grouchy, the final failure of the attempt on
Ireland may be attributed. The wind began to blow foul
on December 22 and never ceased to do so for a full week.
During all this time the remnant of the expedition, consisting of 6,500 soldiers, and less than half of the fleet, lay
at anchor in, or near, Bantry Bay, having made the Irish
coast on the morning of December 21, buffeted and bat-
tered by the winds and waves—"England's only unsubsi-
dized allies." After waiting a day or two in expectation of
being joined by their comrades, so long missing, a council
of war was held and it was determined to land what forces

were present.   Bouvet, the rear-admiral in command, declined to send off his boats in face of the storm, and the
project was abandoned.

Tone proposed to General Grouchy to send part of
the ships, with the troops, around the coast to the mouth
of the Shannon, whence Limerick could be easily reached.
He also suggested other points of landing, but his propositions were all overruled—the chief objector being Admiral Bouvet.   At one time, General Grouchy seemed
resolved to adopt Tone's plan of sailing to the Shannon,
but as it began to "blow great guns" again, the project was definitively abandoned.   During the night of December 28, as well as on the two nights preceding, several
ships cut their cables and were blown out to sea.   On the
morning of the 29th, the signal to sail for France was given
and the expedition was over—the narrowest escape England had had in centuries from losing Ireland forever.   Had
the weather favored Hoche, and could he have landed
anywhere on the coast of Ulster or Leinster, where the
United Irishmen were in full force, he could not have failed
of success.   This was Napoleon's opinion, expressed when
a prisoner on the Rock of St. Helena, and he was the first
of military judges.   The shattered remains of this part of
the fleet and army reached a French port—seven sail of the
former out of the 43 that left Brest—within a week after
the withdrawal from Bantry Bay.   Strangest fact of all
is this: From the time the expedition sailed, until it returned, it did not sight a single English ship of war!   Fifteen days after Tone reached France, the missing frigate,
Fraternite, with General Hoche and the admiral on board,
sailed into the harbor of La Rochelle.   It had been blown
far into the Atlantic, soon after losing sight of the French

coast. Other tardy vessels of the ill-fated expedition arrived from time to time, and, strange as it may appear, a comparatively few of the ships were totally lost.

Wolfe Tone did not hold General Grouchy responsible for the failure to land in Bantry Bay. On the contrary, he defended him after his return to France. Under date of June 20, 1798, in his diary, Tone writes of an interview with the general in these terms: "We talked over the last [Bantry Bay] expedition. He [Grouchy] said he had shed tears of rage and vexation fifty times since, at the recollection of the opportunity of which he had been deprived, and there was one thing he would never pardon in himself—that he did not seize Bouvet by the collar and throw him overboard the moment he attempted to raise a difficulty as to the landing."

The English government and its Anglo-Irish satrap were grievously alarmed over the attempted French invasion, from which they had been rescued by the elements, and, accordingly, their rage against the United Irish Society became fiercer then ever. Several counties were "proclaimed"; the Bank of Ireland was ordered to suspend payments in specie, and the offices of patriotically conducted newspapers were wrecked by Orange mobs, in Belfast, without any interference for the protection of property on the part of the authorities. But the people, in general, maintained their tranquillity, and the Catholics and Dissenters continued to fraternize, still ardently expecting aid from France.

Theobald Wolfe Tone, disappointed but not discouraged by the failure of the Bantry Bay expedition, remained in the French army, and served under General Hoche as chef-de-brigade and aide, in the gallant ranks of the army of the Sambre et Meuse. These two brave men were devotedly attached to each other, and as Hoche considered himself bound in honor to repair the Irish disaster, he became even more earnest in his endeavor to promote a second expedition than he had been in the first instance. France, in 1797, had so much warlike employment on her hands that she could not make a second expeditionary experiment, but the Batavian Republic, now the kingdom of Holland, which was France's cordial ally, had both ships and men to spare. In the month of June, the general informed Tone that John Edward Lewins, an able and trusted agent of the United Irishmen, had arrived in Holland, had sounded the disposition of the Batavian government, then at war with England, and had found it favorably disposed toward going to Ireland's aid with a strong fleet and army. Hoche aided Lewins and Tone in conducting the negotiations, and, before the end of the month, the Batavian (Dutch) commander-in-chief, General Daendels, informed Hoche that all would be ready for action, as regarded an expedition to Ireland, within a brief time. He was as good as his word. Acting with the brave Admiral De Winter, who commanded the Dutch navy, Daendels had placed 15,000 men, 16 ships of the line, 8 frigates, and several transports in fighting condition. He had also collected eighty pieces of artillery, several thousand stand of small arms, and a sufficient store of ammunition. The military chest contained the pay of the soldiers and sailors for three months. France tried to induce Holland to allow 5,000 French troops to take part in the expedition, and to give Hoche the chief command; but this proposition so evidently pained the gallant Dutch leaders, whose hearts were set upon the enterprise, that the magnanimous French warrior waived all claim and left

General Daendels and Admiral De Winter, in their respective spheres, in chief command of the expedition. There was a definitive understanding with the Dutch government, as there had been with the French, that no attempt would be made to interfere with the national independence of the Irish people after the English yoke was thrown off. These matters having been satisfactorily settled, thanks chiefly to the unselfish exertions of General Hoche, the Batavian troops embarked on their ships in the Texel, and waited a favorable wind to drive their fleet to the Irish shore. An English squadron of rather inferior strength, under Admiral Duncan, lay off the mouth of the Texel. At this time the strength of the British navy was greatly reduced, and its very existence threatened, by the "mutiny of the Nore," which occurred among the crews of the English ships of war, lying near the mouth of the Thames. It was a mutiny for higher pay and better food. The government acted with vigor. The ringleaders were arrested, tried by their officers, found guilty and hanged, or otherwise harshly punished. The pay was raised and the quality of food improved. Nautical John Bull, with his stomach well filled, and with a wholesome horror of the halter or the lash, was then ready to fight. But the precious weeks of diversion were lost to the Dutch expedition by persistent adverse winds, which lasted from the beginning of July to the end of August. Wolfe Tone, who was on board the admiral's ship, fretted himself almost to death. The provisions having been, at length, exhausted, the Dutch troops were disembarked, and the expedition was practically abandoned. Again the foul winds proved themselves England's most potent allies. To add to General Tone's distress, he reached, by Daendels's command, Hoche's head-

quarters in the army of the Sambre et Meuse a few hours
before the hero's death, which occurred on the morning of
September 19, 1797. His death was a severe blow to
France, to Ireland, and to human liberty. There were sus-
picions of poison, but no positive proof. Tone, in his
diary, wrote—"Sept. 18-19. My fears with regard to General Hoche were but too well founded. He died this morning at 4 o'clock. His lungs seemed to me quite gone. This
most unfortunate event has so confounded and distressed
me, that I know not what to think, nor what will be the consequences. Wrote to my wife [who with Tone's children
and sister had been in France for a few months] and to
General Daendels, instantly."

"It is impossible," wrote Mitchel, "to overestimate the
importance of the loss which the Irish cause in France sustained through the death of General Hoche. He had thoroughly made that cause his own, through his warm admiration for his Irish aide, as well as from his settled conviction, formed on military principles, that to strike England
in Ireland is the surest and easiest way to destroy her
power. . . . And if he had lived but another year, his influence might have availed to direct upon the coast of Ireland that fine fleet and army which made the unavailing and
disastrous invasion of Egypt."

Rendered desperate by the failure of the enterprise on
which his government had founded such high hopes, Admiral De Winter, on the morning of October 11, the wind
being, at last, fair for his purpose, sailed out of the Texel
and engaged, off Camperdown, the reinforced fleet of Admiral Duncan. The English had the advantage in weight
of metal, but the Dutch fought with their traditional courage. The slaughter was immense, but, finally, the Dutch

fleet was vanquished, Holland fell from her high estate as a
naval power, and Duncan, the successful admiral, became
Lord Camperdown.

The death of Hoche left Napoleon Bonaparte the undisputed title of the premier soldier of France. Promoted to
the office of commander-in-chief of what was known as the
Army of England, he set to work to prepare an expedition
on a large scale, ostensibly for the invasion and subjugation of Britain. He received both Tone and Lewins with
courtesy, and promised the former employment in the event
of an expedition against England. But, in this matter,
Napoleon was not sincere. The dream of an Oriental empire turned his brain. He knew little of Ireland, which he
underestimated, supposing it to be something like his native
Corsica. Nothing could convince him that it had over
2,000,000 of people, whereas it then possessed more than
double that number, and had resources not to be despised.
Napoleon lived to regret his miscalculation. Before he died
he was forced to the conclusion of an antique English poet:

> "He who would England win
> Must with Ireland first begin."

Bonaparte pursued the expedition against Egypt and
gathered Dead Sea fruit. The great fleet and army, which
might have made him victor over England, met with disappointment almost from the first. Nelson made short
work of the former at the Battle of the Nile, and the
ghastly glory of the Pyramids and Aboukir and Mount Ta-
bor hardly compensated for the repulse before Acre, the
dreadful march through the desert, the horrors of the hospital at Jaffa, where the plague decimated the conquerors
of Lodi, and Bonaparte's almost lonely flight from the land

of the Pharaohs back to mesmerized France, which was destined to be still more the victim of her favorite hero's military genius and insatiable ambition. Napoleon was a great soldier, but, in state affairs, he often acted like a magnificent lunatic.

CHAPTER V

Irish Reign of Terror Begins—Execution of William Orr—The Martyr's Name Made Watchword of United Irishmen—Murders and Outrages by the Military—A Terrible State of Affairs

WHILE the French were moving toward Egypt, the English government, relieved from the terror of formidable invasion, was making Ireland a veritable hell on earth. Secret service funds were freely used to produce a loathsome crop of spies and informers, who wormed themselves into the councils of the United Irish organization. In the previous year (1797) William Orr, a respectable farmer of the County Antrim, and a Presbyterian in religion, was arrested on a charge of administering the United Irish oath to a private soldier named Wheatley. The evidence was of the most untrustworthy character, when he came up for trial, and the jury was notoriously a packed one. Whiskey was also admitted secretly to the jury room. The outcome was, under the circumstances, a foregone conclusion. Mr. Orr was found guilty, and was "hanged, drawn, and quartered" in the vicinity of Carrickfergus, not far from where lived his stricken wife, who was about to become a mother. It was afterward proven that Mr. Orr was not the man who administered the oath to Wheatley. His shocking butchery touched all Ireland deeply, and, particularly, the Dissenting population, by whom he was held in such high esteem. "Remember Orr!" became the rallying cry of the United Irishmen. Mr. Peter Finerty, a native of Galway County, published at that period, in Dublin, an able national journal called "The Press." In it there appeared a strong but just criticism of the base methods adopted by the government to secure the legal murder of William Orr. Mr. Finerty peremptorily refused, when asked by the attorney-general, to give the name of the contributor of the article, who wrote over the signature of "Marcus." He was arrested and brought to trial for "libel of the judiciary," alias the Castle government. His legal defender was the great advocate, John Philpot Curran, who delivered on the occasion one of the greatest speeches ever heard in a court-room. His impeachment of the professional informers deserves to live forever. "Will you," he said, addressing the jury, "upon your oaths say to the 'sister' country [England] that there are no such abominable instruments of destruction as informers used in the state prosecutions of Ireland? Let me honestly ask you, what do you feel, when, in my hearing—when in the face of this audience—you are asked to give a verdict that every man of us, and every man of you, know, by the testimony of your own eyes, to be utterly and absolutely false? I speak not now of the public proclamation for informers, with a promise of secrecy and extravagant reward; I speak not of those unfortunate wretches who have been so often transferred from the table to the dock, and from the dock to the pillory. I speak of what your own eyes have seen, day after day, during the progress of this commission [to try political prisoners] while you attended this court—the number of horrid miscreants who acknowledged, upon their oaths, that they had come from the seat of government—from the very chambers of the Castle—where they had been worked upon by the fear of death and hope of compensation to give evidence against their fellows—that the mild, the wholesome, and the merciful councils of this government are holden over those catacombs of living death, where the wretch that is buried a *man* lies till his heart has time to fester and dissolve and is then dug up a *witness!* Is this a picture created by a hag-ridden fancy, or is it a fact? Have you not seen him, after his resurrection from that tomb, make his appearance upon your table, the image of life and death, and the supreme arbiter of both? Have you not marked, when he entered, how the stormy wave of the multitude retired at his approach? Have you not seen how the human heart bowed to the awful supremacy of his power, in the undissembled homage of deferential horror? How his glance, like the lightning of heaven, seemed to rive the body of the accused, and mark it for the grave, while his voice warned the devoted wretch of woe and death—a death which no innocence can escape, no art elude, no force resist, no antidote prevent! There *was* an antidote—a juror's oath; but even that adamantine chain, which bound the integrity of man to the throne of eternal justice, is solved and molten in the breath which issues from the mouth of the informer. Conscience swings from her moorings; the appalled and affrighted juror speaks what his soul abhors, and consults his own safety in the surrender of the victim. . . . Informers are worshiped in the temple of justice, even as the devil has been worshiped by pagans and savages—even so, in this wicked country, is the informer an object of judicial idolatry—even so is he soothed by the music of human groans—even so is he placated and incensed by the fumes and by the blood of human sacrifices!"

Nevertheless, Peter Finerty was found guilty, fined, imprisoned for two years, and forced to give bonds for his "good conduct" for seven years. His business was, of course, destroyed and he died in exile and penury.

The process of disarmament became general in Ireland early in 1798, and this process was facilitated by the proclamation of martial law and suspension of the habeas corpus.

In England, Arthur O'Connor, who, together with Lord Edward Fitzgerald, had negotiated with France on more than one occasion, in the interest of the United Irishmen, was arrested at Margate, while en route to the Continent, in company with the Rev. James Coigley, a Catholic clergyman; John Binns, and a Mr. John Allen. They were tried before a special commission, in May, and all were acquitted, except Father Coigley, who was convicted of high treason and subsequently executed in the usual barbarous manner of the period. He died heroically, saying on the scaffold that he was proud to suffer for his country. Messrs. O'Connor and Binns were subsequently arrested on another charge, and were detained as state prisoners for a long term, no attention whatever being paid to their request for an immediate trial.

The general condition of the "proclaimed" kingdom in the spring of the year 1798 may be gathered from the following excerpt from the memoirs of Miles Byrne, a participant in the subsequent insurrection of that year, who, afterward, became a lieutenant-colonel in the French army, and survived until 1862: "The military, placed on free quarters with the inhabitants," says Colonel Byrne, "were mostly furnished by the Ancient Britons, a cruel regiment which became obnoxious from the many outrages they committed wherever they were stationed; being quartered in houses where the men had to absent themselves, the unfortunate females who remained had to suffer all sorts of brutality from these ferocious monsters. What hardships, what calamities and miseries, had not the wretched people to suffer, on whom were let loose such a body of soldiery as were then in Ireland!"

The blacksmiths of Ireland, accused of furnishing pike-blades, were systematically arrested, as a mode of "striking terror," and their houses and forges burned to the ground. The life of no man, or the honor of no woman, was secure. Even the lives of innocent children were not safe when at the "mercy" of the uniformed fiends who disgraced in Ireland the honorable profession of arms. To be suspected of being an enemy of government was to be deprived of liberty, if not of existence itself. The Irish Reign of Terror was, in many particulars, more revolting than that which prevailed in France five years before, and, as the year advanced, the horrors increased and multiplied. In evidence of what we have here affirmed, we quote the following passages from the Memoirs of Colonel Byrne (which can be found in the public libraries) : "Poor Garret Fennell, who had just landed from England [May, 1798], and was on his way to see his father and family, was met by this corps [Hunter Gowan's Corps of Orange Yeomanry, mounted, called in derision "the black mob"] and tied by his two hands up to a tree; they then stood at a certain distance and each man lodged the contents of his carbine in the body of poor Fennell, at the captain's command. They then went to a house close by, where they shot James Darcy, a poor inoffensive man, the father of five children. The bodies of these two murdered victims were waked that night in the chapel of Munseed, where the unhappy women and children assembled to lament their slaughtered relatives. This chapel was afterward burned. Fennell left a young widow and two children. The cruel deeds took place between our house and the chapel. The day after, May 25, occurred one of the most bloody deeds recorded in Irish history, since the time of Cromwell, at a point distant about three miles from our place. Twenty-eight fathers of families, prisoners, were shot and massacred in the Ball Alley of Carnew [borders of Wicklow and Wexford] without trial. . . . I knew several of the murdered men, particularly Pat Murphy, at whose wedding I was two years before. He was a brave and most worthy man, and much esteemed. William Young, a Protestant, was among the slaughtered.

"At Dunlavin, County of Wicklow, previous to the 'rising,' thirty-four men were shot without any trial—officers, to their disgrace, presiding and sanctioning these proceedings. But it is useless to enumerate, or continue, the list of cruelties perpetrated. It will suffice to say that where the military were placed on free quarters, and where all kinds of crime were committed, the people were not worse off than those living where no soldiers were quartered; for, in the latter instance, the inhabitants were generally called to their doors and shot, without ceremony; their houses being immediately burned or plundered."

The weight of historical testimony of the period shows, conclusively, that the Orange atrocities were encouraged by the infamous government of the time, Grattan himself declaring that "the ministry was in league with the abettors of the Orangemen and at war with the people." Mitchel, commenting on the horrors of that epoch, says: "It is notorious that, while the Irish and English governments have always professed to disapprove the sanguinary principles of the Orange Society, they have always relied upon that body,

in seasons of threatened revolt, as a willing force to crush
the mass of the people, and that even as late as 1848 arms
were secretly issued to the Orange lodges from Dublin
Castle."

Although the grand masters of the Orange fraternity
disavowed enmity to "loyal" men of the Catholic persuasion, the acts of the Orange yeomen, in Leinster, belied their
assertions, for they outdid even the Ancient Britons, of
atrocious memory, in crimes of cruelty and indecency committed against one of the most virtuous populations on the
globe.

CHAPTER VI

The Government Strikes Hard—United Irish Leaders Arrested while
    in Council—Lord Edward Fitzgerald Escapes—He is Finally Cap-
    tured, after a Fierce Resistance—Dies of his Wounds in Prison—
    Loss Irreparable

MARCH 12, 1798, was signalized by the arrest of several leaders of the United Irish Society, at the house
of Oliver Bond—a patriotic merchant—in Dublin. The
traitor on this occasion was one Thomas Reynolds, a silk
mercer, and a property owner in Kildare County, who had
been deemed worthy by Lord Edward Fitzgerald, and Bond
himself, because of his influence among the Catholics, to
be high in the councils of the patriotic conspirators. Reynolds, who was of a plausible disposition, succeeded in
having himself elected treasurer and representative for Kildare, accepted the commission of colonel from the United
Irish directory, and, finally, became delegate to that body
from the province of Leinster. He sold out his associates
for money, and received five hundred guineas "in hand"
as the price of his first information. He negotiated with

the government through a Mr. Cope, a "loyalist" merchant, and revealed to that person the important fact that the Leinster delegates of the United Irishmen would meet at Bond's residence, to mature the plans for an insurrection, on the date already stated. Thirteen delegates fell into the trap, and were arrested by Town Major Swan, assisted by twelve sergeants in civilian costume. In addition, on the same day, Thomas Addis Emmet, Oliver Bond, John Sweetman, William James MacNevin, Henry Jackson, and Hugh Jackson were taken into custody and lodged in jail. Warrants were also issued for Richard McCormick, William Sampson, and Lord Edward Fitzgerald—the latter being known to the government as the commander-in-chief of the United Irish army, from the papers captured at Bond's house. In those papers, many of the plans of campaign were outlined, and the real formidability of the United Irishmen was startlingly revealed. The three gentlemen last named, having had ample warning, managed to escape the fangs of the government sleuth-hounds, for a period.

The vacancies in the national directory were speedily filled, and among those who took active part in remedying the recent disaster were two brilliant young barristers, Henry and John Sheares. These gentlemen were subsequently betrayed to the government by a personal friend and associate, who had held the king's commission as an officer, Captain Armstrong, who actually accepted the hospitality of Henry Sheares, ate at his table, drank of his wine, and played with his children, on Sunday, May 20, 1798. Mrs. Sheares entertained this modern Judas with music, and he was treated as a member of the betrayed family by the aged mother and accomplished sister of the devoted brothers. From this sacred domestic atmosphere, Armstrong went forth and sold his host, Henry, and his brother, John, for pay! They were immediately arrested and speed-ily reached their doom—a cruel and ignominious death. Interred in old St. Michan's Church, which seems to have preserving properties, their severed heads are still to be seen, almost as perfect as on the day of execution, now more than a hundred years ago.

Treason seemed to pursue the United Irishmen from the day of the arrest at Bond's. The date of general insurrec-tion had been already fixed for May 23. The government, evidently, had become aware of that fact, for the pursuit of Lord Edward, who had been in concealment since March 12, became more ardent, and immense rewards were of-fered for his capture. He managed to elude his enemies successfully, although his bodyguard had a few sharp en-counters with them, for many weeks. Once, after having escaped from a surrounded house by connivance, he actually directed a patrol he encountered to hasten to the place he had just fled from if they would arrest "Lord Edward"! The man never knew the meaning of fear. On the 19th of May government was informed by a traitor, who has never been identified, that the dreaded rebel chief was in Dublin, stopping at the house of one Nicholas Murphy, a feather merchant of excellent reputation, on Thomas Street. In the afternoon of that day, Lord Edward, a man named Nelson, whose after conduct exposed him to what may have been unjust suspicion, and Mr. Murphy sat down to dinner together. They seemed to enjoy the repast, but, immedi-ately after the cloth was removed, Nelson excused himself abruptly, and left the house, being, seemingly, in a great hurry. Mr. Murphy was called downstairs on a matter of business, and Fitzgerald was left alone in the parlor. When

Mr. Murphy returned to that apartment, his guest had gone to his room. Thither Murphy proceeded and found Lord Edward lying on the bed with his coat off. He addressed a remark to him, but, before Fitzgerald could reply, the chamber door was flung open, and Major Swan, followed by Captain Ryan and a party of soldiers, entered the room. Swan advanced immediately toward the couch, and a soldier thrust Murphy out of the apartment. The major produced a warrant for Fitzgerald's arrest, warning him, also, that resistance would be futile. Lord Edward sprang up immediately, leveled a pistol at Swan and pulled the trigger. The weapon missed fire. In a second he had drawn a double-edged, twisted dagger, of Oriental make, from beneath his pillow and grappled with Swan, inflicting many painful wounds. Captain Ryan rushed to the major's aid, and fired at the gallant Geraldine, without effect. He then rushed at him with a sword-cane, and his lunge bent the blade on Lord Edward's ribs. The latter was borne on the bed by the shock and Ryan, who was a powerful man, while Fitzgerald was below the medium height, threw himself on the prostrate hero. The latter, roused to fury, grappled with his huge antagonist and they rolled on the floor together. Lord Edward's dagger dealt death blows all over the captain's body, and one wound in the lower part of Ryan's abdomen actually disemboweled him. At this crisis, Major Sirr, followed by several soldiers, appeared, and beheld Fitzgerald making for the door, with the dying Ryan clinging to one limb and the bleeding Swan to the other. The right arm of the Irish leader was raised to give Swan his coup de grace, when Sirr, fearing to close with him, fired a pistol, the ball from which lodged in Lord Edward's shoulder. The raised arm of the latter dropped helpless, and the blood-stained dagger fell upon the floor. Then the soldiers rushed to the assistance of their chiefs, but they were obliged to fell Fitzgerald to the floor, lay their muskets across his legs, wrists and neck, and kneel upon them, before he could be subdued. While lying upon his face, helpless, a dastardly drummer inflicted a severe stab in the back of the neck, which eventually produced fever and hastened the dauntless captive's death. Lord Edward died in a cell of Newgate prison, Dublin, on June 4. In his dying delirium, he fought the battle with Swan and Ryan over again, and the people, standing mournfully on the sidewalks near the jail, could hear him shouting, "Come on! d—n you! Come on!"

Thus perished one of the bravest spirits Ireland has produced. He had in his veins the proud blood not of the Geraldines alone, but also of the Plantagenets, the Stuarts, and the O'Neills. Yet for the sake of Ireland and human liberty—although in his early youth, while an officer in the British army, he fought against America—he yielded up his life. A former comrade in arms, who visited him in prison before he became delirious, reminded him that he had been wounded at the battle of Eutaw Springs in South Carolina. "Oh," observed the chivalrous sufferer, "that was in a very different cause. Then, I was fighting against liberty, now I am dying to establish it in Ireland!" No wonder that the masses of the Irish people adore his memory. He left a beautiful young widow, Pamela, reputed daughter of Philippe Egalité, Duke of Orleans—who perished on the scaffold during the French Revolution—by the celebrated Parisian beauty and leader of fashion, Madame de Genlis. Lady Edward was, therefore, a half-sister of the late King Louis Philippe, of France. Three

children were born of this romantic union. The only son,
Edward Fox Fitzgerald, was educated by the Duke of
Leinster's family, and brought up in a Whig atmosphere.
He became an officer in the English army, and died in
obscurity, about the year 1861. The daughters married
Englishmen of title. The Lady Pamela, herself, had an
unenviable ending. After the lapse of years, she married
an American consul. They lived unhappily and were finally
separated. Pamela survived to be old and died penniless.

Lord Edward's capture and death dislocated, so to speak,
the whole United Irish military machinery. Many of his
papers, containing plans of concentration and attack, fell
into the hands of the government, which was thus enabled
to take counteracting measures. This circumstance, probably, explains why the insurgents, when they finally struck,
were unable to surprise the strong places they had calcu-
lated on capturing with a rush.

So perfect was the spy-system of the Pitt government
that even the State and War Departments of France were
not safe repositories of the United Irish documents, transmitted by trusty messengers to their respective heads. And
when, in after days, the leaders, who made an honorable
compromise with government after the suppression of the
revolt, were examined before a secret committee of the
Irish House of Lords, they were astonished at finding some
of the original manuscripts of their communications with
France in the hands of the Anglo-Irish law officers. Their
compromise consisted in stating frankly to their examiners
the causes that led to the insurrection, and the part they
had individually taken in maturing the conspiracy. As all
of them were in close arrest before the fighting began, their
lives were spared, but they were exiled to and confined in

Fort George, a place of strength in the Scottish Highlands, in April, 1799, and remained there as prisoners until the Peace of Amiens, in 1802, when they were set at liberty, the condition in most cases being that they must not return to Ireland. The names of these persecuted patriots were Thomas Addis Emmet, Arthur O'Connor, William James MacNevin, John Sweetman, Matthew Dowling, John Chambers, Edward Hudson, George Cumming, Samuel Neilson, Thomas Russell, Robert Simms, William Tennent, Robert Hunter, Hugh Wilson, John Sweeney, Joseph Cuthbert, William Steele Dixon, and John Cormick. The creeds of these prisoners were divided thus: Episcopalians, of the anti-Orange element, 10; Presbyterians, 6; Roman Catholics, 4. In the rank and file of the active revolutionists, the Catholics stood first in point of numbers—that is, after the insurrection broke out—the Presbyterians and other Dissenters second, and the Episcopalians third. Nor were the Irishmen who basely fought against their country in 1798 exclusively Protestant. A very large contingent of Catholics fought for George III in the ranks of the militia and regulars particularly; although many of the latter deserted their colors when brought into actual conflict with their own countrymen. These men, when captured by the English, were summarily shot or hanged.

As many of the insurgent colonels had become possessed of Lord Edward's orders, previous to his arrest, they followed them out to the best of their ability, but without the understanding and cohesion so necessary to success.

CHAPTER VII

Outbreak of the Insurrection—Kildare, Carlow, and Other Counties Contiguous to Dublin Spring to Arms—Outnumbered and Outmanœuvred, the People are Quickly Subdued—Massacre at the Curragh

THE signal for insurrection, as understood by the Irish leaders, was to be the stoppage of the regular mail coaches on the principal highroads throughout the country. Accordingly, when the Northern and Connaught mails did not go through, as usual, on the night of May 23, the insurgents in the County Kildare (Lord Edward's home district) rose at once, and, on the morning of the 24th, attacked the jail at Naas, held by a royal garrison under Lord Gosford. This post, like all the others throughout the disturbed sections, including Dublin, had been greatly strengthened without the knowledge of the people. Hence, they attacked a superior force, well protected, and were repulsed, their retreat being accelerated by a charge of the Ancient Briton cavalry, which swept around their flanks and did considerable execution. The insurgent loss was 140 men killed, wounded, and captured, the latter to meet a more cruel death than would have overtaken them in the field. The king's forces, according to their own account, lost two officers and thirty men in killed and wounded. Thus the rebellion opened ominously for Ireland. On the same day, the insurgents, under Doctor John Esmonde, who was also an officer in a yeomanry corps, destroyed, at Prosperous, a militia detachment under Captain Swayne. Dr. Esmonde, who would seem to have been extremely imprudent, was recognized by a yeoman and betrayed to the government agents. He was arrested, tried, convicted, and hanged in Dublin soon afterward. In an action fought with a body of royal troops at Kilcullen the patriots were defeated with heavy loss. At Clane they suffered another serious reverse. On May 25, a party of four hundred insurgents, under Captains Ledwich and Keough, was suddenly attacked, while on the march, near Clondalkin, by Lord Roden's horse, and, in spite of a brave resistance, sustained a complete rout. Their leaders were captured, Keough being dangerously wounded. He recovered, and, through some friendly influence, escaped. Captain Ledwich was immediately tried by drumhead court-martial, found guilty, and hanged. Kildare and Dublin Counties, being mainly level, or gently rolling, gave good opportunity for the use of cavalry by the royal army, which, be it noted, was, at the outset, composed mainly of "loyalist" Irishmen, chiefly recruited in Ulster. Most of them were militia, yeomen, and other irregulars. Thus it was, to a great extent, Irish against Irish—the better armed and disciplined forces, although less numerous than their antagonists, having a decided advantage. Carlow, Dublin, and Kildare were about equally unfortunate in their attempts at overwhelming the royal troops, although determined and bloody encounters occurred at the towns of Carlow, Hacketstown, Monastereven, Rothfarnham, Lucan, Tallaght, Barretstown, Baltinglass, Collon, and Dunboyne. The patriots were successful at Dunboyne and Barretstown, but, although displaying chivalric courage, were worsted in a majority of the engagements, their total loss being appalling, because the victors, once the insurgent formation was broken, rushed in their formidable horse and butchered the fugitives without mercy. In fact, "no quarter" was the recognized order of the day in the royal army. At Carlow, particularly, the insurgents suffered terribly, because of their own imprudence. Their defeat led to the murder of a man entirely innocent of "rebellion," who was supposed to have sympathized with their cause. The victim was Sir Edward Crosbie, a respected gentleman, upon whose lawn, outside the town, the insurgents had mustered before they attacked. He could not prevent their action and did not join in their hostile movement. Other innocent people were subsequently arrested and sustained their guiltlessness before the military tribunals, but in most cases they shared the fate of those taken with arms in their hands. Two hundred respectable citizens of Carlow and its neighborhood were summarily executed before the royalist fury expended itself. The loyalists were particularly frenzied by the repulse of General Dundas's column, with the loss of Captain Erskine and 22 men killed, together with many wounded, on May 24. Left without competent military direction, the insurgents, notwithstanding occasional successes, speedily lost heart, and proceeded to negotiate with Dundas, who promised them quarter if they would lay down their arms. This they agreed to do, and that officer sent General Welford to receive their surrender. Before the latter could arrive at Gibbet Rath, in Kildare, where the capitulated "rebels," to the number of 3,000, had assembled, General Sir James Duff, at the head of a formidable force of horse, foot, and artillery, had reached the vicinity of that place. Although he must have been advised of the surrender, Duff immediately formed his troops in order of battle and advanced upon the Rath. Plowden says, in his history, that one of the "rebels," as the troops approached, caught up his gun, swearing he would not surrender it loaded, and fired in the air. Other historians are silent

regarding this alleged incident. However, the force under
Duff immediately attacked the bewildered people and cruelly
shot or sabred over 300 of them—a perfectly useless and
causeless massacre. We are glad to find the following ex-
oneration of an honorable foe in Madden's "United Irishmen": "No part of the infamy of this proceeding," says the
learned Doctor, "attaches to General Dundas. The massacre
took place without his knowledge or sanction. His conduct throughout the rebellion was that of a humane and
brave man." One of the most spirited engagements fought
in Kildare, previous to the ill-starred surrender, was that at
Rathangan, where the insurgents were ably commanded by
Captain Edward Molloy and Lieutenant James Doorley.
Both of these officers were young men of the heroic type.
They held the town for several days, but were, at length,
their comrades in other places having capitulated, overwhelmed by numbers, and died fighting desperately to the
last.

About 3,000 of the United Irishmen of Dublin and Meath
mustered on the regal hill of Tara, in the latter county, on
May 26. They were attacked that day by a powerful royalist force, composed of Scotch fencibles and Irish yeomen,
horse and foot, and were scattered with some loss, but not
before they had killed thirty-two of their assailants and
wounded thrice that number. Another depressing defeat
befell the insurgents at Dunlavin, where they lost about 350
men. These reverses practically terminated the insurrection in the neighborhood of Dublin. That city failed to
rise, for the very good reason that it had been placed under
martial law soon after the arrests at Bond's, in March.

The reader will think, not without reason, that the metropolitan districts of Leinster made a poor showing in the

field. The records, however, show no lack of physical courage on the part of the vanquished, but reveal an almost total lack of organization and a profound ignorance of military prineiples. Arms—all except shotguns and rude pikes —were exceedingly scarce, and the people had not learned the martial principle of that day—to form square when about to be charged by cavalry. Wellington, in the Iberian peninsula, proved, soon afterward, that it was then possible for a determined infantry to repel, even when in line, a charge of horsemen with the bayonet. In our own times, no general would think of hurling a mass of cavalry at a body of foot equal, or nearly so, in number, and armed with the Mauser rifle, or some kindred weapon. If ordered to do so insane an act, the cavalry would be mown down like grass.

CHAPTER VIII

The "'Rising" of Wexford—Father John Murphy Calls on the People to Defend Themselves—They Defeat the Yeoman Cavalry at Camolin, and Annihilate a Militia Regiment at Oulart Hill

THERE was, of course, much joy in Dublin Castle over the speedy collapse of the local revolt, but the jubilation turned out to be premature. Soon there came bodeful news from the peaceable, easy-going, English-blooded people of the County Wexford—the first portion of Irish soil occupied by the invading Normans and their Welsh subjects, more than six hundred years before. Many old Celtic families, more or less mixed with the invaders through long intermarriage, still remained, but, in general, the Wexford folk were Norman, Cymrian, or Danish by descent. They were slow to anger, but desperate when aroused. Up to this time the United Irishmen had made but small headway

among them. Many Catholics were in the yeoman ranks,
and these, notwithstanding the fidelity to England displayed
by some of their comrades in Kildare and Carlow, Lord
Castlereagh, who had active direction of affairs under the
viceroy, caused to be discharged. All Protestants suspected
of Irish sympathies were similarly disposed of. Then government demanded a surrender of all arms in the hands
of the people. The Wexford baronies of Forth and Shel-
malier, near the coast, were then, as now, peopled by a race
accustomed, as hunters, to carry firearms. Most of these
were immediately secreted, together with such pikes as had
been recently manufactured for an emergency. The Catholic priesthood, with few exceptions, advised, from their altars
and in private, the people to give up their arms, so that they
might escape pillage and outrage at the hands of the vicious
soldiery, who, in the event of refusal, were certain to be
placed at "free quarters" among them. The clergy acted,
unquestionably, from good intention, but they were soon
about to réalize that they had committed a serious political
mistake. The more the people submitted, the more high-
handed became the conduct of their persecutors. Militia
and yeomen, on the pretext of searching for concealed
weapons, entered the houses of the peasants and committed
all manner of unspeakable offences—the helpless females
being mostly the objects their cowardly crimes. Soon the
peaceably disposed county of Wexford was in a tumult.
The virtuous people could stand any oppression rather than
insult to their wives, sisters, daughters, and even aged
mothers. Among the priests who had been most active in
urging the peasantry to disarm was Father John Murphy,
paster of Boolavogue. He, no doubt, sincerely believed that
Ireland could not succeed in throwing off the English yoke

by force of arms—at least just then; but he was greatly
shocked and troubled by the reports of outrages that reached
him daily and hourly through his affrighted parishioners.
Most of the peasantry had begun to cut their hair short
about the year 1798, and, for this reason, the soldiers, and
royalists in general, nicknamed them "Croppies." Whenever one of the latter fell into the hands of the cruel military, a cap made of strong material and plastered with
melted pitch, red-hot, on the inside, was applied to the captive's head and allowed to grow cold and hard. Then it was
torn off, and, of course, most of the "croppy's" short hair
with it. Unprovoked massacres of the people were of daily
occurrence—the chief being those of Carnew and Dunlavin.
The savage Indian was never more ferocious than the royalist soldier in Ireland at that period. His merciless conduct
greatly horrified the law-abiding Father Murphy. He had
been prone to believe that the British soldier was a brave
warrior, not a dastardly assassin of the helpless and innocent. The good Father had been educated on the Continent
of Europe; and, remembering the excesses of the French
Revolution, had a holy horror of popular uprisings. But the
tales of outrage became so frequent that his soul was filled
with sorrow for his afflicted people, and he fervently prayed
to God for light to guide him through the surrounding social and political darkness. Returning from his other parish
of Monageer, on Whit-Saturday, May 26, he found his
church of Boolavogue, the humble parochial house, and the
cottages of several of his parishioners on fire—wantonly ignited by the savage, hard-hearted yeoman cavalry, who
imagined that the people were wholly in their power after
having given up their arms. In the face of this exasperating spectacle, Father Murphy, the amiable and peace-loving,

became transformed—we might say transfigured—into a gifted and resourceful general. His people flocked to him for counsel and guidance. They were bewildered by their misfortunes and terror. "What are we to do, your reverence?" the more resolute asked. "Do!" echoed the indignant priest; "why, die courageously, as becomes Christians and Irishmen, in the field, rather than submit to be butchered in our homes. For my part, if any brave men will follow me, I am resolved to fight and sell my life dearly. We will prove to those cruel monsters that they can not continue their murders and devastations with impunity. Who among you will follow me for Ireland and liberty?" "All, Father—all!" responded the men of the parish.

They had assembled in a wood within sight of the burning buildings, for they dared not show themselves in the open fields, as the fierce yeomen were riding all around, committing arson, murder, and all manner of crime in every direction. The smoke of their many burnings blackened and polluted the sweet May-time air.

On hearing the response of his faithful parishioners, the priest's fine, expressive face flushed with joy. He bitterly reproached himself with having advised his flock to give up their pikes and guns to foes who had neither faith nor honor. He soon broke silence, however, saying to his followers: "Well, my children, I have decided what to do. When night falls, hasten homeward and arm yourselves, the best way you can, with pitchforks and other weapons, and attack the Camolin cavalry on their way back to Earl Mountnorris's place, where they will pass the night after venting their rage on the unfortunate and defenceless country people." (Miles Byrne's Memoirs.)

This plan was put in operation at the appointed time.

The men, when night fell, picked up their hay-forks—
most of them with eight-inch prongs—and such pikes and
guns as they had not given up. Then, under Father
Murphy's orders, they mustered in a wood, formed in
rude array, and marched on the causeway by which the
corps of yeoman cavalry was to approach. He left a squad
of men at a farmhouse on the way, with orders to draw
a couple of carts across the road when the rear of the horsemen had passed. With the main body, he took post behind
the hedges on the roadside, half a mile farther on, having
first taken the precaution to place a strong barricade across
the highway. The cavalry, going at a smart trot, and boast-
ing of the crimes they had committed on the peasantry during the day, returned from their infamous mission about 9
o'clock in the evening. The night was dark enough to
screen the preparations to receive them made by Father
Murphy and his men. Presently, their leading files smashed
into the barricade in their front. Simultaneously, the
priest's voice rang out: "Now, my children, in God's name,
strike home!" The peasant insurgents leaped over the
hedges and closed with their foes. The horsemen fired their
pistols, but, before they could reload, the pitchforks of the
peasants were driven between their ribs! Taken utterly by
surprise, they attempted to retreat by breaking to the rear,
but Father Murphy's men, in that direction, had obeyed
their orders well, and all escape was cut off. The entire
detachment was destroyed, Lieutenant Brodie, who commanded in the absence of Mountnorris, among the rest.
"In short," says Colonel Byrne, "they were literally lifted
out of their saddles and fell dead under their horses' feet!"

The insurgents, by this first victory, got many fine horses,
military equipments, arms, and much ammunition. They

moved on to Camolin Park, the residence of Mountnorris, which they occupied, and there found considerable additional warlike supplies. Among the latter were the new carbines of the slaughtered corps, which had just arrived from Dublin and had not been distributed.

The news of the insurgents' success soon spread far and wide through Wexford, and, by morning and during the ensuing day, which was Whitsunday, May 27 — a day forever memorable in Irish history—thousands of brave peasants, led here and there by some man who had "seen service," flocked around the priest-general and ardently awaited his orders. They soon came. He had heard that the royal troops, having learned of the annihilation of the Camolin yeomanry, showed the white feather and fled from Gorey. In the forenoon of Sunday, he marshaled his 5,000 followers, mostly unarmed, and made a rapid march to Oulart Hill, a gentle eminence, about ten miles from Wexford Town, and five from Enniscorthy, over which rises Vinegar Hill. At Oulart, Father John determined to make a stand, and he spent most of the forenoon in getting his armed men into some kind of military shape. With the foresight of a born general, he sent out mounted scouts to reconnoitre toward Wexford, where the bulk of the enemy's army lay. He also posted pickets in other directions, so as to guard against the possibility of a surprise. Meanwhile, hundreds of the hunted, terrified country-people thronged to the hill—those capable of bearing arms burning to fight for liberty and vengeance. Father Murphy breathed new hope and courage into every fugitive. He kept his eagle eye fixed on the road from Wexford, and soon perceived several strong bodies of yeoman horse, in their scarlet coats, white belts, and glittering in brass and steel, riding cautiously along the causeway and wheeling around the base of the hill, when they reached the by-roads. His videttes had already fallen back, fearing to be cut off by the hostile cavalry. The afternoon was well advanced, when the soldier-priest's keen vision detected a glint of bayonets through the far-away cloud of dust toward the city, and soon a compact body of infantry came in sight, marching at the route step to attack his force on Oulart. He called around him his musketeers and pikemen, all except the sentinels, and said, in his concise and nervous manner: "Men, the enemy are now advancing to engage us, and will soon be within striking distance. The cavalry you observe turning this hill are waiting for the foot to drive you hence in confusion, so that they may cut you to pieces on the plain below. Stand by me bravely and faithfully, and we will surely win the battle. I have devised a plan by which to destroy their infantry. When that is accomplished, the yeoman horse will run away. They are too great cowards to attack us alone." The insurgents, naturally martial, saw that he knew how to lead, and answered his words with a ringing cheer. Meanwhile, the hostile infantry had approached close to the position. They were already at the foot of the hill—so near that the commands of the officers could be plainly heard, while the cavalry, largely reinforced by new arrivals, quite surrounded the base of the eminence. Across the top of the latter, at right angles with the main road, ran an old boundary ditch, which might answer all the purposes of a rude breastwork. The hedges, common to Ireland, ran along the side of the road itself, and there the priestly general posted a force of agile pitchfork-men; for few pikes were in the hands of the insurgents at the battle of Oulart. He led forward his musketeers to meet the enemy.

His instructions were simple, and, therefore, easily comprehended. "We must attack them," he said, "with spirit. After you deliver your fire, fall back to the mearn [boundary] ditch and there shelter yourselves. The infantry will come after you on the run. A few of you rise in the centre and on the flanks, so as to draw their fire. Then, while they are reloading, or if they should charge with the bayonet, rush right on them, fearless of consequences; you will be supported by the pitchforks!" Father John's commands were implicitly obeyed. After delivering their fire against the line of infantry, the musketeers gave ground and retreated rapidly to the boundary ditch, behind which they rallied and crouched, as if in terror. The North Cork, uttering jeers and savage howls, advanced in double time, thinking the "rebels" badly worsted and demoralized. Some of the insurgents showed themselves above the ditch, as directed, and the royalist force fired as one man. Almost at the same moment, the camp-followers, by order of Father Murphy, ran in apparent confusion across the summit of the hill and down the reverse slope. This sight further emboldened the North Cork, but before they could realize their situation, the vengeful pitchforks were searching for their hearts on the flank of the column. The musketeers assailed them in front, and a detached party—for the wondrous cassocked general seemed to forget no point of strategy—attacked them in rear. Astonished, stunned, and overwhelmed, the well-trained militia regiment lost its formation, broke and fled precipitately. A cry of despair rose from the flying mass, but the Wexford blood was up, and no quarter was given. Murder, outrage, nameless insult, had to be avenged, and the vengeance was great and thorough. Of the North Cork regiment, there escaped from that bloody rout only Lieutenant-Colonel Foote, a sergeant, a drummer, and two private soldiers. Major Lombard, the Hon. Captain De Courcey, several lieutenants and ensigns, together with scores of the rank and file, died under insurgent steel on that red causeway. The Cork regiment fought bravely, but inflicted only slight loss on the "rebels." But the yeoman cavalry, under Colonel Le Hunt and other officers, proved themselves poltroons. They fled at full gallop on beholding the destruction of the infantry, but, in a measure, recompensed themselves by burning every house on the line of their flight, and shooting every peasant who came within range of their carbines. Unfortunately, in this sense, their victims were many.

CHAPTER IX

Further Insurgent Victories—Father Murphy, after Desperate Fighting, Storms Enniscorthy—Carthaginian Strategy Wins the Town—Royalists Defeated at Three Rocks and Driven from the Town of Wexford

FATHER MURPHY'S determined little army was much augmented by the Oulart victory. The demoralized royal troops fled toward so many points of the compass that he was, for a period, sore puzzled to decide which group he ought to pursue. He called a council of his officers, and, after some debate, determined to march at once and encamp for the night on Carrigrew Hill—a stronger position than that of Oulart. On the morning of the 28th, he broke camp at Carrigrew and moved his command along the main road by Camolin and Ferns. At the latter place he learned that the bulk of the royalist force had retreated to Gorey and Enniscorthy. He at once resolved to attack the latter town, although knowing that it was strongly garrisoned. His command crossed the river Slaney by the bridge of Scarawalsh and proceeded to attack the town by way of the Duffery gate, its principal entrance. Cavalry and infantry were used by the royalists to defend it. The former remained concealed until the infantry, strongly and securely posted, had disordered, by their fire, the head of the insurgent column, which was composed chiefly of pikemen. Then the horse sallied forth and repelled the attacking body. This manœuvre was repeated several times, and the patriots began to bleed copiously. They fell by the score, but rushed on again and yet again, without victorious result. Father Murphy became anxious. Suddenly he remembered how the Romans and Carthaginians used to employ fierce elephants to smash each other's lines 2,000 years before. Behind his column was herded a drove of steers, for the maintenance of the people. He immediately ordered a band of pikemen to select the wildest and drive them to the front. This was done. Fifty stout fellows, uttering terrific yells, goaded them with their pikes and headed them toward the gate. The defenders, astonished, made a brave show of resistance, but they could not long withstand that combined charge of steers and pikemen, especially as the latter now came on in force. The loyalists of the town opened their doors to some of the flying redcoats, who used the windows as loop-holes and fired on the insurgents. Father Murphy ordered the houses to be stormed. Great mutual slaughter resulted, for no quarter was asked or given, but the insurgents finally triumphed. The surviving soldiers fled in all haste to Wexford. Before they ran, Enniscorthy was in flames, and their flight was accompanied by a large, despairing crowd of old men, scared women, and weeping children. None of the latter need have feared to stay, for Father John Murphy was as merciful as he was brave and able. Indeed, the insurgents, respecting the helpless condition of the unfortunates, did not pursue, and few, if any, non-combatants perished in the fight or retreat. The garrison suffered severely, and lost nearly one hundred killed alone. The loss of the patriots was also severe.

Captain Boyd, a royalist landlord, held a commission in the Wexford (yeoman) cavalry. He arrested, by order of the sheriff and magistrates, on May 27, three popular Wexford gentlemen—Beauchamp Bagenal Harvey, John Henry Colclough, and Edward Fitzgerald—on suspicion of "treasonable" designs. They were conveyed to Wexford jail, where Boyd visited them. After a conference, it was agreed that one of the captives should proceed to Enniscorthy and try to have the insurgents break up their camp recently formed at Vinegar Hill, which stands above that town, and disperse. Mr. Colclough resolved to assume this mission, provided that Mr. Fitzgerald would accompany him. This was finally agreed to. When the emissaries reached the insurgent camp they found it divided as to immediate procedure. Some wanted to attack one place and others another. At last they determined on attacking the town of Wexford, and, detaining Mr. Fitzgerald in the camp, sent Mr. Colclough to the town, there to announce their intention. Thither, accordingly, that gentleman proceeded, and, when the royalist authorities had assembled at the old Bull Ring, then a popular place of meeting, announced to them, from horseback, the intention of the insurgents. After some parley he was allowed to depart, on giving his promise that he would join Bagenal Harvey in Wexford jail next day.

General Fawcett, of the royal army, having been apprised of the danger to Wexford, prepared to march, with a strong force, to its relief. On the morning of May 30, his advance guard, accompanied by a howitzer battery, and commanded by Captain Adams, was attacked at a place called Three Rocks, by the insurgents, and utterly destroyed—the guns becoming a prize of war, most useful to the "rebels." Colonel Maxwell attempted to retrieve the disaster, but was himself defeated with loss, and retired in all haste to Wexford. General Fawcett, greatly discouraged by the fate of Captain Adams's party, had, in the meanwhile, retreated precipitately to Duncannon, leaving the town of Wexford practically uncovered, and at the mercy of the insurgents. The royalists were utterly disheartened and begged Bagenal Harvey, although a close prisoner, to save the town from pillage and massacre. Some of the Orange yeomen had already threatened to put Mr. Harvey and other prisoners (although he and some of the rest were Protestants) to death. But the jail governor barricaded the prison and gave the key to Mr. Harvey. The latter, at the request of the magistrates, issued a brief address to the insurgents, urging them to be merciful to the people of Wexford when they came to occupy the town. A deputation was sent with the document to the insurgent camp, where they were received with respect. While the terms of capitulation were being prepared, most of the officers and men of the royal troops quartered in Wexford shamefully abandoned their posts, leaving their civilian allies in ignorance of their flight. As the "rebel" army approached the town to take possession, the few remaining military threw aside their uniforms, or else secreted themselves, for fear of popular vengeance. When the "rebels" entered Wexford, they at once proceeded to the jail and liberated the prisoners. They were, in general, boisterously good-natured, and decorated most of the houses with green boughs. In their exuberance they insisted that Bagenal Harvey should become their commander-in-chief—a position for which that unfortunate gentleman was absolutely unfitted, both by nature and training. He was physically brave, but had no military perception. The choice proved a most unfortunate one, both for him and his tumultuous followers. The only house pillaged by the insurgents, when they occupied Wexford, was that of Captain Boyd, who had rendered himself especially obnoxious to the people.

The retreating military were not so moderate in their behavior. On the contrary, they plundered, burned, shot, and ravaged indiscriminately in their dastardly flight, and, from the summit of the "rebel" encampment at Three Rocks, the whole country seemed to be covered with blazing, smoking ruins of former comfortable habitations. It is not wonderful, therefore, that the Wexford insurgents were greatly reinforced by the wretched people, who, driven from their once happy homes by a ruthless military mob, sought refuge in the "rebel" camps, many of them filled with recollections that made them burn to be avenged. It was estimated that the insurgents, all counted, numbered 30,000 souls, at least, but only a moiety were armed, so that the actual fighting strength of Wexford at any time did not, in all probability, exceed 10,000 men. With this small force, indifferently prepared for such a struggle, the "rebels" accomplished military miracles, and fully proved that, under more favorable auspices, they would have conquered in the end. Toward the close, the Wexford men had powerful assistance from the adjoining County Wicklow, where

the Byrnes, Michael Dwyer, and Joseph Holt kindled
against the common enemy the flames of war. But Wexford bore the brunt of the battle all through the rebellion.
"If the other thirty-one counties," wrote Mitchel, "had
done as well as Wexford, there would have been that year
an end of British dominion."

CHAPTER X

Insurgent Army Forms Several Encampments—Repulsed at Newtown
Barry—Bagenal Harvey Commander-in-Chief—Bloody Battle
of New Ross—Scullabogue Barn Horror

THE insurgents, in order the better to defend themselves,
and also for the purpose of sheltering, as far as they
were able to do so, thousands of frightened fugitives from
the districts where the soldiers were at their bloody work,
formed encampments at Carrigrew Hill and Carrickbyrne,
in addition to that already established on Vinegar Hill.
The latter was rudely fortified, and some of the captured
cannon were planted in the embrasures to protect it. As
has been stated, this historic elevation rises above Enniscorthy; Carrigrew was nearer Wexford and Carrickbyrne
within a few miles of New Ross. The latter was considered the key to the southeastern counties of Ireland, and
was strongly garrisoned by the royal army.

So many Catholic chapels had been wantonly burned by
the yeomen that, unfortunately, a spirit of revenge sprang
up in the breasts of some of the Catholic insurgents, who,
owing to the necessarily loose character of the military organization of the people, could not be kept under strict
discipline. Some of these ignorant and exasperated peasants took occasion one night to wreck the interior of the

Episcopalian church at Enniscorthy. It was one of the few acts of vandalism that could be laid at their doors; but, none the less, it was villanous and inexcusable. The Irish leaders were much angered by the outrage, and some of the inciters were driven from the camp and otherwise punished. We have not been told, however, that any of the yeomen were even reprimanded for having destroyed thirty places of Catholic worship in Wexford County alone. Mr. Plowden, an impartial historian of the times, says that the total number of such temples burned during the rebellion was sixty-nine.

The "rebels" met with a serious reverse near Gorey on June 1, when a large party, on the road to occupy Ballymannan Hill, was surprised and routed by the garrison of Gorey, which had made a sortie in its desperation. More than sixty of the people fell, while the royalist loss was merely nominal. Another severe repulse was experienced by the insurgents at Newtown Barry, which they bravely attacked, but without order. Having taken the place, they scattered to refresh themselves. Taking advantage of this, the royalists, under Col. L'Estrange and Lieut.-Col. Westenra, returned, surprised the town, and drove out the patriots, with a loss of about 200 men. The loss to the latter would have been much greater had not an officer of the Donegal militia, named Young, lost time at Clonegall in hanging four men, who had nothing whatever to do with the rebellion—a fact which an officer of the North Cork regiment vouched for in vain. But such was the cruelty of the period. Thousands of crimes of a similar character were committed, but there was no word of censure for the murderers from the lips of the authorities. On the contrary, it was well known throughout the army that to be merciful to the "rebels," or "croppies," as they were usually called, meant disfavor in official circles.

After the people had released Bagenal Harvey from Wexford jail, he had become, as previously stated, sorely against his will, their commander-in-chief. A brave and patriotic gentleman, he had had no military training or experience, and, doubting his own ability as a commander, succeeded, as is usually the case, in making others doubt it, too. The insurgent army divided into two bodies. One marched toward Gorey, and, while en route, encountered, at a place called Tubberneering, near Clough, the advance-guard of General Loftus's fine regular brigade, under Colonel Walpole. This battle was short and bloody. The "croppies," being now well provided with pikes, rushed in a furious torrent on Walpole's men, whom they surprised in a narrow roadway, and utterly destroyed the detachment, killing Walpole himself. The English officer was gallant, but inexperienced. Three guns were captured by the "rebels," and General Loftus, scared by his subordinate's fate, and by the annihilation of a body of Antrim militia, which, on hearing the firing, he had sent to his assistance, retreated precipitately, first to Carnew, and subsequently to Tullow, in the County Carlow.

Meanwhile, Harvey and his lieutenants, aware of the importance of capturing New Ross, the gateway to Kilkenny and Waterford, took post at Carrickbyrne, where an attempt was made to put the tumultuous array into some kind of military order. This was partially accomplished when, on June 4, that portion of the Irish forces abandoned Carrickbyrne, and occupied Corbett Hill, within about a mile of the town of New Ross. General Harvey, inexperienced as he was in the art of war, nevertheless evolved the idea of attacking the town from three sides at once, which was a wise enough plan, and, no doubt, would have succeeded had not the ill-fated commander conceived the notion of calling upon the English commander, General Johnson, to surrender the place. He sent his aide, James Furlong, a fine young man, with the message, under flag of truce. Furlong, well mounted and a finished horseman, crossed the intervening space at a gallop, "taking" all the fences and ditches in his way with perfect ease. But the red-coated guardians of Three Bullet Gate did not respect the flag. When Furlong came within range, a brutal soldier leveled his piece and fired. The insurgent officer fell from his horse stone dead. From Corbett Hill the people witnessed the murder, and, without waiting for orders, it is said, one division of the "rebels" rushed, with franctic yells, to the attack. Colonel John Kelly, of Killane, led the head of the attacking column. They met a stout opposition, but penetrated to the town. Sir Jonah Barrington says that they were repulsed and began to retreat when a thirteen-year-old boy, named Lett, who had run away from home to witness the battle, caught up a green flag, and shouting, "Follow me who dare!" induced them to renew the fight. The English cannon, served by veteran gunners, mowed down scores, but the Irish could not be dismayed. With their long pikes leveled low, they charged home the flaming cannon and took them! The royal troops gave way before them, and were driven to the market house, where they made a most gallant stand. Here more cannon were planted, but were so well handled that the insurgents could not capture all of them at once. The slaughter of the people was horrible, for the stubborn Celto-Norman blood in them was thoroughly aroused by the sight of poor Furlong's dastardly murder, and they would not give way. Finally, with a mad rush, they swept the soldiers from their front, and drove them in utter rout across the bridge of the river Barrow into the County Kilkenny. Lord Mountjoy, colonel of the County Dublin Militia, with other officers of the royal army, fell. The casualties of the rank and file were also large, but the insurgents lay dead in heaps before the muzzles of the guns they had so bravely captured. The gutters of New Ross ran red with human blood. Ireland had won the battle by consummate courage. She was about to lose another by the mad fatuity of her peasant heroes. Instead of taking proper precautions, Colonel Kelly having fallen desperately wounded in the last charge, they scattered in search of food and drink, for they were entirely worn out. They found plenty of the latter, at least, and used it freely. Soon many were asleep and helpless. Only a few "slept on their arms." An Irish royalist, named McCormick, observing this, stole over the bridge and notified the English general. Johnson rallied his remaining men and came back over the bridge. The sentinels gave the alarm, and the people, shaking off their torpor, rushed again to battle. Another murderous struggle ensued, and again the soldiers were driven over the bridge. But some of them managed to hold a part of the market house and some houses that flanked it. These, directed by McCormick, kept up the fight. The soldiers again returned and were again repulsed. But the insurgents, who were unaccountably left unsupported by their comrades on the hill, were by this time so tired out that they yielded to the combined effects of fatigue and strong liquor. Many of them entered the dwellings and went to sleep. Again General Johnson came back upon them, and the battle was, in a measure, renewed. Soon the town was on fire in many places, and both the carousers and wounded were burned by hundreds in their beds. The insurgents finally retired to Carrickbyrne Hill, leaving behind them a few dismounted cannon they had captured. Their loss was enormous, and the royal army suffered very severely also. In his bulletin of the affair, General Johnson, alluding to the insurgents, declared that he "had never seen troops who charged with more resolution." And all contemporaneous accounts bear out the statement of the general. The battle of New Ross, according to some writers, lasted ten, and, according to others, thirteen, hours. The final loss of it by the people decided, practically, the fate of the insurrection in the southeastern counties.

The massacre of the wounded and intoxicated "rebels" by the redcoats, after the latter became undisputed masters of the town, led to an act of savage and unjustifiable retaliation by a party of insurgent fugitives, who, it is said, had taken no part in the fight. A number of loyalist prisoners —mainly Protestants—were imprisoned in a barn, at a place called Scullabogue, near the foot of Carrickbyrne Hill. During the night following the battle of New Ross, this barn was set on fire, and the wretched inmates, to the number of about one hundred, were burned to death—a horrible, shocking crime, unworthy of Irishmen, and certainly not perpetrated by the gallant peasants who had fought so heroically, if unavailingly, at New Ross. The crime was committed by the skulkers and runaways of the popular army, not by the real warriors.

CHAPTER XI

Massacre of Wounded Insurgents at New Ross—Mr. Frizelle's Statement—Harvey Resigns Command—Father Roche Succeeds
Him—Indecisive Battle of Arklow

THE insurgents, when they rallied at Carrickbyrne, on
June 6, reproached their involuntary general, Bagenal
Harvey, with incompetency and want of dash.   He was so
much mortified by their accusations and horrified by the holo-
caust at Scullabogue, that he immediately resigned and retired to the town of Wexford, having, first, issued a general
order in which he said the death penalty would be executed
on "any person or persons who should take it upon himself
or themselves to kill or murder any prisoner, burn any
house, or commit any plunder, without special written order
by the commander-in-chief."   And this very order was afterward used by the infamous government as evidence against
Harvey, and was a main cause of sending him to the gallows!

Poor Harvey!   Had he been a trained soldier, he would
have arrested the ringleaders among the mutineers and shot
them, thereby reducing them to obedience, or else compel-
ling them to kill him, which would have been better than
to have died by the rope.   When he had disposed of the
mutineers—that is, if his army supported him—he should
have hunted down the Scullabogue murderers and hanged
every man of them within sight of the remains of their victims.   General Cloney, who took part with the people in
the Wexford campaign, and survived it, says, in his interesting memoirs, that, after the retreat from New Ross, he

found Harvey and several of his officers "lamenting over the smoking ruins of the barn and the ashes of the helpless victims of that barbarous atrocity." Mr. George Taylor, a royalist historian, affirms that General Harvey turned from the scene in horror and exclaimed to those about him: "Innocent people were burned there as ever were born. Your conquests for liberty are at end!"

It is only just, in this awful connection, to state a circumstance that, at least, partially relieves the murderers from the loyalist charge that their crime was committed without provocation and in cold blood. Mr. Plowden, the royalist Catholic historian, relates it thus: "A gentleman of punctilious veracity and retentive memory has assured me that he was present in the [Irish] House of Commons at the examination of a Mr. Frizelle, a person of respectability, at the bar of the House, in the summer of 1798, who was a prisoner in the House of Scullabogue on the 4th of June. . . . He said that he did not know, of his own knowledge, but only from the reports current among the prisoners, what the particular cause was for which the rebels had set fire to the barn. Upon which Mr. Ogle [the Hon. George] rose with precipitancy from his seat and put this question to him, with great eagerness: 'Sir, will you tell us what the cause was?' It having been suggested that the question would be more regularly put from the chair, it was repeated to him in form, and Mr. Frizelle answered that the only cause he, or, he believed, the other prisoners, ever understood induced the rebels to this action was that they had received intelligence that the military were again putting all the rebel prisoners to death in the town of Ross, as they had done at Dunlavin and Carnew. Mr. Ogle asked no more questions of Mr. Frizelle, and he [Mr. F.] was soon afterward dismissed from the bar." History records that the insurgents were not misinformed concerning the conduct of the royal army in New Ross the day and night following the conflict. None of the Irish wounded who were left behind escaped the slaughter. Many were removed to Wexford, among them Colonel Kelly, who so bravely led the assault. When the English finally captured Wexford town, they murdered the colonel, cut off his head, and kicked it as a football through the streets! It was then spiked, with other Irish heads, over the court-house gate. Nothing more atrocious is recorded in the annals of Europe, except the treatment given the mutilated body of the beautiful Princess Lamballe, by the revolutionary mob of Paris, during the Reign of Terror.

But it is the verdict of the patriot leaders, whose expressions on the subject have been handed down, and it is the verdict of every Irish historian, as well, that, no matter what the soldiers did in New Ross, the Irish insurgents should have scorned to imitate them at Scullabogue.

When Harvey resigned, Father Philip Roche—a much abler man—was chosen commander-in-chief in his place. But the people were now dispirited by their failure at Ross, and an attack made on some gunboats in the river was repulsed by the royalists. Subsequently, the insurgent force retired to Lacken Hill and there awaited reinforcements.

Meanwhile, that division of the United Irish army, which had fought victoriously under the orders of Father John Murphy, at Camolin, Oulart Hill, Enniscorthy, and Tubberneering, made its headquarters at Carnew, and, having been somewhat augmented by insurgent bands from the neighboring districts, marched to Gorey on the 8th of June. Next day, under the command—as we are informed by John

Mitchel, who had talked over the event with Colonel Byrne and other survivors—of Fathers John and Michael Murphy, the impatient "rebels" marched on Arklow, in the County Wicklow—a town which was the key to the capital. It is said the Irish numbered 20,000 men, 5,000 of whom had firearms of some pattern—mostly obsolete. They had also three cannon, the battery being commanded by a veteran named Esmond Kyan, who had lost an arm in battle. Now, the insurgents were accustomed to win all their battles with a pike-rush, which hardly any troops in the world could withstand, if the attacking party was boldly led. At Oulart, the people trusted more to the cannon and musketry—in which their partially intrenched enemies, who numbered not more than 2,000 men, had all the advantage. Kyan used his guns with good effect. The musket-men, with a backing of pikes, advanced in two columns to the attack, and maintained a regular fusillade for hours with the English regulars and fencibles. The latter fought with great courage, and the insurgents, who had routed the yeoman cavalry — the latter swimming the river at the risk of drowning, in order to retreat beyond the range of fire— were checked for a time by a charge of regular horse. Nothing daunted, they advanced again and took position in some ditches close to the English lines. The portion of the royal troops—Durham Fencibles, under Colonel Skerritt—who were exposed to their aim, suffered severely, but stood their ground. General Needham, who commanded in chief, thought the rebels too strong for successful resistance on the part of the army and talked of retreat. Colonel Skerritt had faith in the cannon and muskets, as arrayed against pikes and shotguns—for Kyan's guns were short in range —and refused to stir. His firmness saved the day for England. The insurgents charged across the open ground three times, losing hundreds at each attack. This was what Skerritt wanted, because they were then at the mercy of his bullets. In the last charge, Father Michael Murphy, who had led all the attacks, was killed by a cannon-ball. He was a great favorite, and the people who witnessed his fall recoiled to the ditches, and, as night had fallen, made no further effort. The reserve of, at least, 10,000 pikemen was not brought into action, for some reason that nobody has explained—at least to satisfaction. There was no Irish flight from Arklow. Colonel Byrne says the insurgents retired in a leisurely way during the night, having used up all their ammunition. Besides, Captain Kyan, who had commanded their guns, was wounded, his wooden arm having been shot off, and a portion of the stump with it. In truth, Arklow was a drawn battle, in which the Irish, because of having been the attacking party, suffered much more loss than their opponents. They behaved throughout, according to English testimony, with superb courage, as did, indeed, the royal troops. But the failure to take Arklow decided the fortune of the campaign. Dublin was secured to the English interest, and the people who had not yet committed themselves to the revolution remained neutral. Colonel Miles Byrne, who fought at Arklow, maintains that it was an Irish triumph. "How melancholy," says he, in his memoirs, "to think that a victory so dearly bought should have been abandoned, and for which no good or plausible reason could ever be assigned. . . . My firm belief is, to-day [1861], as it was that day, that if we had had no artillery the battle would have been won in half the time; for we would have attacked the position of the Durham Fencibles at the very outset, with some thousand determined pikemen, in place of leaving those valiant fellows inactive to admire the effect of each cannon-shot."

Father P. F. Kavanagh, in his admirable "History of the Insurrection of 1798," says that Father Michael Murphy was the actual commander at the battle of Arklow, and that "Father John" was not present. "It was well known among the old insurgents," says Father Kavanagh, in a foot-note, "that Father John strongly disapproved of the attack on Arklow, and remained behind at Castletown." The absence of this able chief may account for the retirement of the insurgent army, without further conquest, from that town after the death of their heroic, priestly commander.

Father Kavanagh, who sustains Colonel Byrne's assertion that Arklow was an English defeat, says somewhat bitterly in his able book: "The insurgent army received orders to march back to Gorey Hill, leaving their routed foe to pursue his flight unmolested. Had the English soldiers been pursued as they retreated, in panic and disorder, their total rout would have been inevitable; but the occasion was lost and with it the fruits of a victory that cost the lives of so many brave men. The insurgents on their march back to Gorey carried some hundreds of their wounded comrades with them, leaving, unfortunately, many others on the field, who were slaughtered without mercy by the enemy on their return. Not only did those wretches murder the unhappy and defenceless wounded, but they mangled the senseless remains of those whom death might have protected from all but the vengeance of fiends. Imagination sickens at the contemplation of the horrible deeds perpetrated by the Ancient Britons, who, having fearfully mangled the remains of the Rev. Michael Murphy, tore out his heart, roasted and ate it! Does history record another such fiendish deed of the soldiers of any country?"

The truth of Father Kavanagh's statement is vouched for, according to a foot-note, by the Rev. Mr. Gordon, a Protestant clergyman, who, as an avowed loyalist, would not lightly cast an imputation on the king's troops. Tradition states that "all who partook of this cannibal banquet died raving mad."

CHAPTER XII

Battle of Vinegar Hill—Insurgents Fight Gallantly, but are Finally Defeated—Retreat with Small Loss—Mutual Murders in Wexford Town—Retaken by Royalists

MANY skirmishes occurred between the insurgents and the King of England's troops from June 10 to the 19th of that month. On the latter date General Roche's "rebel" camp, on Lacken Hill, was surprised by a strong royalist force which made a forced march from New Ross, but General Thomas Cloney, second in command to Father Roche, was on duty and made such masterly dispositions that the Irish retreated in good order to Three Rocks, where they took up a strong position.

Vinegar Hill, however, was the principal insurgent rendezvous, and the entire disposable Anglo-Irish army was put in march against it. The various columns were led by experienced generals—Dundas, Loftus, Needham, Johnson, Eustace, Argill, Sir John Moore, and Sir James Duff. General Lake retained the supreme command. Moore encountered an Irish force, under Generals Roche and Cloney, at Foulk's Mill, early on the 20th. An engagement of four hours' duration resulted, and, in the end, the insurgents were forced to give ground, but not in disorder. General

Moore acknowledged a loss of more than 200 killed and wounded.

On the following day was fought the celebrated battle of Vinegar Hill, where the formidable remnant of the United Irish main army had mustered for a last stand against the enemy. Sir Jonah Barrington, who may be described as a sort of "national loyalist," thus pictures the conflict in his "Rise and Fall of the Irish Nation": "General Lake [who had decided that 30,000 regular troops were required for the attack] at the break of day disposed his troops in four columns [infantry], while his cavalry were prepared to do execution on the fugitives. One of the columns [whether by accident or design is strongly debated] did not arrive in time at its station, by which [tardiness] the insurgents were enabled to retreat to Wexford, through a country where they could not be pursued by cavalry or cannon. It was astonishing with what fortitude the peasantry, uncovered, stood the tremendous fire opened upon the four sides of their position. A stream of grape and shells was poured upon the multitude. The leaders encouraged the people by exhortations, the women by their cries, and every shell that broke among the crowd was followed by shouts of defiance. General Lake's horse was shot, many officers wounded, some killed, and a few gentlemen became invisible during the heat of the battle. The troops advanced gradually, but steadily, up the hill, the peasantry kept up their fire and maintained their ground; their cannon was nearly useless, their powder deficient, but they died fighting at their posts. At length, enveloped in a torrent of fire, they broke, and sought their safety through the space that General Needham had left by the non-arrival of his column. They were partially charged by some cavalry, but with little execution; they retreated to Wexford, and that night occupied the town."

Sir Jonah forgot to state that the royal cavalry were baffled in their attempt to massacre the fugitives by the timely arrival of a fine insurgent division, under General Philip Roche, Revs. John Murphy and Moses Kearns, and William Barker, which arrived too late to join in the battle, but did noble service in protecting the retreat of the "rebels," who had been engaged on "the Hill."

John Savage, in his " '98 and '48," says that the leaders of the insurgents at the battle of Vinegar Hill were Fathers Philip Roche, John Murphy, Moses Kearns, and William Clinch, together with the lay officers, Edward Fitzgerald, Esmond Kyan, Anthony Perry, William Barker, John Hay, and Garret Byrne. As a prelude to Vinegar Hill, Enniscorthy, after a most gallant defence by the insurgents under Father Moses Kearns and Colonel William Barker, was finally captured by Generals Lake and Johnson, but not until nearly all remaining houses were consumed by fire. General Edward Roche would have arrived in time to restore the fight on the hill, had he not been detained in Wexford by the misconduct of a rabid fanatic, named Captain Thomas Dixon, who organized a band of Jacobins in the city and proceeded to murder the "loyalist" prisoners, despite the vigorous protests of the Catholic pastor and many of his flock. Father Corrin called on God to "show the same mercy to the executioners that they would show to their prisoners," and this solemn appeal had the good effect of saving many innocent lives. The good priest is remembered with honor, even unto this day, by the descendants of those he rescued from an awful doom. After the fall of Wexford, when many good and noble Irishmen perished for having been loyal to their country and liberty, the brutal wretch, Dixon, escaped the penalty due to his crimes against humanity, and died in obscurity long years afterward. In all thirty-six "loyalist" prisoners perished on Wexford bridge. Dixon and his lieutenants were materially aided in their bloody work by two Orange informers, who saved their necks at the expense of their fellows' lives. It is sad to have to state, in the interests of truth, that few "loyalists" risked their lives to save those of "rebels" when the latter were, later on, in the toils of the courts-martial, which rarely showed mercy to any "croppy," high or low.

Wexford town, through its insurgent government, the head of which was the amiable and ill-fated Matthew Keough, decided to surrender to Lord Kingsborough, the chief royalist prisoner, immediately after the defeat at Vinegar Hill. Kingsborough assented to humane terms, and sent despatches to the English generals announcing the fact, but the cruel Lake refused to confirm the agreement, in the following curt note:

"Lieutenant-General Lake can not attend to any terms by rebels in arms against their sovereign. While they continue so, he must use the force intrusted to him with the utmost energy for their destruction. To the deluded multitude he promises pardon, on their delivering into his hands their leaders, surrendering their arms, and returning with sincerity to their allegiance."

This reply was sent by Mr. John Hay, one of the three emissaries of the people who had been deputed to interview Lake. The document frightened the citizens, as well it might, and, as General Sir John Moore was in advance of Lake, with his division, they very wisely resolved to surrender the city to that brave and humane officer, who kept the soldiers from entering the place until their brutal fury had somewhat abated. Several of the prominent insurgent leaders remained in Wexford—a most imprudent step and one attended by melancholy results. Many bands of sanguinary yeomen, defiant of Sir John Moore's merciful orders, sneaked into the city and committed gross outrages on the defenceless people, particularly the unfortunate wounded men. There is only too much reason to believe that Lord Kingsborough, after General Lake's arrival, had an understanding with that brutal imitator of Cromwell. The merciful policy of General Moore was disregarded, and the insurgent chiefs, who were credulous enough to trust to the word of an Anglo-Irish "lord" of the Tory pattern, soon found themselves caught in a trap from which there was no escape. Lake resolved, at once, to "act with vigor"; and he did. He ignored the agreement of the people with Kingsborough, no doubt with the full consent of the latter, and immediately appointed courts-martial to "try" the principal "rebel" chiefs. Bagenal Harvey and J. H. Colclough, having been warned of danger, fled to the Saltee Islands, on the Wexford coast, and sought safety in a cave. Colclough's young wife and infant child accompanied his flight, which was destined to be made in vain. Therefore, the first victim was the heroic, but chivalrously imprudent priest, Father Philip Roche, who shared with the Fathers Murphy the chief glory of the Wexford campaign. Like Roderick Dhu,

"One blast upon his bugle horn
Was worth a thousand men."

Deceived by the promises of the faithless Kingsborough, this hero—a giant in stature—rode into Wexford town and made his surrender in due form, stipulating at the same time for the safety of his associates. Scarcely had he entered the British lines when he was set upon by the brutal soldiery, dragged from his saddle, kicked and buffeted in a most savage manner. Some of the red-coated cowards wound their hands in his long hair, and, in spite of his fierce resistance, in this manner he was dragged, amid the hoots and jeers of the now triumphant "loyalist" rabble, to Wexford jail. He was summarily "tried," and, of course, convicted. Lake gave him no respite. Father Roche was taken at once to the gallows, the rope was placed around his neck, and the plank kicked from under him. His weight broke the noose and another rope had to be adjusted. This time the murderers were successful and the brave priest died with a prayer for Ireland on his lips. The butchery of Father Roche was all the more inexcusable from the fact that he had saved many "loyalists" from the vengeance of the people when they were prisoners at the camp on Vinegar Hill. Colonel Matthew Keough, a Protestant and retired army officer, the insurgent governor of Wexford, and a virtuous, merciful gentleman, quite well on in years, was tried and sentenced with Father Roche. They died almost at the same moment, but Colonel Keough was spared the ante-mortem indignities heaped upon the priest. After death, both bodies were decapitated. The head of Colonel Keough was spiked over the court-house door. Then what remained of him, together with the mutilated body of Father Roche, was thrown over the bridge into the river Slaney, and was seen no more by mortal eyes. Mr. Cornelius Grogan, an aged country gentleman of fortune, who had been forced by the insurgents into their ranks, despite his vehement protests, was accused of having acted as a "rebel" commissary. Conviction followed and he was hanged without mercy. Two of his brothers were in the royal army, and one was killed at Arklow. Mr. Grogan's head was also spiked on the court-house. Bagenal Harvey and John Henry Colclough were hunted down in the caves of the Saltee Islands and brought to Wexford. They abandoned hope at once, and died with becoming firmness. Their heads were placed beside those of their unfortunate former associates. Among the other victims were Captain John Hay, formerly of the Franco-Irish Brigade—the brigade of Cremona and Fontenoy—and Esmond Kyan, the brave artillerist of the battle of Arklow. The sad fate of Colonel Kelly, of Killane, has already been referred to. Kyan was simply murdered, because General Dundas, who was not bloodthirsty, guaranteed his safety on condition of going into exile, but the callous Lake disregarded the honor of his brother officer and fellow-Englishman, as was customary with him.

The shambles—for so the gallows may well be called—were placed on the bridge of Wexford, and it is impossible to say how many victims perished before even Lake's appetite for human blood was finally glutted. "Executions," as they were called, continued throughout the month of June, and even into July.

CHAPTER XIII

Insurgent Army Divides into Two Columns—Fitzgerald and Aylmer March Toward Wicklow and Kildare—Father Murphy Marches on Carlow and Kilkenny—His Capture and Death—End of Revolt in Leinster

AFTER the disaster of Vinegar Hill the insurgent forces of Wexford were divided into two bodies. One division acted under the orders of Generals Edward Fitzgerald, Edward Roche, and Colonel Garret Byrne, while the other, after the ill-starred departure of Father Roche to Wexford, was commanded by Fathers John Murphy and Moses Kearns. As the latter was severely wounded in the defence of Enniscorthy, Father Murphy was in supreme command.

The division led by Fitzgerald and his confederates faced toward Wicklow. A detachment, under Anthony Perry, attacked the British garrison at Gorey and drove it from the town. The main body marched by Monaseed, Donard Glanmullen, Aughrim, and Blessington to Ballymauns, where it was reinforced by the Wicklow men, under Byrne. On the 25th of June they were attacked, in front of Hacketstown, by the royal forces, whom they repulsed with loss, killing Captain Hardy and many soldiers. The British received timely aid and renewed the battle with desperation. After a conflict of nine hours' duration, the insurgents, who feared being surrounded, retreated, carrying off their dead and wounded, together with the wives of Captain Hardy and Lieutenant Chamney, and the grown-up daughters of the latter. All were sent under guard to a place of safety, where they soon rejoined their friends. The wives of Colonels Perry and Byrne, who had fallen into royalist hands, were treated with courtesy, in return, although, in general, the militia, yeomen, and foreign mercenaries did not respect female honor, and thus added to the unspeakable horrors of civil war—if such a designation fit the bloody struggle of 1798. Near Carnew, the "rebels" met and routed a strong party of British horse, killing or wounding nearly a hundred, including two officers. Carnew took the alarm, and they wisely determined to avoid attacking it. At Ballyrahn Hill, on July 2, they had another success, in the open field—placing several officers and seventy men hors de combat; but they failed to carry a fortification in which the fugitive redcoats took shelter. At this period of the insurrection, the insurgents seemed to have no definite plan of campaign. They courted death in battle, but many of them still continued scathless. Sir James Duff's forces blocked their way at Wicklow gap. They gave him a fierce fight, but, nevertheless, were forced to countermarch toward Carnew and Gorey. In order to effect this object, they had to cut their way through the hostile cavalry, which retained its old dread of the formidable pike. Their last combined action was at Ballygullen, where, although greatly outnumbered, they fought with their usual bravery. Savage says, "They repulsed the cavalry and drove the artillery three times from their cannon." Their final rendezvous was at Carrigrew Hill, where they separated—most of them never to meet again in this world.

All the leaders did not return to Wexford. Fitzgerald and Byrne had an idea of arousing Connaught, aided by the brave William Aylmer, of Kildare, and Michael Dwyer, of Wicklow. They were defeated at Clonard, while trying to surprise Athlone, on the 11th of July, and this disaster crushed their new-born hopes. Father Moses Kearns and Anthony Perry, after having survived the dangers of many battlefields, fell into the hands of the British, and were murdered, by process of court-martial, at Edenderry.

Flying detachments of the insurgents had small encounters with the royal army in the country around Dublin, but want of cannon gave the royalists an advantage which could not be overcome. But Edward Fitzgerald and Colonel Aylmer held together enough men to worry the government into consenting that General Dundas should give them terms. "Safety and exile" were the conditions, and they were ac-

cepted. Sir John Moore granted similar terms to Garret
Byrne and General Hunter to General Edward Roche and
Captain John Devereux. The latter and Aylmer became
somewhat famous soldiers of fortune. Devereux rose to the
rank of lieutenant-general in the army of Bolivia, and Aylmer, who had been a colonel in the Austrian service, died
fighting for South American independence, under the orders
of his old friend and fellow "rebel" of '98. Fitzgerald, who
owned a valuable estate in Wexford, sacrificed all for Ireland, and died an exile, in reduced circumstances, in Ham-
burg many years after the rebellion. Byrne, who had contracted a fatal disease during the campaign of Wexford,
passed away at Bath, in England, about the end of the
eighteenth century.

The formidable "rebel" division, under Father John
Murphy, "the Irish Hidalgo," broke camp at Sleedagh,
five miles from Wexford town, early on the morning of
June 22, made a rapid march to Scollagh Gap, in the
Blackstairs Mountains, and, in spite of some resistance
on the part of an English force stationed in the defile,
succeeded in penetrating to the County Carlow. The British made a stand at Killedmond, which Father Murphy
captured. During the fight, the village caught fire and
was wholly consumed. The insurgent force then marched
to Goresbridge, situated on the river Barrow, in the
County Kilkenny, where it encountered the 4th Dragoon
Guards and Wexford militia, who had taken post on the
bridge. The pikemen charged and swept the royalists before them into the town, and out of it, at the other extremity. Major-General Asgill, with a strong body of regulars, arrived too late to retrieve the day, but Father Murphy
prudently drew off his men to the mountain ridge, where

they bivouacked in safety. He next marched upon and attacked Castlecomer, hoping to be joined by a large body of the colliers employed in the neighborhood of the town. In this he was disappointed, chiefly, as is commonly believed, through the treachery of one "General" Gaffney, who professed to be a patriot, but prevented the Kilkenny men from fighting at the battle of New Ross. He repeated the same tactics at Castlecomer, as his treason was still undiscovered. It is related that, after New Ross, Gaffney called on General Lake for a money reward. Even the sanguinary soldier could not stomach the rascal. "Sir," said Lake, "you are a scoundrel! Yesterday you betrayed your country. Tomorrow you would betray me, were I to trust you. Begone, or I shall order you hanged!" Gaffney went.

During the attack on Castlecomer, a conflagration broke out, but nobody has been able to fix the blame for this act of vandalism, because it is admitted that some unknown party deliberately set fire to the dwellings of peaceful people. General Asgill's attack on the "rebels" was, at first, successful. His cannon "raked the streets" and compelled the insurgents to retreat, leaving behind the prisoners taken at Goresbridge. The royal army also retreated, having been seized with panic, and, finally, the insurgents took the town, which they sacked, as most of the inhabitants had shown hostility to them. They failed to find ammunition, of which they stood in sore need, and, as Kilkenny remained passive, they determined to return to the heroic soil of Wexford. They, accordingly, marched back to Goresbridge, and encamped on Kilcomney Hill the night of June 25. In this situation, depressed and disappointed, General Asgill, with his powerful force, found them early on the morning of the 26th, and attacked them from all sides at once. They died in scores, but maintained a bold resistance for an hour and then fled. Their few horsemen covered the retreat. Otherwise, not a man could have escaped. Asgill, with the fury of a dastard, let loose his bloodhounds on the innocent people of the district, and it is recorded that about one hundred and fifty persons were wantonly sacrificed. The royalist historian, Rev. Mr. Gordon, says: "The greater part of the slain were inhabitants of the County [Kilkenny], which had, unfortunately, become the scene of action. They had not joined the rebels nor left their houses, and a great part of the plunder was taken from people of the same description."

The return passage through Scollagh Gap was not as fortunate as the other. Asgill pressed the insurgents hard, but two brave fellows, James Cody and Michael Lacy, who had serviceable muskets and plenty of ammunition, took up a position among the rocks and killed so many of the English cavalry by their accurate fire that the troopers halted in consternation, while most of the "rebels" effected their escape. Father John Murphy, who planned the retreat with his usual ability, having, as is generally supposed, gone back to reconnoitre, attended by an aide named Gallagher, unfortunately fell into the hands of the enemy, probably through an ambuscade. This disaster occurred near the town of Tullow, and thither he and his companion in misfortune were conveyed. A drumhead court-martial speedily decided their fate. A stole and pyx, found in his pockets, revealed the identity of Father Murphy. He was known to be the leader of the insurgent column, and the joy of his fiendish captors knew no bounds. But he and Gallagher remained utterly unmoved. Father Kavanagh, in his "History of the Insurrection," quotes the Carlow Magazine of the period as saying: "Before his [Father Murphy's] execution, he received 500 lashes with a cat-o'-nine-tails, which he endured without a groan. His head was then cut off and his body thrown into a lighted pitch barrel, which was placed at the door of a Mr. Callaghan, a respectable Catholic, in order, as the Orangemen said, that he might enjoy the smell of a roasted priest. His head was stuck on a pole, at the chapel gate, where it remained for a long time after." Mr. Gallagher was, likewise, flogged, and received 600 lashes in all. At intervals he was taken down and offered his life if he would betray his companion. This he nobly refused to do, and so he was finally hanged and beheaded. And this was only a hundred years ago! The executioners in all such cases acted under the orders of those "honorable and gallant gentlemen," the officers of the British army—to a man, in that day, aristocrats and highly "civilized"!

The survivors of the ill-fated Carlow-Kilkenny expedition fell in with some bands of their comrades in Wexford and did a last service for their country by falling upon and exterminating several hundred vile "regulars" and yeomen, chiefly horse, who were engaged in murdering old men and helpless children and in dishonoring the fair maids and matrons of that noble county. The execrable villains were caught red-handed in their crimes and received no mercy. This salutary lesson made the marauders much more cautious than they were accustomed to be, and, thenceforth, the Wexford Reign of Terror began to wane and normal conditions resumed their sway. The Marquis of Cornwallis —the same who surrendered his army at Yorktown to Washington—had arrived in Ireland to assume the dual duties of viceroy and commander-in-chief, on June 21—the day of the battle at Vinegar Hill. Although an intense Englishman, and an enemy of Irish legislative independence, he was not fiercely cruel in his policy, as his predecessor, Lord Camden, had been, and, as soon as the insurrection seemed subdued, he caused milder methods to be pursued toward the people. The latter had been goaded into premature rebellion, and William Pitt's purpose—to creat an excuse for the legislative union of Great Britain and Ireland—had been achieved. His most active Irish ally, outside of Lord Chancellor Clare, the notorious Lord Castlereagh, became "the right-hand man" of Cornwallis in Ireland. The great conspiracy to strangle the Irish Parliament was rapidly maturing, although a very large section of the people were unable to realize that the independence of their country trembled in the balance. Then, as since, too many Irishmen were dazzled by English promises, behind which lurked shame and ruin.

McGee, after referring to many insurgent leaders already dealt with, sums up the finale of the Leinster rebellion thus: "Walter Devereux, the last colleague of Father John Murphy, was arrested at Cork, on the eve of sailing for America, tried and executed.* Months afterward, General Joseph Holt [of Wicklow] surrendered, was transported, and returned after several years to end his life where he began his career. Michael Dwyer alone maintained the life of a rapparee for five long years amid the hills of Wicklow, where his adventures were often of such a nature as to throw all fictitious conceptions of an outlaw's life into commonplace by comparison. Except the fastnesses frequented by this extraordinary man [who finally made terms of expatriation with the government] and in the wood of Kilaughrim, in Wexford, where the insurgents, with the

---

* John Devereux escaped to South America.

last stroke of national humor, assumed the name of The Babes in the Wood, the Leinster insurrection was utterly trodden out within two months of its first beginning on the 23d of May. So weak against discipline, arms, munitions, and money are all that mere naked valor and devotion can accomplish!"

CHAPTER XIV

Ulster's Uprising—Presbyterians of Antrim and Down in Arms—
Battles of Antrim and Ballinahinch—Insurgents Finally
Defeated—Leaders Executed

THE insurrection in Ulster, if judged by the long time occupied in preparing for it, and the numbers actually enrolled and organized, ought to have been much more formidable than that in Leinster. But it was not. The non-arrival of the French and Dutch expeditions, on which so much depended, had dispirited, if not demoralized, a mercurial and impressionable people. Then, their original and trusted leaders, Samuel Neilson and Thomas Russell, were prisoners "in the hands of the enemy." The next in command weakened, and resigned his post. The Rev. William Steele Dixon, of Down, a resolute Presbyterian clergyman, was arrested on charge of treason. The government knew his capture would add to the public distrust and they were not disappointed. Still, there remained a few of the junior chiefs who were determined not to give in without striking a blow. Antrim had for its leader Henry Joy McCracken, a close friend of Wolfe Tone, and a thriving manufacturer of Belfast, while the men of Down reposed their hopes in General Henry Munro and Dr. Jackson. Both counties struck simultaneously. The insurgents, under McCracken, attacked the town of Antrim on the 7th of June. At first successful, they routed a regiment of dragoons and killed Lord O'Neill, several other officers and many rank and file. But a large regular reinforcement soon arrived and the town, after another fierce and bloody struggle, was retaken. McCracken and a few of his officers held together, but the other insurgents immediately dispersed. The unhappy leader was captured soon afterward and duly "hanged, drawn, and quartered," with several other officers of lesser note. This defeat virtually quelled the national spirit of Antrim and it has never since been revived.

Down, also, sprang to arms on the 9th of June, and a body of insurgents, under Dr. Jackson, mustered near Saintfield. They learned that Colonel Stapleton, at the head of the York Fencibles, two regiments of yeomen, and a section of artillery, was marching from Newtownards to give them battle. Jackson set a trap for them, very similar to that set by Father Murphy for the cavalry at Camolin; but an insurgent, beholding the chaplain of the yeomen, a minister named Mortimer, against whom he had a grudge, fired, contrary to orders, wounding Mortimer and effectually warning Stapleton's men of the bad position into which they had been led. The advance-guard was cut to pieces, but the Yorkshire regiment rallied manfully and repulsed an attempt to break their formation. Stapleton, taking advantage of the insurgents' temporary confusion, drew off his remaining troops and effected his retreat in good order on Comber. Jackson's force slept that night in Saintfield. A "rebel" attack made on Portaferry, where a veteran officer, Captain Matthews, commanded, failed, because the enemy had notice of the intended attack, and were materially aided by the well-directed fire of a revenue cutter stationed in the river. On the 12th, the insurgents, under

General Henry Munro—a young officer of great merit—
evacuated Saintfield, and occupied the positions of Wind-
mill Hill and Ballinahinch. The commanding eminence of
Ednevady, above the town, was also garrisoned by Munro.
In this posture, full of confidence, he awaited the combined
attack of a numerous royalist force, composed of Highlanders, militia, and yeomanry, under Generals Nugent and
Barber. The Irish Presbyterians, of which Munro's force
was mainly made up, displayed superb firmness, when, on
June 14, the British finally advanced to the attack. Deficient in everything but valor, the men of Down, exposed
to a deadly artillery fire, to which they had no means of replying, maintained their ground for several hours on the
heights, and finally withdrew without disorder to the position of Ednevady, where Munro had the bulk of his force
and commanded in person. His lieutenants, Townsend and
McCance, were reluctant to abandon the positions they had
so stubbornly defended, but finally yielded to orders. The
British occupied Ballinahinch that night, and the yeomanry,
as usual, disgraced their cloth by killing or torturing all
male suspects in the town, and outraging the unfortunate female relatives of their victims. Creed made no difference
to that satanic banditti—they were quite as ready to defile
the Protestant women of the North as their Catholic sisters
of the South.

The sounds of murder, rapine, and revelry rose high
from Ballinahinch during that awful night, and his officers
urged Munro not to wait for morning, but fall upon the
enemy while engaged in their hellish work. Either because
he feared the issue of a night attack made by an undis-
ciplined force, or, as some say, through a mistaken spirit
of chivalry, which scrupled to take an enemy by surprise,

Munro refused to engage before daylight. This unwise resolution was fatal to his army and himself. Convinced that they would be beaten on the morrow, one regiment of 700 men left the camp and scattered to their homes. The battle began early on the morning of the 13th. Munro, dividing his army into two divisions, bravely attempted to take the town by assault. One body emulated the heroic bravery of their Catholic fellow-"rebels" at New Ross. They had only a few small cannon, which were of little use against the formidable English batteries, and relied mainly on musketry and the pike. After several desperate efforts, the insurgents broke General Nugent's square of infantry and drove it through the streets in fierce disorder. The general, himself, was desperately wounded. Munro, with the other division, also succeeded in entering Ballinahinch from the opposite side, but was met by such a storm of shot and shell that, for a moment, the column hesitated. The ammunition was exhausted, but the pikemen were ordered to charge. The order was obeyed with such resolution that the British cannoneers were forced to abandon their guns, and General Barber concluded that nothing more could be done in the way of resistance. The retreat was sounded and the British abandoned the town in great haste.

But, again, accident, rather than valor, favored the British. Disciplined armies yield to panic, on occasions, but untrained bodies, even the most fearless, are always liable to it. This was the case at Ballinahinch. Great clouds of smoke hung over the town. The insurgents, unable to see what was going on, heard the English bugles sounding the retreat, and immediately concluded that fresh enemies were coming down upon them. A disgraceful and disastrous panic ensued immediately. They paused in their fierce pur-

suit of the flying enemy, who soon perceived what had occurred. Their cavalry wheeled around and made a dashing
charge, while the infantry rallied and marched to the support of the horse. Munro's men broke and ran tumultu-
ously, many throwing away their arms. No quarter was
given by the English, and the slaughter was frightful.
Munro did all that a brave man could to restore order, but
in vain. Nothing could rally the broken mass, and the
pursuers had it all their own way—they were glutted with
carnage. It may astonish some of the Down Orangemen
of our day to learn that their "rebel" forefathers, under
General Munro, carried green flags at Ballinahinch—the
fact being vouched for in Nugent's distorted report of the
engagement. Munro was captured six miles from the field
of battle and taken to Lisburn, of which he was a native.
There he was tried by court-martial and sentenced to be
hanged, with the usual barbaric accompaniments. His
noble courage did not desert him on the scaffold, which
was erected before his own door. It is said that his aged
mother and young wife beheld his martyrdom from an upper window, and waved farewells to him to the last. When
all was over, nature asserted itself. The mother soon followed her gallant son to the grave, and the widow became
a helpless invalid. Henry Munro was only thirty-one years
of age when he suffered death for Ireland, and in Irish
annals no patriot is mentioned with more honor than this
gallant son of Ulster. The cause he loved died with him,
and McCracken, so far, at least, as the northern province
was concerned, for it made no further sign that is worthy
of record.

BOOK X

TREATING OF THE PERIOD BETWEEN THE FRENCH
INVASION OF CONNAUGHT (1798) TO THE RE-COMMENCE-
MENT OF THE NAPOLEONIC WARS WITH ENGLAND (1803)

CHAPTER I

French Invasion of Connaught—General Humbert Lands at Killala—
He Marches on Castlebar and Routs a Much Larger British
Force—Celebrates Victory by Giving a Public Ball

WHILE the events just narrated were occurring in
Ireland, Wolfe Tone, still a staff-general in the
French army, was "eating out his own heart" in anxiety
and sorrow. He repeatedly urged the feeble French Directory, as each succeeding story of Ireland's gallant resistance
reached France, to organize a strong expedition and send
it to the assistance of his countrymen without loss of time.
But Bonaparte had taken with him to Egypt, on a perfectly
profitless enterprise, the main strength of the Republic—
her finest army and most powerful fleet. This circumstance
rendered, for the moment, the Directory virtually helpless.
Therefore, Tone was not summoned to a conference with
the responsible ministers until nearly the middle of July,
when the Irish rebellion was, practically, overcome. Influenced by the arguments of Tone, the Directory finally
resolved to re-form the "Army of England," which might
have been more appropriately called the "Army of Ireland,"
under the command of "the brave Kilmaine," an Irishman
whose family name was Jennings, but who had "grown old
in wars" and was somewhat of an invalid. This force consisted of 9,000 men, under Kilmaine himself; 3,000 with
General Hardy at Brest, and about 1,000 under General
Humbert at Rochelle. The latter, an impetuous and head-
strong officer, brave as a lion, but lacking in sound judg-

ment, soon grew tired of seemingly endless waiting. He "requisitioned" Rochelle for needed supplies, embarked his force on three frigates, and set out on an enterprise almost without parallel in the annals of war for desperate daring. Humbert, who was an intense republican, had his heart in the Irish cause and wished to commit the French Republic by his act and compel it either to abandon or support him. Among the officers of his staff were Captain Matthew Tone, brother of Theobald; Captain Bartholomew Teeling, and Lieutenant Sullivan, a nephew of M. Madgett, of the French War Office. His second in command was General Sarrazin, and his chief aides were Colonels Cherin and Charost. The expedition carried a few small cannon and several thousand stand of arms, for such recruits as might join it in Ireland. There was, also, a store of extra clothing, but little or no money, which, under the circumstances, proved a great disadvantage. The French frigates made the voyage in safety and cast anchor in the Bay of Killala, County Mayo, on the 22d of August. They displayed English colors, which induced the port officer and the sons of the Protestant bishop to board them. All were astonished when they found themselves prisoners of war. Humbert immediately landed his men—all young veterans of the armies of Italy, the Rhine, and the Sambre, and fit for any work that might be required of them. Their entry into Killala was opposed by a small body of yeomanry, whom they speedily put to flight. Then Humbert, at the head of his officers, marched into the court of the bishop's "palace." The prelate spoke French fluently, which simplified matters. He presented to Humbert his family and several Protestant clergymen, his guests, who had come there on diocesan business. The French general assured the bishop that no plundering, or outrage of any kind, would be permitted, and that no levy would be made except for needed supplies, which would be paid for when money arrived on the next vessels from France. Until then, bills on the prospective Irish Republic, guaranteed by that of France, would be issued to all with whom the army might have business dealings. This seemed perfectly satisfactory to the bishop. Humbert established headquarters in the "palace," without, however, disturbing the inmates, and raised the Irish flag of green and gold, with the motto "Erin go Bragh" (braw), which means "Ireland Forever," inscribed upon it.

Humbert, who greatly impressed even the "loyalists" by his courtesy and generosity, remained only a few days in Killala, as he knew time was precious. Leaving a small garrison, under Captain Tone, in the "palace," he took up his march to the town of Ballina, on the river Moy. En route, he was joined by Colonel Blake of Galway, Major Plunkett of Roscommon, and Messrs. Moore, MacDonnell, Barrett, Bellew, O'Dowd, and other influential men of Mayo. The peasantry, who had been partially organized by United Irish refugees from the northern counties, flocked to the general's standard, and he caused to be distributed among them such arms as he could spare from the limited surplus he had on hand. He dressed many of them in the French light infantry uniform, but much of this clothing was found to be too small for the stalwart Celts of Connaught, who seemed like giants beside the short and hardy Frenchmen. Humbert, himself, was a tall, stout man, and some of his officers were also of imposing build and aspect. The Mayo peasants soon fraternized with the good-natured, light-hearted French soldiery, and historians of the time relate the brave efforts the Gauls made to pick up the rattling Irish choruses, mostly sung in Gaelic. One refrain, in English, was a particular favorite with the French, and ran thus:

> "Viva la, the French are coming!
> Viva la, our friends are true!
> Viva la, the French are coming—
> What will the poor yeomen do?"

The French general met with no resistance at Ballina, where all the people seemed friendly, and, after a brief halt, he pushed on toward Castlebar, the county capital. The news of his landing and march had already spread far and wide through the country, carrying either joy or woe with the announcement. Patriot hearts beat high with exultation, while the "loyalists" flocked gloomily by themselves, anticipating the worst. General Hutchinson of the British army succeeded in collecting a splendid force of 6,000 infantry, with a numerous cavalry and several batteries of artillery, and took post about a mile from Castlebar, facing the highroad from Foxford, by which he expected Humbert to approach. He even thought of marching to meet the Frenchman, whose force he well knew was made up of only 800 of his own countrymen and 1,500 untrained Mayo levies. But General Lake arrived upon the ground, and, being senior officer, assumed command, thus upsetting the contemplated forward movement of Hutchinson. Lake determined to accept battle where he stood, not doubting, with his superior force, that victory was within his grasp.

Humbert, having campaigned in La Vendee, was accustomed to a rough country, and inquired of his guides if there was not another route by which Castlebar might be approached than the Foxford causeway. A hardy peasant suggested the mountain trail by the rugged pass of Barnagee, which the British would not think of defending, as it would seem to them utterly impassable. Humbert realized the importance of the information, and, at once, chose the mountain route. His men marched all night right merrily, and, by morning, the head of his column had cleared the mouth of the defile, and beheld before it the powerful British force drawn up in "battle's magnificently stern array," with cavalry on its wings and cannon planted so as to sweep everything in its front. The Mayo men headed the Franco-Irish column, and the hostile batteries opened on them immediately. Several files were knocked over, and as they were unaccustomed to artillery fire, Humbert withdrew them temporarily and sent forward the French veterans. These, on clearing the pass, immediately deployed as skirmishers and manœuvred so as to threaten the British flanks. The Irish supported them. A sharp artillery fire could not retard their advance, nor did the musketry of the enemy have any effect upon their nerves. After exchanging several volleys, they went forward at a run, and the English went backward at the same pace—an unaccountable panic having seized all their force, except a few Highlanders, who attempted to cover the retreat and were finally destroyed in the streets of Castlebar, through which Lake's routed army poured in one tangled mass of horse and foot—the King's Carabineers and Lord Roden's "Foxhunters" leading the procession. About forty of the French Hussars, who had obtained "mounts" at Ballina, pursued them beyond the town. Seeing them unsupported, a squadron of Roden's regiment turned back and charged them successfully. Several of the French were killed, after a most gallant defence, and the survivors retired on their main body. The spot on which the Hussars fell is called French Hill to this day, and on the centennial of the battle, August 27, 1898, a monument was erected by the people to their memory. So rapid was the British flight that their horse reached Tuam, forty miles distant, that same day, and, next day, were at Athlone, about seventy miles from the scene of action. Ever since the peasantry have called the battle "the races of Castlebar." Lake acknowledged a loss of 18 officers and 350 men, killed, wounded, and prisoners, but Humbert reckoned the total at over 600 of all ranks. In addition, they left in the hands of the victors all their cannon—fourteen guns— and five stand of regimental colors, not to mention lesser trophies of their prowess. Humbert and his officers, with French volatility, immediately advertised a ball and supper, to which all the neighboring "nobility, gentry, and merchants," with their families, were cordially invited! No social "function" held in Castlebar was better attended before or since. Ireland seemed back again in the days of the brave and gay St. Ruth, who, as it was said, danced while Athlone was lost.

General Humbert, although fond of society and pleasure, was also an eminently practical soldier. The French, although mainly Celts, like the Irish, are well mixed with Latin blood and inherit their orderly spirit from the conquering Romans. Therefore, magisterial districts were soon established, and a provincial government was formed—the President being Colonel Moore, of Moore Hall, a very influential gentleman. Proclamations to the people, urging them to rally to their flag, and to observe good order, were issued in the name of an Irish Republic. The French made their allies understand that no persecution of "loyalists" would be tolerated, but the records of the times—outside the partisan narrative of the State Church Bishop of Killala—do not establish the fact that such a precaution was necessary. Very little crime of any kind marked the popular uprising in Mayo. The reign of slaughter was deferred until the English finally triumphed. Mitchel, commenting on Humbert's brilliant exploit at Castlebar, says: "From the terror [to the "loyalists"] this handful of French troops inspired, we may form some idea of the effects which might have followed the landing of Humbert's little force anywhere in the south of Ireland, while the Wexford men were gallantly holding their own county; or we may conjecture what might have been the result if Humbert had brought with him ten thousand men, instead of one thousand; or if Grouchy had marched inland with his six thousand men, at the moment when the people were eager to begin the rising, and the English had but three thousand men in the island. It seemed as if England were destined to have all the luck, and either by favor of the elements, or the miscalculations of her enemies, to escape one after another the deadly perils that forever beset her empire."

The same writer calls attention to the fact, also dwelt upon by Sir Jonah Barrington, that the defeat (of the British) at Castlebar was a victory for the viceroy (Lord Cornwallis); it revived all the horrors of the rebellion, which had been subsiding, and the desertion of the militia regiments (meaning those of Louth and Kilkenny), which went over to Humbert when the English ran away, "tended to impress the 'gentry' with an idea that England alone could protect the country"—another casuistic and treacherous argument in favor of the nefarious scheme hatched out in the subtle minds of Pitt and Castlereagh, Cornwallis, and Clare, to bring about that curse and bane of Ireland, "the legislative union."

Cornwallis, aroused to a sense of danger by the crushing defeat of General Lake, begun at once to assemble a powerful army. In doing this he had no difficulty, because there were, then, at least 125,000 troops, of all arms, in Ireland, and all of them had seen more or less service. He soon had 20,000 men under his immediate orders and reinforcements joined him day by day. The French force had not increased and the Irish allies did not show much disposition to operate beyond their own county—"a circumstance," remarks Mitchel, "which greatly surprised and disgusted the French." There was good reason, on the other hand, for Irish surprise and disgust, when the Irish people beheld, after so many boastful promises, that the French Republic had sent them only a few battalions, instead of the great army that had been, virtually, guaranteed by their most trusted leaders. They knew also that, in the event of failure, the French would be treated as prisoners of war, while they would be treated to the knout and the gallows. And the weakness of the French force made this contemplation all the more impressive. Unhappily, the anticipations of the gallant few who took part in the enterprise of Humbert were too speedily realized.

The wretched "Irish" Parliament, which had played into England's hands all through the rebellion, occupied itself with passing measures to compensate "such of his Majesty's loyal subjects as had sustained losses in their property during the insurrection," and appointed commissioners to carry the same into effect. It likewise passed bills of attainder against three dead rebels—Lord Edward Fitzgerald, Beauchamp Bagenal Harvey, and Cornelius Grogan. The eloquence of Curran was vainly exerted to save the estate of Fitzgerald to his widow and children. On this occasion the great advocate said: "I have often, of late, gone to the dungeon of the captive, but never have I gone to the grave of the dead to receive instructions for his defence—nor, in truth, have I ever before been at the trial of a dead man." Further along, referring to the noble descent of Lord Edward, he spoke of his blood—that of the Geraldines—as being "nobler than the royalty that first ennobled it; that, like a rich stream, rose till it ran and hid its fountain!"

The base Parliament also passed Fugitive and Banishment bills, which excepted from amnesty "certain United Irishmen not then in the country and certain others who were to be allowed to exile themselves." And, in addition, the military commanders and paid magistrates kept up the persecution of the people in "the disturbed, or recently disturbed, districts," so that Ireland's wounds were kept open and bleeding, and the exhausted nation was fast reduced to that deplorable moral condition which welcomes "peace at any price."

CHAPTER II

Humbert Leaves Castlebar and Marches Toward Longford—He is Hemmed in at Ballinamuck by Enormous British Force and Compelled to Surrender—Irish Allies Mercilessly Put to Death by Cornwallis's Order

HUMBERT committed a military error in remaining too long at Killala and Castlebar. Had he marched northward immediately after his success at the latter place the event might have speedily proved favorable to his cause. When he finally moved out, heading toward the frontiers of Ulster and Leinster, Cornwallis was already at Hollymount, about fourteen miles from Castlebar. The Franco-Irish force reached Foxford without serious opposition, but, at Collooney, on September 5, it encountered Colonel Vereker—afterward distinguished in the Peninsular War—at the head of the 24th Light Dragoons, two curricle guns, and the City of Limerick militia. The colonel made a good fight, but, in the end, was beaten, with the loss of his cannon and many men, and had to retreat to Sligo. But he had delayed Humbert long enough to give Cornwallis's superior force an advantage in pursuit. It also determined the French general not to attempt the capture of Sligo, which, it is said, he originally contemplated. He turned off by the route of Drumahaire to Manor Hamilton, in Leitrim, leaving three pieces of cannon spiked and dismounted on the road, and throwing five pieces over the Drumahaire Bridge into the river. Rumors had reached Humbert that a large "rebel" force had mustered near Granard in the County Leitrim, and the hope of meeting it, according to some writers, caused him to wheel by his right toward the village of Drumkerkin. The English advance-guard, under General Crawford, fell upon the French rearguard, on September 7, between Drumshanbo and Ballymore. Crawford was smartly repulsed and Humbert continued his march on Granard. He crossed the river Shannon by the bridge of Ballintra the same evening, and halted to rest and refresh his weary troops, for a few hours, at Cloone. On the morning of September 8, he defiled by the village of Ballinamuck, in the county of Longford, but was so closely pursued by General Crawford, supported by a powerful body of British troops under General Lake, that he had not sufficient time to destroy the bridge at Ballintra—a fatal omission. Even after this misfortune, he might still have reached Granard in safety, had not Cornwallis, with the main British army, composed of all arms of the service, crossed the river Shannon at Carrick, and marched to intercept his front by way of Mohill and St. Johnstown. The combined royalist force now numbered over 30,000 men. The situation of General Humbert had, accordingly, become desperate, and he had nothing left to hope for, except to fight to the last for the honor of the French arms, and wring the best terms he could from his thronging enemies. He, accordingly, arranged his forces for battle, and, being attacked on all sides, made a very gallant resistance. It is said that he intended to prolong the struggle so as to allow his Irish allies, who expected no quarter, to escape through a neighboring bog, but his good intention was frustrated by the action of General Sarrazin, who, without consulting his chief, surrendered to the enemy the rearguard of two hundred men which he commanded. In spite of this cowardly, or treacherous, action Humbert held out for nearly an hour longer, and succeeded in capturing Lord Roden and a party of his dragoons. Just then the overwhelming array of Cornwallis appeared upon the field. The French drums beat a parley, and the whole force surrendered and became prisoners of war. The hapless Irish allies, beholding this, and knowing the fate that awaited them if captured, broke their hitherto unconquered ranks and made for the bog that flanked the battleground. Many succeeded in making their escape, but hundreds were overtaken by the British cavalry on the firm soil, and cut to atoms. Some were also made prisoners and were shot or hanged with scant ceremony. A total of about five hundred perished by the sword, the bullet, or the rope. The loss of the British army—always underrated—was reported to be inconsiderable. The French general surrendered a total of 96 officers and 746 non-commissioned officers and private soldiers. Since his landing in Ireland, about 200 men had been rendered hors de combat by wounds or disease. Colonel Blake, of Galway, who had been an officer of the British army, and some ninety ex-members of the Louth and Kilkenny militia regiments, who had joined the French at Castlebar, were hanged on the field of battle by order of the "merciful" Lord Cornwallis. One Kilkenny man defended himself by saying that "it was the army and not he who were deserters; that while he was fighting hard they all ran away and left him to be murdered." The English general thought this good logic, and, it is said, commuted the man's sentence to banishment from Ireland. Captains Tone and Teeling were among the captured, and were conveyed to Dublin, tried by court-martial, and hanged. Great efforts were made in behalf of Teeling, who had been conspicuously gallant and merciful throughout the campaign, but government was inexorable. It ignored a most magnanimous and touching letter in his behalf from Humbert, who greatly admired the fearless young officer and loved him as a son. Teeling conversed carelessly with the British officers, who commanded the death escort, while his scaffold was being made ready, and, mounting it with heroic serenity, died without a complaint or a tremor. Matthew Tone also displayed absolute indifference to his fate, and perished as became a brother of the greatest of Irish revolutionists. Many other Irish leaders, including Colonel Moore, and Mr. Roger Maguire, of Mayo, were sent into exile. The French prisoners, including Lieutenant Sullivan, whose long residence in Paris enabled him to pass for a genuine Frenchman, were exchanged after a tedious detention.

The small French garrison left at Ballina capitulated on hearing of Humbert's disaster. Not so, however, the Irish allies. Although aware that General Trench was sending upon them an overpowering force from two directions—so as to cut off all chance of escape—they resolved to defend the town, and, in doing so, displayed reckless gallantry. In the words of the hostile Protestant bishop, "they ran upon death with as little appearance of reflection or concern as if they were hastening to a show." The English, well supplied with cannon, were speedily upon them. Four hundred were killed, after an engagement which reflected credit upon their courage, if not upon their skill. The survivors fled, but many were shot down in the suburbs of Killala, while others were massacred by a battery of cannon, placed so as to enfilade the line of their retreat along the beach. These men were all pure Celts, "brave among the bravest," and many of them, in after days, driven to enlist by famine and political persecution, formed the famous "Faugh-a-Ballagh" regiments in Wellington's Peninsular army—the best fighting body of men that England ever placed in the field. The unfortunate fellows did not reflect that every victory they won for her, from Vimiera to Toulouse, only served to fasten more securely the English fetters on their native land.

General Trench's victory had the usual accompaniment of the halter. A large number of the captured were summarily executed, the most prominent victims being General Bellew and Richard Burke. And thus terminated the bloody uprising of north Connaught against the traditional foe, and the far more culpable Irish royalists.

The name of James Napper Tandy, because of his connection with the volunteer artillery of 1782, his subsequent services in the United Irish Society, and the mention of his name in a famous Irish ballad, "The Wearing of the Green," is, perhaps, as widely known as that of any other '98 man. Yet, he was a harmless kind of revolutionist, and his attempt to invade Ireland, before Bompart sailed, covered him with a large share of ridicule at the time. He and some other Irish refugees of France procured a small, but fast sailing, vessel and set sail for the Irish coast, hoping to be able to join Humbert. They reached Rathlin Island on September 16, and there learned of the fatal result to the French and Irish at Ballinamuck. Convinced that they could do nothing effective for the cause just then, they scattered some proclamations and, hoisting sail, were fortunate enough to find refuge in Norway.

CHAPTER III

Admiral Bompart's Irish Expedition—Wolfe Tone Accompanies it— Battle of Lough Swilly—The *Hoche,* Overpowered, Strikes its Colors —Wolfe Tone Betrayed and Captured—His Trial, Condemnation, and Death in Prison

THEOBALD WOLFE TONE did not relax his great efforts after the sailing of Humbert's expedition, but applied himself with redoubled energy to the heavy task of inducing the Directory to send at once an adequate force to second the ardent French general's daring experiment. But the French navy was grievously depleted and the French arsenals almost destitute of munitions, because of the empty Egyptian expedition. The news of Humbert's first successes reached France speedily enough, but the 20th of September arrived before the small squadron, consisting of one ship of the line, eight frigates, and a sloop, under Admiral Bompart, with about 3,000 soldiers under General Hardy on board, was ready to put to sea. Wolfe Tone embarked with Bompart on the battleship *Hoche*. On board of one of the frigates were two other Irish patriots, Messrs. McGuire and Corbett, destined to be more fortunate than their illustrious countryman, who afterward distinguished themselves in the French service. Tone was not hopeful of this attempt, but accepted his "manifest destiny" with grim determination. That he was betrayed he knew only too well, for, before sailing, he had read in a French newspaper a full account of the enterprise, with the statement that he himself was on board the *Hoche*. Thus, all hope of secrecy was destroyed by some traitor or fool, and, sometimes, the terms are synonymous. There was no immediate hope that General Kilmaine's large force would be ready for action, so the patriot resolved to go with Hardy, even if he had to be in at the death of the hopes of his country. As usual, the winds fought for England. The expedition was scattered by a storm, and, at last, on October 10, after a cruise of twenty days' duration, Bompart, with only the line-of-battle ship and two frigates and the sloop *Biche,* appeared off the entrance to Lough Swilly. Next morning, before he had time to enter the Lough, or land the small remnant of Hardy's troops, he saw six English sail of the line, a razee of 60 guns, and two frigates, making toward him with all speed. They constituted the formidable squadron of Sir John Borlase Warren. Bompart knew at once that his case was hopeless, but would not strike his colors without a fight, for honor's sake. He signaled the frigates and sloop to attempt retreat through the shallower water, but cleared his own deck for action. A boat was sent from the *Biche* for his last orders. He and his officers counseled Tone to take advantage of the opportunity to effect his escape. "We French," argued the gallant and generous sailors, "will become prisoners of war, but *you*—what will become of you?" The magnanimous patriot was immovable, although death actually stared him in the face. His noble and memorable reply to their well-meant entreaties was: "Shall it be related that I fled, while the French were fighting the battles of my country?" His answer settled the controversy. The *Biche* sailed without him and reached France in safety.

While a portion of Warren's squadron pursued the retiring frigates, some of which were sunk or captured, four battleships and one frigate surrounded the *Hoche,* and one of the most terrible sea-fights on record resulted. Tone obtained command of a gun—one of the officers having fallen—and fought with the grand energy of despair, animated by the highest form of courage. As has been written of another gallant soul: "He seemed to court death, but death fled from him"—only, however, to return and claim him in a far more cruel form. The battle lasted six hours—until the *Hoche* was a pitiful wreck; "her scuppers flowed with blood; her wounded filled the cockpit, her shattered ribs yawned at each new stroke, and let in five feet of water in the hold; her rudder was carried off; her sails and cordage hung in shreds; nor could she reply with a single gun from her dismounted batteries to the unabating cannonade of the enemy." (Mitchel.) When she seemed to be sinking, she struck her colors, and the English poured in to exult in a barren victory. Most of the missing French frigates were soon taken, after a brilliant defence, and only the *Biche,* already mentioned, the *Romaine,* and the *Semillante* escaped capture.

The surrendered French officers were treated with courtesy, on being landed, preparatory to their removal to a place of detention, which was, usually, an English floating prison, or "hulk." The Earl of Cavan, who commanded in the district, invited them to breakfast. They accepted, and among them, according to Mitchel, and other historians, Wolfe Tone sat undistinguished, until a fellow-student at Trinity College, Sir George Hill, who had become an Orange leader, entered the dining-room, accompanied by police officers. Sir George was a magistrate and a rabid hater of all "rebels," no matter what his personal relations with them. His narrow mind could not comprehend the infamy of his action. "Looking keenly at the company," says Mitchel, "he singled out the object of his search, and, stepping up to him, said: 'Mr. Tone, I am very happy to see you!' Instantly rising, with the utmost composure, he replied: 'Sir George, I am happy to see you; how are Lady Hill and your family?' Hill made some inconsequential remark, and the policemen beckoned Tone into an adjoining room. He entered and was immediately set upon by a body of soldiers, commanded by General Lavau. That coward ordered the gallant prisoner to be placed in irons. Tone's indignation overcame him for a moment. He flung off the French uniform, exclaiming as he did so: 'These fetters shall never degrade the insignia of the free nation I have served.' Then he submitted to be ironed, remarking as they were being riveted: 'For the cause I have embraced, I feel prouder to wear these chains than if I were decorated with the Star and Garter of England!' " The arrest occurred at Letterkenny, and, with his feet chained under the belly of his horse, the hero was conveyed to Dublin, escorted by a strong body of dragoons. The escort was commanded by a Captain Thackeray, who said that Tone was the most delightful companion he ever traveled with. He even felt a comfort, prisoner though he was, in being back again on Irish soil, and saluted the people, who thronged to see him, with the greatest cordiality, even singling out many whom he had previously known by name. Captain Thackeray afterward became a clergyman and was rector at Dundalk. From him, Mr. Mitchel told the author, in 1874, the historian learned the particulars of the arrest and pilgrimage of Wolfe Tone—a pilgrimage destined to close in a bloody, and, for a long period, an unhonored grave. Like earlier political martyrs, he was tried by court-martial, although the court of King's Bench was then in session, and, ordinarily, it would have had jurisdiction in such cases—especially as Wolfe Tone had never been in the British military service. The prisoner might have made appeal to the King's Bench, but he, evidently, did not care to survive the ruin of his country. He offered in evidence his French commission of Chef-de-Brigade (colonel), with the brevet of adjutant-general, not to save his life, which he knew his enemies were resolved to take, but to obtain the honorable death of a soldier—by the fusillade. His appeal, which might have moved the coldest, fell upon hearts of steel. A few excerpts from the speech he made to the members of the court-martial deserve reproduction: "From my earliest youth," said he, "I have regarded the connection between Ireland and Great Britain as the curse of the Irish nation, and felt convinced that while it lasted Ireland could never be free or happy. My mind has been confirmed in this opinion by the experience of every succeeding year, and the conclusions I have drawn from every fact before my eyes. In consequence, I determined to apply all the powers which my individual efforts could move in order to separate the two countries. That Ireland was not able, of herself, to throw off the yoke, I knew. I therefore sought for aid wherever it was to be found. In honorable poverty I rejected offers which, to a man in my position, might be considered highly advantageous. I remained faithful to what I thought the cause of my country. . . . Under the flag of the French Republic, I originally engaged with a view to save and liberate my own country. For that purpose I have encountered the chances of war among strangers; for that purpose I have repeatedly braved the terrors of the ocean, covered, as I knew it to be, with the triumphant fleets of that power which it was my glory, and duty, to oppose. I have sacrificed all my hopes in life; I have courted poverty; I have left a beloved wife unprotected, and children, whom I adore, fatherless. After such sacrifices in a cause which I have always conscientiously considered the cause of justice and freedom, it is no great effort, at this day, to add the sacrifice of my life. . . . In a cause like this, success is everything. Success, in the eyes of the vulgar, fixes its merits. Washington succeeded and Kosciusko failed. . . . As to the connection between Ireland and Great Britain, I repeat it—all that has been imputed to me, words, writings, and actions, I here deliberately avow. Whatever be the sentence of this court, I am prepared for it. Its members will surely discharge their duty; I shall take care not to be wanting in mine."

The court-martial, composed mostly of veteran officers—many of them intense royalist bigots—was "visibly affected" by the utterance of the undaunted "rebel." There was a pause, which Tone himself broke by inquiring whether it was not usual to assign an interval between the sentence and execution. The judge advocate replied that the voices of the court could be collected immediately and the result transmitted, without delay, to the viceroy. It was then that Tone made his touching appeal, "I ask that the court should adjudge me the death of a soldier, and let me be shot by a platoon of grenadiers." But Cornwallis, the bedraggled "hero" of the Yorktown surrender, refused the last request of the gallant condemned, and the sentence of the court-martial, that he be hanged within forty-eight hours from the time of sentence, that is on November 12, was ordered to be carried into effect. "This cruelty," observes Mitchel, "he had foreseen; for England, from the days of Llewellyn of Wales, and Wallace of Scotland, to those of Tone and Napoleon, has never shown mercy, or generosity, to a fallen enemy. He, then, in perfect coolness and self-possession, determined to execute his purpose and anticipate their sentence."

As Tone had never been a military man in the kingdom of Ireland, had never borne the king's commission or worn his uniform, the ablest lawyers in the country held the sentence of the court-martial to be illegal. John Philpot Curran, invoking Tone's aged father as a witness, claimed that the King's Bench alone had jurisdiction, and Lord Kilwarden, who presided when the appeal was made, on the morning of the 12th, granted a stay of execution, under a writ of habeas corpus. The humane judge despatched the sheriff to the prison where Tone was confined to acquaint the provost marshal with the fact that a writ was being prepared and that execution must be suspended. The sheriff soon came back, and, addressing the court, said: "My lord, I have been to the barracks, in pursuance of your order. The provost marshal says he must obey Major Sandys. Major Sandys says he must obey Lord Cornwallis." Mr.

Curran announced, immediately, that Tone's father had served the writ of habeas corpus on General Craig, and that that officer "would not obey it." Lord Kilwarden's usually calm countenance became lurid with indignation, as he exclaimed, in agitated tones, "Mr. Sheriff, take the body of Tone into custody, take the provost marshal and Major Sandys into custody, and show the order of the court to General Craig."

Everybody present believed that the court would be defied by the military authorities, who had so long held the upper hand in Ireland. Kilwarden was not, however, the man to be trifled with, as he was an intense respecter of the law, and, besides, felt a personal friendship for Wolfe Tone. The suspense was broken by the return of the sheriff, who announced that he had been refused admittance to the barracks, but was informed that Wolfe Tone had wounded himself dangerously in the neck on the preceding night, and could not be removed with safety. He had written a letter to the French Directory, commending to that body the protection of his family. He also wrote two letters, couched in the most affectionate terms, to his wife, reminding her that she soon would be the only parent of their beloved children. Then, historians of the period say, he attempted to cut his throat with a penknife, while local tradition, likely in this instance to be more accurate, says that he sharpened his last silver coin on his fetters and tried to sever the carotid artery. The failure of the attempt would seem to confirm the traditional statement. He lingered in great agony, stretched on his bloody pallet, without relative or friend to console him in his sufferings, for seven days and nights. Just before he died the French emigrant doctor who attended him whispered that if he moved or spoke he would expire instantly. Tone's reply was characteristic: "I can yet find words to thank you, sir. It is the most welcome news you could give me. What should I wish to live for?" In a second afterward he had ceased to exist. The body was surrendered to relatives, who had it interred in Bodenstown churchyard, in the County Kildare. A cloud of mystery hangs over the last hours of Wolfe Tone, and many have hinted at murder, but, as the English would have preferred to hang him, it is altogether likely that he ended his own life. He had frequently said that the British should never put a rope around his neck, and his desire to shield the French uniform from dishonor, no doubt, intensified his purpose. Ireland, mindful of his great, and almost successful, efforts in behalf of her independence, honors his memory with ardent devotion, and the humble tomb at Bodenstown has become, of late years particularly, a kind of national shrine, to which thousands throng each year. A monument to his memory was projected in Dublin on the hundredth anniversary of his death, November 19, 1898, and before many years, perhaps, it may be completed. Meanwhile,

> "In Bodenstown churchyard there is a green grave,
> And wildly along it let winter winds rave;
> Far better they suit him, the ruin and gloom,
> Till Ireland a nation can build him a tomb!"

The theory has been advanced that had Tone not fatally injured himself, and had Lord Kilwarden's interference been successful, his doom might have been averted, as the French government held many English officers of rank as prisoners of war, and a threat of retaliation might have led to the exchange of the able and gallant Franco-Irish general. Dr. Madden, the learned compiler of the "Lives and

Times of the United Irishmen," says of Wolfe Tone: "Thus passed away one of the master spirits of his time. The curse of Swift was upon this man—he was an Irishman. Had he been a native of any other European country, his noble qualities, his brilliant talents, would have raised him to the first honors in the State, and to the highest place in the esteem of his fellow-citizens. His name lives, however, and his memory is probably destined to survive as long as his country has a history. Peace be to his ashes!"

CHAPTER IV

Demoralization Following Suppression of the Rebellion—Legislative Union with Great Britain Advocated—Virtually Defeated in Irish House of Commons

THE last great act in the bloody drama of 1798, in Ireland, ended with the death of Wolfe Tone. The masses of the people were thoroughly dispirited; the "loyalists," or Ascendency party, were more intolerant than ever; the "nobility and gentry" were frightened out of their senses; the carrion crows of political corruption scented their prey and hung around the Irish Parliament building like buzzards around a dying animal; the official returns of February, 1799, showed that the country was occupied by 32,281 regular soldiers, 26,634 active militia, 51,274 yeomen, or volunteers, as Americans would call them, 24,201 English militiamen, or "Fencibles," 1,500 artillery men, and 1,700 military employees of the commissariat department, making a total of 137,590 effectives— the largest force ever placed by England in the field before the war with the South African republics. According to the same returns, the total cost of suppressing the rebellion and corrupting the Irish Parliament, previously to the passage of the legislative Union enactment, was £21,573,547, or about $106,000,000 in our money of the present day. "The whole of which," remarks the sardonic Mitchel, "was the next year, in the arrangement of the terms of 'Union,' carried to the account of Ireland, and made part of *her* national debt—as if it were Ireland that profited by these transactions." O'Connell, in after years, alluding to this sharp practice, in connection with other matters, used to say: "It was thus that England made Ireland pay for the penknife with which Castlereagh [who died by his own hand] cut his throat!" The national debt of Ireland in 1787 was, according to Sir John Parnell (ancestor of Charles Stewart Parnell), Chancellor of the Exchequer, £3,044,167, or about $16,000,000, and even that amount was complained of as being excessive. In 1794, it was reduced to £2,500,000. In 1804, three years after the "Union," it had been increased, by the benevolent system of British book-keeping, to £53,000,000—$265,000,000! This is anticipating, somewhat, but it will preserve the thread of the subject. When the Consolidation Act of 1816, which united the Irish with the British exchequer, was passed, the funded debt of Ireland was stated to be £130,561,037—$652,805,185! Ireland had to pay, as may be seen, for the "honor and glory" of helping to beat Napoleon, with whom most of her people sympathized, if for no better reason than that he was the arch-enemy of England. "By this [British] management," comments Mitchel, "the Irish debt, which, in 1801, had been to the British as one to sixteen and a half, was forced up to bear to the British debt the ratio of one to seven and a half. This was the proportion required by the Act of Union as a condition of subjecting Ireland to indiscriminate taxation with Great Britain—a condition equally impudent and iniquitous. Ireland was to be loaded with inordinate debt, and then this debt was to be made the pretext for raising her taxation to the high British standard, and thereby rendering her liable to the pre-Union debt of Great Britain!"

The Irish "Rump" Parliament—for it barely represented, or, rather, misrepresented, one-fifth of the Irish nation— the Catholics still remaining excluded from membership— continued its sessions, and mainly occupied itself during the autumn of 1798 in examining Thomas Addis Emmet, Arthur O'Connor, Dr. William J. MacNevin, and other leaders as to the causes that led up to the rebellion. They, with truth and justice, laid the blame on the government of Lord Camden, which goaded the people to madness by endless persecution and the insults offered to and outrages committed upon virtuous Irish females, particularly in those districts where the soldiers were placed at "free quarters" before the outbreak of the insurrection. After completing their testimony, the prisoners were sent, as elsewhere stated, to a Scotch fortress, where they remained until peace was made with France, in 1802. Parliament was prorogued October 6, and "the throne" congratulated that miserable body on the suppression of "the dangerous and wicked rebellion." Military and Orange outrages on the people continued at intervals, and in one notorious case of murder, the perpetrator of which was a yeoman, named Wolloghan, and the victim a peaceable man, who was shot in his own house, Lord Cornwallis was compelled to set aside the findings of the court-martial, presided over by the Earl of Inniskillen, which acquited Wolloghan. The murderer, indeed, received no greater punishment than dismissal from his corps.   The example, however, had the desired effect.   Quiet was restored, and Cornwallis and Castlereagh wanted the country quiet for purposes of their own, which will presently appear.   The country had, in a measure, grown sick of slaughter.   No definite figures as to the total loss of life, including both sides, during the rebellion of 1798, have been published, but many authors have made computations, which range from twenty to fifty thousand killed in the field, hanged, or otherwise sent into eternity.   We think that a total of 30,000 lives sacrificed to the fury of the period is a conservative estimate.

A pamphlet said to have been written by Under-Secretary Cooke, at the suggestion of Lord Castlereagh, setting forth the alleged advantages of a legislative union with Great Britain, was largely circulated throughout Ireland toward the close of the rebellion.   This was for the purpose of preparing the public mind for the fixed intention of the British Minister, William Pitt, to make Ireland a discrowned and degraded province of the British Empire. The question soon came up for general discussion in both public and private gatherings.   Members of Parliament discussed it in their clubs and took sides without loss of time. Many of the fiercest opponents of a union had been bitter persecutors of the defeated revolutionists.   The foremost of these—in fact, he was regarded as the leader of the opposition—was Speaker Foster, who was cordially hated by Lord Clare, Lord Castlereagh, and their venal Unionist followers.   Lord Clare was bitter and unscrupulous.   He knew the needy condition of many of the members of the Irish Parliament, a condition brought about by the extravagant habits which had prevailed in the fashionable circles of the metropolis since the viceroyalty of the Earl of Rutland. Poverty renders most men weak of spirit, and nobody knew this better than Lord Clare. He, accordingly, took time by the forelock in preparing to bait his intended victims. In order to intimidate the bolder spirits, he caused Sir John Parnell, "the Incorruptible," to be dismissed from his chancellorship of the Exchequer, and Prime Sergeant Fitzgerald from the office which he held. Both these gentlemen had expressed themselves as being strongly against the Union. As the members of the Irish bar, in general, were among the hottest opponents of the projected Union, and contained in their ranks a very large proportion of the ablest statesmen in the country, Clare, aided and abetted by Lord Castlereagh, proceeded to mature a plan for their demoralization. Many new and needless legal offices were created to tempt their vanity, or cupidity. Of course, such favors came only through solicitation, and those who solicited became the slaves of the government, or else were turned away officeless. Among other positions, begotten for the foul purpose of political bribery, were two-and-thirty county judgeships—one for each of the Irish counties. The number of bankruptcy commissioners was doubled, with the same object. Foul play was manifest to the dullest, and the Irish barristers soon took alarm. A meeting of these gentlemen was called for December 9, 1798, at the Exhibition House, and was numerously attended. Many King's Counselors were present, some of them having joined in the call for the meeting, at which the Union proposition was to be discussed. Speeches were made for and against the measure, but the most memorable of all was the brief one uttered by Mr. Thomas Goold, who was afterward elected to the House of Commons: "There are," said Mr. Goold, "forty thousand British troops in Ireland [he meant English regiments proper, not the entire royalist force], and with forty thousand bayonets at my breast, the Minister shall not plant another Sicily in the bosom of the Atlantic. I want not the assistance of divine inspiration to foretell, for I am enabled by the visible and unerring demonstrations of nature to assert that Ireland was destined to be a free and independent nation. Our patent to be a State, not a shire, comes direct from heaven. The Almighty has, in majestic characters, signed the great charter of our independence. The great Creator of the world has given our beloved country the gigantic outlines of a kingdom. The God of nature never intended that Ireland should be a province, and by G— she never shall!"

A vote followed Mr. Goold's trumpet blast, and resulted, for the Union, 32—the exact number of county judges recently appointed by Lord Clare—against it, 166.

The merchants and financiers of the capital also held a great meeting at which strong resolutions of protest against the abhorred Union were adopted, and this was followed by a similar meeting and declarations on the part of the faculty and students of Trinity College. And far and wide throughout the whole country other gatherings uttered passionate protest against the contemplated degradation of Ireland from a kingdom to a province.

Parliament met on January 22, 1799, and the viceroy, Lord Cornwallis, opened it in person. The "speech from the throne," carefully prepared in council, avowed the intentions of the government in the following portentous passages:

"The zeal of his Majesty's regular and militia forces, the gallantry of the yeomanry [chiefly manifested against women], the honorable co-operation of the British fencibles and militia, and the activity, skill, and valor of his Majesty's fleets, will, I have no doubt, defeat any future effort of the enemy. But the more I have reflected on the situation and circumstances of this kingdom, considering, on the one hand, the strength and stability of Great Britain, and, on the other, those divisions which have shaken Ireland to its foundations, the more anxious I am for some permanent adjustment, which may extend the advantages enjoyed by our sister kingdom to every part of this island.

"The unremitting industry with which our enemies persevere in their avowed design of endeavoring to effect a separation of this kingdom from Great Britain, must have engaged your particular attention; and his Majesty commands me to express his anxious hope that this consideration, joined to the sentiment of mutual affection and common interest, may dispose the Parliaments in both kingdoms to provide the most effectual means of maintaining and improving a connection essential to their common security, and of consolidating, so far as possible, into one firm and lasting fabric, the strength, the power, and resources of the British Empire."

An address was proposed in the House of Lords, which sustained the viceregal speech and promised to "give the fullest attention to measures of such importance." An amendment proposed by Lord Powerscourt, declaring that a legislative Union would lead to total separation, was defeated by a vote of 46 to 19. Several other amendments of a germane character were offered, but all were rejected, the government party increasing its majority to 49. Finally fourteen of the peers in the minority made formal protest against the Union. Their names, which deserve to be remembered, were Leinster, Granard, Belvidere, Arran, Charlemont, Bellemont, Mountcashel, Kilkenny, Belmore, Powerscourt, De Vesci, Dunsany, Lismore, and the Protestant bishop of Down and Connor.

In the House of Commons, Lord Tyrone, heir to the Marquisate of Waterford, moved the address. It was seconded by Colonel Fitzgerald, who spoke favorably of "strengthening the connection between the two countries." The debate showed a strong opposition to the contemplated Union measure; but Lord Castlereagh, nothing daunted, announced that, at an early day, he would submit a specific motion, bearing on the question of a legislative Union, to the House. The ablest speech made in opposition was that by George Ponsonby, who appealed to the settlement of 1782, and said it was final. He, therefore, moved an amendment to the address, following the passage which declared "the willingness of the House to enter on a consideration of what measures might best tend to confirm the common strength of the empire," to this effect: "Maintaining, however, the undoubted birthright of the people of Ireland to have a resident and independent Legislature, such as was recognized by the British Legislature in 1782, and was finally settled as the adjustment of all differences between the two countries."

Sir Lawrence Parsons seconded the Ponsonby amendment in a vigorous speech, and Prime Sergeant Fitzgerald declared that the Irish Parliament was not competent to vote its own extinction, and with it the rights and liberties of those who created it. Sir Jonah Barrington also waxed eloquent in opposition to the Union; and Sir Boyle Roche —one of the Castle clique—got off one of his most famous "bulls," when, taking the government side, he said: "I am for a union to put an end to the uniting between Presbyterians, Protestants, and Catholics to overturn the Constitution!"

The debate was lengthy and called out many warm speeches on both sides, but, in general, the anti-Unionists seemed to have the advantage. This alarmed Castlereagh, who made an impromptu speech, vague but clever. William Conyngham Plunket replied to him in a very powerful argument—saying, in conclusion: "For my own part, I will resist a legislative union to my last gasp of existence, and with the last drop of my blood; and, when I feel the hour of dissolution approaching, I will, like the father of Hannibal, take my children to the altar, and swear them to eternal hostility against the invaders of their country's freedom!"

Unhappily, although to the last he fought against the Union in the Irish House of Commons, Plunket lived to outlive his sentiments, and to be the stern prosecutor of a patriot (Robert Emmet) who afterward rose in revolt against the same Union which the orator so vehemently opposed. Says Mitchel, grimly: "This gallant speech was often cited afterward against Plunket, and it was remarked that Hamilcar, after that swearing scene, never helped the Romans to govern Carthage as a province."

Finally, after a debate which consumed twenty-two hours, the House divided, on Ponsonby's amendment, with the following result: For the amendment, 105; against it, 106, making a majority of one for the government, which looked, upon the test vote, in the light of a defeat. The anti-Unionists, in the House and outside of it, cheered loudly and long, but Castlereagh had still cards up his sleeve and was determined to try again. Sir Jonah Barrington states broadly that Mr. Luke Fox and Mr. Trench, of Woodlawn, County

Galway—the ancestor of the present Lord Ashtown—were publicly bought on the floor of the House. Otherwise the government would not have had even a nominal majority. He had yet another engine of destruction at his command —the Place bill, which, Barrington says, was "so indiscreetly framed by Mr. Grattan and the Whigs of Ireland" several years before. "That bill," remarks Sir Jonah, "enacted that members accepting offices, places, or pensions, during the pleasure of the crown, should not sit in Parliament, unless re-elected, but, unfortunately, the bill made no distinction between valuable offices which might influence, and nominal offices, which it might 'job'; and the Chiltern Hundreds of England were, under the title of the Escheatorships, of Munster, Leinster, Connaught, and Ulster, transferred to Ireland, with salaries of forty shillings, to be used at pleasure by the Secretary [Castlereagh]. Occasional and temporary seats were thus bartered for by government, and, by the ensuing session, made the complete and fatal instrument of packing the Parliament and effecting a union." Thus, if a venal member, afraid of his constituency, or loth to accept cold cash for his vote, wished to shirk the responsibility of selling his country's independence, the minister could give him an escheatorship, at forty shillings per annum. His acceptance meant his resignation. For a consideration of high office, title, or some other corrupt recompense, his seat was vacated, to make room for a government supporter, who had also made his bargain with the Union "jobbers."

CHAPTER V

Union Proposition Defeated in the Irish Parliament, 1799—Mr. Ponsonby's Decisive Resolution Rendered Negative by Speaker Foster's Technicality—Daniel O'Connell's First Speech Against the Union

THE second debate on the question of a legislative Union between the two kingdoms came up on January 24, 1799. The galleries of the House were filled with spectators, many of them ladies, for the excitement was intense, and affected both sexes and all classes. Outside the walls of the Parliament house an enormous multitude had collected, and their cheers for the opponents of a Union and groans for its champions sufficiently proved that the Irish capital was overwhelmingly against the contemplated act of national suicide. The question was on the adoption or rejection of the address to the throne. Sir Lawrence Parsons led off against the adoption of the document. " 'Annihilate the Parliament of Ireland!' That is the cry," he said, "that came across the water [from England]. Now is the time. Ireland is weak, Ireland is divided, Ireland is appalled by civil war! Ireland is covered with troops! Martial law brandishes its sword throughout the land! Now is the time to put Ireland down forever!—now strike the blow! Who?—is it you? Will you obey that voice? Will you betray your country?"

There were many other speeches, "pro and con," but, apart from Parsons's, the most notable were those of Mr. Plunket and Lord Castlereagh, both of whom were fully aroused. Plunket's speech against the Union was said to have been "the ablest ever heard from any member of that Parliament." Mr. Ponsonby, whose amendment was the alternative to the adoption of the address, also spoke powerfully, and he and Castlereagh exchanged some bitter remarks. On this occasion, Ireland won. The vote stood: For Mr. Ponsonby's amendment, making the Irish Parliament indestructible, 111; for Lord Tyrone's address, favoring the Union, 106: majority against the government, 5. The anti-Unionists in the House cheered vociferously and their shouts were re-echoed in thunder waves by the patriotic multitudes that filled the streets and squares in the neighborhood. Of the members who voted with Tyrone, Sir Jonah Barrington says sixty-nine held offices under government "at pleasure"; nineteen were rewarded with offices for their votes; one member was openly seduced on the floor of the House, and eighteen were commoners created peers, or their wives peeresses, for their votes. Only three were supposed to be uninfluenced.

Mr. Ponsonby "congratulated the House and the country on the honest and patriotic assertion of their liberties, but declared that he considered there would be no security against future attempts to overthrow their independence but by a direct and absolute declaration of the rights of Irishmen, recorded upon their journals, as the decided sense of the people, through their Parliament, and he, therefore, without further preface, moved that this House will ever maintain the undoubted birthright of Irishmen, by preserving an independent Parliament of Lords and Commons, residing in this kingdom, as stated and approved by his Majesty and the British Parliament in 1782."

Lord Castlereagh made protest, but when the question was put by the Speaker, there were but two negative votes, those of Castlereagh himself, and Mr. Toler—afterward the notorious Judge Norbury.

Ireland appeared to be saved, and would have been, had not the Speaker (Mr. Foster), in a moment of most unfortunate particularity, and wishing to be strictly correct, called upon Mr. Ponsonby to come to the table and *write* down his motion accurately. The members were already leaving the chamber as Mr. Ponsonby proceeded to comply with the Speaker's request. All immediately resumed their seats and the government party took advantage of the pause to regain their lost ground. A whisper went around that the motion would bar out all further chance of "negotiation" on the subject of Union, and many needy and avaricious "patriots" did not want it that way.

The Speaker put the motion as written, and the response of the "ayes" seemed sufficient, when Mr. Chichester Fortescue, of Louth, asked to be heard before the resolution should finally pass. He was allowed to speak and declared himself against a Union, but declined to bind himself forever, "as possible circumstances might arise which should render such a measure expedient for the empire."

Mr. Ponsonby, judging that some of the weak-kneed members of his own side might desert him, and fearing defeat, committed the blunder of not pressing the passage of the resolution, which would have put an end for all time to the controversy. Ireland could not have been again menaced by the British minister—at least not in that form— and both Cornwallis and Castlereagh would have been compelled to resign their offices. The motion was not put again, and Ireland, therefore, ultimately lost her legislative independence.

The disaster to the Ponsonby motion discouraged the

anti-Unionists, and they sought to take away one of Castlereagh's arguments by introducing a Regency bill, which provided that the Regent of Ireland should forever be the same personage who exercised that function in England. But Castlereagh was too shrewd for them. He opposed the bill, and it went over until next session, never again to be heard of. The rest of the session was consumed in the passage of certain penal enactments against the late "rebels"—the Loyalist Claim bill was among them.

The proposition of a Union was brought up in the English Houses of Parliament on the same day that it was mooted in those of Ireland. It came in a "speech from the throne" couched in much the same language as that used by Viceroy Cornwallis in Dublin.

Richard Brinsley Sheridan, who represented an English borough, but who was an Irish patriot by instinct as well as education, opposed the measure in the Commons, in his characteristically eloquent manner. He was replied to by Minister Pitt, but was not convinced by his casuistry. Next day, when the usual address was proposed, he appealed to the honor of England and reminded the House of the settlement of 1782, which was supposed to have been final. "The British legislature had acquiesced in it, and, therefore, no other basis of connection should be adopted."

George Canning and Minister Pitt both felt called upon to reply to him, using the customary arguments about the alleged "weakness" and "dependency" of Ireland on Great Britain, which was said to be very anxious for the "safety" of the "sister" island. Both these gentlemen knew full well that Great Britain was the only enemy Ireland had need to fear. In his speech Pitt made a bid for Catholic support by hinting at emancipation, if the Union Act prevailed. He

did not dare to come out openly with a definite promise.
The matter was also debated in the Lords, and, finally, both
Houses sustained the royal propositions, which were those
of Pitt, but awaited the action of Ireland before taking
more definite ground. Pitt, it is asserted by Mr. Mitchel,
sent a private despatch to Lord Cornwallis to carry through
a Union bill in the Irish Parliament, but not to press the
matter until assured of a majority of at least fifty votes.
Sir Jonah Barrington is quoted as having seen and read
the message to the viceroy. Castlereagh, as will be seen,
was fully equal to the task of carrying out the wishes of
Pitt without waiting for so decisive a majority. He had
the treasury at his command, and knew how to make use of
its resources among the unprincipled; and where money
could not do the work, there were titles, offices, and pensions without stint. He took occasion during the Parliamentary recess to play the rôle of public seducer, and did
not shrink from announcing "that every nobleman who
returned members to Parliament should be paid, in cash,
£15,000 [$75,000] for every member so returned [to vote
with the government for a Union]; secondly, that every
member who had *purchased* a seat in Parliament should
have his purchase money repaid to him out of the treasury
of Ireland; thirdly, that all members of Parliament, or
others, who were *losers* by the Union should be fully recompensed for their losses, and that £1,500,000 [$7,500,000]
should be devoted to this service. In other words, all
who should effectively support his measure were, under
some pretext or other, to share in this bank of corruption."
(Mitchel.) The bait, as will be seen, took with the persons concerned, and some of the scoundrels "thanked God
that they had a country to sell."

The attempt to get the Catholics to support a measure of Union that was protested against by twenty-six Irish counties, and was opposed by even the Orange lodges, aroused bitter indignation in the breasts of some members of that denomination. Among those who raised their voices against any bargain with England was a young lawyer named Daniel O'Connell, then in his 25th year, and destined to be, perhaps, the most renowned of all Irish Parliamentary leaders and orators. At a meeting held in the Royal Exchange, Dublin, while the question of a legislative Union was still pending, Mr. O'Connell, in the course of a lengthy and most effective speech, said: "Sir, it is my sentiment, and I am satisfied it is the sentiment not only of every gentleman who now hears me, but of the Catholic people of Ireland, that if our opposition to this injurious, insulting, and hated measure of Union were to draw upon us the revival of the penal laws, we would boldly meet a proscription and oppression, which would be the testimonies of our virtue, and sooner throw ourselves once more on the mercy of our Protestant brethren than give our assent to the political murder of our country. Yes, I know—I do know—that although exclusive advantages [alluding to a speech of Pitt] may be ambiguously held forth to the Irish Catholic to seduce him from the sacred duty he owes his country; I know that the Catholics of Ireland still remember that they have a country, and that they will never accept any advantages as a *sect* which would debase and destroy them as a *people*." Resolutions denouncing the Union were passed at this meeting, and at hundreds of similar meetings, composed of Protestants as well as Catholics, throughout Ireland. A petition against the Union received countless signatures, while one in favor of it was signed only by a few officeholders, place-beggars, and needy adventurers. The people, en masse, were faithful to their country. "What Parliament or Congress" (other than the Irish), asks Mitchel, contemplating the machinations of Castlereagh, "has ever been tempted so? There is no need to make invidious or disparaging reflections; but Englishmen and Frenchmen and Americans should pray that their respective legislatures may never be subjected to such an ordeal."

Castlereagh, although thoroughly base and heartless, was physically brave. He was afraid of the orators of the opposition, and conceived, as dueling prevailed in that day, that the best way to get rid of them was to have them duly challenged and shot, by himself and his colleagues, "at ten or twenty paces." But the orators were also brave, and both sides were inflamed to a white heat of mortal hatred.

CHAPTER VI

A.D. 1800 the Fatal Year of Union with Great Britain—Fierce Debate Over the Measure in Irish Commons—Government Triumphs—Opposition to Act in British Parliament

WHEN the last session of the Irish Parliament began its deliberations on January 15, 1800, the subject of a Union was not made immediately prominent. On the contrary, insignificant measures, such as the government of the Protestant Charter Schools, came up for consideration. The speech of the viceroy was vague in the extreme, and that of the mover of the address, Lord Loftus, whose father, the Marquis of Ely, had received £45,000 ($225,000) for his three "rotten boroughs" from Castlereagh, was vaguer still. The word "Union" had been tabooed, but everybody knew what was coming, and the government corruption mill was still working night and day.

The opposition, led by Sir Lawrence Parsons, always a good Irishman, determined to make the government show its hand. Sir Lawrence, after delivering a notable speech, moved an amendment to the address, "declaratory of the resolution of Parliament to preserve the Constitution, as established in 1782, and to support the freedom and independence of the nation."

Castlereagh replied in measuredly contemptuous tones, and said the project of Union had not been abandoned, but was not referred to by the viceroy, "for the reason that it would be made a subject of distinct communication to Parliament."

The debate that followed was brilliant in the extreme— the genius being mainly on the side of the Patriots. Charles Kendall Bushe and Plunket surpassed even themselves. But the climax came when the illustrious Henry Grattan, who had just been elected by a Wicklow constituency—after an absence of a few years from the House, because of disgust and ill-health—tottered into the chamber, leaning on the arms of George Ponsonby and Arthur Moore; he was too feeble to walk alone. Every member rose when he advanced to his seat. He found himself too weak to rise, and asked the privilege of addressing the House from where he sat. His request was cordially granted. "Never," observes Mitchel, "was a finer illustration of the sovereignty of mind over matter. Grattan spoke two hours with all his usual vehemence and fire against the Union, and in favor of the amendment of Sir Lawrence Parsons. The Treasury Bench was at first disquieted, then became savage, and it was resolved to bully or to kill Mr. Grattan."

He was insultingly replied to by Mr. Corry, but was too much exhausted to make reply at the time—an omission he supplied with interest afterward in the course of that "eloquent war." But the Unionists, notwithstanding the matchless oratory of their opponents, defeated the amendment of Sir Lawrence Parsons by a vote of 138 to 96.

The project of Union was brought formally before the Irish Parliament by Lord Castlereagh on February 15. He advocated the measure at some length and with a vast amount of finesse and sophistry—the latter addressed to the cupidity of the country, not to its patriotism.

He was ably replied to by Sir John Parnell, Peter Barrowes, Grattan, and some others; but when the roll was called on the ministerial motion that the proposed articles of Union be printed, the government won again by a vote of 158 to 115. In the House of Lords, despite the opposition of Lord Charlemont, the Marquis of Downshire, the Earl of Bellamont, Lord Powerscourt, Lord Dillon, Lord Glenworth, Lord Glendore, and the Archbishop of Cashel, the vote on the same proposition stood in favor of government 75 to 26.

The adoption of the articles, one by one, was moved by Lord Castlereagh in the House of Commons on February 21. There was much fine argument by the Patriots, but Castlereagh was cold-blooded and immovable. He would not listen to delay or compromise. He did not care how many counties, or towns, had petitioned against the Union. It must be carried—it was "his Majesty's pleasure" that it be carried. His lordship knew that he carried the majority of that dishonored membership in his breeches pocket.

It was—only at a bigger expense, as the prize was more valuable—the case of Scotland's purchase over again. Castlereagh refused his consent to a dissolution of Parliament, proposed by Sir John Parnell and Counselor Saurin, to test the feeling of such people in the country as had the franchise on the subject. His lordship knew that, in such an event, his case would be hopeless. He even had the hardihood to surround the Parliament houses with British troops, under the pretext of "keeping order"—an unfailing British pretext in Ireland and elsewhere.

We regret to be compelled to state that a few Catholic prelates, deceived by Pitt, Castlereagh, and their agents, declared themselves favorable to the Union, believing that such a measure would forward the cause of Catholic emancipation. They were doomed to a not undeserved disappointment. Their action angered the Catholic priests and laity; but a blunder in their address to the viceroy, who had one eye that never remained fixed for a second, owing to some nervous trouble, made the whole nation laugh, in spite of its apprehensions. They addressed Cornwallis at a public reception and proclaimed themselves Unionists, with quite unnecessary emphasis, remarking, at the outset: "Your excellency has always kept a *steady eye* on the interest of Ireland!" The courtiers endeavored not to laugh, but failed. The viceroy reddened, but said nothing. The Right Rev. Spokesman and his supporters had never before seen Cornwallis, and were thoroughly unfamiliar with his unsteady organ of vision. His lordship, however, plainly assured the delegation that "Catholic emancipation would be immediately made a cabinet question."

The articles of Union, with a few amendments of no vital importance, were adopted in the Irish Commons on March

22 and in the Lords on the 27th of the same month. The address, declaring that they (the Parliament) "cordially embraced the principle of incorporating Great Britain and Ireland into one kingdom, by a complete and entire union of their legislatures," was carried by the usual government majority, and the matter then passed to the British Parliament for an approval already greedily and gladly resolved upon. Ireland was, already, in the toils of the imperial constrictor. It only remained for her bones to be crushed that she might be swallowed by the monster.

In the English Parliament, the proposals for Union, in the shape of the articles adopted by the Irish Parliament at the dictation of the British ministry, were immediately put forward. The Duke of Portland communicated to the House of Lords, on April 2, a message from the throne, bearing upon the Union proposition. The Irish address and resolutions accompanied the royal message.

Lord Holland bravely raised his voice against the projected measure, saying, with heat, that the Union, as formulated, "was evidently offensive to the great body of the Irish people, and if it should be carried into effect against the sense of the nation, it would endanger the connection between the countries, and might produce irreparable mischief."

Lord King voted with Holland against going into committee on the subject, and they were supported by the Earl of Derby. But all opposition was in vain, and eighty-two British peers voted to proceed with the measure in committee, where, of course, everything went as the ministers desired.

Minister Pitt made the motion for a committee in the Commons. He made, also, a very clever speech, and was immediately replied to by Mr. (afterward Lord) Grey, who was a determined English opponent of the Union. In the course of his remarks this honest Englishman said: "The facts are notorious. There are, in all, three hundred members of the Irish Parliament, and, of these, one hundred and twenty are strenuously opposed to the measure; among them are two-thirds of the county members, the representatives of the city of Dublin, and of almost all the towns which it is proposed shall send members to the Imperial Parliament. One hundred and sixty-two members voted in favor of the Union, and, of these, one hundred and sixteen were placemen; some of them were English generals on the staff, without one foot of ground in Ireland, and completely dependent on the government."

He concluded by moving an address to the king, praying him to direct his ministers to suspend all proceedings on the Union until the bona fide sentiment of the people of Ireland regarding the measure was constitutionally declared.

Brinsley Sheridan and some other members supported Mr. Grey, and they were answered by Secretary Dundas and Viscount Carysfort. The result of the division was the defeat of Mr. Grey's motion by a vote of 236 to 30.

As in the case of the Lords, the Commons committee adopted the three first articles of the proposed Union, to the following effect:

Article one defined that the kingdoms of Great Britain and Ireland should be, thereafter, consolidated into one, under such terms and conditions as might be established by the acts of their respective Parliaments.

Article two provided that, from the first day of January, 1801, the two kingdoms should be forever after known as "the United Kingdom of Great Britain and Ireland," and that the royal style and titles appertaining to the imperial crown of the said United Kingdom, and its dependencies, and also the ensigns, armorial flags, and banners thereof should be such as the king, by his royal proclamation, under the great seal of the United Kingdom, should be pleased to appoint.

Article three provided that the succession to the imperial crown of the United Kingdom and the dominions belonging to the same should continue limited and settled (that is, to the Protestant succession) in the same manner as the succession to the imperial crown of the said kingdoms of Great Britain and Ireland then stood limited and settled, according to existing laws, and to the terms of the Union between England and Scotland.

These were the fundamental provisions, and the other articles bore on the details of future government, revenue, and expenditure; the maintenance of the Established Church, the proportion of the "national debt" to be paid by Ireland; the abolition of all duties, after a stated number of years —free trade, in fact, by which the poorer country was inevitably bound to suffer, being quite incapable of competing with wealthy England unless protected by, at least, a moderate tariff.

Other provisions belong to that portion of history generally relegated to the appendix.

It is, perhaps, superfluous to remark that all the articles, after perfunctory debates, were carried through at the pleasure of Mr. Pitt and his colleagues.

Lord Holland sought to pledge the ministry to Catholic emancipation, but was overruled, and the prelates of the Catholic Church, who favored the Union from a purely sectarian standpoint, were obliged to content themselves with the pie-crust promises of Cornwallis and his "Irish" satraps.

On the 9th of May, after all the articles had been adopted, the Houses sent a joint address to the king, stating that they were "ready to conclude a union with the Irish Parliament" on the basis contained in the articles aforesaid.

Soon afterward the articles were framed by the respective Parliaments into a Union bill, which was to be submitted for action immediately. In order to prepare the Irish people for the radical change in their representation, contemplated under the new dispensation, Lord Castlereagh had passed in the Irish Parliament, on May 20, an act for the regulation of elections, to be incorporated in the general act of Union; and this remained in force from the time of the Union until the period of the Reform bill, in 1832, when it underwent a slight modification.

It gave one member each to the cities and towns of Waterford, Limerick, Belfast, Drogheda, Carrickfergus, Newry, Kilkenny, Londonderry, Galway, Clonmel, Wexford, Armagh, Youghal, Bandon, Dundalk, Kinsale, Lisburn, Sligo, Carlow, Ennis, Dungarvan, Downpatrick, Coleraine, Mallow, Athlone, New Ross, Tralee, Cashel, Dungannon, Portarlington, and Inniskillen; two each to the cities of Dublin and Cork; one to Trinity College, Dublin; and two each to the two-and-thirty counties of Ireland—aggregating one hundred representatives in all. The increase of population added five members to the House of Commons, when the Reform measure was adopted. The modification of the boroughs, at a later period, reduced the number to one hundred and three members, and, at that figure, the Irish representation in the London Parliament still remains. There is some talk of reducing the delegation, because of Ireland's decreased population, but constitutional experts declare that such a measure would be clearly against the stipulation of the Treaty of Union, and that it would be both difficult and dangerous to meddle with the arrangement as it stands. Irish representation might, with safety, be increased *above* —as has been already done—one hundred members, but could not be reduced *below* that number, unless the Act of Union is to be considered null and void, in letter as well as in spirit. It is true that the Established Church was guaranteed in perpetuity by the Union treaty, but its abolition by Mr. Gladstone's first memorable administration struck no such vital blow at the arrangement of 1800-1 as the reduction of Irish representation at Westminster would inevitably accomplish.

The rotation in which four Irish bishops should sit in the House of Lords, and the election of 28 representative peers, "by their own order," were also provided for. It was, further, arranged that "if the king should authorize the present Lords and Commons of Great Britain to form a part of the first Imperial Legislature, the sitting members for Dublin and Cork and for the thirty-two counties of Ireland should represent the same cities and shires in that Parliament; that the written names of the members for Trinity College, for the cities of Waterford and Limerick, and other towns before mentioned, should be put into a glass and successively drawn out by the clerk of the Crown, and that of the two representatives of each of those places, the individual whose name might be first drawn should serve for the same place in the first United Legislature; and that when a new Parliament should be convoked, writs should be sent to the respective constituencies, provided for in the Union Treaty, for the election of members in the usual mode, according to the number then adjusted." The ministers did not dare to submit the election to the people, immediately after the outrage committed on their national pride.

CHAPTER VII

Final Agony of the Irish Parliament—England Confirms Act of Union, which went into Effect January 1, 1801—Shameful Bribery of Irish Members

THE Irish people must have been very stupidly led and directed between the periods of the promulgation of the Union scheme and its virtual accomplishment. Too much was left to a Parliamentary minority, without hope of reinforcement, and too little to the masses. The latter should have been organized to make popular anger felt by the traitorous majority in some effective, terror-striking manner. The country's life hung in the balance, and ceremony should have been cast to the winds. It was a desperate case and, therefore, needed a desperate remedy, but true manhood seemed to have then deserted Ireland—for a period.

On May 21, Castlereagh moved for leave to bring in his Union bill, and leave was granted by a vote of 160 to 100. The second reading occurred on the 25th, and the third, moved on the 26th, was stubbornly opposed by Grattan and other leaders of the Patriot section. In concluding his pathetic, but powerful, speech, Grattan said: "The cry of connection will not, in the end, avail against the principle of liberty. Connection is a wise and profound policy, but connection without an Irish Parliament is connection without its own principle, without analogy of condition, without the pride of honor that should attend it; is innovation, is peril, is subjugation—not connection. The cry of disaffection will not, in the end, avail against the principles of liberty. Identification is a solid, an imperial maxim, necessary to the preservation of freedom, necessary for that of empire, but without union of hearts—with a separate government, and without a separate Parliament, identification is extinction, is dishonor, is conquest—not identification.

"Yet I do not give up my country: I see her in a swoon, but she is not dead. Though in her tomb she lies, helpless and motionless, still there is on her lips a spirit of life, and on her cheeks a glow of beauty—

> "Thou art not conquered; beauty's ensign yet
> Is crimson in thy lips and on thy cheeks,
> And death's pale flag is not advanced there!"

While a plank of the vessel sticks together, I will not leave her. Let the courtier present his flimsy sail, and carry the light bark of his faith with every new breath of wind, I will remain anchored here with fidelity to the fortunes of my country—faithful to her freedom, faithful to her fall!"

Mr. Plunket declared that he had no hesitation in saying that "if the wanton ambition of the minister should assail the freedom of Ireland, and compel him to the alternative, he would fling the connection to the winds and clasp the independence of his country to his breast."

Mr. Saurin said: "You can make the Union binding as a law, but you can not make it obligatory on conscience. It will be obeyed as long as England is strong, but resistance to it will be, in the abstract, a duty, and the exhibition of that resistance will be a mere question of prudence."

Mr. Kendall Bushe remarked: "Odious as this measure

is in my eyes, and disgusting to my feelings, if I see it is carried by the free and uninfluenced sense of the Irish Parliament, I shall not only defer and submit, but I will cheerfully obey. It will be the first duty of every good subject. But fraud and oppression and unconstitutional practice may, possibly, be another question. If this be factious language, Lord Somers was factious; the founders of the Revolution were factious, William III was an usurper and the Revolution was a rebellion."

Notwithstanding, the Union bill was, so to speak, "railroaded" to a third reading, and the final vote in the Commons was taken on the measure, June 7, 1800. The House itself was packed to the roof, the streets thronged by an excited populace, who needed but organization and desperate leaders to hurl itself upon the debauched legislature and convert College Green into a Place de la Concorde. But serried lines of steel glittered around the building and scarlet uniforms, by the thousand, glared, like fields of poppies, in the eyes of the spectators. England was in full military, as well as "moral," occupation of the Irish capital. Sir Jonah Barrington, in his graphic "Rise and Fall," thus describes the closing scene:

"The galleries were full, but the change was lamentable —they were no longer crowded with those who had been accustomed to witness the eloquence and to animate the debates of that devoted assembly. A monotonous and melancholy murmur ran through the benches, scarcely a word was exchanged among the members, nobody seemed at ease, no cheerfulness was apparent, and the ordinary business, for a short time, proceeded in the usual manner.

"At length the expected moment arrived, the order of the day for the third reading of the bill for a 'legislative union between Great Britain and Ireland' was moved by Lord Castlereagh; unvaried, tame, cold-blooded, the words seemed frozen as they issued from his lips; and, as if a simple citizen of the world, he seemed to have no sensation on the subject. At that moment he had no country and no God but his ambition. He made his motion and resumed his seat, with the utmost composure and indifference.

"Confused murmurs again ran through the House; it was visibly affected; every character, in a moment, seemed involuntarily rushing to its index—some pale, some flushed, some agitated; there were few countenances to which the heart did not despatch some messenger. Several members withdrew before the question could be repeated, and an awful momentary silence succeeded their departure.

"The Speaker rose slowly from that chair which had been the proud source of his honors and of his high character; for a moment he resumed his seat, but the strength of his mind sustained him in his duty, though his struggle was apparent. With that dignity which never failed to signalize his official actions, he held up the bill for a moment in silence; he looked steadily around him on the last agony of the expiring Parliament. He at length repeated, in an emphatic tone, 'As many as are of opinion that this bill do pass, say aye.' The affirmative was languid but indisputable; another momentary pause ensued; again his lips seemed to decline their office. At length, with an eye averted from the object which he hated, he proclaimed, with a subdued voice, 'The ayes have it.' The fatal sentence was now pronounced; for an instant he stood statue-like; then, indignantly, and with disgust, flung the bill upon the table and sunk into his chair with an exhausted spirit. An independent country was thus degraded into a province —Ireland, as a nation, was extinguished."

But the formal approval of the Irish House of Lords was needed to complete the work of Pitt and Castlereagh, and this, after a debate of no great consequence, was given on June 13, when the bill was read for a third time. The following peers protested against the reading, and gave their reasons in an able document of some length: Leinster, Arran, Mountcashel, Farnham, Bellamore, Massy, Strangford, Granard, Ludlow, Moira, Right Rev. Waterford and Lismore, Powerscourt, De Vesci, Charlemont, Kingston, Riversdale, Lismore, and Sunderlin.

The English Parliament confirmed the action of that of Ireland on July 2. The last separate Parliament of Great Britain was prorogued on July 29, and the royal assent to the Act of Union was given on August 1—the anniversary of the accession of the House of Hanover to the British throne. It went into effect, as already indicated, January 1, 1801, and the new imperial standard was displayed the same day on London Tower, Dublin Castle, and the Castle of Edinburgh. It has remained unchanged since then, "quartered, first and fourth, England; second, Scotland; third, Ireland." The latter country is represented by a harp on a blue field in the lower quarter of the standard next the staff.

In addition, a Union Jack, which also still exists, was adopted, by royal proclamation, as follows: "Azure, the crosses, saltires of St. Andrew and St. Patrick, quarterly per saltire, counterchanged, argent and gules; the latter imbriated of the second, surmounted by the cross of St. George of the third, as the saltire." For elucidation of the mysteries of the foregoing royal jumble, the reader is referred to a book on heraldry.

We can not take a joyful leave of this most villanous of international transactions without giving a summary of the bribery necessary for its accomplishment, taken from the Black List, published by Barrington and other historians of that mournful period. In all Castlereagh and Lord Clare, with the full sanction of Pitt and Cornwallis, disposed of the following "considerations" for votes to produce an artificial majority for the "Union" in the Irish Parliament: Two bishoprics of the Established Church—given for the complaisance of relatives of the beneficiaries who were members of the House of Commons; fifty-nine valuable offices; one hundred and four minor ones—chiefly in the gift of Lord Tyrone, who moved the original resolution for the Act of Union in the Commons; and hundreds of minor positions; fourteen colonelcies—one being to Sir Edward Pakenham, who afterward commanded the British army at the battle of New Orleans, and was defeated and slain in that fight; eighteen peerages, with two "ladyships," given to the wives of venal members; $7,500,000 in cold cash, paid to sixteen political hucksters; seven pensions of the first class, and many more of minor grade; thirty-two county and nine other judgeships; two generalcies, and two baronetcies.

Of the cash purchases, Lord Shannon received for his patronage, in the Commons, £45,000—$225,000; the Marquis of Ely the same amount; Lord Claremorris (besides a peerage), £23,000—$115,000; Lord Belvidere (besides his douceur), £15,000—$75,000; Sir Hercules Langrishe, a similar sum. There were many others, but the examples given will serve to illustrate the methods of the unworthy ministers who thus vilely strangled the legislative independence of Ireland.

Truly, Mr. Saurin was entirely right when he remarked, during the final debate, that such a "Union" was "not binding on conscience; that resistance to it would be, in the abstract, a duty, and that the exhibition of that resistance was simply a question of prudence." We will see how that exhibition was "imprudently," and prudently, manifested by successive generations of Irishmen.

CHAPTER VIII

The Unionist Catholics Disappointed in the Hope of Emancipation—
George III Sits Down on the Proposition—Pitt Ostensibly "Resigns"—Addington Succeeds Him—Peace of Amiens—Renewal of War with France

THE "Jellyfish Catholics"—a minority of that creed—who had supported the Union waited in fond expectation of a distinct ministerial promise of full emancipation. But they waited in vain. George III had much less use for the Irish Catholics than he had for Satan himself. In fact, he hated Catholics as Old Nick is supposed to hate holy water. When Pitt mentioned the matter, he put down his foot and absolutely refused to have the subject introduced into Parliament as a ministerial measure. Pitt, who had served as Prime Minister for seventeen years, and who "loved" the Catholics quite as little as his master, was artful enough to make the king's refusal a pretext for temporary resignation, in order that he might more easily escape from an awkward dilemma. The English peace party was clamoring loudly for a cessation of hostilities with France, and the minister, while he favored war, was not willing to shoulder the responsibility of continuing it. But he did not resign at once. The first new Imperial Parliament met at Westminster January 22, 1801. In the royal speech there was no mention of Catholic emancipation—neither was there any allusion made to it in the address proposed in Parliament to the throne. But Mr. Grey, who had so resolutely opposed the Union Act, moved an amendment, which, among other things, pleaded for "the extension of the British constitution to the Catholics of Ireland, and their restoration to all the rights of British subjects. This," he said, "they had been taught to expect, and this was the least they were entitled to in return for the measure of Union forced upon them by England."

Mr. Pitt answered vaguely, as was his custom, when he did not wish to take prompt action, and he made no reference whatever to either Ireland or Catholic emancipation. He intimated, though, that the honest and courageous Mr. Grey was "afflicted with that spirit of Jacobinism which had recently brought such calamity to the Continental countries of Europe."

But Mr. Grey was not going to be so easily put down. He was aware of the existence of documents, which amounted to a promise of emancipation, sent by Lord Cornwallis before the Union, to the Most Rev. Dr. Troy, Catholic Archbishop of Dublin, and Lord Fingal, an ardent champion of that measure. In March, he moved that the House of Commons resolve itself into a committee of the whole, to take into consideration the state of the country, and alluded to the pledges to the Catholics as having been given without sincerity or authority. He denounced the whole proceeding as base and unworthy, compromising to the dignity of the king, whose word had been pledged by proxy, without his consent.   It was a criminal act in ministers of the crown, and called for drastic inquiry.   But nothing ever came of his motion or his speech.

William Pitt and his colleagues, Lord Grenville, Secretary Dundas, Lord Cornwallis, and Lord Castlereagh, having resigned their respective offices, within six weeks after the passage of the Act of Union, were succeeded by Speaker Addington, who took the position of Premier; and by others not so well known, who formed a new ministry, of which Pitt was shrewdly suspected of being the real head and director.   The new ministers were of his own party, and nothing could have been more polite and complaisant than their bearing toward each other.   Lord Hardwicke was appointed to fill the place of Lord Cornwallis as viceroy of Ireland.

As the Habeas Corpus Act—which meant the suspension of that privilege in Ireland—was to expire on March 25, the ministry brought in a bill for its renewal, and it passed without serious opposition—as many similar bills have since passed.   It was needful, above all things, to keep the bulk of the Irish people down, to browbeat and disarm them. A secret committee of the House of Commons made a sensational report of "dangerous conspiracies" in many parts of the "United Kingdom," but more particularly in Ireland. Such turbulence as existed in "well-disposed" England and Scotland was attributed to the bad example set by Ireland, in the recent rebellion, and more nonsense of a similar pattern.   But the secret committee did not suggest the suspension of the Habeas Corpus in "that portion of the United Kingdom called Great Britain."

Following the Habeas Corpus Act, came sundry Irish "Insurrection Acts," "Crime and Outrage Acts," "Arms [disarming] Acts," and other penal measures which have been visited on Ireland, almost without intermission, in one form or another, from 1801 to the days we live in. Ireland is, to-day, the most thoroughly undrilled and disarmed country in the world. She has neither cannon, nor rifles, nor magazines, nor munitions of any kind—all these are in the hands of England, who holds all her strong places, and whose men-of-war jealously keep guard upon her harbors. No wonder, then, that Ireland must agitate instead of revolt.

But, if Dr. Troy was disappointed about emancipation, as, indeed, he richly deserved to be, for his bargaining with Cornwallis and Castlereagh to enslave his country for a sectarian benefit, Lord Clare, the virtual head of the Protestant ascendency and Unionist party in Ireland, was not less so in his expectations of "Imperial honors." For Pitt had used him, and was done with him. He counseled Minister Addington to give Clare "the cold shoulder" when he sought a higher post in London, and Addington did as he was told. He was snubbed by the Duke of Bedford and other English noblemen openly in the House of Lords, and was told by the former "to his beard" that "the Union had not transferred his dictatorial powers to the Imperial Parliament." Repulsed on all sides, he, at last, perceived the abyss into which he had hurled his unfortunate country and himself. This great, bad Irishman was proud to intensity. The slights offered him in England, which he had so faithfully, if unnaturally, served against his native land, cut him to the core of his cruel and remorseless heart. He pined and died of chagrin, in January, 1802—a year and a day after the passage of the Union Act, which he had done so much to accomplish, went into effect. At his burial, in St. Peter's Church, Dublin, there were strong manifestations of popular hatred. "It is singular," remarks Mitchel, "that the only two eminent men who were within the nineteenth century borne to their graves amid the hootings of the people were the Earl of Clare and the Marquis of Londonderry [Castlereagh], the two able tools of British policy in ruining the independence of their country."

When it became apparent to the dullest that both the English and French governments desired a rest from warfare, for a time at least, Lord Cornwallis was appointed plenipotentiary to arrange peace terms by England and Joseph Bonaparte by France. The preliminaries were signed in London, October 1, 1801; but the peace itself was signed at the city of Amiens, in France, March 27, 1802, the signatories being France, then ruled by General Napoleon Bonaparte as First Consul; Great Britain, Spain, and the Batavian Republic (Holland). The main terms of the treaty were that England was to retain the islands of Ceylon and Trinidad. France was to be given back all her colonies. Malta was to be restored to the Order of the Knights of Malta, Spain and the Batavian Republic were to have back all their colonies, except the islands reserved by England, and the French armies were to evacuate Rome, Naples, and the island of Elba. Nobody of political intelligence believed, however, that this delusive peace would last long. England was too dominant on sea and France on land to permit of it. And Mr. Pitt, directing Addington, his puppet, could easily see the storm gathering in the distance and began taking stupendous measures, in secret, to meet it when it should burst. Lord Whitworth was sent as Minister to France. Soon there were rumors of French naval preparations at Brest, which pointed, it was thought, to a new attempt on

Ireland. England occupied herself in raising regiments of volunteers to aid in her internal defence, and the Orange Yeomanry were augmented in Ireland. England had no notion of surrendering Malta, in spite of the treaty, and Napoleon was not the man to stand any sharp practice where the honor and interests of France were concerned. He had several conferences with Lord Whitworth—ever on the subject of Malta. He would rather, he said, on one occasion, have England in possession of the Faubourg Saint Antoine (in Paris) than of that island. The English government ordered Whitworth to explain to Bonaparte that, since the conclusion of the treaty, circumstances had arisen that rendered the stipulations in regard to Malta incapable of being carried into effect. The final breach occurred at a levee in the Tuileries, on the 11th of March, when Napoleon, before the assembled ambassadors of the nations, reproached Whitworth with England's bad faith, and concluded by saying: "The King of England has promised by treaty to evacuate Malta, and who was to violate the faith of treaties?" The declaration of renewed hostilities between France and England was made public on May 18, 1803. Pitt, who was alleged to have been ill in the interval, resumed the duties of Prime Minister a year later, and bent all his gigantic energies to form that military and political coalition of Europe against Napoleon which began, fatally for Pitt, with Ulm and Austerlitz, and terminated, fatally for Napoleon, at Leipsic and Waterloo.

BOOK XI

TREATING OF PERIOD BETWEEN THE BEGINNING OF ROB-
ERT EMMET'S CONNECTION WITH IRISH REVOLUTIONARY
AFFAIRS TO THE RISE OF DANIEL O'CONNELL, 1802–1810

CHAPTER I

Irish Prosperity Declines—Robert Emmet's Early Career—Cruel Execution of Colonel Despard

THE prosperity of Ireland began to decline immediately following the Union act; manufactures decreased; many people took to agriculture for a living, and "absenteeism," on the part of the "nobility and gentry" who had hitherto made Dublin their fashionable resort, began to be noticeable. They began then, and have continued ever since, to spend the wealth wrung from the Irish toiling masses in London, Paris, or some other foreign capital or social resort. Orange riots broke out in the Irish capital—capital now no longer—in July, 1802, and many people were injured during the disturbances. The English government took advantage of the disorders to make its coercion acts all the more stringent. It believed, or pretended to believe, that the Irish masses were more "disloyally disposed" than ever, and, no doubt, they were, as, indeed, they had every reason to be, seeing that they no longer had a national Legislature—even in name.

The Act of Union, while it destroyed the Irish Parliament, left the viceroyalty intact. There was not a total suppression of distinctiveness, as in the case of Scotland. There were natural obstacles. Pitt and Castlereagh had succeeded in making "a parchment Union"—as O'Connell termed the alleged "Treaty" of that name; but not all England could bridge over the Irish sea. Consequently, the semi-separateness of Ireland had to be acknowledged, even in semi-independence, and she is the only one of the Three Kingdoms, now called the "United" Kingdom, that has a separate designation, retaining, as she does, her ancient name.

Many old members of the United Irish Society who remained in the country continued to hope for French invasion and intervention. At every peasant hearth throughout the island the name of "Young Bony" (Bonaparte) was breathed with veneration. He was known to be England's foe, and that was enough for those simple people. Visions of great fleets sailing into Bantry Bay, and of French cohorts landing, in all the pomp and circumstance of war, to free Ireland, flashed before their ardent minds. And, indeed, it would seem that, about this period, Napoleon actually meditated playing again the role Duke William played in 1066—forming a powerful army on the French coast and crossing it by means of a huge flotilla to English soil. There was, to be sure, the potent English fleet to be considered, but that might, by some means, be eluded or circumvented. Rumors there were, also, of another patriotic conspiracy, which was to embrace the four Irish provinces. The disasters of 1798 had disciplined, not cowed, the people of the counties in which the "rebellion" had raged most fiercely. They had learned that a showy uniform does not always cover an invincible warrior, and that the Irish insurgent, at close quarters, was more than a match for his well-drilled opponent. But the failure of the insurrection had impressed upon the popular mind the folly of partial uprisings, no matter how heroically conducted. They only gave the enemy a good chance to suppress the "rebels" in detail, and at his leisure.

Many of the Irish political prisoners who had been liberated from Fort George, at the Peace, were now in France;

among them Thomas Addis Emmet, who was attended by his ardent and devoted younger brother, Robert, of sadly destined memory; Dr. William James MacNevin, Hugh Wilson, Thomas Russell, and Thomas Corbett. Among these —"the faithful and the few"—the moving spirit was young Robert Emmet. He was the youngest son of Dr. Robert Emmet, and was born in Molesworth Street, Dublin, March 4, 1778. He learned the rudiments of knowledge at Oswald's School, became further advanced at White's Academy, in Grafton Street, and, at the age of fifteen, entered Trinity College, where he soon displayed remarkable ability in the direction of exact science and oratory—rather antithetical habits of thought, because most orators are indifferent scientists. In the Historical and Debating Societies of Trinity College, the youth stood almost without a peer, and among his closest friends was Ireland's celebrated national poet, Thomas Moore, who has left testimony that, even at that early period of his life, Emmet's eloquence was of a most striking and convincing order. He was only twenty years old when the troubles of 1798 began, and there is some degree of doubt as to whether he was affiliated with the United Irishmen, but there is none whatever regarding his adoption of their principles. In the college debates, he always stood for Ireland, and scathed her oppressors in language not diplomatic, but decidedly electrical. He was popular beyond rivalship among his fellows—even those who were opposed to his views. In appearance, he was medium-sized and possessed regularity of features— the cast of his countenance being rather similar to that of Napoleon when First Consul. His eyes were superb, and their fitful flashings revealed the noble thoughts that swelled within his soul. His sentiments, together with those of

other university students, attracted the hostile attention of
the chancellor, Lord Clare, who instituted an inquisition
which sought to make the students State informers against
their college mates, who might be members of the United
Irish Society. Dr. R. R. Madden, in his "Life of Robert
Emmet," says that the latter, on being summoned, wrote a
letter to the board of inquisitors, appointed by the chancellor, denouncing their action and desiring to have his name
taken off the books of the college. This letter he showed
to his worthy father, who entirely approved of it. "The
name of Robert Emmet," remarks Dr. Madden, "without
any reference to this proceeding, appeared in the list of ex-
pelled students." After this event, Robert would seem to have
been taken entirely into the confidence of the older patriots,
and was employed by them in several confidential missions,
having reference to renewed attempts to promote the independence of Ireland. He visited the Continent in this interest, as early as 1800, having first had a long interview
with his brother, Thomas Addis, at Fort George. According to Madden, he visited many places in Switzerland,
France, and Holland, and accompanied John Allen, who had
been tried with Arthur O'Connor and Father Coigley at
Maidstone, but was acquitted, to Spain, stopping, among
other places, at Cadiz. While Thomas A. Emmet was stay-
ing at Brussels, in 1802, Robert arrived at Amsterdam and
met his brother, who came to see him, in that city. Later in
the year, the young man proceeded to Paris, where he spent
several months, was in communication with Talleyrand,
and sought an interview with the First Consul. Madden
tries to make out that the latter's government was willing
to hand over the fugitive United Irishmen in exchange for
the Vendéan conspirators, who threatened Bonaparte's life,

but the idea is far-fetched, and is not to be taken seriously. Whatever his political faults, Napoleon was incapable of such baseness, as his noble defence of Napper Tandy, when the English sought to take him from the Dutch authorities, in order that they might hang him, sufficiently proved. The First Consul threatened immediate reprisals, of a capital character, and Tandy was left to die in peace. It is believed that the elder Emmet and his immediate friends were entirely cognizant of Robert's plans and purposes.

In the autumn of 1802 there were rumors of a conspiracy, hatched in France, it was alleged, to assassinate George III and "overturn the Constitution." The head and front of this so-called plot in England was said to be Edward Marcus Despard, a retired Colonel of the British army, who had served with distinction in various wars, and whose sympathy with the cause of the over-taxed masses was proverbial. By his intimates he was regarded as an eccentric person, honest in his sentiments, but indiscreet in the expression of them. He was a native of Ireland, but had lived in England, or far abroad, during most of his life. Arrested in November, this unfortunate gentleman, and several alleged accomplices, were brought to trial at the Surrey Assizes in February, 1803, on charges of high treason, felonious conspiracy, and other high crimes and misdemeanors, including an intent to murder King George. The celebrated English jurist, Lord Ellenborough, presided at the trial, and refused the chief prisoner permission to make an explanation to the jury at the outset of the trial. The witnesses for the crown were not of a class whose oaths would have been accepted without question on ordinary occasions, but the government needed a victim, and Despard was doomed from the first. In vain did the famous Lord Nelson, fresh from the glories of his great naval victories, testify in the fated colonel's behalf; and his testimony was supported by several other English gentlemen of distinction. When asked to supplement the statements of his counsel by one from himself, Colonel Despard politely, but firmly, declined; he knew it would be of no avail. Lord Ellenborough threw the responsibility of the verdict on the jury in his charge, and the jury, after an absence of half an hour, brought in a verdict of guilty, with a strong recommendation to mercy, because of the prisoner's previous high character. Despard heard his doom pronounced with the firmness of a soldier, who had faced death unflinchingly on many fields; and when asked if he had anything to say against sentence of death being pronounced, remarked: "I have nothing to say now but what I said when first brought to the bar, that I am not guilty." He also denied that he had anything to do with "seducing from their allegiance" six of his alleged associates, condemned by the same court to suffer death with him.

All seven victims were taken from the jail to the place of execution early in the morning of February 20, 1803. They were hanged side by side on a long scaffold specially erected for their immolation. Despard made a brief speech before the drop fell, in which he again denied any knowledge of an attempt to assassinate the king. "But," said he, "although his Majesty's ministers know as well as I do that I am not guilty, yet they avail themselves of a legal pretext to destroy a man, because he had been a friend to truth, liberty, and justice, because he had been a friend to the poor and oppressed."

The populace, assembled around the scaffold, cheered, and the colonel concluded by hoping that "the principles of

freedom, of humanity, and of justice would finally triumph
over falsehood, tyranny, and delusion, and every principle
hostile to the interests of the human race."

After execution, the bodies were taken down, beheaded
and quartered — a most hideous practice. Colonel Despard's beautiful young wife remained with him to the last.
His legal murder left her penniless, but she found a friend
in the noble House of Cloncurry, which, in that and two
succeeding generations, was worthy the historic name of
Lawless. Colonel Despard was sixty years old at the time
of his tragical death. It is supposed that the unhappy man
was enticed into the revolutionary association, called "The
Secret Committee of England," which had branches in
Scotland and Ireland also, and had existed since 1795. It
was from this society Father Coigley carried papers of importance to the French government in 1796. Despard was
feared by the government, because of his love of liberty
and great popularity, and, once they had knowledge of his
connection with a secret political society, having for its
object the overthrow of existing conditions, his fate was
sealed. Adepts as they were in the profession of ruthless
spydom, there was nothing easier than to weave a web of
circumstantial evidence around the object of their hatred,
from which he could no more escape than a hampered fly
from the toils of a strong and cunning spider. They were
shocking times, those of 1797-1803, in Ireland, and, in
truth, wherever the power of George III's government extended. Even long residence in England, and gallant services performed for the crown, as in the case of Colonel
Despard, were insufficient protection against the machinations of unscrupulous politicians. Dr. Madden, differing
from Arthur O'Connor, is of opinion that Despard's plot

was well known to the United Irishmen, and that a simultaneous "rising" in the three kingdoms was contemplated, and would have given the revolutionary party in each a much better chance to divide, distract, and finally overcome the royal forces in the field.

CHAPTER II

Daring Conspiracy of Robert Emmet—His Plans Upset by an Accident—A Prey to Spies and Traitors—Failure of his Attempt at Insurrection—Murder of Lord Kilwarden

EMMET loved Ireland, not as a man loves a country, but as a lover loves a mistress. His country seemed the embodiment of a fair woman, persecuted and reviled, whom he, as a true knight, was bound to rescue from the toils of her oppressors. And when he came to love a fair woman, she seemed to him to be the very genius of Erin, so often, and so fondly, apostrophized by the native poets. Ireland and his Sarah, Sarah and his Ireland, made the sum of his worldly devotion and happiness during the few sad and exciting months that preceded his catastrophe. Sarah Curran was the lovely daughter of a gifted but uncomely sire, John Philpot Curran, whose forensic eloquence was the pride and glory of the Irish bar at that period. How they came to meet, how they came to love, we know not, but Emmet's devoted friend, Thomas Moore, probably fathomed the circumstances and revealed them, in that sad but exquisite lyric, in which he sang—

"—Our hope was born of fears
And nursed 'mid vain regrets;
Like winter suns it rose in tears,
Like them in tears it sets,
Dear Love!
Like them in tears it sets."

But we are anticipating the tragedy. The tears that fell finally were tears of blood.

During the early spring of 1803, the French preparations for the invasion of England had become "open and notorious." Robert Emmet, before setting out for Ireland, by way of Holland, in October, 1802, had had his long-desired interview with Bonaparte, and came to the conclusion that the Peace of Amiens would not be of great duration. Madden says that the impression left on Emmet's mind, by his conversations with Talleyrand and Napoleon, was that neither was very ardent in the cause, but that Talleyrand rather desired the establishment of an Irish republic, whereas Bonaparte's only object was "to aggrandize France and damage England." But he considered that Napoleon, seeing that war with Great Britain was inevitable, was sincere in the purpose he expressed of "making a descent on England at the earliest possible moment, after war had been declared, and that event, he was led to believe, would take place within eight or nine months." This would make the chosen time about the middle of August, 1803; he had been informed by Mr. Dowdall, connected with the Secret Committee of England, of a popular movement being determined on by that body to overthrow the crown and government, and, according to Dr. Madden, he had "assurances of support and pecuniary assistance from very influential persons in Ireland, and, lastly, he depended on the concurrence of several of the most devoted of the Irish leaders in Paris." Emmet was of a sanguine disposition, and spoke freely to those whom he thought he could trust of his intentions. On one of those occasions, according to his able biographer, "he spoke of his plans with great enthusiasm; his features glowed with excitement, and the perspiration burst from his pores and ran down his forehead." Some of his hearers approved of his plans, and some did not; but he resolved to proceed with the task he had started to accomplish without regard to concurrence or opposition. Meanwhile, his brother, Thomas Addis, kept in constant communication with Bonaparte and Talleyrand, both of whom gave him encouraging assurances. An Irish Legion, composed of the exiled United Irishmen, had already been formed for the French service. It was commanded by General Mac-Sheehy, wore a distinctive Irish uniform, and carried a French eagle—the only one ever intrusted to foreign troops—and Franco-Irish flags, having green in the centre, a tri-colored circle, with the letters R. I., standing for "Republique Irlandaise," and the legend "Independence of Ireland—Freedom of Conscience" inscribed on the scroll.

The terms on which the two Emmets sought French aid, and to which Napoleon assented, came out at a later date, in a reply made by the First Consul to a memorial addressed to him by the elder brother. In this document, General Bonaparte said, through his secretary: "He [the First Consul] wishes that the United Irishmen should be fully convinced that it is his intention to ensure the independence of Ireland, and to give full and effective protection to all of them that will take part in the expedition, or that will unite with the French forces.

"The French government can issue no proclamation until a landing shall have been made on the Irish territory. But the general who is to command the expedition will be furnished with sealed letters by which the First Consul will declare that he will make no peace with England without stipulating for the independence of Ireland, upon condition, however, that the army shall have been joined by a considerable body of United Irishmen.

"Ireland shall be treated in everything just as America was treated in the late [Revolutionary] war.

"Every person who will embark with the French army destined for the expedition will be commissioned as a Frenchman, and if he be arrested and not treated as a prisoner of war reprisals will be made on the English prisoners.

"Every corps formed in the name of the United Irishmen shall be considered as forming a part of the French army. In fine, should the expedition be unsuccessful, and the Irish be obliged to return to France, France will maintain a certain number of Irish brigades, and will grant a pension to every person who shall have formed one of the government or authority of the country."

There were other provisions of a less important character, but the impression left on the minds of the United Irish leaders in France, at least, was that, by the strong arm of Napoleon, Ireland was, at length, to retake her lost place among the nations.

After Emmet's failure in Ireland, the French assurances became so strong that the usually conservative patriot, Dr. William James MacNevin, prepared a proclamation to the people of Ireland, calling upon them to prepare to receive the rescuing French. Thomas Addis Emmet, however, was not so sanguine. He saw that France would only act according to her own opportunity, and, some months after his brother's execution, left Paris in despair, and proceeded to Bordeaux, whence he sailed for the United States, September 27, 1804. New York, excepting a few pro-English bigots, like Rufus King, honored him greatly, and he soon rose to a high position in his chosen profession of the law.

He gained much renown at the bar, where his logical eloquence made him potent, and finally won, against all kinds
of mean opposition from inferior minds, the distinguished
office of Attorney-General of the Empire State. He died,
after a brief illness, in 1827. His faithful friend and co-
worker, Dr. W. J. MacNevin, came to America about the
same time as Addis Emmet, distinguished himself in the
practice of medicine, and survived until 1841. Monuments
to the two illustrious patriots were erected by their admirers, and still stand in the graveyard of Trinity Church,
Broadway, New York, and between them is the tomb of the
brave Major-General Richard Montgomery, also an Irishman by birth, killed in the gallant but unsuccessful American
assault on Quebec, December 31, 1775.

From the time of his return to Ireland, October, 1802,
Robert Emmet never ceased to labor for the end he had in
view. It would seem that the two friends on whom he most
relied for financial aid in his enterprise were Messrs. P. V.
Fitzgerald and Philip Long, both of Dublin. Mr. Long advanced altogether to Mr. Emmet £1,400 ($7,000), and the
first payment was made in May, 1803. In addition, the
young revolutionist contributed about the same amount from
his private fortune, which was small, and, with these very
insufficient means, laid his plans for the destruction of the
British government in Ireland! He established a depot in
Patrick Street, Dublin, for the manufacture of military material, and conducted his preparations with such ability that
he had soon a comparatively formidable armament prepared
for the projected insurrection. He would seem to have
ardently believed that the French invasion of England would
occur in August, and he tried to time his operations so as to
take full advantage of the hoped-for event. By the middle

of July, he had got together in his depot the following stores, implements, and weapons of war: "Eleven boxes of fine gunpowder; forty-five pounds of cannon powder; one hundred bottles filled with powder and enveloped by musket balls—a species of shrapnel—covered with canvas; two hundred and forty-six hand grenades, formed of ink-bottles, filled with powder and encircled with buckshot; 62,000 rounds of musket ball-cartridge; three bushels of musket balls; a quantity of tow, mixed with tar and gunpowder, another combustible matter, for throwing against woodwork, which, when ignited, would cause an instantaneous conflagration; skyrockets"—he virtually invented the Congreve rocket—"false beams filled with combustibles, and some ten thousand pikes—mostly 'jointed,' so that they could be carried under the coats of the insurgents without observation until the hour for action came." He also devised small spikes, and spiked planks, to place in the streets along which cavalry were likely to advance—thus displaying a military foresight and capacity which, under more favorable conditions, might have rendered him one of the great commanders of the age. His main idea was to catch the government unprepared, seize on Dublin Castle and several of the barracks, make prisoners of the Lord Lieutenant, the Privy Council, and other chief officers of state, and, having paralyzed British authority at the vital centre, then to rely on a popular rising of the provinces to finish the work of revolution. Madden believes, and with good reason, that this daring plan was modeled after that of the successful Portuguese uprising against the usurping Spanish government, at Lisbon, in 1640, where only "about forty individuals conspired to free their country from the yoke of Spain, and these forty men, strange to say, carried on their secret conferences for several months without an act of perfidy on the part of any of them. Their plans were already in the course of accomplishment, the conspirators were already in possession of the palace, public offices and residences of the ministers, when they were joined by the populace. They had already seized on the vice-queen and Spanish authorities, and put to death the only individual of the ruling powers whose life was sacrificed in the revolution—a degenerate Portuguese, Miguel Vasconcellos, who had been the chief agent of the despotism of their foreign taskmasters. But that revolution was effected by a band of men who acted as if there was but one common mind in all, one common cause, and one hand alone which could crown their efforts with success. The night before the revolution the conspirators assembled—where? In taverns, in public houses, or in each other's houses to revel and carouse? No; they met in the churches of their several localities, which, by orders of the Archbishop of Lisbon, were left open for them [duly attended by approved clergymen] without being lighted up on this occasion. They met, not to conspire, but to pray to God for assistance, and each man of them that night received the Sacrament."

The year afterward (1641), the reader may remember, Roger O'More and Lord McGuire attempted a similar "coup" in Dublin, but were frustrated by the treason of Owen O'Connolly. Emmet may have had this last precedent in his mind also.

Everything in regard to the preparations for revolt proceeded quietly, and, apparently, without observation, until an explosion occurred in the Patrick Street depot on July 16. Major Sirr, who visited the premises, discovered fragments of implements, but did not happen to find the main stores. One of the store attendants had been wounded and was taken to hospital, where, of course, he was subjected to examination by the government authorities. It is believed that no information tending to alarm the Castle was obtained from this individual. However, that there was treachery somewhere after events proved sufficiently. Emmet's original intention was not to strike until August, but the accident of the depot precipitated the event. After that mishap, he supervised matters from a depot in Marshalsea Lane, created to supplement the other, and there, says his biographer, "he lay at night, on a mattress, surrounded by all the implements of death, devising plans, turning over in his mind all the fearful chances of the intended struggle, well knowing that his life was at the mercy of upward of forty individuals, who had been, or still were, employed in the depots; yet, confident of success, exaggerating its prospects, extenuating the difficulties which beset him, judging of others by himself, thinking associates honest who but seemed so, confiding in their promises, and animated or, rather, inflamed by a burning sense of the wrongs of his country, and an enthusiasm in his devotion to what he believed its rightful cause; that had taken possession of all his faculties, and made what was desirable to them seem not only possible, but plausible and feasible."

July 23—always that fatal 23d—was set for "the rising," because Emmet deemed further delay dangerous. On the morning of that day, he held a conference with some of his most trusted officers, and discovered that they were divided in their opinions as to immediate action. Dr. Madden, commenting on this eventful meeting, says: "There was division in their councils, confusion in the depots, consternation among the citizens, who were cognizant of what was going on, and treachery tracking Robert Emmet's foot-steps, dogging him from place to place unseen, unsuspected, but perfidy nevertheless embodied in the form of patriotism, basely employed in deluding its victims, and counting already on the ultimate reward of its infamy. Portion after portion of this plan of Robert Emmet's was defeated, as he imagined by accident, or ignorance, or neglect on the part of his agents; but it never occurred to him that he was betrayed, that every design of his was frustrated, every project neutralized as effectually as if a traitor had stolen into the camp of an enemy, seduced the sentinels, corrupted the guards, discovered the plans, disconcerted the projects, and then left the adversary to be forced into the field and there discomfited."

Matters had arrived at such a pass that one of two alternatives had to be adopted—an immediate rising or the total abandonment of the project. The latter, under the circumstances, would have been the rational mode of action, but Emmet and his closest friends felt they were committed to insurrection, no matter what the consequences. Yet, had he but paused to consider the situation, he must have seen that the measure he contemplated was doomed to failure, almost from the beginning. War is, in many respects, an exact science, and can not depend successfully on mere possibilities. The combinations that bring victory must be in full view of the commanding general. What ought to happen, in the way of fortune, is most frequently that which does not happen in revolution, or warfare of any kind, as patriots and warriors have discovered, mostly to their cost, since first human conflicts disturbed this fair planet. To illustrate: Emmet placed great reliance on armed assistance from Michael Dwyer, the fearless Wicklow insurgent, who still held out against the government, in his native fastnesses, and with whom the leader was in communication. The coward, or fool, who was to have borne him the order to move on Dublin, never delivered it, but stopped at Rathfarnham until after the failure. When the Kildare men, true to their promise, came into the city, they were met by a traitor who told them the rising was postponed, and they returned to their homes at five o'clock that same afternoon. Two or three hundred of the Wexford veterans of '98 also came to the capital, and remained there during most of that fatal night, but no orders ever reached them. A strong body of men assembled at the Broadstone in readiness to act when a rocket signal was fired, but no rocket was fired, and they, in consequence, remained inactive. These facts show that Emmet had provided for a sufficient force to carry out his project—at least in its first details—but he was betrayed at every point —either by persons bribed to betray him, or by poltroons terrified at the prospect of a hazardous and sanguinary struggle. Never was insurgent leader placed in so terrible a position as brave, confiding Robert Emmet. The consummation of the catastrophe is best narrated by the biographer already quoted:

"It is evident that Emmet to the last counted on large bodies of men being at his disposal, and that he was deceived. At 8 o'clock in the evening he had eighty men, nominally under his command, collected in the depot at Marshalsea Lane. In the neighborhood, several of the leaders were assembled at Mr. John Heney's house, 41 Thomas Court, and refreshments were not wanting, while messages were passing backward and forward between his house and the depot. At a public house in Thomas Street, kept by John Rourke, there were crowds of country people drinking and smoking, in the highest spirits, cracking jokes and rallying one another, as if the business they were about to enter on was a party of pleasure. Felix Rourke kept constantly passing backward and forward between this house and his brother's, dressed in plain clothes; at no period was he dressed in the 'rebel' uniform, as had been sworn by the approvers on his trial. About 9 o'clock, when Robert Emmet began to reflect on the failure of all his preparations, the holding back of the people on whom he mainly reckoned, Michael Quigley rushed into the depot and gave an alarm which proved to be a false one. He said: 'We are all lost, the army is coming on us!' Then it was that Robert Emmet determined to meet death in the street, rather than wait to be cooped up with his followers in his den, and massacred there, or captured and reserved for the scaffold. He put on his uniform, gave his orders to distribute the arms, and, after sending up a single rocket, sallied into Thomas Street, with about eighty men, who were joined there by, perhaps, as many more before they were abreast of Vickar Street. The design of Emmet was to attack the Castle. The greater part of the gentlemen-leaders were not with Robert Emmet; several remained at Heney's, others were at the house of John Palmer, and elsewhere in the immediate vicinity of the scene of action, waiting, I presume, to see if there was any prospect of success, or any occasion for their services, that was likely to make the sacrifice of their lives of any advantage to their cause.

"The motley assembly of armed men, a great number of whom were, if not intoxicated, under the evident excitement of drink, marched along Thomas Street without discipline, with their ill-fated leader at their head, who was endeavoring to maintain order, with the assistance of Stafford, a man who appears to have remained close to him throughout this scene, and faithful to him to the last. Between the front ranks and the rear, there was a considerable distance, and it was in vain that Stafford and others called on them repeatedly, and sometimes with imprecations, to close their ranks, or they would be cut to pieces by the army. They were in this state, about half-past 9 o'clock, when Robert Emmet, with the main body, was close to the old Market House. The stragglers in rear soon began acts of pillage and assassination. Among others they attacked, and desperately wounded, a custom-house officer named Leech, who, however, made his escape and recovered from his wound. Over these drunken wretches—few, but ferocious—Robert Emmet, far in advance, could exercise no sway. Their bad passions were inflamed by drink, and their excesses finally destroyed any faint hope that remained of making the insurrection even decently formidable. The majority of the men who followed Emmet were brave and humane, and disdained to bring discredit on their cause by acting like murderous banditti."

When Emmet was nearing the Castle, where the guards for the first time since 1798 had been doubled that very evening—showing that definite information of Emmet's project must have reached the government in due season—a carriage, containing a lady and two gentlemen, entered Thomas Street and headed toward the Castle. Near Vickar Street, the same rascally squad of stragglers that had made the attack on Leech rushed upon the vehicle, and made the driver come to a standstill. The fellows demanded to know who were the occupants, and the older gentleman replied: "It is I, Kilwarden, Chief Justice of the King's Bench."

This reply, at any other time, would have been sufficient to let the coach pass on, because Lord Kilwarden, who had attempted, as will be remembered, to save Wolfe Tone, was the most popular judge in all Ireland; but a drunken ruffian, named Shannon, who had a fancied grievance against the great jurist, exclaimed: "You are the man I want!" and plunged the blade of his pike into Kilwarden's body. Then the chief justice was dragged from the carriage and received other wounds. His nephew, the Rev. Richard Wolfe, was murdered before his eyes. The Hon. Miss Wolfe, daughter of Lord Kilwarden, remained in the vehicle in a fainting condition, but no violence or insult was offered her by the assassins. Finally, a young gentleman, who seemed to be a leader, said by some actors in the emeute to have been Robert Emmet himself, appeared upon the scene, took the unfortunate young lady from the coach and led her through the mob to a neighboring house. For a brief period she rested there, and then proceeded to the Castle, where, it is said, she conveyed to the authorities the first information of the murders committed in Thomas Street. A patrol proceeded to the spot immediately, and found Lord Kilwarden gasping on the pavement. His nephew, Rev. Mr. Wolfe, was quite dead. Kilwarden was taken to the watch-house on Vickar Street, where he lingered for some time in great agony. Major Swan, who had some prisoners in charge, was determined to make reprisals. "What are you going to do, Swan?" asked the dying judge. "I am going to hang these rebels, my lord," answered the major. Almost with his dying breath, Lord Kilwarden said: "Let no man be put to death but by the laws of his country!" And the prisoners, by these noble words, were saved. James Hope, one of the captured insurgents, has

left a narrative of these happenings, which is quoted by
Dr. Madden. After enumerating many of Kilwarden's
good deeds, Hope says: "Had I been there, I would have
risked my life to save Lord Kilwarden from hurt or harm."
The learned doctor believes that the assassinations in
Thomas Street were not the result of wild impulse, but the
work of "wicked men in the ranks of the insurgents, for the
purpose of defeating and disgracing their proceedings."
We sincerely hope his diagnosis of this most lamentable
case is correct, for we would hate to believe that any man
who drew the sword in the cause of Ireland could be guilty
of so dastardly a crime.

The unhappy Emmet had halted his party at the market-
house and tried to restore order, but "tumult and insubor-
dination prevailed." When he heard of the attack on Lord
Kilwarden, he turned back and did what he could to prevent further outrage. But the spectacle of the assassins'
work broke his spirit and destroyed all hope. When he
returned to the market-house, the city was thoroughly
alarmed, and the soldiers were already marching to clear
the streets. Then his men did what they should have done,
when they found that Emmet's plans had totally miscar-
ried, earlier in the evening—dispersed before the fire of
the military, and fled in all directions. Emmet and a
few other leaders — profoundly grieved and disgusted—
escaped to Wicklow. At the Coombe, one part of the insurgents made a stand; Colonel Brown and two members
of the Liberty Rangers were killed by them; but, in attacking the guard-house, the "rebels" were unsuccessful and
lost several men. It became known before morning that
Lord Kilwarden was en route to the Castle to attend a specially called meeting of the Privy Council, hastily sum-

moned because of startling news of the insurrection, conveyed by express from Kildare, according to Mr. Emmet's own statement, when he met his cruel and unmerited death.

CHAPTER III

What Emmet had Hoped to Accomplish—Disappointed at Every Turn
—His Return to Dublin after Escaping to Wicklow—Heroic
Devotion of his Servant, Anne Devlin

IN justice to the memory of Emmet, we feel impelled to give a summary of his plans, as revealed in a paper left for the information of his brother, and addressed to him, before his execution. The letter was committed to the care of a government official, either Dr. Trevor, who attended the revolutionist while in jail, or Under Secretary Marsden. At all events, it never reached Thomas Addis Emmet, and was rescued from oblivion by the son of John Philpot Curran in the well-known biography of his illustrious father. As the document was acknowledged by competent witnesses to be in the handwriting of Robert Emmet, there can be no doubt of its authenticity. Subjoined is the summary of the "Plan of Insurrection and Cause of its Failure":

It was comprised under three heads—Points of Attack, Points of Check, and Lines of Defence. The points of attack were to have been the Pigeon House Fort, the Castle of Dublin, and the artillery barracks at Island Bridge. The first-named point called for 200 men, armed with blunderbusses and jointed pikes, who were, under some commonplace pretext, to surprise and seize the sentries and open the gates to their associates. The second point—the Castle —called for a like number of men, similarly armed, who were to enter the Castle yard in coaches, or sedan chairs, as

drivers, footmen, passengers, or carriers, surprise the sentinels and seize the gates. The Lord Lieutenant and other
high officers, together with the bulk of the artillery expected
to be captured, were to be sent, under escort, to the commander in Wicklow, in case the insurgents might be finally
forced to retreat. At Island Bridge, the insurgent force
was to have consisted of 400 men, well armed, who were
to surprise the barracks and seize the cannon, caissons, and
other warlike munitions. There were to have been rocket
signals for all these attacks, and the details were narrowly
entered into in Emmet's document.

Points of check were to be established at the old Custom
House, in Parliament Street, Crane Lane, and the streets
opening on Essex Street, and the place of assembly was to
have been at the Coal Quay. Many other important points
were also chosen for this purpose. It is not necessary for
the purpose of this history to say anything about the projected lines of defence. All showed good military judgment, and there is no doubt that Emmet had, throughout,
the skilful advice of Wolfe Tone's stanch friend, Captain
Thomas Russell, who took an active part in the preparations for revolt.

After detailing, with manly simplicity, the many disap-
pointments and vexations he had encountered, he concluded
his communication, with undesigned pathos, thus: "Had I
another week—had I one thousand pounds—had I one thousand men, I would have feared nothing. There was redun-
dancy enough in any one part to have made up, if complete,
for deficiency in the rest; but there was failure in all—
plan, preparation, and men.

"I would have given it [the emeute] the respectability of
an insurrection, but I did not wish uselessly to shed blood.

[Napoleon's very excuse twelve years afterward for not having again fought after the Waterloo disaster.] I gave no signal for the rest [of the men summoned to action] and they all escaped.

"I arrived time enough in the country to prevent that part of it which had already gone out with one of my men to dissuade the neighborhood from proceeding. I found that, by a mistake [?] of the messenger, Wicklow would not rise that night; I sent off to prevent it from doing so the next, as it intended. It offered to rise, even after the defeat, if I wished it; but I refused. Had it risen, Wexford would have done the same. It began to assemble, but its leader kept it back till he knew the fate of Dublin. In the state Kildare was in, it would have done the same. I was repeatedly solicited by some of those who were with me to do so [that is, give the signal for revolt], but I constantly refused. The more remote counties did not rise, for want of money to send them the signal agreed on.

"I know that men without candor will pronounce on this failure without knowing one of the circumstances that occasioned it; they will consider only that they predicted it. Whether its failure was caused by chance, or by any of the grounds on which they made their prediction, they will not care; they will make no distinction between a prediction fulfilled and justified—they will make no compromise of errors—they will not recollect that they predicted, also, that no system could be formed, that no secrecy nor confidence could be restored, that no preparations could be made, that no plan could be arranged, that no day could be fixed without being instantly known at the Castle; that government only waited to let the conspiracy ripen and crush it at their pleasure, and that on these grounds only did they predict its miscarriage. The very same men that after success would have flattered will now calumniate. The very same men who would have made an offering of unlimited sagacity at the shrine of victory will not now be content to take back that portion which belongs of right to themselves, but would violate the sanctuary of misfortune, and strip her of that covering which candor would have left her." This interesting document was signed "R. E."—the initials of the martyr-patriot's honored name.

One of Emmet's most daring associates was John Allen, of Dublin, who escaped to France soon after the fiasco, and entered the service of Napoleon. He participated in the great campaigns of that matchless general against the coalition, and rose to the rank of lieutenant, afterward to that of captain, by sheer merit. In Spain, he led the French stormers up the breach of Rodrigo, and, having gained the summit, although severely wounded, turned around and saluted the supporting army with his sword. This brave action gained him a colonelcy. Soon afterward, he was made prisoner by the Spaniards, and was confined on a rock near Corunna, where he lingered for weary years, but was finally exchanged and returned to France in time to take part in Napoleon's campaign of Germany in 1813, and was present at Leipsic and Hanau. Afterward, he fought at Montmarail and Laon, remaining faithful to Napoleon to the last. When "the last of the Cæsars" returned from Elba, Allen joined him immediately and took part in the fatal campaign of Belgium. At the second Restoration, the English government had the hardihood to demand his surrender, and the base Bourbon government, which did not dare to give him up on French soil, sent him under an escort of gens d'armes toward the Belgian frontier, where the English guard was waiting for him. The gens d'armes were Frenchmen—all old soldiers, who respected the uniform of the prisoner. On the final march, before delivery, they halted for the night at a village and asked permission to sup with Allen. This was cordially granted. Supper ended, they escorted him to his place of close confinement. On reaching there, the sergeant said to him: "Monsieur le Colonel, the room in which you are to be confined is strong, but one of the iron bars of the window is loose; we trust you will not escape!"

Allen did not need a second hint. He had no difficulty in reaching the street, carrying a bundle and his own sword, which the kind-hearted policemen had left in the room. The colonel sought the Army of the Loire, then commanded by Davout, but it was so thinned by the wholesale desertion of Napoleon's veterans, who would not serve the Bourbons, that he found no shelter there. He left France for a period, but Ireland offered him no asylum, as, if recognized there, he would have been hanged for participation in Emmet's revolt. He became a wanderer for some years, but, when the foreign army of occupation withdrew from France, he returned to Paris and demanded his half-pay as a colonel, which was given him. Then he had the daring to visit Ireland—so changed by war and wounds and toil that even his own relations failed to recognize him, especially as he bore an assumed name. He met Major Sirr, the notorious persecutor, face to face on the street, but even that Castle Argus, whose memory was phenomenal, had no suspicion of Allen's identity—most fortunately for the latter. Finally, the colonel induced his two aged sisters—one of them totally blind—to proceed with him to France. All three settled in Normandy, where they lived and died in peace—

their one regret being that their dust could not repose in Irish soil. John Allen was one of the most remarkable—certainly one of the bravest—men of the 1798-1803 epoch, and his name should ever be honored by his countrymen as a synonym of patriotism, devotion, and valor. Other brave men of the period were Henry Howley, who killed Colonel Brown of the Scotch Fusileers, the night of the rising, in fair fight, and Dennis Lambert Redmond, both of whom suffered death at the hands of the common hangman.

Robert Emmet, according to the statement of his loyal housekeeper, Anne Devlin, published in Madden's work, came back to the lodgings he had formerly occupied in Butterfield Lane, accompanied by Nicholas Stafford, Michael Quigley, Thomas Wylde, John Mahon, John Heney, and some others. She observed them coming "just as she was sending off a man on horseback with ammunition in a sack and bottles filled with powder." This was about eleven o'clock on the night of July 23. "Anne called out: 'Who's there?' Robert Emmet answered: 'It's I, Anne.' She said: 'Oh, bad welcome to you; is the world lost by you, you cowards, that you are to lead the people to destruction and then to leave them?' Robert Emmet said: 'Don't blame me —the fault is not mine.' They then came in. Quigley was present, but they did not upbraid him. Emmet and the others told Anne afterward that Quigley was the cause of the failure."

From Butterfield Lane, after resting, the fugitives proceeded toward the Wicklow mountains, where they halted at the house of a Mr. Doyle. Thence they went to the widow Bagnal's, where they awaited the coming of letters from Dublin, which Anne Devlin and a Miss Wylde brought to them in a conveyance. They found Emmet and his associates "sitting on the side of the hill; some of them were in their uniforms, for they had no other clothes."

Robert Emmet, heedless of the danger of his course, insisted on returning toward Dublin with Anne Devlin and her companion. He parted with them in the suburbs, but did not say where he was going to spend the night. A few days afterward, however, he sent for Anne Devlin and requested her to take a letter from him to Miss Sarah Curran, his promised wife. He was then lodging at Harold's Cross, in a house kept by Mrs. Palmer. It was not long before Major Sirr had positive information of Emmet's place of abode, and Madden asserts that the informer was a Wicklow man named Lacey who had been engaged in the '98 rebellion, and was, therefore, trusted by the insurgent chief. Sirr was told to give one rap on the door, when it would be opened, and he would find Robert Emmet in the parlor.

Meanwhile a troop of yeomanry horse, attended by a magistrate, made a descent on the Butterfield Lane house, where they found Anne Devlin, whom they immediately seized upon. Emmet had been going some time under the name of Mr. Ellis, and the informer had advised the magistrate of the fact. The woman was then about twenty-four years old, an intelligent peasant, but entirely unlettered. What followed is best told in the words of Dr. Madden, because the average reader may need authentic evidence to enable him or her to believe that such infamous savagery could have existed in Ireland only a century ago.

"The magistrate," says the Doctor, "pressed Anne to tell the truth; he threatened her with death if she did not tell. She persisted in asserting her total ignorance of 'Mr. Ellis's' acts and movements, and of those of all the other gentlemen. At length the magistrate gave the word to hang her, and she was dragged into the courtyard to be executed. There was a common car there; they tilted up the shafts and fixed a rope from the backband that goes across the shafts, and while these preparations were making for her destruction, the yeomen kept her standing against the wall of the house, prodding her with their bayonets in the arms and shoulders, till she was all covered with blood, and saying to her, at every thrust of the bayonet: 'Will you confess now? Will you tell now where is Mr. Ellis?' Her constant answer was: 'I have nothing to tell; I will tell nothing!'

"The rope was, at length, put about her neck; she was dragged to the place where the car was converted into a gallows; she was placed under it, and the end of the rope was passed over the backband. The question was put to her for the last time: 'Will you confess where Mr. Ellis is?' Her answer was: 'You may murder me, you villains, but not one word about him will you ever get from me!' She had just time to say: 'The Lord Jesus have mercy on my soul!' when a tremendous shout was raised by the yeomen; the rope was pulled by all of them, except those who held down the back part of the car, and, in an instant, she was suspended by the neck. After she had been hanging for two or three minutes, her feet touched the ground, and a savage yell of laughter recalled her to her senses. The rope around her neck was loosened and her life was spared. She was let off with a half-hanging, was then sent to town and brought before Major Sirr.

"No sooner was she brought before him than he, in the most civil and coaxing manner, endeavored to prevail on her to give information respecting Robert Emmet's place of concealment. The question continually put to her was: 'Well, Anne, all we want to know is, where did he go to from Butterfield Lane?' He said he would endeavor to obtain for her the sum—he did not call it a reward—of £500, which, he added, 'was a fine fortune for a young woman,' only to tell against persons who were not her relations; that all the others of them had confessed the truth —which was not true—and that they were sent home liberated—which was also a lie. The author [Dr. Madden] said to her, with becoming gravity, 'you took the money, of course?' The look the woman gave [this was in 1843, when she was old, poor, and broken] was one that would have made an admirable subject for a painter—a regard in which wonder, indignation, and misgiving of the seriousness of the person who addressed her were blended—'Me! take the money—the price of Mr. Robert's blood! No; I spurned the rascal's offer.' "

Major Sirr tried more persuasion, but in vain. He even repeated to her the language she had used to Emmet and party the night they reached Butterfield Lane after the failure, which, Madden thinks, goes to prove that one of the party with the unfortunate leader must have been an informer. Finally she was sent to Kilmainham jail, and was still confined there when Emmet was arrested and brought to the same prison. The prison surgeon, Dr. Trevor, came to her one day and, in a kindly way—for a purpose—said she needed some indulgence and would be allowed to take exercise in the jail yard. This "worthy" had had frequent conversations with her about Emmet, but she pretended never to have known him. The turnkey took her to the yard, and the first person she saw there was Robert Emmet, walking rapidly up and down. Their paths crossed and recrossed several times, and she almost fainted from apprehension, because she felt that the keen eyes of the government agents were upon both of them. When, at last, Emmet looked full in her face, she frowned, as if in anger, and raised a finger warningly, but in such a manner that the gesture seemed involuntary to those who may have observed it. Emmet, with the instinct of genius, understood instantly, but a half smile, like a gleam of sunshine, illumined his expressive countenance for a moment as he passed on without further sign of recognition. And so the trap set for the faith and honor of Anne Devlin by a degraded doctor—a disgrace to his noble profession—failed, and she was relegated to her cold and gloomy cell, from which she did not again emerge until the day following Emmet's cruel execution, when her guards had the brutality to take her through Thomas Street, en route to the Castle, where she was to be re-examined, and halted at the place of skulls on which he died. The rude scaffold remained intact, and Anne Devlin's horrified eyes beheld the coarse planks besprinkled with the blood of the young hero she had served so faithfully. Anne's aged father and mother and a brother and sister were all confined in Kilmainham, "on suspicion," while she was a prisoner, but she alone suffered rigorous treatment, chiefly because of the villanous influence of Dr. Trevor, on whom she never failed to pour out the vials of her wrath when he came near her. "It relieved my mind to tell the wretch what a rascal I thought him," was her explanation to her friends in after days. Her case was finally brought to the attention of the viceroy, who ordered her jailers to show her more courtesy, and the head jailer's wife, although a native of England, did much to ameliorate her condition. Dr. Trevor did all he could to persecute her, and even the members of her family. Her brother died under his treatment, and his misconduct became so notorious, at last, that public opinion, aroused by an address issued by the state prisoners from Kilmainham jail, compelled the authorities to check the petty tyrant, who would seem to have been of the same class of cranky despot as Sir Hudson Lowe, the jailer of Napoleon at St. Helena.   Neither Anne Devlin nor her kindred regained liberty until after the death of Pitt in 1806.   Then Anne was much broken in health and rendered prematurely old by the hardships, indignities, and sorrows she had endured in her country's cause.   Her uncle, Michael Dwyer, called "the Wicklow outlaw" by the foes of Irish liberty, had surrendered, on compromise, to the government in 1803, having held his native hills for five years against all their forces.   His life was spared, but he was transported to Botany Bay penal settlement.   On a false charge, he was transferred for six months to Norfolk Island, and thence to Van Dieman's Land.   This was under the régime of Governor Bligh.   When Bligh died, his successor, Governor McQuarry, permitted Dwyer to return to Sydney and appointed him high constable.   This post he held for eleven years, became prosperous and owned an extensive farm.   Four faithful comrades shared his exile—Hugh Byrne, Martin Burke, Arthur Devlin, and John Mearn.   He died in 1826, and, quite recently, a number of Irish-Australians erected a monument over his grave.   Michael Dwyer was a peasant hero, bold, dashing, and original —"a natural-born" general, and a guerilla chief whose countless exploits belong rather to the region of romance than sober history.   The English soldiery, who fought against him so often, respected his bravery and ability. When he surrendered, Captain Hume promised that he would be allowed to go to America, but the government overruled the soldier's promise, and the gallant outlaw was transported for life instead.

Anne Devlin, "that noble creature," as Dr. Madden truly terms her, survived in penury—more shame for the rich among her countrymen—until 1855, when she finally sank to rest, and was buried by a few thoughtful Dublin men in the cemetery of Glasnevin, near the O'Connell memorial round tower. A few years later, a small monument was placed above her remains. To the last hour of her life, she preserved her feeling of affection for the martyr of 1803, always speaking of him as "Mr. Robert." Anne Devlin, peasant as she was, was nobler of soul than any Irish woman mentioned in history—unless St. Brigid. Moore did not honor her in any of his matchless melodies, as he did Sarah Curran, whom misfortune forced to marry an English officer. Anne Devlin would have died first. She had in her the proud, indomitable spirit of the Spartan mother, and her fearlessness when she believed herself to be in the presence of a cruel and degrading death, in 1803, proved that she could have died as heroically in the cause of liberty and in the midst of flames, as did Joan of Arc in the cathedral square of Rouen.

CHAPTER IV

Arrest of the "Rebel" Chief—His Imprisonment and Trial—His Defiance of Norbury and Barbaric Execution

ROBERT EMMET, betrayed, almost beyond question of doubt, by the man Lacey, already mentioned, was arrested at Mrs. Palmer's house, Harold's Cross, on the evening of August 25, 1803. He attempted resistance, but was knocked down and overpowered by the myrmidons of

Major Sirr, whose part in the arrest of Lord Edward Fitzgerald will be remembered. The prisoner had passed, while at Mrs. Palmer's, under the name of Hewitt, although Sirr says, in his narrative of the arrest, that he gave also the alias of Cunningham. An important paper, which he was preparing to send to the government, fixing the blame for the recent uprising on himself and exonerating his associates, was seized at the lodgings. Sirr pretended that he did not know the person of Emmet, but when the latter was taken for examination to the Castle, he acknowledged who he was. Several other persons, among them one of Emmet's near relatives, St. John Mason, who would seem to have had no part whatever in the revolt, were already in custody, and many more were subsequently arrested. The government, eager "to make an example," did not long delay the trial of the principal offender. Emmet was carried, under guard, from Kilmainham jail to Green Street courthouse, on the morning of September 19, to be "tried" before a special commission of judges, namely Lord Norbury, "the Irish Jeffreys," Mr. Baron George, and Mr. Baron Daly. The charge against the prisoner was high treason, the 25th of Edward III—far enough back, it will be admitted. His counsel were Messrs. Ball, Burrowes, and McNally— Leonard McNally, who is more than suspected of having been a traitor to and informer against his unfortunate and confiding client. The attorney-general, Mr. Standish O'Grady, was, of course, the chief prosecutor, and he was supplemented by the solicitor-general, and no less a personage than Counselor William Conyngham Plunket, who made the famous "father of Hannibal" speech against the Union, in 1800, and who was familiarly known to the Dublin populace as "Hamilcar" Plunket. The usual crop of vile informers—some the paid spies of government and others who informed to save their worthless necks—sprang up on this occasion, as they do on all such occasions, in every land where conspiracy ends in failure. Lord Macaulay, commenting on the Rye House plot in the reign of Charles II, says: "Cowardly traitors [when the plot was discovered] hastened to save themselves by divulging all, and more than all, that had passed in the deliberations of the party." We do not quote this statement of Macaulay for the disparagement of Englishmen, whom the same author has described as "poor conspirators," but simply to show that a very common, and very unjust, British charge against Irishmen, namely that they furnish more traitors to their fellows than people of other races, should not be lightly accepted. It has been too much the habit to charge all the weaknesses and errors of humanity in general to the Irish race alone, simply because it has been, after many heroic struggles, vanquished, and rendered impoverished by the operation of laws intended not to protect but destroy its liberty and prosperity.

The trial of Emmet lasted from early morning until 10 o'clock at night. Then Norbury charged the jury, but not with his usual rancor, although with sufficient force to secure conviction. The verdict of "guilty" was given by the jurors without leaving their box, and then the Court put the usual question to the prisoner as to whether he had anything to say against sentence of death being pronounced upon him. The response was a speech of most thrilling eloquence. It survives only in fragmentary form, and, for the most authentic version, the world is indebted to Dr. Madden. Emmet seemed particularly desirous of denying that he was, in any sense, an emissary of France, and, in our opinion, was a little too severe in describing the political conduct of that noble and progressive country, to which the cause of human liberty, both in the New World and the Old, owes so much. Lord Norbury interrupted the prisoner several times, but only succeeded in kindling into fiercer flame the fire of his forensic genius. Emmet protested against being described as the head and front of the offending, as he was by the ungracious Plunket, a trimmer and backslider. He revealed, in retracting this accusation, that able and leading Irishmen, who had not lived up to the courage of their convictions, were in the conspiracy with him. His memorable words, after one of Norbury's characteristic interruptions, were these: "I have been charged with that importance in the efforts to emancipate my country as to be considered the keystone of the combination of Irishmen, or, as it has been expressed, 'the life and blood of the conspiracy.' You do me honor overmuch. There are men concerned in this conspiracy who are not only superior to me, but even to your own conceptions of yourself, my lord; men before the splendor of whose genius and virtues I should bow with respectful deference, and who would not deign to call you friend—who would not disgrace themselves by shaking your blood-stained hand." (Interruption by the Court.) Emmet again essayed to proceed, but Norbury again broke in, to remark that the prisoner "had the honor of being a gentleman by birth and that his father had filled a respectable situation under the government; that he had had an eldest brother [Temple Emmet] whom death snatched away, and who, when living, was one of the greatest ornaments of the bar"; had he lived, Norbury continued, he would have taught the prisoner "to admire and preserve that constitution [?]

for the destruction of which he had conspired with hostlers, bakers, butchers, and such persons whom he had invited to council when he had created his Provisional government." Emmet's memorable reply and peroration were in the following terms:

"If the spirits of the illustrious dead participate in the concerns of those who were dear to them in this transitory scene, dear shade of my venerated father, look down on your suffering son, and see has he for one moment deviated from those moral and patriotic principles which you so early instilled into his youthful mind, and for which he has now to offer up his life.

"My lord, you are impatient for the sacrifice. The blood which you seek is not congealed by the artificial terrors which surround your victim—it circulates warmly and unruffled through its channels, and in a little time it will cry to heaven—be yet patient! I have but a few words more to say—I am going to my cold and silent grave; my lamp of life is nearly extinguished; I have parted with everything that was dear to me in this life, and for my country's cause, with the idol of my soul, the object of my affections. My race is run—the grave opens to receive me, and I sink into its bosom. I have but one request to ask at my departure from this world—it is the charity of its silence! Let no man write my epitaph; for as no man who knows my motives dare now vindicate them, let not prejudice or ignorance asperse them. Let them rest in obscurity and peace, my memory be left in oblivion, and my tomb remain uninscribed, until other times and other men can do justice to my character. When my country takes her place among the nations of the earth, then, and not till then, let my epitaph be written. I have done."

Lord Norbury, who, strange to say, manifested some emotion, then sentenced Robert Emmet to be hanged next day, Tuesday, September 20, at the hour of noon. The sentence was carried out accordingly, and the place of execution was in Thomas Street, at the end of Bridgefoot Street, and nearly opposite St. Catherine's Church. He was taken from jail to the fatal spot in a close carriage, escorted by horse and foot. It is said that Miss Curran, seated in another close vehicle, waved him an eternal adieu, which he returned, as he passed by on the way to eternity. He was accompanied to the rude scaffold, improvised out of barrels, planks, and beams, by two clergymen of the Episcopal Church. Although his hands were tied, he mounted the steps with alacrity and vigor, and said to the people, in a sonorous voice: "My friends—I die in peace, and with sentiments of universal love and kindness toward all men." "He then," says Madden, "shook hands with some persons on the platform, presented his watch to the executioner, and removed his stock." (We suppose his hands had been temporarily untied for that purpose). "The immediate preparations for execution were then carried into effect, he assisted in adjusting the rope round his neck, and was then placed on the movable plank underneath the cross-beam." The tragedy followed immediately, and, within a few minutes, the brave and noble enthusiast had ceased to live. But English law was not satisfied even then. Scarcely was life extinct when the hangman drew the body back to the scaffold and subjected the corpse to the process of decapitation. The executioner then grasped the severed head by the hair and displayed it to the multitude as that of "a traitor, Robert Emmet." Soon afterward the dogs in Thomas Street were lapping the victim's blood. Some people steeped their handkerchiefs in it, and preserved them as sacred relics. There is a question as to Emmet's place of burial, some asserting that it was in St. Michan's Churchyard, and others in Glasnevin. Moore's beautiful and tender lines embalm the memory of the martyr:

"Oh, breathe not his name, let it rest in the shade,
Where, cold and unhonored, his relics are laid.
Sad, silent, and dark be the tears that we shed
As the night dew that falls on the grass o'er his head.

"But the night dew that falls, tho' in silence it weeps,
Shall brighten with verdure the grave where he sleeps,
And the tear that we shed, tho' in secret it rolls,
Will long keep his memory green in our souls!"

His friend, Thomas Russell, whom he had sent to create a diversion in Ulster, failed in his mission, and was arrested and executed at Downpatrick, dying with the utmost firmness, and glad not to longer survive the associates to whom he had been so faithful. Miles Byrne, whom Emmet had sent to France with a message to his brother, escaped the fate of most of his comrades, and lived to win glory under the eagles of Napoleon. Many others joined him in his honorable exile, and served with credit in the Irish Legion of the First Empire. And so the curtain falls on the catastrophe of 1803.

CHAPTER V

Napoleon Gives Ireland Fresh Hope, but the Disaster to the French
Fleet at Trafalgar Mars his Plans—Irish and Continental
Policy of Charles James Fox

NAPOLEON, no doubt, was sincere enough in his intention of invading England after the breach of the Peace of Amiens if his fleets had served him better. His Irish Legion was much augmented by fugitives from Ireland after Emmet's collapse. General Augereau was appointed to command the expedition intended to operate in Ireland, and General Arthur O'Connor, of '98 fame, was attached to his personal staff. There was much hoping and longing among the Irish military exiles, but month after month rolled by and no forward movement was made from either the great camp at Boulogne, or the smaller one near Morlaix, in Bretagne, where most of the Irish soldiers were assembled. But the military exigencies of France continued to grow, and the Irish Legion was ordered on active service along the Rhine, and afterward in Holland, where it aided in defeating the large English army sent to Walcheren under the command of the Duke of York, whose only claim to lead so large a force was that he happened to be a younger son of George III. Time passed on. The French fleet assembled at Brest, and, although intended for Ireland, was sent to operate elsewhere. Trafalgar was fought, and lost, by France. The English navy again ruled the seas, and the intrigues of Pitt armed Russia and Austria against Napoleon, recently (December 2, 1804) crowned Emperor of the French. What followed belongs to general history. Suffice it to say here that when the Grand Army turned its back on the camp of Boulogne, and marched to the Danube, all hope of French intervention in Ireland was at an end.

The English had it all their own way in the "United" Parliament, as far as Ireland was concerned. Her national debt continued to increase, and her taxation grew in proportion. Presbyterian republicanism in Ulster was placated by an increase of the Regium Donum (royal grant), which gave a comparatively snug living to the previously half-starved ministers of that denomination. The Catholics, or rather their credulous leaders, continued to be deluded by promises, but there was no emancipation. On the contrary, the Pope's praise of Napoleon for having restored the Catholic worship in France was made a pretext for further hounding and abusing them—as if the Irish Catholics, either then or since, had the slightest influence on the political actions of his Holiness. The English made the Pope a bugbear when they wanted an excuse for persecuting the Catholic Irish. They courted his power and "spoke him fair" when they thought they needed the Pontiff to check Irish "disloyalty" to the British system in Ireland. And it took both the Pope and the Irish Catholics a long time to understand this policy, which continues, although with perhaps less effect, to this day. Attempts were made in 1804-5, by Lord Fingal and other liberal Irish gentlemen, both Protestant and Catholic, to have a bill for further "Catholic relief," which meant emancipation, introduced in both the House of Lords and the Commons, and, notwithstanding the best efforts of Fingal, Fitzwilliam, Charles James Fox, and Henry Grattan, who had become a member of the Imperial Parliament, the proposition was badly beaten in each body.   Pitt, now fully restored to power, acted perfidiously, as, indeed, might have been expected from the father of the "Union" measure.

It was the unwholesome era of slavish Catholic petitions to a Parliament that hated and despised the very name of Catholic, and we turn away from it in disgust.   Honest judges were prosecuted and punished in Ireland for seeking to protect unarmed Catholics who were wantonly assailed by armed Orangemen—the successors of the ferocious yeomanry.   For censuring Lord Abercorn—leader of the Orangemen in Ulster—Judge Fox was practically ruined in health and fortune, and Judge Johnson, for the alleged castigation of the "Irish" government in a pamphlet, a la "Junius," was forced to retire on a pension.   Napoleon's successes against England's allies on the Danube and in Moravia caused the prestige of Pitt to visibly decline, and some of his adherents, including Castlereagh, were defeated for Parliament.   His vanity was greatly piqued, and he died of " a broken heart" on January 23, 1806.   In him Great Britain lost one of her greatest ministers, and Ireland the deadliest enemy that had ever held the high office of Prime Minister—excepting, perhaps, Lord John (afterward Earl) Russell of later times.

Then followed the combination known as the Grenville-Fox ministry, Lord Grenville being First Lord of the Treasury and Charles James Fox Secretary of Foreign Affairs. A proposal made by Castlereagh to have national honors paid to Lord Cornwallis, who had died in India, brought out opposition from an Irish member, Mr. O'Hara, who bluntly stated that he could not consistently vote for such honors to the man who had brought about the unfortunate union between Great Britain and Ireland, which he hoped

would, some day, come under the consideration of the
House, and either be entirely rescinded or greatly modified.
In fact, Mr. O'Hara was the first member of the British
Parliament who breathed the sentiment of Repeal of the
Union, which became afterward so formidable. He moved
that a monument to Cornwallis be not concurred in.

Charles James Fox, who supported the motion of Castlereagh, said that "he agreed with Mr. O'Hara in character-
izing the Union as one of the most disgraceful transactions
in which the government of any country had been involved."
On the strength of Fox's words, several Dublin corporations got up petitions for repeal, but when that statesman
was challenged by an English member to explain his attitude a little later, the adroit minister said that "while he
adhered to every syllable he had uttered relative to the
Union, on the Cornwallis motion, and reprobated a thing
done, he said nothing prospectively. However bad the
measure had been, an attempt to repeal it, without the most
urgent solicitation from the parties interested, should not
be made, and, hitherto, none such had come within his
knowledge."

"Even so early," comments John Mitchel, "did it become apparent that neither English Tory nor English Whig
would ever listen to any proposal for the undoing of that
shameful deed. Gradually, as time has worn on, men of
all parties in England have become willing to admit that
the Union was a foul act, foully accomplished, yet no British minister, of any party, would dare, for his head, to pro-
pose that it be undone. It was thus, in 1806, on the accession of Mr. Fox to office, that the first whisper was heard
of that demand." Yes, and just eighty years afterward,
the late Mr. Gladstone brought in his modified Repeal meas-

ure—the Home Rule bill, which was defeated through the defection of Lord Hartington, Joseph Chamberlain, and their associates. It passed, in a modified form, the House of Commons in 1893, and was extinguished in the House of Lords. Whether it will be again revived, is a mystery of the future which can not now be penetrated. Much depends on the union and resolution of the Irish people. Divided and irresolute, they can accomplish nothing.

Lord Hardwicke, one of the very worst viceroys that ever reigned in Ireland, left that country after five years' service. He was so unpopular, that only three expressions of regret at his departure were uttered by the country he had afflicted. "He sailed from the Pigeon House," says a historian, "on the 31st of March, 1806, and many a curse went after him."

The Duke of Bedford succeeded Hardwicke, and from him the Irish, and the Catholics particularly, had "great expectations," which, as usual, were doomed to be disappointed. Mr. Mitchel—not at all wont to praise Englishmen—says Fox had a noble nature, and, had he seen Irish misgovernment with his own eyes, would, undoubtedly, have remedied many of the grosser grievances; but, unfortunately, English interests were paramount in his mind, as was but natural, and his régime did not last long enough to give much chance to effect reforms. England expected him to put an honorable period to the war with France, and this task he set himself to accomplish. Lord Lauderdale carried Fox's proposal to the French government, but failed in his efforts for peace. Mr. Fox's health had been failing for some time—as he had been a dashing gentleman who "burned the candle at both ends," after the manner of the days he lived in—and he died, sincerely lamented by millions in Great Britain and outside of it, on September 13, 1806, and thus, as Mitchel puts it, "relieved the administration of the embarrassment of the presence of one honest man."

CHAPTER VI

Increase of Irish Debt—Administration of the Duke of Bedford—Catholic Petitions—King George's Bigotry—The Duke of Richmond and Orange Ascendency

UNDER the rule of the Duke of Bedford, as of his predecessor, the Irish debt increased right rapidly, so much so as to alarm even the Unionists, but the evil of the Union once accomplished, England felt that she could afford to despise Irish discontent and remonstrance. The Maynooth grant, however, was increased by the British Parliament from £8,000 to £13,000 per annum. It was opposed by the anti-Catholic element, headed by Mr. Percival; but Lord Howick's eloquence convinced the majority of the wisdom of the concession, when he explained that he "supported the measure on the large principle of connecting the Irish Catholic with the State. It was then particularly necessary to promote the domestic education of the Catholic clergy, as an institution of great extent [the Irish College] had been founded in Paris, at the head of which was Dr. Walsh, a person of considerable notoriety, with a view to re-establish the practice of Irish Catholic education at that place, and to make that education the channel of introducing and extending the political influence of the French government in Ireland." This Irish college had the imperial sanction of Napoleon, and hence the alarm in England caused by its foundation. English and Scotch Catholic students were also admitted to its privileges.

Another measure proposed by the politic Lord Howick was the Catholic Officers' bill, which would allow gentlemen of the Catholic faith to purchase and hold commissions in the British army and navy. On this proposition, George III, who was in one of his periodical "tantrums," resolutely "sat down" and even demanded the resignation of the ministry, because they would not pledge themselves "never, under any circumstances, to bring forward any measure whatever respecting Papists." The mad old king was egged on to this precious piece of despotism by his two sons, the Dukes of York and Cumberland, both rabid upholders of the Orange faction in Ireland. The ministry resigned, not, however, without some protest from their supporters; and a new cabinet, anti-Catholic in the extreme, was formed, with Mr. Percival as Chancellor of the Exchequer. Castlereagh became Colonial Secretary and also Secretary of the War Department. Lord Camden was made President of the Privy Council, and George Canning—the only liberally disposed man in the new ministry—Secretary of Foreign Affairs. The recall of the Duke of Bedford from the viceroyalty of Ireland was decided on, as he was considered, on very slender grounds, to be favorable to the Catholic claims. The Duke of Richmond became his successor, and Sir Arthur Wellesley, afterward the renowned Duke of Wellington, who had returned from India with the laurels of Assaye upon his brow, was made Chief Secretary for Ireland. Sir Arthur had few superiors as a general, but, as an Irish patriot, he belonged to the very rearmost rank, then and until the hour of his death. Lord Eldon became Chancellor of England and Lord Manners, formerly Baron Sutton, of Ireland.

The Catholics of Ireland were taken somewhat by surprise, as they had counted on favorable legislation under the former ministry, and had prepared a petition for complete emancipation, which they confided to their ever consistent friend, Henry Grattan. That great man consulted with Richard Brinsley Sheridan and other friends of the Irish Catholics in Parliament, and the consensus of their opinion was that the bill, or petition, had better be withheld until a more favorable condition of affairs justified its presentation. The aged John Keogh presided at a Catholic meeting held in Dublin, and both he and Daniel O'Connell, whose gigantic figure now began to loom gloriously on the horizon of Irish affairs, advocated postponement, in conformity with the advice of Grattan and Sheridan. After some opposition, the postponement was agreed to, and the Catholic committee dissolved. Lord Fingal was deputed to present an address, setting forth the respect in which the Catholics held the viceroy, to the Duke of Bedford; and, when that peer and his duchess left Dublin, the ever "too easily deluded" populace unhitched the horses from the carriage and drew the distinguished pair to the wharf, where they embarked for England.

"The Ascendency" was in its element anew under the Duke of Richmond's administration of Ireland; and the British Parliament occupied itself in passing numerous insurrection, coercion, and disarming acts for the "sister island"—ostensibly to suppress agrarian secret organizations, known, according to locality, as "Threshers," "Shnavests," "Caravats," and "Terry Alts." These organizations were, unfortunately, often guilty of forceful, and even sanguinary, acts, in protecting their fellows from eviction, or searching for arms at the residences of the landlords and their followers, but, in good truth, the blame was far less on their side than on that of the government, whose harsh and absolutely unjust land laws drove them to desperation. The relations between landlord and tenant in Ireland, at that time, and, indeed, for seventy years afterward, and, in some instances, even now, were, and are, conducive to public demoralization. There have been many reforms since 1870, but much evil still exists, and much arduous labor on the part of the Irish leaders and people will be necessary to bring about a condition of affairs favorable to perfect public tranquillity. The latter will never be thoroughly attained until Ireland's legislative independence—the only rational alternative to total separation—is recognized and established. It is our personal opinion, and we think it is shared by a majority of the Irish race, that separation and a republican form of government in Ireland would be best for both nations. It is certain, however, that Ireland, as a great majority, will never be satisfied until, at least, the status the country enjoyed from 1782 to 1801, "with modern improvements," is restored.

The Catholics got up still another petition to Parliament "for the repeal of the remaining penal laws" against them. At the meeting in Dublin, which formulated the petition, an attempt was made to have it postponed, but Daniel O'Connell, impatient of the degrading delay, sprang to his feet, and, in a brief but powerful speech, declared for immediate action. His voice, young as he then was, prevailed, and the petition, on motion of the gallant Count Dalton, was adopted. Lord Fingal took the document to England and had difficulty in finding a member of the House of Lords to present it. When it was finally presented by Lord Grenville, it was unceremoniously laid on the table. Grattan presented it in the Commons, but Percival and Canning

had it thrown out, because of a trifling informality. It is
very pleasant to bear testimony, in this connection, to the
generous conduct of many Irish Protestants, of all classes,
who petitioned the British Parliament to knock the penal
fetters off the limbs of their Catholic fellow-countrymen.
But such noble Protestants were regarded in England—that
is governmental England—with even less favor than the
Irish Catholics themselves, and their petitions followed the
others into the imperial waste-basket. In order, further, to
show its animosity to the Catholics of Ireland, Parliament,
at the suggestion of the ministry, cut down the Maynooth
College grant from £13,000 to £9,250.

Lord Fingal had, at least, the quality of perseverance,
and determined not to give up the Catholic petition. A
new one, properly signed, was sent to him in London, and
there, on the advice of timid friends of the Catholic cause,
he interpellated a clause into the document, which gave the
crown the right of veto in the nomination of the Irish
Catholic prelacy. Dr. Milner, who was then an agent for
the Irish bishops in London, but who had no authority
relative to the veto from them, or from the Irish laity,
united with Lord Fingal in authorizing Messrs. Henry
Grattan and George Ponsonby to present the Catholic petition with the veto amendment. Lord Grenville presented
the petition, also, as amended, in the Lords. In Ireland,
among the Catholics, the proposition raised a perfect cyclone of denunciation, and the agitation was scarcely less
in Great Britain. There were countless speeches delivered,
and pamphlets written, on the subject, in both countries.
The advocates of the veto contended that it would strengthen
"the bonds of union" between the two countries, and would
guarantee the loyalty of the Catholic people to the sov-

ereign. The opponents of the projected measure deprecated
"the introduction of royal and Protestant power, connection and influence into the constitution and perpetuation of
a Catholic hierarchy, to the utter exclusion of which the
Irish Catholics ascribed that almost miraculous preservation" of the said hierarchy. The controversy raged for
many years, and Daniel O'Connell was a steadfast opponent of the veto, from the first moment it came to his
knowledge; and his views were sustained by all that was
bravest and brightest in the Catholic body of Ireland. The
Irish Catholic prelates met in regular national synod in
Dublin, September 14 and 15, 1808, and adopted the following resolutions :

"It is the decided opinion of the Roman Catholic prelates
of Ireland that it is inexpedient to introduce any alteration
in the canonical mode hitherto observed in the nomination
of the Irish Roman Catholic bishops, which mode long
experience has proved to be unexceptionable, wise, and
salutary.

"That the Roman Catholic prelates pledge themselves to
adhere to the rules by which they have been hitherto uni-
formly guided; namely, to recommend to his Holiness only
such persons as are of unimpeachable loyalty and peaceable
conduct."

Well, as may be seen, the bishops, to the number of
twenty-three, were against the veto, and signed the resolutions; but there were three prelates who dissented from the
majority, and refrained from signing. The Irish Catholic
prelates of to-day would never think of holding "unimpeachable loyalty" to such a creature as George III a leading virtue in a candidate for the prelacy. As for peaceful,
or "peaceable conduct," no Irish bishop had violated the

peace, such as it was, since Bishop Heber MacMahon drew the sword for Ireland in the days of Cromwell. Truly, the iron rust of the penal laws had entered deeply into the souls of the Irish Catholic prelates of the first decade of the nineteenth century. However, the Catholic people were grateful for the resolutions they adopted, and, at many public meetings, declared they would rather remain unemancipated than suffer their Church to be enthralled by the English crown. The government abandoned the veto plan for a period, but it came up often afterward during O'Connell's struggle for emancipation, and was repulsed every time it showed itself by the force of Irish public opinion, marshaled solidly by that great leader.

CHAPTER VII

Orange Violence—Formation of a New Catholic Committee—O'Connell Rises Rapidly to Leadership—Agitation to Repeal the Union

THE Duke of Richmond's policy was to protect violent Orangemen in the commission of crime against Catholics, and to punish to the last extremity such of the latter as might be so rash as to retaliate. He was an "Ascendency" viceroy with a vengeance, and frequent horrible murders were committed by the Orange fanatics, none of whom was ever brought to justice. Sir Arthur Wellesley, soon about to take command of the British armies in the Spanish Peninsula, was thoroughly in touch with the viceroy in this indefensible policy.

In the beginning of 1809, a new Catholic committee, to take charge of Catholic interests, was organized in Dublin, but, owing to the Convention Act, passed by Parliament to prevent Irishmen from assembling as delegates of the people, as in 1782-83, great care had to be exercised, in order to protect the personal liberty of the members. O'Connell was the man for the occasion, and he framed an ingenious resolution, disclaiming popular representation, which baffled the drastic designs of the Richmond government.

Lord Fingal again pressed a Catholic petition on Parliament, leaving out the veto feature; but Henry Grattan, strange to relate, favored the veto, because he thought it would bring emancipation speedily, and, in any case, he was always suspicious of French influence over the Pope, and he, unhappily, detested "French principles." This detestation was one of the causes why Ireland lost her independence. Had Grattan been cordially with the United Irishmen, the rebellion of 1798 might have been a successful revolution. Although he presented the petition in the Commons, he did not heartily support it, and, on going into committee, it was refused by a large majority. The same fate befell the document in the House of Lords. This double defeat occurred in 1810, and the younger and more active of the Catholic chiefs saw that to present petitions, without any kind of "force," moral or physical, behind them, was to court insult added to injury. This was Daniel O'Connell's policy, and his rapidly rising star made all others "pale their ineffectual fires." Soon after the rejection, the Catholic committee met again, and thanked the venerable John Keogh for his "long and faithful services to the cause of Catholic emancipation." An address, signed by Daniel O'Connell, as chairman, was issued to all the Irish Catholics, urging upon them "a new and more combined form of political action." "The programme of action presented in this address," observes Mr. Mitchel, "is substantially the same as that which was followed up by O'Connell, under several successive names, throughout all his agitations—local organizations holding frequent meetings and corresponding with a central committee in Dublin. All proceedings were to be peaceful and legal; yet there was the *hint* of a possibility that millions of people, steadily denied their rights, might, in the end, be driven to extort them with the strong hand."

Alderman Hutton, in the Corporation of Dublin, which was then composed exclusively of Protestants, made a forceful speech in which he depicted the hapless condition of Irish business and finances since the passage of the Union Act, and he offered resolutions which declared that the true cure for all the evils complained of would be the immediate repeal of that measure. Although much opposition was made, the resolutions were adopted by a majority of thirty.

On requisition of the Grand Jurors of Dublin, Sir James Reddall, one of the two high sheriffs of the city and county, called a meeting of the freemen and freeholders to "consider the necessity that exists of presenting a petition to his Majesty and the Imperial Parliament for a repeal of the Act of Union." The meeting was held in the Royal Exchange on September 18, 1810, and was made memorable by a speech delivered by O'Connell, which impressed his auditory and the Irish nation more deeply than any that had been delivered since Grattan moved his Declaration of Irish Rights nearly thirty years before. That speech placed the orator undisputedly at the head of the Irish Catholics, and he was equally regarded as the national leader by patriotic Irish Protestants. His speech was printed, and, accompanied by his portrait, was distributed throughout the country, through the agency of the central and local Catholic committees, by the thousand. Its main burden was that the Union Act caused all the misery Ireland was enduring and that public policy, not less than ordinary justice, demanded its repeal. And resolutions to that effect were unanimously adopted. A petition was also prepared for presentation to Parliament. Like all such presentations, nothing came of it, except a debate, which, sufficiently inconsequential in the House of Commons, was made memorable in the House of Lords by the illustrious English poet, Lord Byron, who described the measure brought about by the combined action of Pitt, Cornwallis, Lord Clare, and Castlereagh, as "the union of the shark with its prey."

About this time, George III grew wholly insane, and "George, Prince Regent," again resumed the reins of government; for, in those times, the occupant of the British throne wielded much more influence than at present. The Regent, as was his custom, made frequent pledges of friendship to the Catholic leaders when he was out of power, but now, being in power, he coolly turned his back upon them, and retained Percival and all their other enemies in office. It is broadly asserted that the Regent was influenced in his double-dealing conduct by the Marchioness of Hertford, a bigoted woman, with whom he is alleged to have been on terms of immoral intimacy.

Meanwhile, Sir Arthur Wellesley, on the battlefields of the Peninsula, had risen to the rank of Lord Wellington, and the Secretaryship of Ireland had, in the interim, been held by his relative, Wellesley-Pole, who was an intense enemy of the Catholic committee, who, indeed, quite scandalized his ideas of "loyal propriety." After a vain effort to squelch the said committee, he returned to England and was succeeded in office by one of his own kidney, the famous Sir Robert Peel, who organized the Irish, now the "Royal Irish," Constabulary, and also "reformed" the Dublin metropolitan police, whence the term "Peelers" applied by the Irish people to both forces ever since.

Mr. Spencer Percival, the anti-Catholic premier, was killed by an English maniac in the lobby of the House of Commons in 1812, and was succeeded by Lord Liverpool, with both Canning and Castlereagh in his cabinet. Ireland, under *all* English régimes, continued to decline steadily in material prosperity. In this year, John Philpot Curran, who contested unsuccessfully with General Needham the borough of Newry, said on the hustings, while reproaching the Irish "nobility and gentry," who opposed him bitterly: "By that reciprocal animosity [creed against creed and class against class] Ireland was surrendered; the guilt of the surrender was most atrocious—the consequences of the crime most tremendous and exemplary. We put ourselves into the condition of most unqualified servitude; we sold our country, and we levied upon ourselves the price of the purchase; we gave up the right of disposing of our own property; we yielded to a foreign legislature to decide whether the funds necessary to their projects or their profligacy should be extracted from us or furnished by themselves. The consequence is that our scanty means have been squandered in her internal corruption, as profusely as our best blood has been wasted in the madness of her aggressions, or the feeble folly of her resistance. *Our debt has, accordingly, been increased more than tenfold*—the common comforts of life are vanishing; we are sinking into beggary; our poor people have been worried by cruel and unprincipled prosecutions, and the instruments of our government have been almost simplified into the tax-gatherer and the hangman."

Yet all his melancholy eloquence fell unavailingly on those

who had votes, however it may have moved the disfranchised masses. The Habeas Corpus Act continued to be suspended regularly, or irregularly, as occasion might demand; and the insurrection act, under one name or another, was almost perpetual. Even Henry Grattan, who was a great stickler for "law and order," voted on, at least, one occasion for a coercion bill, because agrarian troubles were rife in the South of Ireland.

BOOK XII

DEALING WITH THE PERIOD FROM THE DOWNFALL OF
THE GREAT NAPOLEON TO THE ACCESSION OF WILLIAM IV

CHAPTER I

Grattan's Last Work for the Catholics—Downfall of the Great Napoleon—O'Connell's Characteristics as an Orator and Statesman —George IV's Irish Visit

THE last great effort of Henry Grattan to emancipate his Catholic fellow-countrymen was made in the first session of the newly elected Imperial Parliament in 1813. His bill omitted the odious veto provision, and provided that Catholics should sit in Parliament and hold office, the Lord Chancellorship of either England or Ireland, and the viceroyalty of the latter being specially excluded. The English Catholics, who have always been, as a body, opposed to Irish independence, aided by Monsignor Quarantotti, a household representative of the Pope, and very much under British Catholic influence, sought to have the veto clause again inserted in the bill. The Irish priests and people resisted fiercely. O'Connell mercilessly scored Monsignor Quarantotti, and, in one of his matchless popular addresses, exclaimed: "I am a Roman Catholic, but not a political slave of the Papacy. We, Irish Catholics, take our religion from Rome, but not our politics!" In these fierce controversies, O'Connell was reluctantly compelled to differ from Henry Grattan, whom, however, he treated with great courtesy. But the quarrel over the veto had the effect of disgusting the sensitive leader of 1782, and the brilliant orator of that radiant era was now an old and greatly broken man. Ireland needed a younger and more vigorous leader, and she felt she had found him in the then dashing and daring Daniel O'Connell.   The bill was finally with-drawn, and, thereafter, Grattan left Catholic interests in other hands.

Events hastened on with magical speed. Napoleon, after dazzling mankind, both as a soldier and ruler, committed the monumental folly of going to war with Russia, merely on a point of vanity, certainly not one of necessity.   His huge army, having a contingent from nearly all the West-ern nations of Europe, crossed the Niemen, in June, 1812, not less than 450,000 strong; and recrossed it in December of the same year less than 40,000 men.   The rest were dead under the snows of savage Muscovy, or else prisoners in the hands of the Russians.   His enforced allies, the Prus-sians, deserted him at the first opportunity, and, after the disaster of Leipsic, in the succeeding year, the whole of Europe, practically, fell upon him.   The Austrians had tried, before Leipsic, to arrange a peace, as Napoleon was married, having divorced "the excellent Josephine" in 1810, to Maria Louisa, daughter of the Emperor of Austria; but the great conqueror refused all peaceful advances—some of which, no doubt, were insincere—with fierce scorn—the outcome of his imperial and military pride.   The Saxons turned upon him in the very crisis of the battle of Leipsic, in which they were his allies; and the Bavarians and Rhen-ish Germans also became hostile, so that he had, practically, no friends in Germany.   Then he fell back on the Rhine, having cut his way through the Bavarian army, under Mar-shal Wrede, at Hanau, and recrossed that famous river with a sadly diminished force.   To add to his misfortunes, typhus fever broke out among the soldiers, and spread among the French villages in which they were quartered, sweeping off thousands.   His defence of France, in 1814, when he was greatly aided by the skilful valor of Marshal Ney, was most brilliant, but, after many splendid victories, he was finally, because of the treachery or stupidity of Marshal Marmont, who uncovered Napoleon's line of defence on the Essonne River, compelled to abdicate at Fontainebleau, April, 1814. He had gloriously fought 300,000 men, for months, with a mere remnant of his once powerful army, and his military reputation was not, therefore, clouded by his reverses, but his standing as a statesman was greatly lowered, and he had lost the confidence of some of the greatest minds of France, formerly his devoted friends. The fallen emperor was sent to the island of Elba, where he remained less than a year, returning to France, which he knew was tired of the restored Bourbon dynasty, with the handful of his old soldiers that had followed him into exile. Then came the Hundred Days of imperial power resumed, for all of France, except La Vendée, submitted when he appeared, and the Bourbons, placed upon the throne by the bayonets of coalesced Europe, were compelled to fly from French territory. Then followed the brief, but murderous, campaign of Belgium—a country in which Napoleon commanded for the first and last time in his marvelous career; the crowning disaster of Waterloo, and the cruel exile of Napoleon to the volcanic "rock of St. Helena," in the fateful year, 1815. His victor, the Duke of Wellington, was born in either Dangan Castle, County Meath, or the city Dublin, in May, 1769, exactly 600 years after his paternal ancestor came over with Fitzstephen; and his mother's forebears had resided in the country for more than three centuries. Yet, the duke was a bitter foe of Irish independence, and had no love whatever for his Catholic countrymen, too many of whom, to their disgrace be it

recorded, helped to win his many victories. Napoleon's
fall proved a curse to Ireland, not that he cared very
much for her cause at any time, because of his ignorance
of her condition and resources, but because it left England
free to work her will in the hapless island. Catholic emancipation was postponed by Wellington's triumph for fourteen years longer, despite the titanic labors of the indefatigable O'Connell, but the great agitator never paused for
a moment in the work he had set out to accomplish. He
labored night and day to infuse fresh life into the almost
"inert mass" of his Catholic countrymen, inspiring the
brave, shaming the cowardly, and confirming the wavering. He was now the most popular legal advocate in Ireland, having taken the place as a defender of the persecuted
people formerly occupied by Curran. His speech defending the publisher, John Magee, against a government suit
for libel, in 1813, is a masterpiece of manly, virile, un-
ornate, Demosthenic eloquence, and should be read by every
student of the art of oratory. O'Connell's style was all
his own—he borrowed from nobody, he imitated nobody,
and he could command the attention, at any time, of any
audience, high or low, learned or illiterate. As he spoke
Gaelic fluently, he had no difficulty in making himself thoroughly understood by the Celtic Catholic peasantry, who,
at that time, were accustomed to be spoken to in their
native tongue. Thousands of them, owing to the old penal
laws against education, understood no other. O'Connell,
as a popular orator, fully understood the value of simple
speech to the multitude. The Irish peasant might have admired Grattan, still more Curran or Sheil, who could, occasionally, come near to the earth, but neither could have
moved him as did O'Connell, who knew so well every emo-

tion of the changeful Celtic temperament and the elastic Celtic mind. He was, sometimes, even rude and brusque, when speaking of the enemies of the people, and his humor, although always mirth-provoking, was often rather the reverse of elegant. In the realm of banter, he could not be beaten, whether by a learned judge, a king's counselor, or a fluent fish-wife. Then, he had a magnificent figure, an irregular but attractive countenance, a flashing Irish blue eye, a winning smile, and a voice whose modulation was the perfection of prose-poetry, as its range was the acme of a powerful conveyance of vocal sound. He knew the weaknesses, as well as the virtues, of his people, and often flattered them overmuch—something they would not have endured from other leaders, for no people are so quick to perceive the ludicrous side of sentiment. His sarcastic philippics against the Dukes of York and Cumberland, "the Iron Duke," "Scorpion Stanley," and "Orange Peel" often made those worthies wince, notwithstanding the rank and power they held. O'Connell was, in all respects, intensely human, profoundly religious, at the same time, and a lover of the beauties of nature, whether animate or inanimate. He had married his lovely relative, Miss Mary O'Connell, early in life, and no couple were ever more devoted to each other's happiness. Several sons and daughters blessed the marriage, but the mantle of the sire did not fall on the shoulders of any of his descendants. O'Connell's greatest fault was a too profuse expression of loyalty to the British crown, especially after the accession of Victoria. His ingenuity in changing the title of his various associations, as one after the other was suppressed by "government," showed him to be a most self-reliant and resourceful tactician. We have always considered, without wishing to throw discredit on

O'Connell's sincerity, that many of his profuse professions of devotion to the British sovereign were "put on" for purposes of policy. In order to effectively fight the Parliament, he had to appear friendly to the throne. But "the throne" was never friendly to him.

Grenville in his gossipy memoirs takes occasion, more than once, to throw imputations on O'Connell's personal courage. His career does not justify such a charge. In 1815, when he spoke of "the beggarly Corporation" of Dublin, one of its members, a needy person, named D'Esterre, challenged him. O'Connell abhorred dueling, from a moral standpoint, but, after consultation with friends, accepted the challenge. The parties fought with pistols, about twelve miles from Dublin, in December, 1815, and O'Connell mortally wounded D'Esterre at the first shot. He was perfectly cool throughout, but the death of his opponent greatly affected him, and, thenceforth, he eschewed the duello, as a matter of principle. It is said that he settled a pension on the widow of D'Esterre. If so, the act was creditable to his humanity, but his victim has been charged by Irish historians—at least by inference—with having purposely provoked O'Connell to fight, being himself a crack shot, with the object of ridding the government of so dangerous and able an enemy. However, D'Esterre's fate, allied to his early memories of the horrors of the French Revolution, while a student in France, made the agitator morbid on the subject of bloodshed in his older age. It is unjust to dub such a man a physical coward. He was simply of a temperament too humane for the foes he had to fight and the almost unheard-of difficulties he had to contend against. But he manifested no timidity of any kind, moral or physical, during his long and brilliant and successful struggle for Catholic Emancipation. Daniel O'Connell had a great, loving, fatherly heart, and, whatever the political errors of his old age, Ireland, considering his earlier services, can well afford to forgive them, and, indeed, has both forgiven and forgotten them.

Ireland was visited by famine in 1817, although she was making large exports of all kinds of provisions to Great Britain. The proceeds thereof did not go into the pockets of the people, but those of the "English garrison" landlords, who spent them lavishly in "high living" at the various European capitals, particularly London. And this has been the case during every so-called "Irish famine"—of English manufacture—since that period.

William Conyngham Plunket, of doubtful fame, introduced a bill for Catholic Emancipation in the Imperial Parliament, February 28, 1821. It was furiously opposed in the Lords by the Duke of York, and in the Commons it fared but little better. In short, it was disastrously defeated. Henry Grattan had passed away in the previous year—"ever glorious Grattan," as Byron called him—and was interred in Westminster Abbey. England honored her constitutional foe in death, but Ireland was bereaved of his ashes.

George IV made a visit to Ireland in August, 1821, and received from the again "too easily deluded" people "a great ovation"—O'Connell and Fingal, whom he had repeatedly deceived in regard to Catholic claims, taking a leading part in it, from motives of "policy." O'Connell, Mitchel says, went so far in the line of "toleration" as to drink at a Dublin banquet, given in the king's honor, the Orange "Charter toast." We are sorry O'Connell did this, if he did, because it was an act of needless self-humiliation.

Every Orangeman present at that banquet, and even King George himself, would have gladly seen him hanged.

This degrading Dublin exhibition of toadyism drew from the caustic pen of Byron his renowned "Irish Avatar," in which he told, as a friend of Ireland, willing even, although an Englishman, to fight for her independence, some wholesome, if unpalatable, truths, which Irishmen might study with advantage at the present day.

Worst of all, ancient Dunleary, from which George sailed for England, "with tears"—those of a crocodile—"in his eyes," changed its name to Kingstown," and a monument, happily very ugly, marks the spot where his "false, fleeting, perjured" person last lingered on Irish soil. O'Connell decorated him with a wreath of shamrocks as he was going up the boat ladder. All this tomfoolery was enacted in the hope of winning the perfidious monarch to a friendly feeling for Catholic Emancipation, but the crowned confidence man again duped the Irish Catholics, and, in fact, made them appear abased and ridiculous in the eyes of the world. O'Connell, in after years, painted a very uncomplimentary word-picture of George IV, and the latter reciprocated by calling the agitator, as he approached him at a levee, in a stage whisper, as an aside to a satellite, "that d—d scoundrel!" These are not pleasant revivals, but, as they happen to be true, they form a genuine part of this history and fully illustrate the obsequiousness and hypocrisy of the period dealt with. Daniel O'Connell was not entirely free from the duplicity induced by a penal heredity, but he had enough stalwart virtue left in his nature to conquer the lingering serf that still slightly fettered his great spirit, and burst the chain that had, for centuries, galled the Catholics of Ireland.

CHAPTER II

Monstrous Debt Piled upon Ireland by Great Britain—Suicide of Castlereagh—Attempt on the Part of Government to Pension the Catholic Priesthood—The Bribe Rejected with Scorn

THE act of the Imperial Parliament, which consolidated the British and Irish exchequers, was passed five years before the visit of George IV to Dublin, and had greatly enhanced the national debt of Ireland—incurred for wars foreign to her interests, and in which she was reluctantly obliged to participate. "The English debt," comments Mitchel, "had not quite doubled [during those wars], while the Irish debt was more than quadrupled, as if Ireland had twice the interest in forcing the Bourbons back upon France that England had, and also in destroying the commerce of America. Thus, in 1816, when the Consolidation Act was passed, the whole funded debt of Ireland was found to be £130,561,037, about $653,000,000; by this management of the Irish debt, which had been, in 1801, as one to sixteen and a half to the British, was forced up to bear to the latter the ratio of one to seven and a half. This was the proportion required by the Act of Union as a condition of subjecting Ireland to indiscriminate taxation with Great Britain—a condition equally impudent and iniquitous. Ireland was to be loaded with inordinate debt, and, then, this debt was to be made a pretext for raising her taxation to the high British standard, and thereby rendering her liable to the pre-Union debt of Great Britain!"

The famine of 1822 followed fast on the departure of George IV from Ireland, as if his visit had brought with it a curse and a blight. Many people starved to death, but the exportation of food to England did not, therefore, slacken. Thousands on thousands were unemployed and suffering the worst privations, and myriads were obliged to subsist on the scanty crumbs of overworked charity. The government, as usual, did as little as possible to alleviate the distress. No official returns of death from starvation were kept, but it is certain that the population was much diminished before the scourge passed away. Bad times aggravated the agrarian warfare. Secret societies flourished among the peasantry, who, exasperated by want and oppression, killed many evicting landlords and their agents. These acts were followed by "special commissions" and numerous hangings of the offenders, or of men said to have been the offenders, for the agents of government were not particular about being strictly accurate, as long as "an example" was made of somebody. Then followed more insurrection and disarming acts, all of which the late royal guest of Ireland signed most willingly. In this year, also, the wretched traitor, Robert Stewart, Marquis of Londonderry, better known as the notoriously infamous Lord Castlereagh, cut his throat with a penknife. The masses of the English nation hated him almost as bitterly as the Irish, because of his uniform, cold-blooded support of all tyrannical legislation. The man was "born bad"—as vile a monster as the worst that disgraced the Reign of Terror period of the French Revolution. He instinctively battled against liberty wherever it showed itself. When his coffin was borne to Westminster Abbey—the proudest peers of Britain, among them the Duke of Wellington, being the pall-bearers—the funeral procession was hooted by the London mob, who, at least, were decent enough to feel that the

bones of the Judas should not be laid beside those of brave
and honorable men. The Tory historian, Alison, says that
"the savage miscreants [meaning the London populace]
raised a horrid shout." One historian, commenting on Alison's statement, says: "Future ages will probably pronounce
that in all the mob of London was no such dreadful mis-
creant as the man then borne to his grave." Lord Byron,
who detested the "noble" rascal, wrote several of the most
caustic of his epigrams upon the suicide:

> "So Castlereagh has cut his throat at last! The worst
> Of this is—that his own was not the first!"

And yet again he wrote:

> "So *he* has cut his throat! He! Who?
> The man who cut his country's long ago!"

The Marquis of Wellesley, elder brother of the Duke of
Wellington, and a much nobler character and abler statesman, became viceroy of Ireland in the year that saw the
last of Castlereagh. Because he did not ferociously exercise
the powers vested in him, and, further, because he was
known to be favorably disposed toward "the Catholic
claims," as their demand for justice was called, he soon became very unpopular with the yellowest section of the rabid
Orange faction. He was charged in their newspapers with
being "leagued with O'Connell, the Pope, and the Devil"—
the first-named personage being, in their estimation, the
most formidable enemy of the group to the "Ascendency"
element. The Orange fanatics went to the extreme of assailing Lord Wellesley in his box at the theatre, but did not
succeed in injuring him. Several were arrested, and "tried"
before an Ascendency judge, and an Orange jury, properly
packed, and all were acquitted, greatly to the disgust of
decent Protestants as well as Catholics.

Soon afterward, O'Connell organized, with the able help of Richard Lalor Sheil—one of the greatest of the world's polished orators—the Catholic Association, to which several peers, including Lord Killeen, son of the Earl of Fingal; Lord Gormanstown, and Lord Kenmore, sent in their adhesion—Killeen alone taking active part in the movement. The older and more conservative Catholic peers avoided the association, as they favored the slavish "veto," and considered O'Connell's stalwart sentiments "too strong" for their Whiggish taste. The first meeting to form the association was held at an inn in Dublin—only twenty people attended. But O'Connell, supported by Sheil and the able and aggressive Doctor Dromgoole, was not discouraged. He knew he had a vast and potent power still to call upon and wake to action—the Catholic priesthood, so long persecuted and proscribed. Some of the prelates were the first to respond to the call of "the great disturber," as the Thunderer called O'Connell; that is, when it did not call him a "ruffian." The Right Rev. Dr. Doyle, Bishop of Kildare and Leighlin, over the signature of "J. K. L.," fired the Catholic masses with the ablest pamphlets and letters of the time. In one of them he said that the circumstances demanded stern action, and that the Catholic clergy could not be depended upon to preach peace, if Catholic rights were longer withheld. He concluded by saying that "if a rebellion were raging from Carrickfergus to Cape Clear, no sentence of excommunication would ever be fulminated by a Catholic prelate." Some Maynooth professors—who received government support—issued a protest against Bishop Doyle's "extreme views," but the people paid no attention to it, and prelates, priests, and people—boldly led by the tireless O'Connell—were not long in "bracing themselves up to the act of their own deliverance." Even the quiet, peace-loving Archbishop of Dublin, the Most Rev. Dr. Murray, exclaimed, in the pulpit of the Marlborough Street cathedral: "The contemplation of the wrongs of my country makes my soul burn within me!"

O'Connell now appealed to the Dissenters, or Nonconformists, of Ireland, who also suffered proscriptions and penalties, because they were not members of the Church of England, or, rather, the Irish Established Church, to aid him in gaining reforms for all. The Presbyterians, in particular, responded cordially, and gave their full sympathy to the movement for Catholic Emancipation, the accomplishment of which, they knew, would bring the reforms they longed for. The sensitive British government again took alarm, and, in 1825, a law for the suppression of "unlawful associations in Ireland" was passed by Parliament. O'Connell immediately advised the dissolution of the Catholic association, at which the blow was aimed, but immediately reorganized it, under the name of The New Catholic Association—greatly to the disgust and disappointment of Mr. Secretary Goldburn, who had introduced the bill. The next step tried by government was to prepare a bill to pension the Catholic clergy, in order to secure their influence in favor of English methods in Ireland, as had been partially accomplished with the Presbyterian ministers when they accepted the increased Regium Donum.

The bill provided the following scale of payment out of the imperial treasury: Bishops, £1,000 ($5,000) each; deans, £300 each; parish priests, £200, and curates, £60 each. Of course, the Irish clergy saw through the venal scheme at once, and they and their people, almost without exception, protested against the unholy and unwholesome bribe. There was no mistaking Irish sentiment on this point, and the bill —of which Sir Robert Peel was the putative father—was defeated by the Lords, after having passed the Commons. It was not, however, regard for Irish feeling, but crass bigotry, mainly enkindled by the fanatical Duke of York, then heir presumptive to the throne, which caused its defeat in the House of Peers. "Never, so help me God!" shouted this miserable scion of hybrid royalty, "will I allow the claims of the Catholics!" and the Lords, as in duty bound, warmly applauded him.

O'Connell visited London, with Sheil, Mr. Richard O'Gorman and Sir Thomas Esmonde, about this time, to protest against the enactment of further laws for the suppression of Catholic associations. That of which O'Connell was the organizer had recently presented a courteous address to the aged Archibald Hamilton Rowan, of United Irish fame, upon his return to Ireland. When Mr., afterward Lord, Brougham moved that O'Connell and Sheil be "heard for their cause" at the bar of the House of Commons, Sir Robert Peel made a vehement speech in opposition, and almost insulted O'Connell, who, he said, was the leader of an association which "presented addresses to attainted traitors," meaning Hamilton Rowan. Brougham replied, but the opposition was too strong, and the matter dropped. Mitchel and other writers claim that O'Connell, at this period came, for the first time, under that fatal Whig influence which, ultimately, marred and thwarted his grand career. The persuasions of the Duke of Sussex, reputed to be a friend of Catholic Emancipation, although a brother of the Duke of York, Brougham, the Duke of Norfolk, and other Whig leaders, induced him, it is alleged, to favor acceptance of an Emancipation measure, with what were called two wings attached to it—namely, the payment of the Catholic clergy, and the disfranchisement of the "forty-shilling freeholders." He soon discovered that he was on thin ice. The defeat of the pension bill by the House of Lords covered his retreat gracefully, and he never again countenanced the dependency of the clergy on the government in any shape. Unfortunately, he was not so firm regarding the forty-shilling franchise question.

Events now rushed rapidly onward toward the crisis of Catholic Emancipation. In some districts, the influence of the Catholic Association succeeded in electing liberal Protestants, instead of Orange Tories, to Parliament, greatly to the rage of the Ascendency faction. There was much trouble between Orangemen and Catholics in Ulster, and even in Dublin, where raged for several days and nights the famous polemical controversy between the Rev. "Father Tom" Maguire and the Rev. Mr. Pope, an eloquent English divine, of Protestant persuasion. The "acute stage" of the discussion was reached when the sacraments were touched upon. Father Maguire showed himself an invincible theologian, and Mr. Pope a pulpit orator of the first rank; but the Catholics of Ireland hold, now, as they did then, that "Father Tom" "laid the Englishman out cold."

Attempts to spread discussions of the kind throughout the country were prudently discountenanced by Dr. Doyle and other leading Catholic prelates, and the many challenges of church militant Protestant clergymen were, thenceforth, disregarded, so that controversies became not alone unfashionable, but unpopular.

Meanwhile the Catholic cause had been winning much sympathy abroad, especially in France and the United States. The French press gave O'Connell its almost undivided support, and, in America, auxiliary Catholic Associations were formed, and much money subscribed and sent in aid of the movement. Many of the States of Germany, as well as Spain, Portugal, Italy, and Belgium, also manifested active interest in the Irish struggle, and England, as usual when her game is interfered with, became violently enraged.

CHAPTER III

Crisis of the Struggle for Catholic Emancipation—O'Connell Stands for
County Clare and Enters Parliament—Peel and Wellington
Yield for Fear of Civil War—Emancipation Won

THE sudden death of Lord Liverpool, in 1825, made George Canning, who had spoken in favor of Catholic Emancipation in the Commons, Prime Minister. Because of his speech, Sir Robert Peel, the Duke of Wellington, Lord Eldon, and other high Tory members of the outgoing ministry, declined to serve with the new premier. Canning formed a new cabinet, which favored concessions. The Marquis of Wellesley was recalled from Ireland, and Lord Anglesea, who had made much reputation as a dashing cavalry leader in the Peninsula, and at Waterloo, became viceroy in his stead. The last volley fired by the French in Napoleon's final battle deprived Anglesea of his right leg. According to Greville, who had the story from the lips of the Iron Duke himself, the earl, then, of Uxbridge, was riding on his right hand side, when, suddenly, Uxbridge cried out, profanely, "By G—, I have lost my leg!"—"Have you, by G—?" responded Wellington, and rode ahead as if nothing extraordinary had happened. Sir Fitzroy Somerset, who afterward, as Lord Raglan, commanded the British army in the Crimea, lost his right arm by the same volley which had maimed Anglesea. He was riding on Wellington's left. Had either shot struck the duke himself, it is quite probable that, although Waterloo was then hopelessly lost, the French would have rallied around their emperor and prolonged the war—perhaps to a successful issue. The Marquis of Anglesea was noted in Ireland as a man of pleasure rather than of executive capacity. His chief secretary was Lord Francis Leveson Gower.

George Canning, who had many fine qualities, died in August, 1827, and was succeeded by the inconsequential Lord Goderich, who failed to form a lasting cabinet, and was supplanted, in January, 1828, by the more vigorous Duke of Wellington. Sir Robert Peel was a member of his cabinet—Home Secretary—and both were, then at least, apparently irreconcilable foes of Catholic Emancipation. Another noted member of this ministry was the late Lord Palmerston—a born politician and constitutional timeserver.

When the Parliamentary session of 1828 opened, a petition from 800,000 Catholics prayed for the repeal of the Test and Corporation Acts, which, for a hundred and fifty years, had prevented Protestant Dissenters from holding public office. Dissenting Protestant petitions came in praying for the emancipation of the Catholics, but the bulk of the Established Church Episcopalians, in the three kingdoms, and particularly the faculties and students of the universities—from which better things were to be expected—sent in counter petitions. Lord John, afterward Earl, Russell, who, at that period of life, and for long after, affected to be a great reformer, fought ably for the repeal of the odious enactments petitioned against by the 800,000 Catholics, and, in the end, they were wiped from the statute book. The old Iron Duke, who was an honest bigot, politically rather than religiously—for he was never noted for piety, and could be as profane as a mule driver on occasions—shook his head and looked severe; he felt that the end was not yet. Sir Robert Peel, more of a politician than a sectarian champion, began to waver, but still kept up an appearance of stiff opposition to further reform. Some members of the cabinet, dissatisfied with the duke's inflexibility, resigned their portfolios, and the Hon. Vesey Fitzgerald, member for Clare County, accepted the presidency of the Board of Trade. According to British custom, when a member accepts an office under the crown, he is compelled to vacate his seat, until re-elected, which is generally the result of a new appeal to the electors. Mr. Fitzgerald lost no time in issuing his address to the Clare electors, with whom he was quite popular; he had the support of the leading aristocrats and landed proprietors of the country, and stood well with the Catholic clergy and laity, because he was known to be a cordial friend of Emancipation. He was also the son of that eloquent Prime-Sergeant Fitzgerald, who had so vigorously protested against the Union at the meeting of the Dublin bar, in 1799, and had been deprived of his office in consequence.

The Irish people, when not influenced by greater considerations than friendship for a candidate for public honors, are hard to detach from their favorite leaders. They loved Vesey Fitzgerald, but they loved Ireland, and Emancipation, more. Lord John Russell, and other Whig leaders, who felt under obligations to the Wellington Ministry for not having too strenuously opposed the repeal of the Test and Corporation Acts, endeavored to induce O'Connell and the Catholic Association not to put up a candidate against Mr. Fitzgerald. O'Connell was rather inclined to adopt the treacherous Whig suggestion—he had not yet fathomed the depth of their statecraft—but his attempt to have a resolution declaring opposition to Mr. Fitzgerald's candidacy in the Association rescinded, was defeated. Now arose the question as to who should be the candidate of the Catholics. He had to be a Protestant, and the celebrated Major "Fireball" MacNamara, who had been O'Connell's second in the duel with D'Esterre, was their first choice. But the major was averse to opposing Mr. Fitzgerald, on account of personal relations, and the deputation sent down from Dublin to Clare returned disappointed. And the aristocrats of that county waxed jubilant, declaring that "no gentleman would stoop so low as to accept the patronage of the Catholic Association." This stirred the hot blood in the veins of O'Connell and his friends, and, after a consultation in the historic house of the agitator, in Merrion Square, he issued an address to the voters of Clare, declaring himself their candidate—the first Catholic who had dared to do so, or who, in fact, had a chance to do so, since the reign of James II.

The Clare election of 1828 was the most memorable in Irish annals. It put to the hardest test the fidelity of the people to principle before material interest. It brought the brave peasantry of Clare—notably the forty-shilling free-holders—face to face with their landlords, who were, then, the arbiters of life or death in their relations with the "ten-ants-at-will," which most of the rural voters were. Undeniably, the influence of the Catholic prelates and priests had much to do with the splendid display of moral heroism on the part of the people when the issue was squarely made. A great majority of the clergy came from the farming class, and, of course, had the full confidence and support of their flocks, who did not forget the splendid devotion of the priesthood to their forefathers in the blackest night of the penal times. All the priests of Ireland were not patriots, in a national sense, but the majority were, as they are still, and not one of them, of course, was opposed to the struggle for Catholic Emancipation.

When Daniel O'Connell entered the canvass for the representation of Clare, he was in his fifty-third year, and in the full prime of his wonderful power as a popular orator. His chief lieutenants were the gallant O'Gorman Mahon, a Catholic gentleman of Clare, of the most noble bearing and chivalrous character; Mr. Thomas Steele, a patriotic, but rather eccentric, Protestant gentleman, who absolutely worshiped the great Catholic leader; "Father Tom" Maguire, the vanquisher of the eloquent Parson Pope; "Honest Jack" Lawless, editor of "The Irishman"; Richard Lalor Sheil, and the Rev. Father Murphy, with other Catholic clergymen of Clare County.

On the side of Vesey Fitzgerald were ranked the whole body of the aristocratic element, headed by the great family of the O'Briens of Drumoland and Inchiquin; the haughty Vandeleurs and the "fighting MacNamaras." "Tom" Steele, afterward, absurdly enough, O'Connell's "Head Pacificator" in Conciliation Hall, having an eye to the practical, as well as the patriotic, sent word in advance into Clare that he was willing to exchange shots with any landlord who might feel himself aggrieved by the interference of "strangers from Dublin" with his tenantry. And O'Gorman Mahon made it quite plain that he, too, was willing to "burn powder" in the same cause. As both these gallant Irish gentlemen were known to be men of their word, the sensitiveness of the Clare aristocrats to the interference of O'Connell's friends became sensibly diminished.

The O'Connell orators canvassed the county from parish to parish—the agitator himself being the central figure. The meetings were generally called on Sundays after Mass, and the pastors usually presided over these "chapel-yard" gatherings. As O'Connell spoke Irish as fluently as English, he had a wonderful power over his ardent and simple auditory, which few of even his most gifted colleagues possessed. He went through Clare, like a moral cyclone, and the O'Briens, the Vandeleurs, the Fitzgeralds, and the Mac-Namaras, with their several followings, were swept before him like so much chaff. His easy, yet powerful, eloquence fascinated the men; his pathos made the women weep, and his inimitable humor sent even his sternest foes into convulsions of laughter. Woe to the opponent on whom O'Connell inflicted a nickname—it followed him to the grave. Speaking of Sir Robert Peel, who was his personal enemy—a challenge having once passed between them—he said: "Orange Peel can smile sometimes, but the smile reminds me of sunshine on the plate of a coffin!" And he denounced that stinging orator, who was always his opponent, and the enemy of Ireland, Mr. Stanley, afterward Earl of Derby, as "Scorpion Stanley." Others have laid claim to the nicknaming of Wellington as the "Iron Duke," but the designation of the great soldier and vehement Tory bears all the earmarks of O'Connell's sarcastic genius. The "monster meeting," held in Ennis, the capital of Clare, was the climax of the great campaign. The town presented a festival appearance, and was garlanded with green boughs and laurel wreaths—the picturesque precursors of victory. Sheil, in his graphic description of the scene, in "Sketches of the Irish Bar," bears testimony to the order and sobriety of the people. Mitchel says of them: "There was no drunkenness, no angry language, and no man ventured—so strong was public opinion—to raise a hand against another upon any provocation. O'Connell at length appeared, with two or three friends, and there was one continuous roar from 30,000 throats. Women cried and laughed, strangers who had never seen one another before wrung each other's hands, and from every window ladies—Mr. Sheil says 'of great beauty'—waved hands and handkerchiefs. No wonder that such a tempest of patriotic zeal whirled away Mr. Fitzgerald's own tenants out of the hands of their marshaling bailiffs; nor that one wave of O'Connell's arm left Mr. Vandeleur deserted by his whole array of freeholders. Sir Edward O'Brien's feudal pride was mortally hurt by the defection of his people, and he shed tears of vexation; but his son, William Smith O'Brien, then member for Ennis, though his family pride may have been hurt by such a result, was not inconsolable, being, indeed, a contributor to the 'Catholic Rent,' and one who, at all times, valued justice and fair dealing more highly than the broad acres and high towers of Drumoland."

The result of the contest may be briefly stated: When the polls closed—the vote being an open one, and not by secret ballot, as is now the condition—O'Connell had received 2,057 votes, and Vesey Fitzgerald 1,075. The announcement was received with frantic cheering by the excited people, many of those who had voted against O'Connell, because of their landlords' influence, joining in the applause. The assessor of election, a Mr. Keating, endeavored to show that no Catholic could be legally returned, but the objection was not sustained, on the ground that Parliament alone could decide on the question of eligibility when the customary oaths were tendered in the House of Commons. And Daniel O'Connell was, therefore, proclaimed duly elected.

This great moral triumph fell like a bombshell in the Tory camp of the "United" Kingdom. The Clare aristocrats were dazed by their defeat. The people throughout Ireland were wildly jubilant, as well they might be. O'Connell's return to Dublin was in the nature of a triumphal progress. Indeed, at that period, he was, really, "the uncrowned king" of Ireland, and he so remained for many a year afterward. "Honest Jack" Lawless, on his way back to Belfast, where his newspaper was published, narrowly escaped being murdered by the infuriated Orangemen, at Ballybay, but, owing to the strenuous exertions of the Catholic clergy, and the repeated expostulations of General Thornton, the military commander of the district, the disagreeable incident passed by without serious results.

Wellington and Peel saw that the hour had come to give way. The latter had been wavering for some time, for his political insight was keen, and the old duke felt the necessity of retreat from his original position—one of uncompromising hostility to Catholic claims—keenly. But these British ministers well knew that they had to choose between Catholic Emancipation and civil war—all Ireland, except the Orange faction, being, practically, united against them, and all the Catholic, and most of the Protestant, nations of the word being in full sympathy with the Irish demand for civil and religious liberty. Peel did not stand long on ceremony. He saw plainly how matters stood and accepted the situation with philosophy. Parliament met in February, 1829. The king's speech, prepared, most likely, by Peel, recommended "the suppression of the Catholic Association and the subsequent consideration of Catholic disabilities, with a view to their adjustment and removal."

The Catholic Association, having performed its work, dissolved itself at once, thus saving a "paternal" government both time and trouble, and there could be no difficulty about reorganizing it, under some other name, at any time, if it should be deemed necessary.

On March 5, Sir Robert Peel moved to go into committee of the whole House, "for consideration of the civil disabilities of his Majesty's Roman Catholic subjects."

The debate on the subject was long and vehement, but Peel was insistent, and the motion prevailed by a large majority. But the vote sent alarm through the souls of the "professional Protestants" of the Three Kingdoms. Petitions from all interested sources poured in upon Parliament, and the arguments used against the emancipation of the Catholics were of the most frivolous, hysterical, and ridiculous nature. Not one of them is worthy of reproduction —all breathe unchristian bigotry and revolting selfishness. Even the Orange descendants of some of the petitioners might blush at the reproduction of their forebears' anti-Catholic fulminations in this more liberal age.

Sir Robert Peel was too calm a politician to be moved from his purpose by the clamor of hot-headed bigots or Ascendency axe-grinders. No Englishman knew better the strength of the Irish demand, and he zealously sought to impress his belief on the sodden brain of the wretched bacchanalian king. He used, for a long time, every argument in vain, George IV swearing vehemently that he would yield only at the very last extremity. An attempt was made by the faithless monarch to dismiss the Wellington-Peel ministry, and appoint an anti-Emancipation one in its stead. The ministers at once sent in their resignations. The monarch was not a person of much resolution, and he saw instantly that he had made a mistake. Therefore, he humbly begged the cabinet officers to withdraw their resignations, which they did immediately. They were then, he told them, "at liberty to proceed with the measures of which notice had been given in Parliament." These were the relief measures, for the benefit of the Catholics, already referred to. The vacillating, ungenerous conduct of George IV excited the contempt of all decent people in Great Britain and Ireland.

O'Connell had already arrived in London to demand his seat as the Catholic member for Clare County, but, finding out the plans of the cabinet for immediate emancipation, he decided not to embarrass its action by forcing an issue in the House of Commons.

The act of Catholic Emancipation was speedily introduced by Sir Robert Peel, minus the veto and priest-pensioning provisions; but it was accompanied by another act—which proved, in after times, death-dealing in its effects on a brave and confiding peasantry—for the total disfranchisement of all the forty-shilling freeholders of Ireland! These were the men who, in Clare, had elected O'Connell, in spite of their landlords, and now, in reward for their courage and patriotism, they were to be again reduced to the condition of helotry. And this was deliberately done by the British minister, in order that the Irish constituency might be made more amenable to governmental influence in future emergencies.

After much acrimonious debate, the Catholic Relief bill passed to its third reading in the House of Commons, on

March 30, by a majority of 36.   In the House of Lords,
the Duke of Wellington moved its second reading, on
April 2, stating frankly that he urged the necessity of
its passage "in order to prevent civil war." Very violent
debates followed, but, finally, the third reading was passed
by a majority of 104.   It was then sent to the king for signature, and it is said that he wept with rage when forced
by the logic of events to comply with the wishes of his
ministers.   And so Catholic Emancipation—except as regarded the succession to the crown, the Lord Lieutenancy
of Ireland, and the Lord Chancellorship, since, however, included under the act—was finally accomplished.

O'Connell, before the passage of the act, was further restrained from seeking to take his seat, because of a pending
petition against his election by the malcontents of the Fitzgerald party in Clare.   The committee of the House, soon
after Emancipation was carried, reported O'Connell duly
elected.   But Peel, who mortally hated O'Connell, took advantage of a mere technicality, and when O'Connell, introduced by Lords Ebrington and Duncannon, went to the table
of the House to take the new oaths, Sir Robert meanly
raised the point that, as O'Connell was elected before the
passage of the Relief bill, he should he required to take the
old and offensive obligations.   The clerk, accordingly, tendered to O'Connell the already abrogated oath of supremacy,
namely, that the King of England was head of the Church;
and the other indecent objuration, namely, that "the sacrifice
of the Mass is impious and idolatrous." He refused to take
them, and, at the bar of the House, asserted his right to sit
and vote as representative from Clare County.   But the
House had the indelicacy to support Peel's point of privilege.   The old oaths were again tendered him.   He carefully

read them over—sad, stupid stuff they were—and then, raising his powerful voice, so as to be heard by all, said: "One
part of them I know to be false—the other I do not believe
to be true!"

Then he retired, first bowing to the Speaker, and a new
writ issued for election in the County Clare.

CHAPTER IV

Irish Peasant Voters Disfranchised—Singular Apathy of O'Connell—
George IV Passes Away and William IV Succeeds—"National"
School System—The Irish Leader and the Whigs

THE forty-shilling freeholders were immediately disfranchised in Ireland, although the qualification remained
in force in Great Britain; and O'Connell has been censured
for not having made vigorous protest against this great injustice to the very class of Irish voters to which he owed his
crowning triumph. Mitchel states that it is not on record
that he made any protest whatever. This disfranchisement
robbed the Irish small farmers of their last weapon of defence against "felonious landlordism," and many of the
evils suffered by the poor people afterward may be justly
traced to Sir Robert Peel's treacherous piece of legislation.
The county qualification for voters in Ireland was raised,
at the same time, to £10 per year—five times the amount of
qualification required in England.

O'Connell made one of the worst mistakes of his career
in not sustaining "the gallant forties," as they were popularly called, but he was so eager for Emancipation that other
causes seemed, by comparison, unimportant in his eyes. Had
he thought the matter over, his great mind would have
speedily recognized the deep grave dug for Ireland's inter-

ests by Peel in the passage of that infamous act. Even Lord Palmerston opposed it, supported by some other members of the Commons, saying that, "If the forty-shilling freeholders of Ireland had been corrupt, like those of Penrhyn, in Wales, their disfranchisement might be defended; but the only offence of the persons against whom the bill was directed had been that they exercised their privilege honestly and independently, according to their conscience." But no English rose has ever been presented to Ireland, unless accompanied by many thorns.

Many sapient Irish writers assert that O'Connell, at heart, considered Catholic Emancipation a trivial reform, more apparent than real, and that the leading ambition of his life was repeal of the Union, which alone could free his country from the blight of British preponderance in her internal, as well as external, affairs. He so asserted, soon after his return from England, and declared that the great victory to be achieved would be the restoration of the Irish Parliament, on broader principles. When he came to agitate this question seriously, he missed the vote of the forty-shilling freeholders. But many important places, under the British crown, were now open to the Irish Catholics, and Ireland being a needy country, as she could not help being, considering her history, many hungry Catholic barristers, and others, who had hitherto stood by O'Connell, because they could not help themselves, might now be expected to fall away from him and look for the loaves and fishes of government "patronage." And this expectation was not disappointed, because the British government has always had a most unpleasant faculty of converting every pretended Irish "benefit" into a new method of corruption. We may say, without wishing to give offence, that, since 1829, the number of Irish Catholic political renegades from national principles—owing entirely to the acceptance of place and pension from the British crown—has been sufficient to justify O'Connell in asking God "to pardon him for having emancipated such fellows."

Two great grievances still affected the Catholics of Ireland—the support of the Protestant Established Church, and the forceful collection of tithes, which resulted from such support. About this time, what was known as "the Tithe War" grew in intensity, and approached a bitterness equal to that of the agrarian warfare, which still continued at intervals.

There was no opposition to the return of O'Connell, when he went back to Clare for re-election, but he did not take his seat in the Commons immediately, as Parliament was prorogued until winter. The session of 1830 opened February 4, but Parliament was speedily dissolved, and a new election followed. O'Connell, in order to defeat the powerful Beresfords, allowed another candidate to stand for Clare, while he himself appealed to the electors of Waterford County. He was triumphantly returned, and the haughty Beresfords were correspondingly humiliated, much to the popular satisfaction. The House of Beresford was noted for greed and courage, in about equal proportion, and held more Irish offices, by crown appointment, than any other of the leading Anglo-Norman families.

The death of George IV occurred in 1830, and he was succeeded by his brother, William IV, popularly known, because of his early voyaging in the navy, as "the sailor king." William was as stupid and ridiculous as George had been faithless, vapid, and dissipated, but, morally, he was a decided improvement on his notorious predecessor.

His reign was marked by the passage of the Electoral Reform bill in England, which was greatly aided by O'Connell and his Irish following, then rather limited, in the House of Commons. In this reign, also, was begun the so-called "National" school system in Ireland—a system carefully devised by government to denationalize the rising and future generations of the Irish people. It was, perhaps, just a little better than no system at all, which had hitherto been the condition. Irish history was carefully excluded from its curriculum, and all mention of English injustice and rapacity was also omitted. So rigid was the censorship that some allusions to Poland's brave struggle for liberty, which crept into one of the text-books, were, on revision, expunged—the leading members of the educational board in Ireland being the Most Rev. Dr. Wheatly, Protestant Archbishop of Dublin, an Englishman, and Mr. Carlisle, a native of Scotland.

The "Tithe War" reached the climax of intensity during the earlier years of William's short régime. Three notable massacres occurred—one at Newtownbarry, in Wexford; another at Carrickshock, in Kilkenny, and a third at Rathcormack, in Waterford. At Carrickshock, the people were partially prepared for resistance, and defeated the armed police with considerable loss, but the other affairs were simply butcheries of the unarmed peasantry, and spread added horror of English rule far and wide throughout the land.

O'Connell's new associations for forwarding of the cause of Repeal of the Union, to which he now gave his earnest attention, were industriously suppressed, but, following his time-honored tactics, he formed others, and boasted that he could, figuratively speaking, "drive a coach and six through any act of the Imperial Parliament directed against the liberties of the people." Nevertheless, he was prosecuted, but defended himself so ingeniously that the government finally allowed the proceedings to go by default.   Owing to the tithe agitation, and resultant slaughters, the Habeas Corpus Act was again suspended, and a still more drastic coercion act was passed; but the indefatigable O'Connell grew still more daring as difficulties multiplied.   At last, William IV, by advice of his ministers, recommended, in a speech from the throne, that the tithe question be taken under consideration.   A committee of the Lords was appointed to investigate and report back upon it.   This, after some delay, they did, and, in the second year of the succeeding reign (1838), the tithes for the support of the clergy of the Established Church were, by act of Parliament, made a charge upon the land, "payable, in the first place, to the parsons by the landlords, and then leviable on the tenants, by distress, along with the rent. Thus, the parsons were relieved from the necessity of coming into immediate collision with the farmers, and raising bloody riots to come at their tenth sheaf and tenth potato." (Mitchel.)   And so the unhappy people continued to be robbed, but under another name.   An improved coercion act was passed under the Whig administration of Lord Grey, by which the Lord Lieutenant was empowered to suppress, and disperse, any meeting he might deem dangerous to the public peace—a power which that functionary did not hesitate to exercise whenever a pretext was afforded him.   In 1834, Daniel O'Connell, in order to test English liberal sentiment, brought up in Parliament the question of repealing the Union Act of 1800.   The motion for considering the proposition was, after a debate of four days' duration, overwhelmingly defeated in the Commons. The Lords, not to be outdone, rejected it unanimously, and carried an address to the king which declared their "unalterable resolution to maintain the integrity of the empire." O'Connell had had his first sharp lesson in dealing with the English Whigs, who were under obligations to him on account of the Reform bill, and who were among his most violent opponents on the question of Repeal. But he was destined to experience much more of their ingratitude, which was, in the end, to prove fatal to the cause of Repeal, and to himself. In one of his impulsive outbursts, the great orator denounced them as "the base, brutal, and bloody Whigs!" Notwithstanding, by a singular contradiction of his strange nature, he had a leaning toward them to the very end of his career.

BOOK XIII

DEALING WITH THE PERIOD BETWEEN THE PASSAGE
OF THE REFORM BILL TO THE FALL OF O'CONNELL
AND DEFEAT OF "YOUNG IRELAND", 1832-1845-1848

CHAPTER I

Accession of Victoria—"Deadliest Reign Since Elizabeth"—O'Connell
Coquettes with the Whigs—Agitation for Repeal of the Union
Renewed—Some Mistakes of the Great Leader

VICTORIA I, daughter and heiress of Edward Duke of
Kent, succeeded her uncle William on the throne in
1837. She was a mere girl, but, from the moment of her
accession, showed a will of her own, which sometimes, according to Greville, caused embarrassment to her ministers,
particularly on the question of "ladies of honor" in her
household. Her reign, according to Mulhall, the statis-
tician, was destined to be "the most destructive in Ireland
since Elizabeth." In May, 1838, the new tithe law, already
dealt with, was enacted; and, in July of the same year, the
hateful English Poor Law system, hitherto unknown in Ireland, was passed by the British Parliament, in defiance of
Irish public opinion, represented by O'Connell, many of
the Catholic prelates, and a large number of high-spirited
Protestant gentlemen. This system, no matter what may
have been the original purpose of it, has proven itself to be
a machine for the wholesale manufacture of paupers, and
has done more to humiliate and degrade the poorer classes
of the Irish people than all the confiscations of Elizabeth
and James, the massacres of Cromwell, and the penal laws
of Anne and the House of Hanover.

A Municipal Reform Act, much needed, in Ireland especially, was, after many vexatious postponements, passed in
1840, and, under it, Daniel O'Connell was elected Lord

Mayor of Dublin—the first Catholic who had enjoyed that honor since James II held court in the Castle. The agitator delighted in tormenting the Orangemen, who abhorred him, by appearing as often as possible "in state," wearing a scarlet cloak, trimmed with ermine, and an enormous gold chain, which recalled King Malachi, and "the collar of gold, which he won from the proud invader." Age had not yet begun to tell on O'Connell, and he was, apparently, in the full flush of manly vigor, and had that boundless good humor which generally accompanies perfect health of mind and body. His speeches abounded in logic and humor. In the latter quality he never had a rival on any platform—

> "That easy humor blossoming
> Like the thousand flowers of spring."

Even some of the Tories and Orangemen, who hated his principles, could not help loving the man. With the masses of the Catholic people, O'Connell possessed an influence which has never been attained by any other popular leader. His word was law, and crime hid its diminished head wherever he appeared. He was never greater than at this period of his wonderful political career.

Two Whig viceroys ruled in Ireland during the earlier years of the reign of Victoria, when the able Lord Melbourne was Prime Minister. These potentates were Lords Normanby and Ebrington—the former a "fine old English gentleman," remarkable for bonhomie and hospitality. Ebrington, although usually urbane, was not so much in favor with the high livers of Dublin. Both "cultivated" O'Connell, who, considerably disappointed, if not disheartened, by the unsuccessful outcome of his motion in favor of Repeal during the late session of Parliament, fell back a little from

his bolder policy, and began to look for "justice to Ireland"
from the Whig administration. "Conciliation" became his
motto, and many of his personal and political friends—
some of whom were needy—benefited by obtaining places
under the crown. This policy he sought to justify by argu-
ing that it was "better to have a friend than an enemy in
power." The people did not quite like this style of argument, but, as they had implicit faith in the wisdom of O'Connell, the masses made little or no objection to his course.
About this time, too, the ministry sought to tempt the agitator himself with offers of high and profitable office. The
pleasant sinecure of the Mastership of the Rolls was held
out to him as an inducement to put himself under obligation to the enemies of his country's independence. He rejected the proffer politely but firmly, saying, in his pecul-
iarly open way, that "he would, doubtless, much enjoy so
comfortable a berth; but that Ireland still needed his services, and he could not desert her cause for any office in the
gift of the crown." This noble reply to a seductive offer
is sufficient vindication of O'Connell against the mean and
malignant charge made by his foes—namely, that he fo-
mented the Emancipation and Repeal agitations for the
"rents" levied for the support of the movements, and not
through motives of patriotism. If ever man truly loved
his country for conscience' sake, making due allowance for
human failings, that man was Daniel O'Connell.

In 1839, the tireless agitator established the Precursor
Society, signifying that, if the Whigs did not grant justice
to Ireland, the organization was merely the harbinger of a
more radical association. As might have been anticipated,
the Whigs did not do justice, and had no thought of doing
justice, to Ireland, although, for two years, O'Connell was

their ally, particularly during the administration of Lord
Normanby, whose war against the Orangemen brought
about a vote of censure in the English Parliament. This
caused his resignation, and he was succeeded by Lord Ebrington, who is chiefly remembered as a viceregal letter-opener.
Ebrington, notwithstanding his courtly manners, was, on
this account, hated most cordially in Dublin, while, on the
other hand, Normanby, who also had had his hand in the
post-office pie, enjoyed an amazing amount of popularity.
But the time had come again for the Whigs to be turned out
of office in favor of the Tories. This occurred in 1841,
when the latter came into power with Ireland's and O'Connell's vindictive enemy, Sir Robert Peel, as Prime Minister.
Meanwhile ejection of tenants from their holdings and emigration on a large scale went hand in hand—the exodus
averaging 100,000 per annum, although the great famine
had not yet thrown its sable shadow on the land.   Mr.
Smith O'Brien, M.P., who was then acting with the Whigs,
made an estimate of Ireland's absentee landlord drain, and
statistically proved that, at this period, Ireland lost $25,000,-
000 a year from that cause alone.   It was no wonder, therefore, that the Irish peasantry, who were the wealth creators,
were truthfully described as "the worst fed, the worst
clothed, and the worst housed people in Europe."   And
Mitchel, dwelling on the ante-famine distress, which was
as nothing to what was so soon to follow, says: "The poorhouses, which had been built under the new law, were all
full; the farmers were paying their tithes to the landlords,
with no possibility of escape, for the bailiffs were always at
the door, and the tithe was levied along with the rent; the
'national' schools were teaching Irish children that there is
no such thing as nationality, and that it is a blessed privilege

to be born 'a happy English child.' Thus the mature and highly elaborated policy of the enemy toward Ireland was in full and successful operation at every point, when, in the spring of 1843, O'Connell announced that it was the 'Repeal Year,' and proceeded to infuse into that movement an energy and power greater than any of his organizations had ever possessed, even in the days of the old Catholic Association."

His outlined policy was formidable. In the first place, he and several of his colleagues declined to go to London and take their seats in Parliament, preferring to arouse the people in every corner of the island to a sense of the danger which menaced the country from the hostile operation of the more recent British enactments, particularly the Land and Poor Law Acts. It was, at last, clear to O'Connell's mind that there was no hope for Ireland except in an immediate repeal of the Union, and this became the war-cry of the Irish people. He called for 3,000,000 enrolled repealers, and soon every parish had its "Repeal Warden," and every priest in Ireland became a propagandist of the new effort for legislative independence. Many patriotic Protestants, who were tired of English misrule, joined the movement also, but thousands of them hung aloof, influenced by the false representations of demagogic bigots, who told them it was not a repeal, but a "Popish" agitation. The prominence of the priests, which was inevitable, gave color to the lie, although the disturbers well knew that O'Connell would gladly welcome Protestant clergymen, of all sects, into the ranks of the Repeal Association. Although an intense Catholic, there was nothing of the bigot in the nature of Daniel O'Connell. The latter opened the campaign of 1843 by moving, in the Dublin Corporation, a resolution for the adoption of a petition to Parliament demanding a repeal of the Union with

Great Britain. This he supported by a powerful speech, in which he recounted the foul means by which the Union Act had been carried, and the long array of evils that had come upon Ireland since its passage. He wanted the status of 1800 restored—Ireland to have her House of Peers and House of Commons, the sovereign of Great Britain to be also the sovereign of Ireland. He left no point untouched, and his speech on that occasion was, perhaps, the ablest he ever delivered on that subject. He had not yet begun to "wither at the top." Although opposed by Isaac Butt, afterward "the Father of the Home Rule Movement," and other able conservatives, the resolution was carried by a vote of 41 to 15. The Corporation of Cork, within a week, adopted a similar resolution.

The English and Irish Tory and Whig press now became alarmed and began to abuse O'Connell in a most virulent manner. The agitator threw himself into the provinces, and rallied the people around him at the "monster meetings" by the hundreds of thousands. Father Mathew's temperance movement had made great headway throughout Ireland, the apostle having been strongly backed by the agitator, so that the Irish masses were in a condition of sobriety and discipline most creditable to behold. At least forty of these great gatherings were held in different parts of Ireland during 1843, but the most notable were those of Tara, Mallow, in Cork, and Mullaghmast in Kildare. The lowest estimate of the Tara gathering was 250,000 people, and the highest 800,000, which was, probably, not far from the truth. The "O'Connell Police," organized by the Repeal Wardens and the priests, kept superb order, so that not a single crime or violent act disturbed the harmony of the meetings. Horsemen came in great numbers, finely mounted, and in ordered array, and these were known as the Repeal Cavalry—men of the same stock as those who had fought so gallantly at the Boyne and at Aughrim. At one meeting, it was estimated that 25,000 horsemen were on the ground. Even the men on foot marched with something of military precision, for soldiering is an instinct with the Irish, and these circumstances produced great alarm in England, until, in an evil moment, O'Connell promised that Repeal would be obtained within six months, and, in the same breath, foolishly announced that he was "a disciple of that sect of politicians who believe that the greatest of all sublunary blessings is too dearly purchased at the expense of a single drop of human blood!" Ireland and the Irish, France and the French, America and the Americans, were amazed by this kind of talk, which, virtually, gave away the whole programme of action to the British ministry. The latter knew, now, they had nothing to fear from O'Connell but words, and words never counted for much with England, unless there were bayonets and cannon balls behind them. Neither Great Britain, nor Ireland, nor the world outside of them, then knew that O'Connell was in his decline—softening of the brain had already set in, and the alert, undaunted leader of 1828 had become the feeble paretic of 1843. This is the whole explanation in a nutshell of O'Connell's ridiculous pusillanimity, so unworthy of his former great career, in the so-called Repeal Year. Charles Gavan Duffy, in his "Young Ireland" and "Four Years of Irish History," has made known the facts in the case, and has, thereby, rescued the memory of Daniel O'Connell from a mass of reproach that would be otherwise justified.

In England, the Repeal movement was regarded with some alarm by the public, but the ministers felt, after

O'Connell had declared himself, quite at their ease. They knew he did not mean to fight, and, further, that no man in Ireland could give the order to try the issue of battle against the forces of Great Britain but himself. Then, again, he had pledged Repeal within six months. The ministers soon devised a plan to make him break his word to the people. They knew they ran no risk in doing so. O'Connell had drawn his own sting. English statesmen declared in Parliament that "Ireland was insatiable in her demands" and "concession had reached its limits." Her interests, they said, could not be considered apart from imperial policy. "Much as I abhor civil war," said Sir Robert Peel, in the House of Commons, "I would prefer that alternative rather than consent to the dismemberment of the empire." In reply to Mr. Berral Osborne, who quoted a statement of Lord Althorpe, in which that nobleman declared that legislative independence should be granted to Ireland if her representatives unanimously demanded it, Sir Robert said he "did not think Lord Althorpe had made such a declaration, but, if he had, he [Peel] was not prepared to abide by it."

This sentiment of the Prime Minister was received by the Commons with every mark of enthusiastic approval—a few Irish, and Radical British, members dissenting from the views of the majority.

CHAPTER II

Famous Monster Meeting at the Rath of Mullaghmast—O'Connell's Versatile Eloquence—He Could Sink or Soar at Pleasure —Foundation of the "Young Ireland Party"

THE condition of Anglo-Irish politics, as stated in the preceding chapter, had reached the "deadlock" stage, when O'Connell convened the Mullaghmast meeting, which was held October 1, 1843. The attendance was vast, and the agitator appeared on the platform in his robes of office as a Dublin alderman. The sculptor, John Hogan, presented him with an antique Irish head-dress, saying, "Sir, I only regret that this cap is not of gold." Hence, O'Connell came to be called "Ireland's uncrowned king." His speech at Mullaghmast was in his best vein. He made fun of Chancellor Sugden, who had recently revoked the commissions of Irish magistrates who took the chair at, or attended, Repeal meetings. The list included O'Connell himself, Lord Ffrench, and other men of note. Smith O'Brien, although not then a Repealer, surrendered his commission in protest, and his example was followed by many other magistrates. The agitator appointed all who were dismissed, or who resigned, "Arbitrators," to settle legal disputes among the people. "Sugden!" exclaimed O'Connell. "What an ugly name the fellow has! Is there a man among you who would call a decent-looking pig Sugden?" Then he grew truly eloquent. "Our ancestors," said he, "suffered through confiding in the English [he alluded strongly to the massacre committed on the rath where he spoke in the reign of Elizabeth, and to the later slaughter at "Gibbet rath," in the neighborhood, during 1798], but we never will confide in them. There is no division among us. We shall stand peaceably side by side in face of every enemy. Oh, how delighted was I in the scenes which I witnessed as I came along here to-day! How my heart throbbed, how my spirit was elevated, how my bosom swelled with delight at the multitude I beheld, and still behold, of the stalwart and strong men of Kildare! I was delighted at the activity and force I saw around me, and my old heart grew young and warm again in admiring the beauty of the dark-eyed maids and matrons of Kildare! Oh, there is a starlight sparkling from the eye of a Kildare beauty, that is scarcely equaled in the sky, and could not be excelled the whole world over! Remember that you are the sons, the fathers, and the brothers and the husbands of such women, and no traitor or coward would have the smiles, or the heart of one among them all! I am in a country celebrated for the sacredness of its shrines and fanes. I am in a country where 'the bright lamp of Kildare's holy fane' burned, with its sacred fire, 'through whole ages of darkness and storm'—that fire which, for six centuries, burned before the high altar, without being extinguished, being fed continuously, without the slightest interruption; and it seemed to me to have been not an inapt representation of the continuous fidelity and religious love of country of the sons and daughters of brave Kildare. Have I any teetotalers [*i.e.* ultra-temperance men] here? [Cries of "Yes, yes, all!"] Yes, it is teetotalism that is repealing the Union. I could not afford to bring you together—I would not dare to bring you together—only that I have the teetotalers—the Father Mathew men —for my police! Ireland! Land of my forefathers! How my mind expands, and my soul walks abroad in something of majesty, when I contemplate thy loveliness, the fidelity of thy sons, and the purity of thy daughters! Oh, what a scene surrounds us! Land of the green valley and the rushing river! Nature herself has written her grandest characters in the fertile fields, the verdant plains, and the purple uplands that environ us! Let any man run around the horizon with his glance and tell me if created nature ever produced anything so bright and so lovely, so undulating, and so teeming with the fruits of the earth? Her water power is sufficient to turn the machinery of the whole world. Oh, my friends and countrymen, Ireland is a land worth fighting for, worth dying for; but, above all, it is a country worth being tranquil, determined, and obedient for. Be guided by me, my countrymen, and you will soon see prosperity, in all its gradations, spreading through a happy, contented, religious land. Yes! I will hear the hymn of a happy people go forth at sunrise to God, in praise of His mercies, and I will see the evening sun set down amid the uplifted hands of a pious and free people. Every blessing that man can bestow, and religion confer, upon the faithful heart shall spread throughout the island. Stand by me, join with me—I will say, be obedient to me—and Ireland, the land of your fathers and mine, shall be prosperous, respected, and free!"

We give the foregoing extracts from O'Connell's Mullaghmast speech, because we consider it one of his most characteristic deliverances—grand, rugged, natural eloquence—with no suspicion of the midnight oil about it—an eloquence picturesque in outline as his own beloved Kerry mountains, and bold and free of utterance as the unchained winds of the wild Atlantic. In nearly all of his speeches,

O'Connell quoted liberally from the writings of his famous friend, Thomas Moore, the foremost of Ireland's poets, whose wondrous melodies did so much to soften aristocratic England toward the cause of Catholic Emancipation. The agitator made good use of the lyrics of the great Irish bard throughout the agitation for Repeal. In fact, he made almost trite the well-known verses—

> "Remember thee! Yes, while there's life in this heart
> It shall never forget, all lorn as thou art,
> More dear in thy sorrow, thy gloom and thy showers,
> Than the rest of the world in its sunniest hours.

> "Wert thou all that I wish thee, great, glorious, and free,
> First flower of the earth and first gem of the sea,
> I might hail thee with prouder, with happier brow,
> But, oh! could I love thee more deeply than now?

> "No, thy chains as they rankle, thy blood as it runs,
> But make thee more painfully dear to thy sons,
> Whose hearts, like the young of the desert bird's nest,
> Drink love in each life-drop that flows from thy breast."

O'Connell's fiercest speech was delivered at Mallow in the county of Cork, where he addressed 200,000 men. Referring to a recent meeting of the British cabinet he said: "They spent Thursday in consulting as to whether they would deprive us of our rights, and I know not what the result of that council may be, but this I know, there was not an Irishman in that council. I may be told the Duke of Wellington was there [groans]. Who calls *him* an Irishman? [Hisses and groans.] If a tiger's cub were dropped in a fold would it, therefore, be a lamb? . . . Suppose for a moment that England found the Act of Union to operate not for her benefit—if, instead of decreasing her debt, it added to her taxation and liabilities, and thus made her burden more onerous, and if she felt herself entitled to call for a repeal of that act, I ask Peel and Wellington—and let them deny it if they dare, and if they did, they would be the scorn and byword of the world—would she not have a right to call for a repeal of that act? And what are Irishmen that they should be denied the same privilege? Have we not the ordinary courage of Englishmen? Are we to be trampled under foot? Oh, they shall never trample me, at least!"

At these words, the enormous gathering broke into a passionate storm of cheering, which did not cease for several minutes, and many cried out: "The word, O'Connell! the word!" by which they meant the signal for revolution, which he alone could give. He bowed his acknowledgments, with the dignity of a monarch, and resumed by saying:

"I was wrong [cries of "No!"]—they may trample me under foot ["Never, never!" and renewed cheering], I say, they may trample me, but it will be my dead body they will trample on, not the living man!"

These words evoked another enthusiastic demonstration, and the people began to think that O'Connell, after all, would throw off the mask of peace, seeing that all hope of constitutional relief was vain, and appeal, however reluctantly, to arms. The chances, in 1843, were largely on his side. The British army in Ireland amounted to about 35,000 men, and nearly half the rank and file were Irishmen, who, in spite of their scarlet coats, had Irish sympathies. Some regiments, while on the march, had met the agitator in his carriage, and, placing their shakos on their bayonets, shouted "O'Connell and Repeal!" Even some of the police were known to be friendly to the cause.

"Brown Bess"—that clumsy, short-ranged old musket—was then the weapon of the armies of all Europe. The Irish were nearly 9,000,000 strong, and could easily have placed 1,000,000 fighting men, from eighteen to sixty, in the field. Before such a force, even though but poorly armed and unprovided with cannon, the British army, even though backed by artillery, could not have stood for a week. It might have held Athlone and Limerick, and a few other fortified points, including Cork, but Dublin would certainly have fallen before the fury of a popular uprising. The Irish people were, as yet, unbroken by famine, pestilence, the poor-house, and emigration, so that all their native courage remained; and what soldiers they are, particularly when aggressive, the whole world, which has witnessed their valor in every clime, can attest. But O'Connell was not a soldier, and both brain and blood were chilled by age.

Jointly with the speeches of O'Connell, who was the sole great orator of the earlier Repeal movement—Sheil having dropped out of it—the Irish national spirit of the time owed its rise and spread to the sentiments of the "Nation," a weekly newspaper of surpassing ability, which had been established in Dublin in October, 1842, by Charles Gavan Duffy, Thomas Davis, and John Blake Dillon. This great paper speedily won an international reputation, and its leading articles were quoted in nearly every language of Europe, while, in America, it soon had a large and growing constituency. It attracted to its brilliant pages the contributions of the brightest intellects of Ireland, regardless of creed or racial origin. Its aim was to unite all Irishmen, Protestant and Catholic, or whether of Celtic, Danish, Norman, or Saxon descent, into one grand confederacy for the re-establishment of Irish independence. Foremost among its contributors were its three founders; John Mitchel, an Ulster lawyer and writer; Thomas MacNevin, Thomas Darcy McGee, John O'Hagan, Richard Dalton Williams, John Savage, J. K. Ingram, Michael Joseph Barry, Denny Lane, James Clarence Mangan, Dennis Florence McCarthy, Maurice Richard Leyne, Michael Doheny, Rev. John Kenyon, Rev. C. P. Meehan, Thomas Francis Meagher, John E. Pigot, Richard O'Gorman, Jr., Thomas Devin Reilly, and many other youthful enthusiasts—all, or nearly all, men of the highest accomplishment, members chiefly of the legal profession, or else devoted to the arts or literature. Their prose and verse teemed with heroic sentiment and breathed heroic resolution. One of themselves laid down their principles in concise form, thus:

> "There's not a man in all the land
>   Our country now can spare,
> The strong man with his sinewy hand,
>   The weak man with his prayer;
> No whining tone of mere regret,
>   Young Irish bards, for you!
> But let your songs teach Ireland yet
>   What Irishmen should do."

All of the gifted "Young Irelanders," as they were called, did not appear on the stage of Irish politics at once, but joined from time to time, between 1842 and 1848—one of the brightest periods of Irish intellectual progress. Even the women caught the patriotic flame, and some of the best poetry that appeared in the "Nation" emanated from the pens of "Speranza" (Lady Wilde), "Eva" (Mrs. Kevin Izod O'Doherty), and "Mary" (Miss Mary Downing). Among the later contributors were, also, John Martin, of Rostrevor; Joseph Brenan, of Cork, and James Finton Lawlor, of the

King's County—a strong writer on agrarian questions. Their chosen leader, at the outset, and up to the time of his premature death, in 1845, was Thomas Davis, a graduate of Trinity College, a Protestant in belief, and the son of a Welsh father and an Irish mother. He was a young man of extraordinary mental power. John Mitchel, in one of his numerous works, calls him "an imperial genius," and, truly, the scope of his knowledge and the diversity of the subjects on which he wrote with such amazing grasp and power go far to confirm the designation applied to him by his almost equally gifted friend and comrade. Davis believed, and rightly believed, that Irish history, language, art, and literature should go hand in hand with the struggle for a restored nationality, and, in this fine combination, he succeeded in enlisting nearly all of Ireland, for some of those who were not Repealers were vehemently attached to their country's language and letters. These Davis never repulsed. Love of Ireland was his ruling passion, and he had the rare power of finally infusing into all who came in contact with him his own patriotic spirit. His death, at the very outset of his career, was an irreparable loss to his country.

These bright young Irishmen were the ardent allies of O'Connell, but they deprecated, in private, his conservative policy, his declarations of attachment to the sovereign, and his uncalled-for snubs to America and France when leading men in both countries proffered their assistance if a resort to other means than "moral force" became necessary. O'Connell was fiercely opposed to negro slavery in the United States and elsewhere, and his prejudice against the French dated from the time of his flight from their country at the period of the Reign of Terror.

What alarmed the government even more than the "monster meetings" was the system of arbitration established by O'Connell, which, virtually, took all civil cases out of the hands of the magistrates appointed by the crown, as the people preferred to adjust their differences in "O'Connell's courts." He also proposed to call a Council of Three Hundred, composed of the leading men of the different counties of Ireland, to assemble in Dublin late in the autumn, to discuss the formation of the new Irish Parliament, which he felt assured he was about to obtain, as a result of the current agitation. This plan was contrary to the Convention Act —only repealed in Parnell's time—which forbade the assemblage of deliberative bodies of a national character in Ireland. Peel and Wellington well knew that the hour had come to strike an effective blow against the Repeal movement, if they did not wish to see O'Connell and his followers masters of the Anglo-Irish situation. The question in their minds was, Would O'Connell show fight or back down? They, evidently, knew that he was declining, or they would never have committed themselves to the policy they immediately adopted.

CHAPTER III

The British Government Grapples with the Repeal Agitation—Clontarf Meeting Proclaimed—The "Projected Massacre"—O'Connell and his Associates Tried for "Conspiracy" and Imprisoned—The Verdict Reversed

THE imperial Parliament was prorogued (adjourned) soon after the Tara meeting, and the queen's speech, composed by her ministers, of course, dealt with the toll-road riots in Wales, and promised inquiry and reform in that principality, while it lectured Ireland on the "discontent and disaffection" which prevailed there, and declared the sovereign's intention, "under Divine Providence, to maintain the Union." In this instance "Divine Providence" was to be represented by the bullets, bayonets, and cannon of the British army.

The last "monster meeting" of the long series was called to assemble on the ancient battlefield of Clontarf, two miles outside of Dublin, on Sunday, October 8, 1843. At dusk on the preceding day a government proclamation was posted on the walls of the Irish capital, forbidding the projected meeting, and was signed by the Chief Secretary, the commander-in-chief in Ireland and the Privy Councilors. All magistrates and officers, "and others whom it might concern," were charged to aid in the execution of the law and stop the gathering. The London "Times" sounded the keynote of English sentiment at this period, when it declared: "Even were the Union gall to Ireland, England must guard her own life's blood, and sternly tell the disaffected Irish, 'You shall have me for a sister or a subjugatrix; that is my ultimatum.'" This was the Tory side of the controversy, and the Whig sentiment found expression in the London "Chronicle," which said: "True, the Union was coarsely and badly accomplished, but stand it must. A Cromwell's violence, with a Machiavelli's perfidy, may have been at work, but the treaty, after all, is more than parchment."

It is not illogical to assert that Ireland, on October 7, 1843, was justified in believing that the Peel-Wellington government contemplated a massacre next day on the sands of Clontarf. The country people were already on the march to the rendezvous from all parts of Leinster. It was a perfectly legal meeting, as the English law lords subsequently declared, but legality was nothing to the British government when it resolved to crush a movement that meant the legislative independence of Ireland, if it was not immediately checked. The Dublin garrison was 6,000 strong, not to mention the Orangemen, who, O'Connell said, were the persons whom the suppression of the meeting might concern, appealed to in the proclamation. The agitator was taken by surprise. His nerve forsook him at the crucial moment, and unfortunately for his country and himself, he resolved to back down. Of course, it must be said in his justification, that the masses pouring into Clontarf were utterly unarmed, and must be slaughtered by the thousand if they came in conflict with the military, nearly all of whom marched out of Dublin during Saturday night, and were in position at Clontarf next morning. There was a chance that the Irish soldiers, at least, might refuse to fire upon the unarmed people, but O'Connell was not in a mood to take a chance of that kind. For himself he had no fear, but he shrank back in horror at the thought of exposing the simple people, who so trusted in him, to massacre. He remembered, also, that the English army did not hesitate to slaughter their own countrymen at the Chartist meeting held near Manchester several years before. How, then, could he place any reliance on the humanity of British soldiers where the Irish only were concerned? Having chosen his course, he set about turning back the multitudes with his old-time energy. The Head Pacificator, as poor Tom Steele was absurdly designated, the Repeal Wardens, and the Catholic clergy all served as members of the Liberator's staff, and rode all night over all the roads converging on Dublin to halt the people and thus avoid a conflict. They were thoroughly successful, and, when morning dawned, the British uniform only was visible on the plains of Clontarf. Therefore, the "projected massacre," as Lord Cloncurry not inaptly called it, was prevented. The Rev. Father Tyrrell, a vehement Repealer, died soon afterward, because of overexertion in his efforts to save his parishioners from English fury. Dwelling on the Clontarf incident, John Mitchel, in his "Last Conquest of Ireland (Perhaps)," says:

"If I am asked what would have been the very *best* thing O'Connell could do on that day of Clontarf, I answer: To let the people of the country come to Clontarf—to meet them there himself, as he had invited them—but, the troops being almost all drawn out of the city, to keep the Dublin Repealers at home, and to give them a commission to take the Castle and all the barracks, and to break down the canal bridge and barricade the streets leading to Clontarf. The whole garrison and police were 6,000. The city had a population of 250,000. The multitudes coming in from the country would, probably, have amounted to almost as many; and that handful of men between ——! There would have been a horrible slaughter of the unarmed people without, if the troops would fire on them—a very doubtful matter— and O'Connell himself might have fallen. It were well for his fame if he had; and the deaths of five or ten thousand that day might have saved Ireland the slaughter, by famine, of an hundred times as many."

Within a week after the Clontarf suppression an inspector of police called on O'Connell and eight of his associates, and demanded bail for their appearance in court on a charge of conspiracy. The bail was furnished.

The action of the government did not, apparently, damp the ardor of the Repealers, who had great accessions to their ranks from unexpected quarters. O'Connell himself appeared to take the matter coolly, and was merry at the expense of the Lord Lieutenant at the weekly meetings of the Repeal Association. He made the people laugh over "the Clontarf war," and ridiculed the law officers, and all concerned therein, saying he would shame them, and, says Mitchel, "come triumphantly out of the prosecution [which he did]; and that he would, thereafter, hold the Clontarf meeting and call together the Council of Three Hundred— neither of which he ever did."

The State prosecutions did not close until near the end of May, 1844, and the alleged conspirators indicted were, Daniel O'Connell, M.P.; John O'Connell, M.P., his son; Charles Gavan Duffy, editor of the "Nation"; Rev. Father Tyrrell, of Lusk, who died while trial was pending; Rev. Father Tierney, of Monaghan; Richard Barnet, editor of "The Pilot," a Catholic publication; Thomas Steele, Thomas M. Ray, secretary of the Repeal Association, and Dr. John Gray, editor of the Dublin "Freeman."

The indictment, according to popular statement, was "thirty-six yards long"; but whether that was true or otherwise, the fact remains that it was "the longest indictment ever seen in any court." The chief charge was "conspiracy," although all O'Connell's meetings had been public, and the object of the conspiracy was alleged to have been the bringing of the laws and their administration into public contempt, and to excite hatred and dissension between various classes of the queen's subjects. The overt acts alleged in the indictment were the speeches delivered by O'Connell, the appointment of Repeal Arbitration Courts, and articles and poems published in the papers of the editors indicted.

Meanwhile, late in 1843, the new Repeal meeting-place, "Conciliation Hall," situated on Burgh Quay, Dublin, had been opened, and the first gathering was presided over by a Protestant gentleman, John Augustus O'Neill, of Bunowen Castle, County Galway, and sympathetic letters were received from many wealthy aristocrats, including Lord Ffrench, Sir Charles Wolseley, Sir Richard Musgrave, Caleb Powell, and last, and most important, William Smith O'Brien, of Cahermoyle, Limerick, destined to be the leader of the abortive revolutionary movement of a later period.

Mr. O'Brien, who was a member of Parliament, had previously acted with the Whigs, but he became disgusted with the whole British system of government in Ireland after the Clontarf episode, and, although a large landholder, threw himself ardently into the popular ranks, in the hour of doubt and danger. In the letter which announced his adhesion to the Repeal cause, he said, among other things: "I would be unworthy to belong to a nation which may claim, at least, as a characteristic that it exhibits increased fidelity in the hour of trial, if I were to delay any longer to dedicate myself to the cause of my country. Slowly, reluctantly, convinced that Ireland has nothing to hope from the sagacity, the justice, or the generosity of the English Parliament, my reliance shall be henceforth placed upon our own native energy and patriotism."

O'Connell seemed greatly rejoiced at the accession of Mr. O'Brien, and alluded to him publicly as "the lineal and worthy descendant of Ireland's greatest monarch, King Brian of Kinkora, who had destroyed the Danish power over his country at the battle of Clontarf," a description which was strictly true.

The trial of the conspirators was proceeded with before a carefully packed jury—all Catholics and all national Protestants being excluded, and the twelve chosen men being mainly members of the Orange Order, more hostile to the independence of the land they were born in than even the English themselves. And O'Connell, in a speech in Parliament, while his sentence was pending, made this same charge, in substance. The proceedings were extremely tedious, lasting in the Court of Queen's Bench, Dublin, from November 2, 1843, to the beginning of February, 1844. The Chief Justice, in summing up, charged against the accused—an unpleasant habit of "Irish" judges—and even alluded to the defendants' counsel as "the gentlemen on the other side"—a bull which exposed him to ridicule, but did not alter the result. The jury, without much delay, brought in a verdict of "guilty" against all the "conspirators," but sentence was not passed immediately. O'Connell was allowed to attend Parliament before judgment was pronounced. This part of the farce was delayed until May 30, when the eight surviving defendants were sentenced to imprisonment, for an indefinite term, in Richmond Bridewell, outside the city, where they suffered no oppression beyond being deprived of their liberty. For three months they were the heroes of the country, and held regular levees in the prison—all the leading people of Ireland, and many from Great Britain, calling upon them to express sympathy. The people would have rushed to their rescue, but O'Connell still counseled peace and submission for six months or a year longer, and promised that, if they but obeyed him faithfully, the government would be baffled and Repeal must surely follow. An appeal had been taken from the Court of Queen's Bench to the House of Lords on a writ of error, and the matter was argued before that body on September the 2d and 4th. Out of nine English judges, whose opinions were asked, eight were for letting the judgment stand, but Lord Coleridge dissented. Lord Chancellor Lyndhurst and Lord Brougham, both bitter haters of Ireland and O'Connell, sustained the views of the majority, but Lord Chief Justice Denman came out against the decision, and said that, if the judgment were to stand, trial by jury in Ireland must be regarded as "a mockery, a delusion, and a snare." He was sustained by two other "law lords"—namely, Cottenham and Campbell—who, like himself, were Whigs and glad to get a slap at their Tory associates. The "lay lords" attempted to get in their votes on a legal question, but were rebuked by Lord Wharncliffe, President of the Council. Then they left the chamber, and the votes of the five "law lords" were taken. Lyndhurst and Brougham were beaten, and the notoriously unfair "judgment" stood reversed.

O'Connell and his associates were liberated from Richmond Bridewell on the 8th of September, 1844, and the event was made the occasion of great rejoicing in Dublin and throughout Ireland. The released agitator was escorted by a large and orderly procession from the prison to his residence in Merrion Square. As his carriage passed in front of the old Irish Houses of Parliament, in College Green, the procession halted. O'Connell stood up in the vehicle and pointed, with emphatic gesture, to the splendid portico. He repeated this action again and again, "turning slowly round and gazing into the faces of the people, without a word." His meaning was so palpable that the multitude broke into a storm of cheers. It was a fond and grand expectation, doomed to cruel disappointment. Although he had triumphed over his enemies, and held all Ireland "in the hollow of his hand," more than ever before, O'Connell came out of Richmond Penitentiary a broken man. Says Mitchel, in dealing with this period:

"I am proud of my people, and have always regarded with profound admiration the steady faith, patient zeal, self-denial, and disciplined enthusiasm they displayed for these two years. To many thousands of those peasants the struggle had been more severe than any war; for they were expected to set at naught potent landlords, who had over them and their children the power of life and death—with troops of insolent bailiffs and ejecting attorneys, and the omnipresent police; and they did set them at naught. Every vote they gave at an election might cost them house and home, land and life. They were naturally ardent, impulsive, and impatient, but their attitude was calm and steadfast. They were an essentially military people, but the great 'Liberator' told them that 'no political amelioration was worth one drop of human blood.' They did not believe the formula, and, in assenting to it, often winked with their eyes; yet steadily and trustfully, this one good time, they sought to liberate their country peacefully, legally, under the advice of counsel. They loyally obeyed that man, and would obey no other. And when he walked in triumph out of his prison, at one word from his mouth, they would have marched upon Dublin, from all the five ends of Ireland, and made short work with police and military barracks."

But he did nothing of the kind. On the contrary, he proceeded to remodel the Repeal Association on a still safer basis, and even went so far as to say he preferred federalism to Repeal. In short, he fell back from his first line of operations as soon as he had won the legal battle in the House of Lords. Rapidly advancing paresis is the only charitable excuse for such unworthy conduct on the part of the once brave and great leader. Healthy opposition, developed under the leadership of O'Brien and Duffy, prevented him, for a time, from further contradicting the general wisdom of his career.

CHAPTER IV

Decline of O'Connell's Political Genius and Power—Death of Thomas Davis, Leader of "Young Ireland"—Smith O'Brien Becomes Head of that Party—Beginning of the Great Famine

IT is really painful to dwell on this portion of O'Connell's life, and to mark the decay of his masterful intellect, little by little. He did not seem to know his own mind, and, again, he began to speak kindly of the Whigs. Young Ireland did not entirely please him—it was too progressive and too independent—and, while he admired the literary prowess of the members of that party, he abhorred their uncompromising spirit and military tendencies. They had but small respect for "moral force." The only real life that remained in the Repeal movement was infused into it by the Young Irelanders, who had now William Smith O'Brien, although then a few years over forty, at their head. There arose on the horizon a war-cloud, which gathered in America over the Oregon boundary question, and Sir Robert Peel openly declared that he sent "a message of peace to Ireland" in view of the pending difficulty with the government of the United States. This "message" consisted, chiefly, in an enlargement of the government grant to Maynooth College, where young Irishmen were educated for the priesthood, and the establishment of three Queen's Colleges—non-sectarian branches of the Dublin University—one in Cork, another in Galway, and the third in Belfast. The "Nation" and Young Ireland generally favored the colleges, for the benefit of higher education, but O'Connell, the able Archbishop

of Tuam, Most Rev. John MacHale, and the majority of
Old Ireland, as the O'Connell wing of the Repealers came to
be called, denounced them as being "godless." A small
section of Young Ireland, headed by Mitchel, was against
them, "not because they were godless, but because they
were English." But this element did little in the way of
opposition and caused no scandalous division on the question. However, both bills passed in Parliament in due
course, and that ended the controversy, which did not fail
to leave a vicious sting behind. O'Connell had much to say
in Conciliation Hall about "rash young men," and his followers were bitter on the "young infidel party"—a false
and scandalous designation. The death of Thomas Davis,
already referred to, occurred about this time—the fall of
1845—and thereby Young Ireland lost its "central fire" and
Ireland, as a whole, her ablest writer and organizer. O'Connell, although he had differed from Davis, entertained for
him a deep affection, and so expressed himself in a pathetic
letter from his home in Kerry to the secretary of the Repeal Association. John Mitchel succeeded Davis as principal political writer of the "Nation" and soon became famous
as an editor, with the soul of Wolfe Tone and the pen of
Dean Swift. The American war-cloud blew over, because
of the backdown of the United States government, which
thus surrendered a valuable portion of the rich territory
of Oregon to the English, who showed great disposition to
fight us on that question.

The terrible potato-blight, which precipitated "the great
Irish famine," began in October, 1845, and did not entirely
expend itself until six years later. It was known as "the
black rot," and, in one night, the sole support of fully three
millions of the poor agricultural people of Ireland was almost

totally destroyed. And the foul odor of the decaying vegetable, bulb and stalk alike, filled the air with the fetid breath of pestilence. Ireland contained immense herds of cattle, great flocks of sheep, huge droves of swine, but these either belonged to the landlords, who were, as a majority, unfriendly to the people, or else had to be sold in the British markets to pay the landlords their exorbitant rents, including the Established Church tithes. These rents were drained out of Ireland to the amount of from twenty to twenty-five million dollars annually, and were spent, for the most part, in England or on the European Continent, because the Irish landlords were too often absentees, who took no interest in their country, or in those whose fate, in great measure, depended upon them. The agents, or rent collectors, they employed to look after their Irish estates were, mostly, hard, harsh men, many of them aliens, and were, if possible, more exacting and tyrannical than even their employers. At that time the Irish land laws were the most drastic in the world, and any failure to pay the rent on the day appointed, or even a refusal to "stand a raise," when the "holding" was already overtaxed, meant eviction, the poor-house, or else famine graves, to such "tenants at will" as did not have enough money to pay their passage to America, or elsewhere out of Ireland.

O'Connell, Smith O'Brien, and other Irish members of Parliament attended the autumn session to urge the government to take action for the relief of the people, and, after some quite unnecessary delay, due to English mistrust, fostered by a prejudiced press, some relief was given by Parliament, but in amount and manner of application wholly inadequate to the desperate crisis which had to be faced immediately. Mitchel claims that the government had been

cognizant of the advent of famine long before its presence
in Ireland was admitted, and that Sir Robert Peel took advantage of the awful situation to break the strength of the
Repeal movement and thus bring Ireland to her knees without risk to Great Britain.

Distress caused some not unnatural discontent among
the class chiefly affected by the potato-rot, and Peel asked
the Parliament to pass a very severe coercion act, but, because of the Whigs' jealousy of the minister, they united
themselves with the Irish members in defeating the measure,
although they were prompt, on their accession to power, to
bring in a more drastic bill themselves. O'Connell became
a changed man, both physically and mentally, after his release from prison. His manner toward "Young Ireland"
became captious and critical, and writers of the period as-
cribe the irritation he showed against that party to the
malign influence of his favorite son, John, who was a dwarf,
whereas his sire was a giant. Parliament, somewhat because
of the arguments of O'Connell and O'Brien, appointed a
couple of commissions to inquire into the relations existing
between landlord and tenant in Ireland. The more note-
worthy of the two was known as "the Devon Commission,"
because Lord Devon happened to be its chairman. Several
months were consumed in the investigation, and when,
finally, the report appeared, in a condensed form, it was,
to all intents and purposes, a special plea for the landlord
system in Ireland, and gave impetus to the "clearance," or
ejectment, system, which rendered the people homeless by
the thousand.

Mr. Mitchel summed up the result thus: "Such was the
Devon Commission programme—Tenant Right to be disal-
lowed; one million of people to be removed, that is swept

out on the highways, where their choice would be America, the poor-house, or the grave. The 'integrity of the empire' was to be menaced no more by half-million Tara meetings; those ordered masses of the 'Irish enemy,' with their growing enthusiasm, their rising spirit, and their still more dangerous discipline, were to be thinned, to be cleared off, but all in the way of 'amelioration.' They were to be ameliorated out of their lives. There was to be a battue of benevolence. Both government and the landlords had been thoroughly frightened by that vast parade of a nation, and they knew they had only been saved by O'Connell, and his peace principle, and O'Connell was not immortal."

But the famine grew rapidly in volume, and 1846 saw it almost in full tide. The government appropriated several millions of pounds sterling for the establishment of public works in Ireland, and this policy was supposed to be a measure of relief for the destitute. But the business was so bunglingly administered that the unfortunate poor derived comparatively little benefit from the scheme. No doubt, a majority of those who voted for the measure in Parliament were actuated by benevolent motives, as were also many generous British persons who subscribed liberally for the relief of the famine-stricken, but Sir Robert Peel stands accused of callousness, and even inhumanity, in not attending to the warnings given him by many Irish members of Parliament, who saw the glaring defects of the relief system his government had inaugurated.

The administration of relief measures in Ireland placed 10,000 clerks and inspectors on the pay roll, and these officials ate up a large proportion of the money voted by Parliament in salaries. The defeated Coercion bill had been introduced by Sir Robert Peel in advance of the bill to repeal the Corn Laws. Irish opposition, aided by the Whigs, delayed, and, as has been stated, defeated the first measure. "In vain," says the historian already quoted, "it was represented to them that this was only delaying Corn Law repeal, which would 'cheapen bread.' " O'Brien replied that it would only cheapen bread to Englishmen, and enable them to devour more and more of Irish bread and give less for it. (This was because a duty which operated for the benefit of Irish grain as against foreign imports was removed when the Corn Laws were finally repealed.) However, notwithstanding the final defeat of the Coercion measure, for that session, the corn was made free of duty, and the Irish grain raiser, who had hitherto sold at a fair profit in England, had now for competitors all the grain, or corn, growing nations of the world, just, as in later times, the Irish raiser of flocks and herds has had to contend with the cheap meats sent from this and other countries to the "United" Kingdom. The English Protectionists were angry with Peel for embracing free trade—for up to 1846 Great Britain was a highly protected country, and their votes went with the Whigs and the Irish to oust him from office on the Coercion question. He resigned on the 29th day of June, 1846, and was succeeded by the Whig Prime Minister, Lord John Russell—destined to be a veritable scourge to and destroyer of the Irish race. Sir Robert Peel, although defeated in Parliament, was idolized by the English masses, on account of his "cheap bread" policy, and because he had "put down" O'Connell. When he left the House of Commons to retire to his Tamworth estate, the streets of London were thronged with people, who uncovered out of respect for him as his carriage rolled by. He had reached the English heart by way of the English stomach—always sensitive to good treatment. But, while he had filled the English stomach, he had left myriads of Irish stomachs void and aching. Yet, it must be acknowledged that of the two statesmen in whose hands the fate of Ireland was placed during the awful famine period, Sir Robert was the better disposed toward the famine-crushed people. He had displayed his enmity toward a free press in Ireland by causing the Dublin "Nation" to be prosecuted, because, in replying to an English editorial on the value of the railroads recently constructed in Ireland in the matter of rapid concentration for the suppression of rebellion, it had pointed out how the Irish could use the roads in self-defence and for the destruction of their enemies. This prosecution failed, because the government was ashamed to pack the jury after the O'Connell episode, which was still fresh in the public mind. Some Repealers were allowed on it, and there was, of course, a verdict of acquittal. Another tyrannical act of the Peel government was the imprisonment of Smith O'Brien in the cellar of the House of Commons, because he had refused to serve on the Railroad Committee—feeling that he could better serve his people in Ireland. A majority of the "Old Ireland" party in Conciliation Hall looked upon Mr. O'Brien's action as rather Quixotic, thus sustaining English sentiment, but the "Young Ireland" party in that hall voted him an address of confidence and sent a deputation to London who presented the document to the distinguished prisoner. He was soon afterward released, and returned to his home duties.

A new act for Outdoor Relief was passed by Parliament, with what was known as "the Quarter-Acre Clause" added on. It provided that if any farmer holding land applied for Outdoor relief, he must first give up all his land, except a quarter of an acre, to his landlord. This made ejectment still easier, and many farms were given up without even the formality of a notice to quit.

"On the 6th of March, 1847," says the historian of "The Last Conquest," "there were 730,000 heads of families on the public works. Provision was made by the Outdoor Relief Act for dismissing these in batches. On the 10th of April, the number was reduced to 500,723 heads of families. Afterward, batches of 100,000 or so were, in like manner, dismissed. Most of these had now neither house nor home, and their only resource was in the Outdoor Relief. For this they were ineligible if they held but one rood of land. Under the new law, it was able-bodied idlers only who were to be fed; to attempt to till even a rood of ground was death. Steadily, but surely, the 'government' people were working out their calculation, and the product anticipated by 'political circles' was likely to come out about September, in round numbers, *two millions of Irish corpses!*"

CHAPTER V

The Famine Slaughter in Ireland—Food Exported from the Starving Country to England—Whig Alliance Gets Repealers Fighting—"Peace Resolutions"—Meagher's "Sword Speech"—"Young Ireland" Secedes from O'Connell

MITCHEL, who had every opportunity to be correctly informed on the subject, asserts that 300,000 persons died in Ireland by famine, or fever produced by famine, in the year 1846, and the death-rate from the same causes multiplied exceedingly during the succeeding year. The Whig government, which had been so glibly "liberal" toward the Irish while the Tories were in power, pretended to do much to stay the visitation, but, in reality, their mechanism for relief was even worse than that of the Peel administration.   While the government was importing cheap corn ("yellow meal" corn) into Ireland from America, splendid consignments of Irish wheat, beef, mutton, pork, and poultry were daily shipped to Great Britain, and American captains of dismantled war vessels, which had been laden with food and sent to Irish ports to deliver it for the benefit of the starving, were astonished to view the excessive, and extraordinary, exportation of the choicest of food-products from a country which the English government calmly allowed the outside world to believe was a blasted waste.   It is computed that enough provisions were sent from Ireland to Great Britain, during 1846, to feed 10,000,000 people for the period of one year.   A native government would, under such conditions, have closed the ports against export.   But the English army was there, in full strength, to keep the ports wide open for the benefit of the English garrison, to wit the exterminating landlords. There was no need to "pass the hat" for Ireland if Ireland had been under a native government.   And this is true of that country in every period of what has been well termed "artificial famine."

And while famine and pestilence were holding high carnival in Ireland, the English people—even the laborers —were living in clover, so to speak.   The consumption of tea, coffee, and currants largely increased.   There was work for everybody who desired to work, and the Sunday plum-pudding graced the table of every English workingman, until it became an aphorism that "the exact correlative of a Sunday dinner in England is a coroner's inquest in Ireland."

The most momentous moral event that occurred in Ireland during 1846, was the secession of Young Ireland from "Old Ireland" in the July of that year. The quarrel, which had been slumbering for some time, was forced to an issue by the introduction at the weekly meeting of the Repeal Association, in Conciliation Hall, of the Peace-at-any-price resolutions introduced by O'Connell in person, doubtless at the suggestions of his factious and intriguing son, John— whose brother, Maurice, next to the Liberator himself, the ablest man of the O'Connell family—declined to attend the meeting at "the Hall" because "the Young Liberator," as he was called, virtually ruled there. The particular sentiment in the resolutions that immediately led to the secession was couched, substantially, in these terms: "That under no circumstances were men justified in seeking political ameliorations by other means than moral force." In another sentence it was declared that the Repealers of Ireland "abhorred and stigmatized the sword." The Young Irelanders were willing enough to uphold "moral force" while there remained a reasonable chance of repealing the Union by that method, but they refused to bind themselves to the absurd pledge that they must not resort to physical force, even as a last resort. The sad truth is, O'Connell had made a compromise, almost an alliance, with the Whigs, and even allowed Richard Lalor Sheil, who had accepted office under the Russell administration, to be elected in the borough of Dungarvan, County Waterford, without opposition. Smith O'Brien, Mitchel, Meagher, and other Young Irelanders, had vehemently protested against this surrender to the Whigs, and also against place-begging, which had again come into practice. O'Connell, therefore, wished to get rid of them, and of the "Nation" newspaper which represented them; and there can be no doubt that the obnoxious resolutions were introduced for the purpose of driving "the rash young men," as he called them, out of the Repeal Association.

He was not present when the final debate occurred, but his son John was. The proceedings lasted two days, and the orators on both sides almost exhausted the resources of eloquence in their arguments. By far the most brilliant speech of the occasion was delivered, in opposition to the Resolutions, by Thomas Francis Meagher, then in his twenty-third year—the same who, in 1861-63, commanded the Irish Brigade in the Army of the Potomac during the Civil War. His effort has been called the "Sword Speech," and, in prose, is a companion piece to Koerner's celebrated "Sword Song." A few excerpts will serve to illustrate its scope, as well as the style of the youthful orator: "The soldier is proof against an argument, but he is not proof against a bullet. The man who will listen to reason, let him be reasoned with; but it is the weaponed hand of the patriot that can alone prevail against battalioned despotism. Then, I do not condemn the use of arms as immoral, nor do I conceive it profane to say that the King of Heaven, the Lord of Hosts, the God of Battles! bestows His benediction upon those who unsheathe the sword in the hour of a nation's peril.

"From that evening on which, in the valley of Bethulia, He nerved the arm of the Jewish girl to smite the drunken tyrant in his tent, down to this day in which He has blessed the insurgent chivalry of the Belgian priest, His Almighty hand hath ever been stretched forth from His throne of light to consecrate the flag of freedom—to bless the patriot's sword. Be it in the defence, or be it in the assertion of a people's liberty, I hail the sword as a sacred weapon; and if it has sometimes taken the shape of the serpent and reddened the shroud of the oppressor with too deep a dye, like the anointed rod of the High Priest, it has, at other times, and as often, blossomed into celestial flowers to deck the freeman's brow!

"Abhor the sword—stigmatize the sword? No, my lord [the Lord Mayor of Dublin presided], for in the passes of the Tyrol it cut to pieces the banner of the Bavarian and through those cragged hills struck a path to fame for the peasant insurrectionist of Innsprück!

"Abhor the sword—stigmatize the sword? No, my lord, for at its stroke a giant nation started from the waters of the Atlantic, and by its redeeming magic, and in the quivering of its crimson light, the crippled colony sprang into the attitude of a proud Republic—prosperous, limitless—invincible!

"Abhor the sword — stigmatize the sword? No, my lord, for it swept the Dutch marauders out of the fine old towns of Belgium — scourged them back to their own phlegmatic swamps, and knocked their flag and sceptre —their laws and bayonets, into the sluggish waters of the Scheldt.

"My lord, I learned that it was the right of a nation to govern herself—not in this hall, but upon the ramparts of Antwerp. This, the first article of a nation's creed, I learned upon those ramparts, where freedom was justly estimated, and the possession of the precious gift was purchased by the effusion of generous blood.

"My lord, I honor the Belgians, I admire the Belgians, I love the Belgians for their enthusiasm, their courage, their success, and I, for one, will not stigmatize, for I do not abhor, the means by which they won a citizen king, a chamber of deputies—"

At this point the young orator was interrupted by John O'Connell, who was driven mad, for the moment, by the applause bestowed upon Meagher by the audience. In effect, he said that either the Association must cease to exist or Mr. Meagher and those who agreed with him to be members of it. Smith O'Brien protested and Meagher attempted to resume his speech, but John O'Connell again interrupted him—the Lord Mayor, who would seem to have been a poor stick, permitting the outrage.

Thereupon, O'Brien, Mitchel, Meagher, and their friends rose in a body and left the hall. It proved to be a fatal step, both for their country and themselves, but they were fairly, or unfairly, driven to it. Free speech being denied them, on the most absurd of pretences, they could only appeal to the public. This they did very soon, and the result was a newer, and bolder, and, we may add, brighter Repeal Association, known as "The Irish Confederation."

CHAPTER VI

Ireland Asks for her Own Money to Check Famine—England Insists on Begging for her, Instead of Acting Generously and Justly— Increase of Famine Horrors—Death of Daniel O'Connell

IT has been claimed by able writers on the greatest of numerous Irish famines that had England, by her Parliament, made a grant of £20,000,000—$100,000,000—for the relief of Irish distress, in 1846, the horrors of that year could have been prevented, and there would have been no recurrence of the danger in the years immediately following. The Irish leaders of the time, however they may have differed otherwise, were united on this one point—they begged no alms for Ireland from England or from foreign nations. The English themselves did all the begging that was done, both in their own country and outside of it. O'Connell, O'Brien, and their colleagues in Parliament asked that Ireland's surplus contribution to the imperial revenue be devoted to purposes of relief, but this was refused. It enraged the government to be reminded of the fact that Ireland contributed any revenue at all, whether surplus or otherwise. Instead, the ministry, through Parliament, tacked still another tax on Ireland, in the shape of a "Labor-rate Act." It was, plainly put, merely an addition to the existing "Poor rate." The British treasury advanced money to give employment. This was not a donation, as many have supposed. It was provided by law that the money so advanced—although Ireland was entitled to a large portion of it out of her own tax contribution—was to be repaid to the British Exchequer within ten years, and this was why the Labor rate was added to Ireland's other burdens—burdens that would have been immediately mitigated by a friendly or native legislature. No period of Irish history is more exasperating to the Irish race than this. First, the people were beggared by vicious legislation, and, next, they were made to appear as paupers, when they were, in reality, borrowers from the imperial treasury, to which their ill-fated country contributed—as it still contributes—much more than the inadequate advance allowed for the famine crisis.

But protests, explanations, and expostulations on the part of the Irish members were vainly uttered. Lord John Russell, "the vicious and victorious economist," had everything his own way in Parliament, and Ireland, overflowing with plenty, was surrendered to famine and pestilence—the most

glaring political crime of the nineteenth century. No wonder that when deaths by starvation multiplied beyond ordinary enumeration, hundreds of coroners' juries throughout Ireland returned verdicts of "wilful murder against
John Russell, commonly called Lord John Russell, the British Prime Minister." The landlords continued their barbarous clearances, and the wail of the emigrants, on their
sad way to the seaports, where they were to take ship for
foreign lands—mainly the United States—mingled with
the caoine ("keen," or funeral cry) of the myriads who
wept tears that wither above the thousands of famine-slain
corpses consigned to coffinless graves! In some parishes a
hinged coffin was used, so as to give some appearance of
decency. When the remains were lowered in the grave, a
spring allowed the bottom of the casket to swing down-
ward. The body was thus allowed to fall into the pit.
Then the coffin was withdrawn, to be used again, and yet
again, for the same ghastly purpose; while the earth was
shoveled hastily on the remains of the unfortunate thus
economically interred! The Whigs, in order to emphasize
their sway, and to further awe the discontented, passed,
in 1846-47, the most stringent coercion act placed upon
Ireland since the time of George I. It was, virtually, a
curfew, as well as a disarming, act, which bound Ireland
hand and foot in a bed of torture, while the English ministry held a clinic in their Parliament to illustrate how
easily a recalcitrant patient might be starved below the
resistance point. In fact, within one year, the soul was
starved out of Ireland. Her very valor fled, or found expression in eloquent words rather than necessarily desperate
acts. O'Connell was in his dotage. He could no more
than make protest. A judgment had fallen upon the

prophet. The "drop of blood," whose shedding might have, were the sacrifice timely made, freed his country, had festered into a mountain of putrefaction. To him Ireland had become a virtual Himmon—a vale of slaughter. The dim remains of his genius were further clouded by remorse. In January, 1847, he left his country's shores forever. In February, he uttered his last appeal in her behalf in the English House of Commons. Even the brutal majority of that body listened to their once formidable, now broken, enemy with respect. The voice that thundered at Tara, with the resonance of kingly power, had fallen to a feeble treble—just as the war shout of '98, on the hills of Wexford, had sunk into the tremulous wail above the famine graves of '47.

Soon afterward, the aged and unhappy man, accompanied by one of his sons and his chaplain, Dr. Miley, betook himself to the Continent of Europe in the hope of recuperation, mental and corporeal. But no relief came. Everywhere along the route, the people thronged to greet the Catholic Liberator, but he heeded not their plaudits. The leonine head was sunk on the ample bosom. The brilliant eyes of azure gray, that had so often flashed with potency, melted with pathos, or sparkled with humor, were dim as the blue waters of a lake under a clouded sky. He desired to reach Rome—to give up the ghost where perished the first Pope, and where, two hundred and fifty years before, Ireland's greatest soldier, Hugh O'Neill, had laid his weary heart to rest in hopeless exile. But death summoned O'Connell at Genoa—Genoa the superb—in Italy. There, on May 15, 1847, while the Irish famine was at the floodtide of its horrors, Daniel O'Connell, the greatest of Irish statesmen and the weakest of Irish revolutionists, died.

Dr. Miley received his last wishes—his heart to Rome; his body to Ireland. It was a pious, but not a noble, bequest. A man may offer his soul to his Church, which is the agent of his God, but his heart, of right, belongs to his country. However, his will was accomplished. That "heart of melting ruth" reposes in a golden urn within the precincts of St. Peter's. The body, which received in Ireland the grandest welcome ever given to the remains of mortal, and which was accompanied to the tomb by the mightiest funeral battalia that ever shook the ancient streets of Dublin with their solemn tread—the body of the great O'Connell reposes in Glasnevin Cemetery, and above the sarcophagus which enshrines it rises a majestic "pillar tower," which, as was said of himself, when standing sublime on mountain heights, "looks far and wide into the island, whose struggles and whose glory shall be forever associated with his name."

CHAPTER VII

Lord Clarendon Viceroy—The Famine Grows in Destructiveness—
Ravages of Typhus Fever—Heroic Conduct of the Irish Priests—
John Mitchel Secedes from the Irish Confederation—The French
Revolution—Irish Sympathy—"Treason-Felony" Bill Passed

LORD CLARENDON, Viceroy of Ireland under the Russell ministry, was a Whig "conciliator" of the Catholics. Among his appointees from members of that persuasion was J. H. Monahan, a lawyer, who was created attorney-general. It was needful that this official should also be a member of Parliament, and, as a vacancy occurred in Galway City, Monahan addressed the electors as a Whig, while a country gentleman, named Anthony O'Flaherty, became the nominee of the Repealers. Young Ireland sent down Mitchel, Meagher, and others from Dublin to help out O'Flaherty, but some of the Galway freeholders were venal, and sold out for Whig money. After a contest which lasted five days, Monahan proved victorious by a very few votes. In that day, terrorism and corruption at the polls did not so nearly involve the loss of a seat as in our own times, and Mr. Monahan went to Parliament and became a judge in after days.

After the death of O'Connell, the Repeal Association dragged out a slowly, but surely, decaying existence. John O'Connell's leadership was distasteful to many of his father's friends, and one by one they dropped away, or else joined the ranks of Young Ireland or the Irish Confederation— the name under which it organized. Smith O'Brien became its chief—a brave man, a good man, honest and utterly devoted to the cause, but lacking in the daring moral qualities which can alone make any leader, whether he employ moral or physical force, a successful revolutionist. His ablest associates were, as a writer and keen caustic debater, John Mitchel; and as an orator, "in the highest sense of that term," Thomas Francis Meagher. These two men were of the first magnitude in their respective orbits, with Thomas Darcy McGee, Richard O'Gorman, Jr., Charles Gavan Duffy, John Blake Dillon, Michael Doheny, and Maurice Richard Leyne—O'Connell's nephew—were little behind them in point of merit. The "Nation" became quite as brilliant as in the days of Davis, and, as Mitchel was chief editorial writer, gradually assumed an aggressive national tone that greatly enlarged its constituency and enhanced its influence. Several public meetings of the Confederation were held in Dublin during 1847, and, at them, Meagher delivered addresses unequaled for power and bril-

liancy since the days of Grattan and Sheil. He even made
a deep impression on the ferocious Orangemen of Belfast,
and his speech on the occasion of his visit to that city is regarded as one of the masterpieces of oratory uttered in the
English tongue.

Sparkling speeches and ringing poems did not, however,
disturb the policy of the Russell administration, which continued its deadly work with the remorselessness of a mow-
ing machine. The strength of Ireland fell before it. Ruins
of the houses of the evicted peasantry disfigured the island
throughout its extent. The poorhouses were full to burst-
ing. The roadsides were mile-stoned with the nameless
dead, and loads of hideous pine coffins, provided, in the later
stages of the famine plague, by the "Poor Law Unions,"
startled the traveler in the rural districts. These coffins
were entirely unpainted, and had no interior lining. Typhus fever—about as revolting and contagious as the Black
Death itself—spread in many districts, and was not confined solely to the poor. Many men, not of the working
classes, set superb examples of courage in attending the
sick and burying the dead. The whole body of the Catholic clergy, prelates as well as priests, exposed themselves to
the worst effects of the scourge in administering the sacraments, or providing for the corporeal wants of the afflicted.
A large percentage of these noble gentlemen fell victims to
their glorious zeal. Many of the Protestant clergy also
showed heroic devotion to the suffering Catholic people, the
more so, as the famine did not so largely prey upon the
non-Catholic population, although many of the latter died of
typhus. Busybody "philanthropists," who were too small
of mind to dissociate charity from creed, annoyed the poor
sufferers by forcing Protestant Bibles upon them in the

midst of their misery. But this was a comparatively small class, except in the remote seacoast villages, and the meddlers were frowned upon by the better Protestant element, who did not believe in the soul's salvation by a sectarian Bible, fortified by a bowl of soup.

As the Irish Confederation did not seem to advance much beyond the policy of the Repeal Association, and as Charles Gavan Duffy objected to John Mitchel's revolutionary artifices, the latter severed his connection with the "Nation," and, in February, 1848, established a paper of his own, called the "United Irishman." This publication he filled with his own spirit, and it soon outstripped all contemporaries in popular favor and general circulation. He was assisted, editorially, by Thomas Devin Reilly—a brilliant and fiery writer, who subsequently died while editing a newspaper in Washington, D. C.—and others of his own way of thinking. He attacked the English ministry; he attacked the viceroy and "the Castle Gang"; he attacked the landlords; he smote the peace preachers — including some of the clergy—hip and thigh. He declared that "the life of a peasant was worth the life of a peer." He exposed the bogus "trial by jury" methods, as exemplified in the case of O'Connell and his colleagues, and, in short, he tore up "government" and "society" in Ireland as they had not been uptorn since the time of Swift. In regard to the crops, he advised the people to feed their families and themselves first, and give a reasonable part of what remained to the landlords. "Hold the harvest" was his watchword. In addressing the Protestants of Ulster—himself being one of them—he grew powerfully eloquent. "The Pope may be Antichrist, as you claim," wrote Mitchel, "but, at least, he does not issue writs of ejectment in Ulster!"

Unable to stomach the more moderate policy of Smith O'Brien, Dillon, and others, Mitchel seceded from the Confederation, followed by his friend, Devin Reilly. Meagher, in the debate which preceded this action, took sides with O'Brien. He did not believe the time set for revolution opportune, while England was at peace, and Ireland weakened by famine and pestilence as she was. "Is an insurrection probable?" he asked. "If probable, is it practicable? Prove to me that it is, and I, for one, will vote for it this very night.

"You know well, my friends," he continued, "that I am not one of those tame moralists who say that liberty is not worth a drop of blood. Men who subscribe to such a maxim are fit for outdoor relief and nothing better. Against this miserable maxim, the noblest virtue that has served and sanctified humanity appears in judgment. From the blue waters of the Bay of Salamis; from the valley over which the sun stood still and lit the Israelite to victory; from the cathedral in which the sword of Poland has been sheathed in the shroud of Kosciusko; from the convent of St. Isidore, where the fiery hand that rent the ensign of St. George on the plains of Ulster has crumbled into dust; from the sands of the desert, where the wild genius of the Algerine so long has scared the eagle of the Pyrenees; from the ducal palace in this kingdom, where the memory of the gallant and seditious Geraldine enhances, more than royal favor, the nobility of his race; from the solitary grave which, within this mute city, a dying request has left without an epitaph—oh! from every spot where heroism has had its sacrifice, or its triumph, a voice breaks in on the cringing cowards who cheer this wretched maxim, crying out: 'Away with it! Away with it!'"

"Inciting to insurrection" was called "sedition" in Ireland previous to 1848. In February of that year, Louis Philippe, the Orleanist King of the French, was hurled from his throne by a popular revolution. The Second Republic was immediately proclaimed, with M. Lamartine as President. All Europe became infected with a desire to revolt. There were uprisings in Prussia, in Austria, in Poland, in Italy, and elsewhere. And Ireland, despite her depleted condition, also became excited, particularly in the chief cities. Revolutionary clubs, of which the nucleus had existed for some years, were formed in Dublin, Cork, and other places of importance. These Mitchel counseled to procure arms, whether guns or pikes made little difference, as "Brown Bess" was not a repeater, nor had it a long range. The advice was heeded. Gunsmiths did a thriving secret business, and thousands of pike-heads were quietly manufactured by patriotic blacksmiths. The handles were cut by trusty rural confederates in the groves of ash trees with which the country abounded. Even Gavan Duffy and the "Nation" newspaper grew more warlike.

Meagher, before the outbreak of the French Revolution, had tried to become member of Parliament for his native city of Waterford, hoping to form an independent party in the House of Commons, but, through a combination of the Whigs and Old Irelanders, he was defeated by Sir Henry Winston Barron. Mitchel, although the young orator's firm friend and admirer, publicly, in his newspaper, prayed for his defeat, saying, in the same connection: "If Mr. Meagher were in Parliament, men's eyes would be attracted thither once more; some hope of 'justice' might again revive in this too easily deluded people."

Meanwhile, the Dublin clubs, fired to enthusiasm by the

teachings of Mitchel, who also published papers on military evolutions in the "United Irishman," continued to arm. It was estimated that, by the middle of March, they numbered 10,000 men, indifferently armed and imperfectly drilled, but capable of great things in a sudden uprising, which their idol was laboring to bring about.

The Irish Confederation, at a public meeting held on March 15, in Dublin, moved, through Smith O'Brien, an address of congratulation to the victorious French revolutionists, which was carried without dissent. A similar address was adopted by a mass meeting of the citizens of Dublin, and Messrs. William Smith O'Brien, Thomas Francis Meagher, and Edward Hollywood—the latter representing the Trades of Dublin—were elected a deputation to go to Paris and present them to Lamartine. The day after the latter of the two gatherings, O'Brien, Meagher, and Mitchel were called upon by a police magistrate and asked to give bail to stand trial for seditious conduct. They gave the required bail, and, immediately thereafter, the delegates started for Paris. There they were received by Lamartine —a poetical admirer of England—who treated them politely but coldly and made but vague reply to their addresses. But the people of Paris greeted them fraternally, and many offers of assistance in men, money, and material were made in case of need. As a matter of fact, the government of Lamartine was even more anglomaniacal than that of Louis Philippe, or, rather, M. Guizot, and this was one of the many reasons why it did not long endure.

On his way home from Paris, Smith O'Brien dropped into the London Parliament chamber. It would seem that the law against sedition was not sufficiently stringent for the purpose of convicting Irishmen who wanted to repeal the Union by other than "moral" means. Therefore, a new measure was required, and, on this, which was "railroaded through" within twenty-four hours from the time of its introduction, "the faithful Commons" were working hard when the Irish leader entered the House. The bill, known as the Treason-Felony Act, which placed Irish political offences on a plane with arson, burglary, and other heinous offences, was a Whig invention, but had full-fledged Tory support. O'Brien rose to protest against it, and was met with a storm of howls, cat-calls, and other vulgar noises, which, at first, drowned his voice. But he persisted, and compelled the enemies of his country to listen to some wholesome truths. One sentence from his speech deserves to live: "If it be treason to profess disloyalty to this House, and the government of Ireland by the Parliament of Great Britain—if that be treason, I avow the treason!"

But, all the same, the bill became a law by tremendous majorities, and thenceforth every Irishman who resented the usurpation of his country's government by the Parliament of an alien nation was, in sight of the "law," a felon, either convicted or unconvicted, according to circumstances.

The three delegates to Paris met in Dublin, after O'Brien's return from London, and Meagher, in the Music Hall, presented the Irish Confederates with "a magnificent tricolor of green, white, and orange—symbolizing all the Irish parties—surmounted by a pike-head." This flag is still recognized as the national ensign by the revolutionary Irish element.

As many non-Catholics held aloof from both the Repeal Association and the Irish Confederation, because of alleged fear of clerical control—for many Catholic priests were members of both, and particularly of the first named—Protestant Repeal clubs, or associations, were formed in Dublin, Drogheda, Belfast, "and even in Lurgan, a great centre of Orangeism." The government, however, manipulated matters in such a way that the Orange element became more furiously "loyal" to the English interest than ever, and the crop of outrages in Ulster showed that the ferocious spirit of 1798 was not entirely subdued in the descendants of the yeomanry of that period. These fanatics were told, of course, that repeal of the Union meant the sway of the Pope and that "brass money and wooden shoes," as in Jacobite days, would be their portion. They could not see that their country was being robbed, ruined, and starved to death by the existing English system of government.

CHAPTER VIII

Failure of "Sedition" Prosecutions—John Mitchel Arrested and "Tried" under New "Treason-Felony" Act—His Jury Carefully Packed—Bold Speech in Dock—Excitement in Court—Failure to Rescue—Transported Beyond the Seas for Fourteen Years

O'BRIEN and Meagher were tried immediately on charges of sedition, but, as the juries were not, for that time, carefully packed, both were acquitted, amid great popular rejoicings. The case with Mitchel, however, was desperate. He was the only Irish leader the government really feared. He knew what he wanted, and he said it. Either Clarendon or he must fall, and the Treason-Felony Act gave the viceroy the weapon he needed to get rid of his intrepid enemy. The "United Irishman" had become a great power in the land, and to crush both its editor and itself became a labor of love with Lord Clarendon. Acting

on the advice of the astute Attorney-General, Monahan, the
indictments, two in number, for sedition against Mitchel
were abandoned, and, on the 12th of May, he was arrested
by policemen, in his own house, on a charge of Treason-
Felony.   The "trial" was hurried onward—no pains being
spared by government to secure a properly packed jury of
"True Blue" Orangemen—and both Ireland and Great
Britain awaited the result with unconcealed impatience.
Should Mitchel be acquitted the English usurpation in Ireland might be fatally endangered.   Should he be convicted
—the question was, Would rescue and insurrection follow?

The jury panel was industriously weeded of Catholics
and liberal Protestants, by the sheriff, but Englishmen,
servants of the Lord Lieutenant, in the sense of being
patronized by him, were freely admitted.   As the crown, in
Ireland, possessed the power of unlimited challenge, the
selection of twelve men, warranted to convict, was by no
means a herculean task.

Mitchel was brought into court from Newgate prison, on
May 25, and was placed in the same dock where Emmet
stood before Norbury forty-five years gone by.   He was
defended by old Robert Holmes, Emmet's brother-in-law,
the eloquent Nestor of the Irish bar.   Baron Lefroy, a
rank old Tory, was the presiding judge.   Mitchel himself
says in his "Last Conquest":

"The crown used its privilege of peremptory challenge
to the very uttermost.   Every Catholic, and most Protestants, who answered to their names, were ordered to 'stand
by.'   There were thirty-nine challenges: Nineteen Catholics—all the Catholics who answered to their names—were
peremptorily set aside, and twenty other gentlemen, who,
though Protestant, were suspected of some national feel-

ing, were also set aside; that is to say the crown dare not go to trial with me before the people, Catholic or Protestant. The twelve men finally obtained by the sifting process had among them two or three Englishmen; the rest were faithful slaves of the Castle and all Protestants of the most Orange dye."

The "overt acts" were proven by Mr. Mitchel's speeches and writings, and, notwithstanding the scathing eloquence of Counselor Holmes, he was found guilty. "Never before," says Mitchel, "had the government of the foreign enemy and the Irish people met in so plain an issue. Never before was it made so manifest that the enemy's government maintains its supremacy over Ireland by systematically breaking the 'law'—even its own law; by turning its judicial trials into solemn farces, its ermined judges into bad actors, and its fountain of justice into an obscene 'mother of dead dogs.' "

When asked what he had to say against sentence being pronounced upon him, Mr. Mitchel replied that he had not been tried at all. Baron Lefroy said that the prisoner's statement was tantamount to charging the jury with perjury. Mr. Mitchel retorted that he made no such charge, but that he did charge the sheriff—another name for the queen—with empaneling only those who were well known to be his (the prisoner's) mortal enemies.

Baron Lefroy then, in a partisan address, sentenced Mr. Mitchel to transportation beyond the seas, in the British penal settlements, for a period of fourteen years. Then the undaunted "felon" responded in the following "words that burn":

"The 'law' has done its part, and the Queen of England, her crown and government in Ireland are now secure—pursuant to act of Parliament. I have done my part also. Three months ago, I promised Lord Clarendon and his government, who hold this country for the English, that I would provoke him into his courts of justice, as places of this kind are called; that I would force him, publicly and notoriously, to pack a jury against me, to convict me, or else that I would walk a free man out of this court, and provoke him to a contest on another field. My lords, I knew I was setting my life on that cast, but I knew that, in either event, victory should be with me, and it is with me. Neither the jury, nor the judges, nor any man in this court, presumes to think that it is a criminal who stands in this dock [murmurs of applause, which the police endeavored to repress]. I have shown what the law is made of in Ireland. I have shown that her Majesty's government sustains itself in Ireland by packed juries, by partisan judges, by perjured sheriffs—"

After an interruption from Baron Lefroy, who said he could not sit there to listen to a repetition of the offence for which the prisoner had been sentenced—Mr. Mitchel proceeded thus:

"What I have now to add is simply this: I have acted all through this business, from the first, under a strong sense of duty. I do not repent anything I have done, and I believe the course I have opened is only begun. The Roman who saw his hand burning to ashes before the tyrant, promised that three hundred should follow out his enterprise. Can I not promise for one, for two, for three? [indicating as he spoke Reilly, Martin, and Meagher]. 'Promise for me' 'and me' 'and me, Mitchel!' rose around him in commingled tones of earnest solemnity, passionate defiance, and fearless devotion, from his friends and followers; and, embracing the exciting scene at a glance, he cried with proud eagerness—'For one, for two, for three? Aye, for hundreds!' "

A scene, continues the narrative, of intense excitement followed, in the midst of which the judges fled from the bench in terror, Baron Lefroy shouting, "Officers! officers! remove Mr. Mitchel!" The prisoner was huddled off, waving his hand to his friends, two of whom, Meagher and Doheny, were arrested for giving vent to the feeling impossible to suppress at such a moment. After they had been discharged, and order had been restored, Counselor Holmes rose to add his defiance to that of the prisoner, concluding with these words: "I now say, with deliberation, that the sentiments I expressed with regard to England are my sentiments, and I here avow them openly. The attorney-general is present—I retract nothing. These are my well-judged sentiments—these are my opinions as to the relative position of England and Ireland, and if I have, as you seem to insinuate, violated the law by stating these opinions, I now deliberately do so again. Let her Majesty's attorney-general do his duty to his government, I have done mine to my country."

The noble old advocate was not prosecuted. In the conviction of John Mitchel, the government had won a sufficient victory. That same afternoon of May 27, 1848, loaded with fetters, placed in a police van, and under a strong escort of dragoons, he was taken to an armed steamer lying in wait for him in the river Liffey, near the custom-house, and put on board, without any attempt having been made at a rescue—more shame to those who prevented the Dublin clubs from acting, as they wished to do. Meagher, usually so ardent, was made use of by the more timid, to discourage a rising—a course he afterward bitterly regretted. Many ardent spirits, seeing that Mitchel was kidnapped, so to speak, without as much as a struggle, quit the clubs and the whole movement in disgust. "Will you wait," exclaimed Robert Ward, at a club meeting, "until heaven showers down muskets upon you? Until the Almighty, himself, sends down angels to pull the triggers for you?"

An attempt was made by some of the Confederate leaders to get Mitchel, the day before his trial, to issue an address from Newgate asking the clubs not to attempt a rescue. This he, with characteristic courage, refused to do.

"When will the *time* come?" demanded John Martin, Mitchel's school-fellow and faithful comrade—"the *time* about which your orators so boldly vaunt amid the fierce shouts of your applause? If it come not when one of you, selected by your enemies as your champion, is sent to perish among thieves and murderers, for the crime of loving and defending his native land—then it will never come—*never!*" Martin was entirely right. The time never came—for that generation at least.

Mitchel was first exiled to Bermuda and subsequently to Van Dieman's Land, or Tasmania, whence he escaped to the United States, in 1853. He lived mostly in the Southern States, and, when the Civil War broke out, took their side of our great family quarrel. One of his sons, Captain John Mitchel, was killed while in command of Fort Sumter, after it fell into Confederate hands. Another son, Willie, a mere lad, fell in Pickett's celebrated charge on the Federal lines at Gettysburg, July 3, 1863. Another son, Captain James Mitchel, has long been a high official of the New York Fire Department, and his children inherit the spirit of their grandsire. John Mitchel, after having been elected member of Parliament for Tipperary—a position he sought merely to annoy the British government—was declared ineligible by vote of the House of Commons. He was about to make another contest when death came upon him at the home of John Martin (who had married his sister), in the County Down, March 19, 1875. Within a week Martin followed him to the grave. Mitchel is buried at Newry. His last words to those gathered around his deathbed were typical of his life and character—"I have never made peace with England!"

CHAPTER IX

Partial Demoralization Following Mitchel's Exile—Leaders are Irresolute and Procrastinate—Government Acts—Habeas Corpus Suspended—Abortive Attempt at Insurrection—Leaders Arrested and Condemned to Death—Sentence Commuted—Young Ireland in Literature

AFTER the transportation of Mitchel, the revolutionary spirit in Ireland seemed, in a measure, to decline. Patriotic men felt that a great error had been committed in not attempting, at least, the rescue of the gallant prisoner. Many members of the Dublin and Cork clubs lost confidence. Able and patriotic priests, such as the Rev. John Kenyon, of Tipperary, who was strongly in favor of rescue, dropped completely out of the movement. This clergyman, who was a profound scholar and a most eloquent orator, never fully recovered from the chagrin of Mitchel's unopposed exile, and he never forgave some of the Young Ireland leaders—including Meagher—for the share they had had in keeping the clubs of Dublin from taking action. Meagher, in a speech delivered some days after

John Mitchel's forcible expatriation, found it necessary to explain his position in the matter, and nobly took all the blame to himself, whereas the people well knew he had been influenced by older and more experienced leaders. "To the end," he exclaimed, "I see the path I have been ordained to walk, and, on the grave which closes that path, I can read no coward's epitaph!"—a gallant vaunt which his after career, as a heroic American general, amply redeemed. But the clubs continued to drill, and the leaders visited and addressed them. All were waiting for the harvest to ripen, so that the prospective patriot army might have an ample commissariat. The government, ever watchful, knew well the purpose of Young Ireland's delay, and resolved not to lessen its vigorous measures of repression.

As the "United Irishman" had been suppressed by order of the viceroy, a new paper, to take its place, was started, under the name of the "Irish Tribune," and of this publication, Kevin I. O'Doherty—a patriotic young physician— and Richard Dalton Williams—a gifted medical student —became the chief editors, assisted by another medical man, of literary tastes, the late Dr. Antisell, of Washington, D. C. Soon afterward, John Martin started still another national organ, which he called the "Irish Felon." The tone of both journals was intense, and gave the Castle government great annoyance. Devin Reilly was Martin's editorial lieutenant, and his capacity for writing "felonious" articles was simply unmeasurable. The "Tribune" and the "Felon"—following Mitchel's course—constantly counseled the people to arm and prepare for what was coming. The popular leaders made pilgrimages to the smaller towns, and even the rural districts, to arouse the masses. They pursued this line of operations somewhat too openly, and their purpose to "strike in the autumn" was too well advertised. Lord Clarendon—smooth old Whig that he was—could not be caught napping. His detectives and spies were ubiquitous, and gave him ample information of every step taken by the patriots. He felt called upon to ask Parliament to suspend the Habeas Corpus Act in Ireland, so as to give him a still freer hand in the matter of suppression. Parliament responded to his request without delay, and thus the last plank of the so-called "constitution" was destroyed. The famine still continued its deadly work, particularly among the class who had hitherto, in all ages, filled the ranks of the patriot armies that had fought for Ireland—the small landholders, or "tenants at will," who were the lineal descendants of the gallant clansmen of other generations.

Lord Clarendon made immediate use of his augmented power. The "Tribune" and "Felon" were seized upon and confiscated, and their editors locked up in Newgate prison. Prominent leaders throughout the country were arbitrarily arrested. In Waterford and Carrick-on-Suir, the people came very near to bloody collision with the soldiers, but, again, the Young Ireland chiefs procrastinated and kept procrastinating, until they tired the people out. The English government was determined, as in 1798, to compel an outbreak before the popular forces were prepared for the struggle. Warrants were issued for the arrest of Smith O'Brien, Meagher, Doheny, and other noted men, so that they had to leave Dublin to avoid arrest, which would have left the people without recognized leaders. Mr. O'Brien was visiting in Wexford when the Habeas Corpus was suspended. Within a few days he was joined by Meagher and John Blake Dillon. After consultation, finding Wexford unprepared, they determined to betake themselves to Kilkenny. Michael Doheny, Terence Bellew MacManus—who was the Irish leader in Liverpool, England—Patrick O'Donoghue, an energetic club organizer of Dublin, and several other proscribed patriots, flung themselves into Tipperary, and sought to arouse the people to resistance. They had few arms and no resources whatever. Richard O'Gorman, Jr., with some chosen associates, sought to stir up Limerick and Clare, but met with scant encouragement. The peasantry seemed to feel instinctively that the time for a successful insurrection had gone by. Moreover, they were dispirited by poverty and famine, and were quite shrewd enough to see that the young enthusiasts who had come among them were not the ideal chiefs of a "rebel" array. Smith O'Brien, who was then about forty-five years old, and of imposing appearance, alone seemed to possess any influence with the rural population. His aristocratic lineage, and the absolute unselfishness of his espousal of the people's cause, also had their effect upon the peasantry.

O'Brien and his friends made a halt at Callan, in Kilkenny, on July 24, and surprised a troop of the 8th Royal Irish Hussars, while they were engaged in cleaning their accoutrements or grooming their horses. Instead of making them prisoners and seizing on their arms and animals, O'Brien had the folly to allow them to escape, and even called for "three cheers" for them. After this exhibition, the Callan people could not be led to believe that an insurrection was seriously intended, and who can blame them? Next day, the fugitives found themselves in Tipperary County, where they were joined by several men from Dublin, who had also "taken to the hills." At Killenaule, a barricade was raised, and Dillon had command of it. Toward noon, on July 27, a party of the Irish Hussars, under an officer, approached the barrier, and the commander ordered the obstruction removed. Dillon asked if he had a warrant to arrest Smith O'Brien. James Stephens—afterward the famous Fenian chief and organizer—who stood beside Dillon, covered the officer with a rifle, and would have fired had not Dillon prevented him. The hussar finally assured Dillon that he had no warrant for O'Brien or any other person. The barricade was taken down and the troop passed on.

From Killenaule, the leaders directed their steps toward "the Collieries," near Ballingarry, where, they were assured, the people were ripe for revolt. About 2,000 men, poorly armed, assembled there on Saturday, July 29, while the rain was falling in sheets. The men were cold and hungry, and proposed to kill the cattle of a neighboring landlord and roast the carcasses on an iron gate, to be laid across a fire. O'Brien peremptorily refused, but gave what money he had in his possession for the purchase of bread. The people now began to murmur. "What was the use of following so impracticable a leader?" they asked each other. "If his conscience was so tender, why could he not issue scrip to the owner of the cattle, redeemable by the Irish treasury, in case the insurrection succeeded?" The priests, too, were hostile to the belated movement. They could see no chance of success—even the most resentful and hopeful. Some had never believed in revolution, but even those who were aggressively patriotic, having witnessed Smith O'Brien's peculiar tactics, counseled the people to go home and quit an enterprise foredoomed to defeat. And most of the people took their advice. Those who did not, rallied around O'Brien on Ballingarry Common, and breakfasted on dry bread. About the time the meal was finished, a runner came into camp all breathless, with the information that Captain Trant, at the head of fifty policemen, was in full march from Mullinahone to arrest Smith O'Brien. All, at once, stood to such arms as they had, which were not many. Soon the police column came in sight, but the crowd on the common, because of the commingling of women and children with the men, looked more formidable than it really was in the eyes of the officer. Instead of marching right on, he caused his little column to wheel to the right up a by-road, which led to the strong stone house of the widow McCormick, on the hill of Farrenrory. O'Brien and his followers pursued the fugitives, but could not intercept them. They entered the McCormick house, and immediately, by aid of crowbars, which they found in the yard, knocked holes in the walls to shoot through. Trant left his magnificent gray charger standing at the back door. The people surged around the house and sought to storm it. O'Brien begged them to desist, until he had parleyed with the officer. To do this, he was obliged to climb on a window-sill. While in the act of parleying, a shot, as some claim, a stone, as others say, was either fired or flung at the policemen in the upper story. A volley was the reply. Two countrymen fell dead, and several were wounded. The people retired a little, but did not run. O'Brien slowly walked across the open space to join his followers. He was not fired upon. Then Terence Bellew MacManus attempted to demolish the rear door under cover of a cart-load of hay. He fired his pistol into the door several times, but the damp weather kept the timber from igniting. Then he sought to fire the hay, but the rain had soaked it thoroughly. Meanwhile, the police exhibited

Mrs. McCormick's little children at the windows. This was too much for the humane O'Brien. He could not endure to see innocent little ones exposed to the risk of cremation, and, at once, ordered MacManus to desist.

At this crisis, news came of a larger body of police, aided by dragoons, marching to relieve their comrades. The people were directed to disperse. O'Brien, himself, after some persuasion, was compelled to mount Captain Trant's charger in order to escape immediate arrest. No further effort at fighting was made at Ballingarry, and the whole affair was turned into ridicule by the hostile British press. Thackeray, himself, became brilliant on "the Modern Brian Boru, or the Hero of Mrs. McCormick's Cabbage Garden." And this was the outcome of nearly half a century of "agitation."

Of course, England knew, quite as well as Ireland, that the strength of the subject nation had not been tested at all. As to Irish courage, England has never questioned it, except when it has been exercised against her. Ireland had suffered in her leaders. O'Connell, with the very best intentions, had demoralized her by his peace-at-any-price policy, in the day of her strength; whereas O'Brien committed the mistake of appealing to her valor when her courage was at its lowest ebb, owing to famine, pestilence, and continued defeat.

Nothing formidable in the way of insurrection followed the Ballingarry fiasco. All the leaders became hopeless fugitives. O'Brien, Meagher, MacManus, and O'Donoghue were speedily arrested and lodged in Clonmel jail. Although large rewards for their capture had been offered by the government, not a man, or woman, outside the police or their agents, could be induced to betray them. England's servants had to do their own dirty work on this occasion. In Dublin, the jails were packed with prisoners. Charles Gavan Duffy, Stephen Joseph Meany, Walter Meyler, and many other literary men, were sent to keep company with Martin and O'Doherty in Newgate. Doheny, O'Gorman, Devin Reilly, Dillon, and other proscribed leaders succeeded, after many adventures, in escaping to France or America. James Stephens and John Kavanagh, both of whom had been severely wounded at Ballingarry, were concealed by the faithful people until they recovered and were enabled to escape to the Continent.

John O'Mahony, a young gentleman-farmer, who had a large personal following on the borders of Cork, Limerick, and Tipperary, aided by John Savage, the poet, planned to rescue the state prisoners from Clonmel jail later on, but the plot was discovered and baffled. O'Mahony escaped by leaping from the court-house window to the ground—a distance of nearly thirty feet. He was as agile as Uncas in the "Last of the Mohicans." Failing at Clonmel, he made an attack on Glenbower police barracks, but the garrison was reinforced and he was compelled to raise the siege after some blood had been shed. A price was put on his head, but he eluded his enemies, reached Paris in safety, and subsequently settled in New York, where he became colonel of a volunteer regiment, and, later, organized the Fenian Brotherhood, of which he was elected president, or Head Centre.

In September and October, the state prisoners were tried by "special commission" at Clonmel. O'Brien, MacManus, Meagher, and O'Donoghue were all found guilty of high treason, on police testimony, and sentenced to be "hanged, drawn, and quartered." This sentence was soon commuted to transportation beyond the seas for life.

In the summer of 1849, all four were sent in a sloop-of-war to Van Dieman's Land, or Tasmania, whence Meagher and MacManus, in 1852, escaped to the United States. O'Brien, proudly refusing all compromise, and failing in an attempt to escape, was, finally, granted an unconditional pardon, in 1856, and returned to Ireland. He made a tour of this country soon after his release, but took no further active part in Irish politics. This honest, chivalric, but unfortunate patriot died of a liver affection, contracted while in exile, in June, 1864. No nobler or truer Irishman ever sprang from the soil his forefathers had gloriously reigned over. In regard to the commutation of the sentence originally imposed on Mr. O'Brien and his associates, it has been stated that clemency was due to the magnanimous action of General Sir Charles James Napier, the conqueror of Scinde, rather than to the humanity of the queen's advisers. At the period of the Reform agitation in England (1832) Sir Charles happened to hold the command-in-chief of the army. Lord John Russell's private secretary presumed to "sound" him, by letter, as to whether he would, in case of emergency, march his forces on London and coerce the aged king, William IV, who was fiercely opposed to Reform, into acquiescence. Napier considered the communication an insult to his honor and loyalty as a soldier and gentleman, and so bluntly, as was his habit, informed "Lord John" and his colleagues, assuring them, at the same time, that if ever the lives of British subjects were placed in jeopardy by a charge of high treason, while any of the Whig conspirators against the crown held office under it, he would make use of the letter to save the culprits. As the cousin of Lord Edward Fitzgerald he could do no less; and he kept his word. When the proceedings opened at Clonmel, Sir Charles placed the communication in the hands of the state prisoners' counsel, and, dreading the effect of exposure, the Russell cabinet gave way on the point of capital punishment.

The trial of Charles Gavan Duffy came to naught, for the reason that the late Lady Wilde, "Speranza" of the "Nation," avowed herself the author of the article headed "The Die is Cast," for which he was prosecuted. This she did in open court and defied the government to "do its worst" to her. "Come, call your guards," she exclaimed, "I am ready for the sacrifice!" But the attorney-general thought it wiser not to molest the noble enthusiast. She died only a short time ago, widowed, aged, and in poor circumstances.

Martin and O'Doherty were both tried for Treason-Felony and sentenced to ten years' transportation each. Martin profited by the Amnesty of 1856 to return to his country, while O'Doherty became attached to the land of his exile, and now, in his old age, is a leading surgeon and physician of the Australian colonies. Many more humble leaders suffered also at the hands of the government, but some of the prosecutions were abandoned, for lack of evidence, or else because the law officers wished to economize. And thus, in utter failure, terminated the well-intended, but ill-timed, attempt of "Young Ireland" at insurrection. And yet no name is dearer to the hearts of the Irish people than the name of "Young Ireland." Although they reaped no laurels in the field, they crowned their unhappy country with the bays of intellect. No land ever produced a group of men more brilliant or more devoted to a principle. In the realm of oratory, Meagher has had few rivals, and hardly a superior; nor were McGee, O'Gorman, and Doheny much behind him in thrilling eloquence. In poetry,

James Clarence Mangan, whose works should be more extensively read, ranks with Coleridge and Edgar Allan Poe. In some respects, his writings outrank those of both. Many of his poems have what may be termed a ghastly grandeur. As writers of popular ballads, no country has given birth to the superiors of Thomas Davis, Dennis Florence Mac-Carthy, John O'Hagan, Joseph Brenan, Charles Gavan Duffy, John Savage, John Kells Ingram, Michael Joseph Barry, Martin MacDermott, Bartholomew Dowling, M. J. McCann, J. De Jean Fraser, Francis Davis, Maurice Richard Leyne, Richard Dalton Williams, Edward Walsh, Arthur Gerald Geoghegan, Denny Lane, and, we may add, Mary Eva Kelly, Ellen Mary Downing, and Lady Wilde. These ladies were called the "Three Graces of the Nation." Nor does this long list dispose of all who might justly claim to take high rank among the exemplars of Irish literature in the English tongue. The great Gaelic savants, O'Curry and O'Donovan, who mainly translated the "Annals of the Four Masters," and other valuable historical manuscripts, can hardly be classed among the Young Irelanders, but belonged to their period. The same is also true of John Cornelius O'Callaghan, author of "The Green Book," which first refuted the slanders of the Williamite writers against Irish valor, and of the inestimable "History of the Irish Brigades in the Service of France," a monument to the courage of Irish soldiers in exile, which time itself can not destroy. McGee's "Popular History" is a most valuable contribution to Irish annals. So also is Mitchel's continuation of McGeoghegan's history. Duffy's "Young Ireland" and "Four Years of Irish History" throw light upon some of the most interesting of more recent happenings in Ireland—particularly the closing days of O'Con-

nell. In his youth, Justin McCarthy, the historian of "Our
Own Times," was affiliated with Young Ireland. The young
writers revived and revivified the intellect of Ireland, which,
barring O'Connell, Lalor Sheil, and Thomas Moore, had
sensibly declined, from the Union period down to 1842.
Had there been no "Young Ireland," Ireland's place in literature would not be the respectable one it holds to-day.
Never was a political party so free from the inevitable
vices of all politics. The poets, writers, and orators of
"Young Ireland" fulfilled, to the best of their great ability,
the promise of their chosen organ, the "Nation" newspaper,
"to create and foster public opinion in Ireland and make
it racy of the soil."

BOOK XIV

DEALING WITH THE PERIOD BETWEEN THE EXILE
OF SMITH O'BRIEN AND HIS ASSOCIATES AND THE
PASSAGE OF THE LAND PURCHASE BILL, 1848–1903

CHAPTER I

Humiliation of Ireland Following the Abortive Insurrection of 1848—
The Curse of Political Apathy—Miserable Condition of the People

POLITICAL apathy settled upon Ireland immediately following the blasting of all her great hopes and high aspirations. Within a few years, she had sunk from her proud attitude of national demand upon her tyrant to the lowly condition of a nation defeated, humiliated, and, worse than all else, despised by her foes and pitied by her friends. She had lost, according to the computation of the statisticians of the period, at least 1,250,000 of her people by starvation and typhus fever, and this, too, without having made resistance in any way worthy of her former valor. No damage had been inflicted on her enemy. It was a sorry outcome, for which most of the leaders, not the faithful and trusting people, were responsible. There had been want of judgment—utter want of resolution—in the councils of the chiefs. Of all the popular leaders, Mitchel alone had passed through the ordeal with credit. Had his brave advice been acted upon, although success was more than doubtful, an insurrection of respectable proportions would certainly have resulted, and the military honor of Ireland, as in 1603, 1691, and 1798, would have been saved a blot. Never in all her previous history had she been discredited in the field—made an object of ridicule to England and a byword to the world at large. True, neither her courage nor her strength had been really put to the test, but the British press, which then had the ear, as well as the eye, of mankind, wrote of the abortive rebellion as if that were all Ireland could do in the matter of resistance. The failure lowered Irish spirit both at home and abroad. The press of England pursued the millions of fugitives out of Ireland to other lands with atrocious libels. The ignorance which English laws had promoted; the poverty which British enactments had enforced, were alike made subjects of ribald reproach to the victims of injustice instead of to the authors of their misery.

The roads leading to the ocean became black with people—young men and women mostly, the very flower of the population—fleeing from their desolated homes to the emigrant ships, which were to bear them across the seas, and thousands of them found deep, deep graves in the mighty ocean. It became a ghastly saying that the bed of the Atlantic, from the Cove of Cork to Sandy Hook, was paved with the bones of Irish emigrants, victims of ship fever, who had been thrown overboard, with sacks for shrouds and weights attached to sink them "a thousand fathoms low." The poorhouses and the Union infirmaries were filled with paupers and patients in all stages of moral and physical decay. The sombre wings of the giant raven of famine still blackened the Irish sky; and the Union coffins, piled in their hideous starkness on the undertakers' carts, were grim reminders of the unchecked slaughter which still raged among the hunger and fever-scourged people. The very winds bore blasts of death along with them, for the potato continued to rot and taint the air with a fierce putridity. But live-stock, grain, butter, eggs, and poultry were still heavily exported to the British markets—they were not for such as the Irish, who, as the queen's husband and one of the queen's uncles remarked, "could live on weeds and grass." Most of the landlords had fled to "foreign parts," but their agents remained behind to harry the people. They and their bailiffs, aided by the sheriffs and police, and often by the soldiers, put the pick and crowbar into active service, and thousands of humble peasant homes were leveled every week for non-payment of rents that had gone far beyond the scale of moderation and justice. A mania for "clearance" seemed to have taken hold of the "owners of the soil." The fad was to banish the people, in order to make room for cattle. Indeed, an English viceroy of Ireland, at a somewhat later date, said, at a public banquet, that Ireland's natural destiny was to be "the fruitful mother of flocks and herds"—that is, a stock farm to raise prime meats for the English table. But the evicted people were flung out on the roadside—some to die in the damp ditches, for neighbors were forbidden, under penalty of eviction, to give them shelter; some to enter the workhouse; those who had a little money to emigrate, and the young men who had neither means nor prospect of work to enlist and help England to impose upon others the chains that rankled the blood of their own unfortunate country. The fate of many of the lovely young Irish girls—they of the raven hair and azure eyes, or of the golden locks and Spanish orbs—is too harrowing a subject to be dwelt upon. And, then, to think of the multitude of innocent Irish children, and tiny babes, who sank, starved off the face of the wrong-blasted island, into graves whence their ashes cried for vengeance! Oh, proud England! of all the shameful chapters of thy crime-stained history, this is, surely, the most begrimed. No Englishman who has a human heart can read the record without blushing for his country. Not all Englishmen are heartless—many of them are among the noblest and most generous of the human race—but, in their dealings with Ireland, as the government, since 1832, has represented the sentiment of the nation, the English people, as a body, have not been either wise, or just, or magnanimous. Had they been, they had made a greater conquest than Agincourt, or Blenheim, or Waterloo.

CHAPTER II

Agrarian Warfare—Landlords and Agents Shot—Tenants Hanged— Irish Political Traitors—Mitchel's Summary of Famine and Exodus

OF course there were many cases of retaliation for eviction and banishment on the part of the peasantry, and agrarian conspiracies, with which even the Arms and Coercion Acts could not successfully grapple, existed in many parts of the country. A few landlords, and many agents and rent warners, were killed by desperate victims of their tyranny. These acts were committed, for the most part, in the fertile counties of Tipperary, Limerick, West Meath, and Roscommon, where the lands were valuable for the raising of horned cattle and sheep, and were, therefore, considered too good for the "mere Irish" tenants-at-will. Government sent out special judicial commissions to try the peasants "arrested on suspicion" of having shot their persecutors, and the judges, aided by packed juries and skilful hangmen, made sad havoc in the ranks of the people. So long as "examples" were made, the courts were not particular as to the evidence against their victims. It was necessary, in their judgment, to "strike terror," and thus for every landlord or landlord's satrap who fell, half a dozen peasants were "hanged by the neck until dead," although many of them were entirely innocent of the offences for which they were executed. It was a case of "making the innocent suffer for the guilty."

Many of the landlords had been "high livers" and wofully extravagant. Some had been lenient to their tenantry, and fell short of their former incomes. Both these classes had borrowed largely in England, on the credit of their estates, and at various rates of interest. Under the system in vogue at the time of the famine and exodus in Ireland, they could obtain little or no relief from their embarrassments. In the Parliamentary session of 1848-49, the Encumbered Estates enactment was passed, and, soon, many old "demesnes" passed from their owners, under the hammer. It was thought, at first, that most of the property transfers would be made to English and Scotch investors. Yet, out of a total of about £3,750,000—$18,750,000—only £319,486—$1,597,430—came from British purchasers. The latter were afraid to buy in Ireland, because of the occasional "potting" of landlords by the "Terry Alts," and the very name of Tipperary, where that style of warfare was most common, made people in Great Britain grow pale. Therefore, most of the encumbered lands were bought by the Irish moneyed classes, and they were, as a rule, quite as hard, and even more unreasonable, in their dealings with the tenants than their predecessors in ownership. This subject will be further dealt with a little later on.

Queen Victoria made a visit—the first of her reign—to Ireland, in August, 1849, while yet the people were starving, rotting from pestilence, and emigrating by the myriad. The flunkeys of Dublin, as usual, received her with enthusiasm, but the body of the people remained sullen and made no manifestation of either welcome or hostility. They remembered that "her Majesty" had subscribed less than the Sultan of Turkey to relieve the famine victims. One Dublin gentleman, Mr. O'Reilly, of South Great George's Street, ran up an ink-black flag, with a crownless harp, to the summit of his house. He also put black curtains on his windows, and had "Famine" and "Pestilence" printed upon them. At the dead of night, the ever-ready police invaded his home, removed the flag, tore the curtains from the windows, and carried Mr. O'Reilly off to prison. How long he remained there, we have no record of; but he, no doubt, truly represented the honest sentiment of Ireland in regard to the "royal visit." When, on the same trip, Victoria visited the Cove of Cork, the slaves of the municipal council changed the fine old name of the place to the commonplace designation of "Queenstown." One reason why the visit passed off quietly was the hope among the people, generated by government agents, that Victoria would pardon the state prisoners. But she didn't, nor had she any intention of so doing. The ministers considered Smith O'Brien and his associates a good riddance, and it was not the shrewd queen's game to quarrel with her advisers over the fortunes, or misfortunes, of half a dozen "Irish rebels." The crown, however, threw a sop to "respectable"—that is, "loyal"—Catholics, by making N. B. Wyse, of Waterford, ambassador to the Court of Greece and More O'Farrell governor of Malta. Other favors were granted to several Catholic barristers, and, shame to relate, even former orators of Conciliation Hall, and writers of ballads for the "Nation," were not above wearing the English livery—for a consideration. Having abandoned all hope of a national revival, these political philosophers consoled themselves by swathing their limbs in English bank-notes, so that the provincial fetters might not gall them. Two of the best "rebel" ballad-writers

—O'Hagan and Barry—afterward became judges, and the former, in Fenian times, is said to have sentenced a patriot to a term in jail for singing, in the streets, a "seditious" song of the "honorable" Court's composition!

"The Last Conquest of Ireland (Perhaps)" thus sums up the famine slaughter, and, with that summary, we close the chapter:

The census of Ireland, in 1841, gave a population of 8,175,125. At the usual rate of increase, there must have been, in 1846, at least 8,750,000; at the same rate of increase, they ought to have been in 1851—according to the estimate of the census commissioners—9,018,799. But in that year, after five seasons of artificial famine, there were found alive only 6,552,385—a deficit of about 2,500,000! . . . In the first place, the decrease did not *begin* until 1846 —there had been till then a rapid increase in the population; the government returns not only ignore the increase, but set the emigration of *ten* years against the depopulation of *five*. This will not do. We must reduce their emigrants by one-half—say to 600,000—and add to the depopulation the estimated increase up to 1846—say half a million. This will give upward of 2,000,000 whose disappearance is to be accounted for—and 600,000 emigrants in the other column. Balance, unaccounted for—*a million and a half!*

In 1861, mainly through emigration, the result of eviction, the population had fallen to about 5,750,000; in 1871, to 5,125,000; in 1881, to 4,750,000; in 1891, to 4,525,000; in 1901, to 4,476,000; in 1911, to ——?

God alone can answer our note of interrogation.

CHAPTER III

Russell's Drastic Coercion Act—The Insulting Ecclesiastical Titles Bill—Orange Outrages—A "Noble" Lord Lies Officially—Systematic Letter-Opening

IN spite of the reduced condition of Ireland, Lord John Russell thought it necessary to still further coerce her people. Therefore, he had passed—for the English Parliament rarely fails to grant any hostile legislation the Premier may suggest for Ireland—a new coercion law, under the title of "An Act for the Better Prevention of Crime and Outrage in Ireland," which extended the powers of magistrates and policemen to further annoy and oppress the people, under the pretext of searching for arms—an abuse often pressed beyond the limits of common decency, where modest females were concerned. A curfew clause, which required everybody not duly authorized by the magistrates to remain in the house after sunset—that is, in the "proclaimed" districts—rendered this law more than ordinarily odious, and led, as such laws always do, to evasion and conspiracy.

Religious rancor was stirred, in 1851, by the introduction of Lord Russell's Ecclesiastical Titles bill in Parliament. It was brought about by a rescript from Pope Pius IX, which districted Great Britain and Ireland into archdioceses and dioceses; and ordering the prelates who had jurisdiction in them to assume their proper titles. This was truly shocking to the English conscience, and the Pope, wearing horns, of course, loomed large and terrible on the political horizon of "Protestant England." He had attacked, the bigots said, the independence of the country, and there was an immediate howl for a penal enactment which would do away with Catholic assumption of equality before the law. "Lord John" accordingly introduced a bill which provided, as he thought, against further "Papal usurpation" in the "United" Kingdom. It absolutely prohibited the assumption of the title of any existing see, or of any title whatsoever, from any place in Great Britain and Ireland, under a penalty of £100 ($500) for each such offence. While the bill was on its passage, the Whigs, headed by Lord Russell, went out of office, and the Tories came into power, with Lord Derby—O'Connell's "Scorpion Stanley" —as Prime Minister. The Tories took up the measure with zeal. Floods of oratorical bigotry swept through both Houses of Parliament—Whigs and Tories making common cause against the few Catholics and Liberals in Westminster. The bill was rushed through by immense majorities, but the Catholics of both Great Britain and Ireland spurned it to a man. John McHale, the great Archbishop of Tuam, whom Daniel O'Connell has called "the Lion of the Fold of Judah," in defiance of the enactment, read the Papal rescript from the pulpit of his cathedral. In the course of his sermon, he invited any informer, or priest-hunter, who might be present, to note his deliberate defiance of the infamous law, and to earn his hundred pounds reward by giving information to the government. He, also, took care to sign himself "John, Archbishop of Tuam," whenever he had occasion to issue a circular or publish a letter. He was never prosecuted. The newly created English cardinal subscribed himself "Nicholas, Cardinal-Archbishop of Westminster"; and their example was followed by all the Catholic prelates throughout the three kingdoms. The bigoted and cowardly government backed down from its arrogant position, and, within a few months, the Ecclesiastical Titles bill was as little heard of as if it had never been enacted.

A slight extension of the electoral franchise had been given to Ireland by the Russell administration, and was based on the Poor Rate, as the freehold qualification had virtually ceased to exist, owing to the depopulation and impoverishment of the country. But, notwithstanding, the proportion of qualified voters in Ireland remained ludicrously small, when compared with that of Great Britain, which, although much the richer island, had a far lower qualification.

Orange outrages were rife in Ireland during 1850-51, and culminated in a bloody riot at a place called Dolly's Brae, in the County Down, where several Catholics were killed by the armed idolizers of King William. The attack was planned at a dinner given to the Orangemen by Lord Roden, at his country-seat. The fanatics were primed with drink, and their host made them a speech of the "True Blue" order, in which, of course, the Pope figured as a designing enemy of the "loyal" elect. Lord Roden did not actually advise his hearers to attack the Catholics, but his address and the liquor they had taken, combined, stirred up their worst passions, and, fresh from the banquet hall, they imbrued their hands in the blood of their fellow-countrymen. They were actually led by an Orange magistrate named Beers.

The outrage stirred up such indignation throughout the country that the viceroy was compelled to take notice of it. An able lawyer, who acted as a Commissioner to make due inquiry, was sent down from Dublin. Government hoped for a whitewash of the Orangemen, but, instead, the Commissioner, who happened to be a just man, threw the blame on the leaders of that body, and the Lord Lieutenant was compelled to deprive both Lord Roden and Magistrate Beers of the commission of the peace.

During a debate in the House of Lords on this subject, Lord Clarendon denied that the government had furnished arms to the Orange lodges, in 1848, when there was danger of a popular outbreak, but his denial was taken as being perfunctory, because it was notorious that arms had been shipped from the Castle armories, in Dublin, to Belfast and other Orange strongholds in Ulster at that period. Moreover, English viceroys are really expected to lie officially, and lie hard, for "the better protection of his Majesty's government in Ireland." The English functionary in Ireland—particularly in Secret Service matters—makes quite a distinction between an official and a social untruth. A "noble lord," who would scorn to look over the shoulder of a friend engaged in writing a private letter, has no hesitation in opening any letter addressed to a suspected person in Ireland, or out of it, for that matter. Nearly all the recent viceroys of Ireland have been expert letter-openers.

CHAPTER IV

The Encumbered Estates Act and its Disappointing Result—The Cause
of Tenant Right Betrayed by Irish Traitors for Fat Office
under "the Crown"—General Public Disgust

EVICTIONS and emigration were such common evils
in Ireland during the "fifties" and early "sixties,"
that people took them almost as matters of course—all
but the boldest of the harried peasants, who frequently appealed to the "wild justice of revenge." Many of the
landlords, who had lived extravagantly both at home and
abroad—particularly abroad—could no longer draw high
rents from the impoverished people, and so piled debt upon
debt against their lands. Their creditors, as early as 1848,
had become clamorous, and, in August of that year, as previously stated, the English Parliament passed, and the queen's
sanction was given to, the Encumbered Estates (Ireland) bill.
An attempt made to extend its provisions to England was
defeated by the government. The first petition for sale, under the act, was filed in October, 1849, and, thenceforth, the
sale of embarrassed estates became a common event in Ireland. Many of the oldest families in the island—Milesians,
Normans, and Saxons—fell victims to the greed of creditors,
who had often forced their trade upon them in the hour of
prosperity. Among the great families that suffered in this
connection were those of Kingston, Gort, Ffrench, and Martin, of Connemara. To recapitulate, the absolute orders
for sale amounted to 3,341. The Irish purchasers—mainly
"middle-class" mercantile people who had saved money—
numbered 7,180; and of English and Scotch purchasers

there were 309. The total sales amounted to £20,475,956 ($102,379,780), the English and Scotch paying about one-fifth of the entire sum. This social revolution—for such, indeed, it was—displaced a heavy proportion of the "flower" of the old aristocracy, who, with all their faults, had some Irish virtues, and turned some of the fairest portions of the country over to "shoneens" and "half sirs," who were even more severe on the tenants than the ancient proprietors of the soil. The people at large derived no benefit from the transfer. Many old retainers ended their days in the poor-house, and emigration, the handmaiden of eviction, went on at a more alarming rate than formerly. The heiress of the Martins, beggared by the Encumbered Estates Act, died on board a common emigrant ship in New York Harbor. Her grandfather, known as "the King of Connemara," had been a noted duelist; betrayed his country at the time of the Union, and was a boon companion of George IV, when that worthy was Prince Regent. The late A. M. Sullivan, M.P., claims in one of his histories, "New Ireland," that the change in ownership compelled Irish tenants to be more methodical in their payment of rents, but, nevertheless, this enforced strictness did not tend to make the relations between landlord and tenant more cordial. On the contrary, agrarian outrages became more frequent than ever, and "Captain Rock" answered the writs of ejectment with a blunderbuss, at short range. Many landlords died by the bullet and many peasants by the rope, during this period and long afterward. There is hardly anything in the history of mankind more ghastly than the story of the warfare between the landed proprietors and the tenant farmers in Ireland. The London "Times," with its habitual brutality, rejoiced in the rapid decrease of the Irish population, and predicted that, within a few years, "a Celtic Irishman would be as rare in Connemara as is the Red Indian on the shores of Manhattan." This prophecy has not been quite fulfilled, but the system that occasioned it, although modified, tends toward its final accomplishment. Emigration from Ireland to all parts of the world—chiefly to America—still keeps on, and weakens the country, as the flow of blood from a punctured artery debilitates a wounded person.

About 1850, the grievances of the Irish tenants stung into action the farmers of Ireland from Antrim to Cork, and from Dublin to Galway. Protestant and Catholic organized together for the purpose of securing what they called "Tenant Right"—intended to give the tillers of the soil some legal foothold on their farms. There had been, by precedent and tacit consent, a certain Tenant Right in Ulster, since the time of the Protestant settlement of that province, but it was deemed to be insufficient. The other provinces had no tenant right in any form, and were absolutely at the mercy of the landlord class.

The good understanding between the Ulster farmers and their Catholic allies of the South and West came very near being disrupted by Lord Russell's Ecclesiastical Titles bill, already dealt with, but, fortunately, the Whig ministry was defeated on a clause in the Militia bill, by a majority of eleven, and went out of power in February, 1852. Lord Derby succeeded Russell as Premier, and announced that a new Parliament would be necessary to settle existing public questions. The old one was, accordingly, dissolved, in June, and, by August, all the constituencies had chosen their representatives. Ireland, animated by the hope of land reform, elected fifty, or more, Tenant Right members, and among the more prominent were John Francis Maguire, of Cork; Frederick Lucas, a worthy namesake of the Lucas of the Patriot epoch in the eighteenth century; Charles Gavan Duffy, renowned both in literature and in politics; John Sadlier, afterward a bankrupt banker and suicide; William Keogh, who became a traitor to his country, and, attaining to the ermine, made a name upon the Irish bench second in infamy to the inhuman Norbury only. Many of the newly elected members had already served a term in the House of Commons, and had there fought the Ecclesiastical Titles bill so vehemently, in the previous Parliament, that the English press called them "The Pope's Brass Band," while the Irish newspapers, having faith in their popular professions, styled them "the Irish Brigade." Keogh, in particular, was regarded with great favor in Ireland. He was handsome—of the Napoleonic type of countenance—learned, eloquent, and profuse in his patriotic utterances.

Mr. Sharman Crawford—an advanced Liberal Protestant, from Ulster—had introduced in the House of Commons a bill which would have extended the provision of "the Ulster Right," with needed amendments, to the whole of Ireland, and this bill had been supported by Keogh, Sadlier, and other members of the "Brass Band." Mr. Sullivan thus explains the Ulster system:

"Substantially, it was a right of continuous occupancy by the tenant at a fair rent—one not raised by reason of any value added to the soil by the tenant's industry or outlay. . . . This tenant right was bought and sold daily; that is, the outgoing sold to the incoming tenant his interest in the farm. On a farm of fifty acres, an Ulster tenant has often obtained twenty years', sometimes thirty years', purchase of the margin between his rent and the valuation, probably a sum of £3,000 ($15,000). If a landlord wished to evict a tenant, he could do so by buying up from him the tenant right of the farm. He could, of course, evict for non-payment of rent, or other reasons, but in every such case he was bound to hand over in cash to the evicted tenant any balance remaining out of the marketable value of the tenant right of the holding, after deducting the amount of rent, cost, or damages legally due. Under this system, unknown or unrecognized by law outside of Ulster, that province bloomed like a garden, and became the home of thrift and plenty, of contentment and prosperity, even before the energy of the people, applied to manufacturing industries, had opened for them new paths to wealth."

In demonstrating the difference in prosperity between Ulster and its sister provinces, this historian says: "Why had the efforts of the tenant class elsewhere to obtain like rights been so steadily and vehemently resisted? Because Ulster was a 'Plantation Colony'; because, in Ulster, the plantation landlords got their lands on implied or express condition of 'planting' them—rooting a population to the soil; whereas elsewhere [in Ireland] the policy of the time was to up-root, to clear away, the Catholic natives. Even where, in the other provinces, the uprooting became too odious, or too dangerous, there still remained this much of its essence, in strong contrast to the Ulster custom, namely, the axiom that the tenant had *no* right of continuous occupancy, held only from year to year on the landlord's sufferance, and was not regarded in law as owning a shilling's worth of even his own outlay. If *he* drained or improved, so that bog land worth two shillings an acre was made corn [grain] land worth as many pounds, the landlord was legally en-

titled to call that improvement his own, and to make that
tenant pay two pounds an acre for that land. What could
come of such a system as this, the cruel opposite of the Ulster Right, but a state of agriculture and a state of society
the reverse of that which smiled on the northern province?
Negligence in place of thrift, squalor in place of comfort
and neatness, hovels in place of houses; insecurity, mistrust,
ill-will, hostility between landlord and tenant; a hatred of
the government, and a deadly hostility to the law that drew
this line of distinction, this line of oppression and wrong between the Protestant North and the Catholic South. If,
happily, the evils one would have thought inevitable were
not everywhere visible, it was in spite of the system, not because of it. If the landlord did not in every case appropriate,
in the shape of a raised rent, the fruits of the tenant's industry, it was because that particular landlord, or family, was
more honest than the law."

A moving cause of the affiliation of the Ulster farmers
with their brethren of the Catholic provinces, in support of
Tenant Right, was the harsh conduct of some of the landlords, who, taking advantage of the hard times and fall in
values, which practically annihilated the Ulster tenants'
margin of profit on their farms, sought to drive the thrifty
yeomen to the wall, in order that they might purchase their
"right" at the lowest possible figure. "Before the landlord's
interest could be affected," remarks Sullivan, "to the extent
of a shilling, the tenant right, equal in value to the fee
simple, should first be consumed. The rent was, always, a
first lien on that tenant right, and as long as at auction it
would fetch a penny more than the rent, the landlord was in
no way to suffer by bad times."

Notwithstanding the fine victory of the Irish Tenant

Right League at the polls, the organization was fated to have the cup of promise dashed from its hand by the base desertion of some leaders most trusted by the people, and strongly vouched for by several of the much deceived Catholic hierarchy. William Keogh, who had sworn by his God, at a banquet held in Athlone, Archbishop McHale presiding, to be true to his country against all temptation, sold himself to the Aberdeen ministry, which had come into power as a result of the general election, for the Irish solicitor-generalship. John Sadlier, another blasphemous "patriot," accepted the Lordship of the Treasury; and Edmund O'Flaherty, who had been regarded as incorruptible, accepted the position of Commissioner of Income Tax. Richard More O'Farrell, another traitor in whom the Irish people reposed confidence because of his previous high character, was bribed by a foreign appointment. These rascals, and some others, auctioned off the interests of their country to the Earl of Aberdeen—a spectacle, unfortunately, not without precedent in Irish Parliamentary history before that event, and not lacking in close reproduction since. The Catholic prelates, who had used their influence for the election of the renegades, felt deeply mortified, all the more so as the faithless members had adopted, with their confrères, the following resolution at a general conference of Irish commoners held in Dublin on September 8, 1852:

"*Resolved,* That, in the opinion of this conference, it is essential to the proper management of this cause that the members of Parliament who have been returned on Tenant Right principles should hold themselves perfectly independent of, and in opposition to, all governments which do not make it part of their policy, and a cabinet question, to give to the tenantry of Ireland a measure embodying the principles of Mr. Sharman Crawford's bill."

Lord Aberdeen, succeeding the Earl of Derby as Prime Minister, on December 20, formed his cabinet immediately, and scooped, as we have shown, the most powerful members of the "Pope's Brass Band" into his ministerial net. Their seduction was accomplished within twenty-four hours, and the hopes of the Irish tenants were blasted for a full generation. Among the Irish members who remained faithful to the people were Charles Gavan Duffy, Frederick Lucas, and George Henry Moore—the eloquent patriot who so long represented Mayo in Parliament. But they were disgusted and disheartened, and, after some brave but futile efforts to reform the broken Parliamentary ranks, were, within a few years, forced to conclude that the cause for which they had zealously labored was, for that time, at least, hopeless. Charles Gavan Duffy bade farewell to Ireland on the 6th day of November, 1855, and emigrated to Australia, where he achieved political distinction, and eventually became Premier of the flourishing colony of Victoria. In his valedictory address, delivered in Dublin immediately before his departure, he justified, to his own satisfaction at least, his voluntary exile by saying that "unless and until the existing conditions changed, there was no more hope for Ireland than for a corpse on the dissecting table." His acceptance of the title of "Sir" from the British crown did not increase his popularity among his fellow-countrymen—especially those of them who remembered his fatal difference with John Mitchel in 1847-48.

Archbishop McHale, and other able Irish prelates, did not hesitate to express their absolute disapproval of the course taken by the place-begging traitors. Many of the priesthood were also bitter in their denunciation of the betrayers of the country, but, unfortunately, Cardinal Cullen, who was, virtually, brought up in Rome, was more of a churchman than a patriot, and did not view the Catholic renegades as unfavorably as did John of Tuam. His influence at the Vatican was all-powerful, and the indignant clergy were speedily prohibited from taking any part in public affairs—on the side of the people, at least. This state of things originated the popular dislike of Cardinal Cullen, in a political sense, and it is safe to say that, with possibly two exceptions, he was the most unpopular Catholic dignitary that ever held sway in Ireland.

John Sadlier, who was the prime mover in the treason to Ireland, became a desperate speculator, was involved in disgraceful lawsuits, which compelled his resignation as Lord of the Treasury, forged deeds and other securities to sustain his Tipperary bank, mainly supported by farmers and working people generally, and finally, to escape the disgrace of his exposure, committed suicide by swallowing prussic acid on Hampstead Heath, London, Sunday morning, February 17, 1856. His fall ruined thousands of trusting peasants, many of whom were made insane by their irreparable losses.

Edmund O'Flaherty, another traitor to his country, stole £15,000, and fled to parts unknown. Keogh, of "So-help-me-God" infamy, was elevated to the bench, which his misconduct disgraced. After a long career of tyranny, he became insane, and ended his dishonored career by cutting his throat in a Belgian madhouse.

The infamies of the venal members of the "Brass Band" sank so deep into the national core of Ireland that, for long years afterward, Parliamentary agitation became a stench in the nostrils of the people, and the younger generation began to think of some other means, more to the taste of Irishmen, of achieving the independence of their country.

One of the most notable events of the period was the attempted abduction of a beautiful young English lady, Miss Eleanor Arbuthnot, by Mr. John Carden, a landlord of extensive property in the County Tipperary. The young lady was a relative, by marriage, of the famous Gough family, of which the great Field Marshal, Sir Hugh Gough, was the head. Carden had been a notorious evictor, and was looked upon as what, in these days, we might term a "crank." He had laid siege to the heart of the fair damsel with an ardor that smacked strongly of lunacy. He pursued her without regard to time or place, and this misconduct on his part, combined with the hard fact that he was nearly three times her age, steeled the young lady against his advances. Even his enemies acknowledged that it was a case of incurable love. Driven desperate, at last, by Miss Arbuthnot's peremptory refusal of his offer of marriage, he resorted to criminal means in order to effect his purpose. One Sunday morning, backed by half a dozen hired ruffians, he attempted to kidnap her while on her way home from church with her sisters and a Miss Linden. The ladies were in a close carriage and were driven by a man named John Dwyer, who proved himself a hero, as did also a young farmer, named McGrath, who, on hearing the women scream, rushed into the fray with all the splendid impetuosity of the national character. These were reinforced by a herd named Smithwick. Carden fought furiously, but was fiercely resisted by Miss Linden, who smote him in the face repeatedly, blinding him with his own blood. The enraged ruffian would not desist, even when he was hit on the temple by a large stone hurled at him by McGrath.

His hirelings soon lost heart, as reinforcements for the weaker party began to arrive, and, notwithstanding their leader's maniacal taunts and threats, they, at long run, forced him into the vehicle provided for the abduction, and drove off at a tremendous pace—the carriage being drawn by blooded horses—toward his castle of Barnane, under the shadow of Devil's Bit Mountain. Before reaching it, the whole party were overhauled and arrested—not without stout show of resistance—by a party of police, commanded by an inspector named McCullagh. At the next Clonmel Assizes Carden was tried, found guilty of attempted abduction, and sentenced to two years' imprisonment, with hard labor, in the county jail. He served out his sentence, but punishment did not quell his love for Miss Arbuthnot. He pursued her after his release, and died faithful to his idol, who, although among the most beautiful of women, never married. Her celibacy was not due to any affection she bore her eccentric adorer, but rather proceeded from her disgust with mankind because of his mad performances.

Abductions were rather common in Ireland, among both rich and poor, in the eighteenth century, although the penalty was severe, sometimes death; but Carden's was the only really notorious attempt at such a crime made by a man of some prominence during the nineteenth century; and the fact of the rarity of the offence of abduction drew all the more attention to his villanous escapade. It is alleged that the plot, counting expenses in preparing for the contemplated outrage, and making suitable arrangements for securing his intended victim after her abduction, cost the amorous lunatic—for such he must have been—about $125,-000. Some writers on the subject place the amount at a higher figure.

CHAPTER V

James Stephens and the Phœnix Conspiracy of 1858—He and O'Mahony
Organize the Fenian Movement—Fatal Delay of the Leaders
—Stephens's Dramatic Arrest and Escape

IN the summer of 1858, James Stephens, a daring and
accomplished native of the city of Kilkenny, who had
acted as an aide to John B. Dillon at Killenaule and to Smith
O'Brien at Ballingarry—both places in Tipperary—during
the brief and abortive "rising" of 1848—James Stephens,
we say, visited the town of Skibbereen in the County Cork,
on a secret mission. He had escaped to France after the
failure, and, in Paris, met with John O'Mahony, who had
also been compelled to leave Ireland in the disastrous "year
of revolutions." Both these highly educated Irish gentlemen moved in the most influential French political circles,
and became acquainted with the leading revolutionists of
Europe—Italians, Hungarians, and Poles—who thronged
the French capital at that period. The young Irishmen,
charmed by the subtle revolutionary methods of their European confrères, became convinced that Ireland could be
freed only by secret conspiracy, which would promote thorough organization of the people. And they set themselves
to the task—O'Mahony undertaking to organize the Irish
people in America and Stephens those living in Ireland and
Great Britain. In Skibbereen the young men had established a Literary Society of no common merit, and their
leader was a young school-teacher, who afterward became
famous in Irish history, Jeremiah Donovan, as he was
commonly known in his earlier career, but now universally
recognized under the style and title of O'Donovan Rossa—

the latter designation coming from the barony of Ross, in which he was born. He was a strongly built, tall, and prepossessing man, well versed in Irish lore and a fluent Gaelic scholar. "Rossa," as he is now known to all the world, possessed a peculiar magnetism. Although one of the fiercest and most uncompromising of Irish "rebels," his manners almost approached a feminine softness, except when taunt or insult aroused the lion slumbering in his heart. Age and misfortune subsequently had their effect on his disposition, but, in the earlier days of his career, he was, in most respects, a reincarnation of Shane the Proud. His moral ascendency over the young men of the Literary Society was unbounded, and Organizer Stephens took advantage of his sway to start, under the poetic name of the Phœnix Society—symbolical of Ireland's political resurrection—the first "Circle" of the Irish Revolutionary—afterward called the Irish Republican—Brotherhood in the town of Skibbereen. The title was subsequently abbreviated to "the I. R. B.," and became known more widely to fame as the "Fenian Brotherhood." The organization soon spread to all the neighboring towns, and even some of the rural districts in the counties of Cork and Kerry—the enlistment of patriotic recruits being much facilitated by the knowledge that the Sepoy Mutiny in India, which had been in sanguinary progress for more than a year, had nearly stripped Ireland of British regular troops.

The enthusiastic young "rebels" felt confident that, with a few months of preparation, counting also on Irish aid from the United States, which O'Mahony had promised, they would be able to dispose to their satisfaction of the half-hearted constabulary and raw militia to whom the holding of Ireland for the British crown was temporarily committed.

But England's all-observing spy system was not slow in getting on the trail of the youthful conspirators. Imprudent articles and letters published in the Dublin "Nation," and some hot denunciations of the political objects of Rossa and his friends by Bishop Moriarty, of Kerry—who became the most unpopular Catholic prelate Ireland has known—hastened on the climax. Government, toward the end of 1858, swooped down on the "Phœnix Men," or Fenians, with the result that Rossa, O'Sullivan Agreem, and about forty other bold enthusiasts were arrested, mainly on the information of a spy and traitor known to enduring infamy in the South of Ireland as "O'Sullivan Goulah." This rascal was the chief witness against O'Sullivan Agreem, who was first placed on trial. The latter was, as a matter of course, found guilty and sentenced to ten years' penal servitude. As the evidence against the other conspirators was even stronger than that against "Agreem," the counsel and influential friends of the accused suggested a compromise with the law officers of "the crown." This, after great hesitation on the part of O'Donovan Rossa and other of the prisoners, was agreed to, and, in consideration of their pleading guilty, the representatives of the government agreed that O'Sullivan Agreem should be immediately released from penal servitude. Notwithstanding, he was kept in prison much longer than was anticipated by his comrades, who compromised with the government solely for the purpose of achieving his liberation. Sentence was suspended upon the compromisers, "during good behavior." "Agreem" was finally released, disabled both in body and mind. The poor man, who lived just long enough to witness the blight of his early hopes, died in the United States about A.D. 1870.

The Civil War between our Northern and Southern

States terminated in April, 1865. This meant the disbandment, including both contestants, of about 1,500,000 soldiers, thoroughly inured to the hardest kind of warfare. Hundreds of thousands of Irishmen, or the sons of Irishmen, born in this country, belonged to both armies—that of the Union having the larger number. The leading Irish generals on the Union side were Major-General James Shields—also highly distinguished in our war with Mexico—Brigadier-General Thomas Francis Meagher, the Irish patriot orator of 1848; Major-General Philip H. Sheridan—who, however, never took much interest in the Irish movement; and General B. F. Mullen. Major-General Michael Corcoran—one of the founders of the Fenian movement in America—had been killed by a fall from his horse, while commanding the Legion that bore his name, in December, 1863; and Brigadier-General Thomas A. Smythe—the most promising of all these heroes in a military sense—had fallen in almost the last battle fought between North and South in Virginia. On the Southern side the most renowned Irish generals had been Major-General Patrick Clebourne, killed at Franklin, Tennessee, early in December, 1864, and Major-General Joseph Finegan, of Florida. From the State of New York there went forth to the war, among others, the following exclusively Irish regiments: 37th Irish Rifles; the 63d, 69th, and 88th Infantry; from Massachusetts, the 9th and 28th; from Connecticut, the 6th; from Pennsylvania, the 69th and 116th; from Ohio, the 10th; from Indiana, the 35th; from Illinois, the 23d and 90th; from Wisconsin, the 17th; and from Missouri, the 7th. There were many others, but those enumerated will serve to show the patriotic spirit of the Irish-American population of the Civil War period.

Naturally enough, when the fighting in America was done with, these warriors turned their eyes toward Ireland, where, they were assured, "a rising" against the English power was soon to occur. Stephens and O'Mahony, the Fenian leaders in Ireland and the United States respectively, made practical overtures to a large number of the officers, and, by the fall of 1865, quite a military staff had gone from America to Ireland to prepare the people for the expected armed revolution. But treason had revealed the plans to the British government. In September, 1865, the police swooped down upon the office of the "Irish People"—the Fenian organ published in Dublin—and arrested there Messrs. O'Leary, Kickham, and Luby—the supreme council of the order. The type was seized upon and all the machinery and other property confiscated. James Stephens, the able but despotic head of the movement, escaped for a time and lived for two months, as a private gentleman, under the name of Herbert, in a suburb of the Irish metropolis. His place of refuge was finally discovered by detectives, who "shadowed" Mrs. Stephens while she was returning to her home from a shopping expedition to Dublin. The house was, at once, placed under observation, and, one fine morning, the police surrounded it and succeeded in arresting Stephens, Duffy, and other leaders, who were, at once, taken to Richmond prison, where already lay O'Donovan Rossa and the other prisoners captured in September.

Mr. Stephens, throughout, manifested the most complete unconcern, and when arraigned before the magistrate, previous to final committal, said: "I have employed no lawyer in this case, because in making a defence of any kind, I should be recognizing British law in Ireland. Now, I deliberately and conscientiously repudiate the existence of that law in Ireland—its right or even its existence in Ireland, and I defy any punishment, and despise any punishment, it can inflict upon me. I have spoken it."

The English press sneered at what it termed "the mock heroics" of the prisoner, but within two weeks he had made good his vaunt. With the connivance of the hospital superintendent, John J. Breslin, and the night watchman, Daniel Byrne, and assisted by outside friends, he effected his escape on the night of November 24, 1865, lay for nearly three months concealed in the house of a poor woman named Mrs. Butler, in Dublin, and, at last, managed to get on board a sloop in Dublin Bay, which bore him in safety to France. The fidelity of Mrs. Butler will be all the more appreciated when we state that the government had offered $5,000 for the recapture of Stephens, but that noble heart could not be corrupted. Like Anne Devlin, the housekeeper of Robert Emmet, she remained faithful to the last, and, like her, too, she died in poverty.

Both Breslin and Byrne, who principally managed the escape of James Stephens, were sworn members of the Irish Revolutionary Brotherhood, and regularly attended meetings of the organization in Dublin. Many other petty officials were also affiliated with the omnipresent Fenians, and thousands of soldiers and sailors, who "loved their country before the queen," joined the "rebel" ranks, and many of these devoted men afterward paid the penalty in penal servitude. The Irish Celts in the British service rarely enlist for any love they bear the conquerors of their native land, but rather from love of adventure, or through the pressure of penury. While, in general, willing to fight for British pay against any other foreign power, these peculiar mercenaries "draw the line" at Ireland, and many of them met the fate of mutineers in 1798 rather than turn their guns against their kindred. At the funeral of Terence Bellew MacManus—one of the '48 men whose remains had been brought back from America for interment in Glasneven Cemetery—in November, 1861, all Dublin was startled to observe at least 1,000 red-coated soldiers marching in the great procession—but without arms of any kind—and saluting, by uncovering their heads, the house in Thomas Street where "Lord Edward" had made his glorious fight at the time of his arrest, sixty-three years before; and also the site of the immolation of Robert Emmet in front of St. Catherine's Church. The soldiers' demonstration at the MacManus obsequies was, from the revolutionary standpoint, most ill-advised, because it exposed their secret devotion to Ireland to the gaze of the hostile government, but they could not be restrained.   Later on in the movement, the organizing work done among the military by Edward Duffy, "Pagan" O'Leary, an ex-soldier of the French Foreign Legion named John Devoy, and other active and enterprising conspirators, put Dublin, practically, in the hands of Mr. Stephens, if he only had had the wisdom to strike before "the Castle" got thoroughly on its guard. The time to have "risen" was in July or August, 1865, while the British government was still apathetic, or incredulous; but it was not the first time that procrastination proved to be the ruin of the national cause. In an article dealing with the military disaffection the "Times" said, with a tone of alarm: "Sedition has eaten its way to the very foot of the throne."

Breslin and Byrne were suspected by the authorities of complicity in the escape of the Fenian chief, but nothing could be proved against the former. His companion kept, most imprudently, some criminating documents in his desk, but nothing that related to the rescue. He was imprisoned for a time, but was finally liberated, and made his way to New York, whither Breslin had preceded him.

Stephens had been a severe censor of O'Connell's policy, and yet he fell into the same pitfalls—only much more unjustifiably. Many things may be pardoned in a mere agitator which can not be overlooked in a revolutionist. O'Connell said that 1843 was "the Repeal Year." The government threw him into prison, and when he came out "the Repeal Year" had gone by forever. The shadow of the jail lay heavy upon his aged heart, and he could not rally from his despondency, which his country shared with him. Stephens stated that 1865 would be "the Year of Action." He, too, was consigned to a prison cell, from which, as we have seen, he almost miraculously escaped. The "Year of Action" went by and the opportunity returned no more. It is true that the broken ranks of the Irish Revolutionary Brotherhood were re-formed, and that new chiefs were chosen, but the documents found in the "Irish People" office, at the time of the seizure, and at Stephens's house at the time of his arrest, together with the secret information liberally supplied to the government by Pierce Nagle, who had been a trusted employee of the "Irish People" Company, and afterward by a wretch named Corrigan, who called himself Corydon, revealed most of the plans, and also the places where the organization was strongest. The new cry of the chiefs was to keep on getting ready for action, but to await aid from America—a vain expectation, because, outside of the Irish military and the Fenian order itself, America had no notion of doing anything practical for the sake of Ireland, although, at that time, most of the American people sympathized with her cause.

CHAPTER VI

Progress of the Revolutionary Movement in America—Division of Sentiment in Regard to Policy—Final Split of the Roberts-Sweeney and O'Mahony "Wings" of the Fenian Brotherhood

THE Revolutionary Brotherhood in Ireland — always hopeful while a single chance of success remained— turned their eyes wistfully westward, hoping to see the promised ships of their American kindred sailing for their deliverance across the broad Atlantic. Many were the prophecies of olden days cited to make it appear that Ireland's freedom would come from the land of the setting sun, but the watchers, like their ancestors of the preceding century, who bent their eyes southward, kept their long vigil in vain, for no friendly fleet appeared on the ocean horizon.

In the United States the Fenian Order, which had held its first national convention at Chicago in 1863 — both Stephens and Kickham having been present as delegates from the Irish organization—continued to grow in strength and influence. A second convention was held at Cincinnati, Ohio, in January, 1865, at which about 500 "Circles," in good standing, were represented. John O'Mahony was rechosen "Head Centre," or President, and a Council, or "Senate," of fifteen prominent members of the Brotherhood was elected to assist in governing the movement in America. O'Mahony, although an honest man, and a devoted patriot, was somewhat of a despot. He soon quarreled with leading members of the "Senate," and the cause suffered by the quarrel. A third convention, at which 800 Circles in good standing were represented, met in Philadelphia, in October, '65. Two men, destined to alter the policy of the Fenian society, attended this gathering. One was Colonel William R. Roberts, a rich merchant of New York City, and the other was Brevet Major-General Thomas W. Sweeney, then holding a commission as major in the regular army of the United States. Both were practical men, and saw that to attempt an invasion of Ireland, without a fleet to back them, was a visionary scheme. On the other hand, Canada, which was then almost as much a part of the British Empire as Scotland or Wales, presented a shining mark to the military revolutionists. Instead of having to cross a broad and stormy ocean, patrolled by the formidable fleet of the enemy, there lay between the Fenians and the territory of Great Britain, for the most part, lakes easily navigable by steamer, or even sailing-vessel, rivers moderately wide, and, in some sections, as northern New York, Vermont, New Hampshire, and Maine, an artificial boundary undefined by any natural obstacle. "On to Canada!" became, then, the war-cry of the Roberts-Sweeney "wing," while "On to Ireland!" was the slogan of O'Mahony and his followers. However, the line of divergent policies was not strongly drawn at the Philadelphia convention, where Colonel O'Mahony was re-elected without opposition "Head Centre" of the Fenian organization, while Roberts became a member of the "Senate." "Strained relations" between the Head Centre and his Council soon became apparent, and few who knew the inside workings were surprised when, early in 1866, there came a secession. Two conventions were then held. One reconfirmed O'Mahony as Head Centre, while the other elected Colonel Roberts as President, with a reorganized Senate, and General Sweeney as "Secretary of War." Before this consummation was arrived at, there had been "criminations and recriminations" between the rival parties. The "O'Mahony wing" was charged with wilful extravagance, because the headquarters had been moved from a back street in the lower part of New York City to a commodious house on an uptown square, known as "the Moffat Mansion." An absurd attempt to capture an island in the St. Lawrence, which ended in ignominious failure, covered O'Mahony, who had hardly anything to do with the project, with ridicule, and shook the faith of many of his own followers in his wisdom. Some, even, did not scruple to question his honesty, but of this no just man could doubt. O'Mahony was despotic and visionary, but he truly loved Ireland. He lived a life of penury, and, about a decade after the ruin of his cause, died in poverty. His body was sent to Ireland, and now reposes in beautiful Glasnevin, beside the relics of many another baffled patriot.

Meanwhile, the "Roberts wing," which had the larger following, continued to organize. Over twenty regiments of infantry were formed from the veterans of the great war, reinforced by members of the militia, or national guard, and also by independent battalions and companies of "Fenian volunteers." Vast quantities of arms and ammunition were purchased, at a nominal figure, from the American War Department, which, now that the internecine strife was over, was glad to dispose of them, at a sacrifice. The Fenian military organization was particularly strong in New York, Pennsylvania, Indiana, Illinois, Kentucky, Iowa, Nebraska, and Wisconsin. Missouri was also well organized, and there were regiments, or parts of regiments, placed on a war footing, in Tennessee, Georgia, and other Southern States. Kansas raised a regiment of cavalry, which was supplied with everything but horses. The latter were to be "requisitioned" in Canada. "Civil organizers" addressed great mass meetings night after night, throughout the Union, and "military organizers" were swearing in new battalions, or companies, day by day—apparently with the full knowledge and consent of the United States authorities. In fact, General Sweeney retained his commission as a major of regular infantry for some time after he had accepted the position of secretary of war and commander-in-chief of the Irish Republican, or Fenian, army. Such proceedings would be impossible at the present day, because American national sentiment has undergone a wonderful change. In 1866-67, the American people abhorred England for her treacherous course during the Civil War, and were still mourning the loss of their ocean commerce—destroyed by English-built cruisers, manned by British sailors, and armed with English cannon, while flying the Confederate flag. The American government sympathized with its people, and, it must be confessed, did very little, at the outset, to discourage the Fenian menace to Canada—probably because it wished to frighten England into a settlement of the *Alabama* Claims, resulting from damage done to our shipping by the cruisers already alluded to.

It may be asked, and very reasonably, Why should Canada have been held responsible for English misrule in Ireland? The Fenians did not hold Canada responsible, any more than Australia or New Zealand, but it was the only portion of British territory they could attack with a tolerable chance of success. It was garrisoned mainly by British regulars, and it had been the asylum of bank-raiding Confederates during the late American rebellion. There, also, had obnoxious "rebels," who proposed to introduce the plague of yellow fever in New York and Philadelphia, by means of infected clothing, after detection and flight, found a refuge and a home. It has been, for generations, the policy of England and her dependencies to foster and cherish the "rebels" of all other countries, and to deal cruelly with their own. Individual Englishmen may not be callous or inhuman, but their government, which represents them corporatively, certainly has been, and is. It is a reproach to the boasted civilization of England that she has never yet shown mercy to a beaten foe, but, on the contrary, as in the quite recent case of the Mahdi of the Soudan, whose tomb was violated by General Kitchener's order, has frequently pursued him beyond the portals of the grave.

CHAPTER VII

Invasion of Canada by the Fenian Vanguard under Colonel John O'Neill — General Sweeney's Tactical Blunder — Battle of Ridgeway, June 2, 1866—Utter Defeat of the Canadians

THE order to invade Canada at different points along the Great Lakes, the Niagara, the St. Lawrence, and the geographical frontier was given by General Sweeney to his lieutenants in the last week of May, 1866. By a singular fatality he ordered his rear, or southern, line to move first, leaving his front, or northern, line without positive command to make a forward step until the men from Tennessee, Kentucky, Indiana, and a portion of Pennsylvania, had started for "the front"—thereby needlessly alarming the whole country. Had he made use of the New York and Illinois troops, in the first place, matters might, eventually, have gone better for his cause. Those two States were, with perhaps the exception of Pennsylvania, better organized than the others, and were close to the contemplated scene of action—the first intention having been to hurl the New Yorkers across the Niagara River against Fort Erie, Hamilton, and Toronto, and to use the Illinoisans as a flanking force at some vulnerable point on Lake Huron or Lake Ontario. There were to have been simultaneous movements against Kingston and other places facing the New York and New England frontier. Chicago had the finest regiment in the Fenian army—almost all veterans— but, at the critical moment, it did not have the means of transportation. Sweeney wanted to purchase cannon, and the treasurer of the Fenian district of the city remitted him, by order of the State officers of the Brotherhood, $40,000. When the call came, it was found impossible to raise the money on short notice, but, on the news of the first skirmish, the amount was furnished by all classes of the Irish-American element within a few hours. But the mishap prevented the regiment from taking an active part in the campaign, although it reached Buffalo, fully one thousand bayonets strong, a few days too late to be of service. The disappointment of both officers and men was bitter, and many of the latter sought homes in other cities, rather than return to Chicago without having encountered the enemy.

Detachments from Nashville, Tenn., Louisville, Ky., Cincinnati, O., Indianapolis, Ind., Pittsburg, Pa., and other places, rendezvoused at Buffalo on the evening of the 30th of May. Colonel John O'Neill, of Nashville, was the senior officer present, and immediately assumed command. Aided by the Irish vessel-men of the city, many of whom were members of the Fenian Order, he soon had the means of crossing the Niagara River at his disposal. The command was ordered to assemble at a point called Lower Black

Rock, three miles below Buffalo, on the night of the 31st. Four canal boats, with tugs to tow them across the deep and rapid river, were in readiness, and at 3.30 o'clock in the morning of June 1, the invasion of Canada by the Fenian vanguard was begun. O'Neill's force landed at a little village called Waterloo, which took its name from the more famous Belgian hamlet. The wakeful inhabitants were, very naturally, startled by this martial apparition, which was wholly unexpected. The colonel called at once upon the Reeve of the town and requested him to convene the most influential citizens. This was done as speedily as possible. O'Neill, in a brief speech, assured them that life and property would be rigidly protected, and that all he asked from them was provisions for his men. These were promptly supplied. One of the Canadian delegation asked the colonel to explain the object of the invasion. O'Neill answered that the Fenian troops had come into the country, not to injure the Canadian people, but to overthrow British rule on the American Continent. "Then," observed his questioner, "you will need more men than you seem to have along with you to accomplish your object." "That may be," replied the colonel, "but, at all events, we will do our best."

Lieutenant-Colonel Starr, who commanded O'Neill's advance guard, occupied, by order, the village of Fort Erie, and the dismantled fortification of like name in the neighborhood. He raised the green flag on the desolate ramparts, and cut the wires connecting Fort Erie and Waterloo with Port Colborne and the interior. O'Neill placed guards on the public buildings and issued strict orders against intrusion into private houses and pillaging. The men who composed the command were, in the main, honest enthusiasts, who needed no such restraint, but their commander had an eye to effect on the Canadian people, who had been led to believe by their pro-British press that the Fenians were a band of assassins and robbers.

Colonel O'Neill moved out from Waterloo at 10 A.M. and went into camp at Newbiggin's Farm, on Frenchman's Creek, four miles down the Niagara, where he rested until 10 P.M. Here he was informed by Captain Donoghue, commanding the scouts, that he had come in contact with the British videttes, on the Chippewa road, that afternoon. The enemy, he said, retreated at sight of his party. Later information from Lieutenant-Colonel Hoy reported the British advancing to attack O'Neill in two strong columns—one from the side of Chippewa, and the other from the direction of Port Colborne. Many stragglers had followed O'Neill's movement across the river, most of whom had no interest in the cause, and some of whom had, perhaps, an eye to booty. O'Neill's order undeceived them, and, seeing the approach of danger, several of them secured small boats and returned to the American side. The commander promptly burned their arms, for fear they might fall into the hands of the British. He had remaining between five and six hundred men, who would follow him anywhere, and dare everything. He found himself in a perplexing position, but decided that the only thing to do was to attack one of the columns and defeat it, before the other could reinforce it. Accordingly, at 10 P.M., he broke camp and marched briskly in the direction of Chippewa, but changed direction about midnight, and turned into the Limestone Ridge causeway, leading toward the hamlet of Ridgeway, where he hoped to encounter the Port Colborne column. Lieutenant-Colonel Starr, with the vanguard, came up with the British scouts about 7 A.M. on June 2, and drove them back on their skirmishers, who were deployed over about half a mile on both sides of the highroad, not far from Ridgeway town. O'Neill hastened to the front and was warned that the British were receiving reinforcements by the whistle of the engine which drew the train from Port Colborne. He made his dispositions without delay, threw forward skirmishers, and posted his main battle-line behind a rail fence on the road leading to Fort Erie, which ran parallel with the British position. For half an hour, a sharp fusillade was maintained between the two skirmish lines, without visible advantage to either side. O'Neill suddenly became aware that the opposing force, which greatly outnumbered his own, was extending its main line of battle on both flanks, so as to surround him and cut off his retreat. He meditated ordering an attack on their centre, but feared he could not force it out of the thick neck of woods which it occupied. But the crisis had now arrived. He must either draw the British out of the timber and try his chances on more favorable ground, or be beaten where he stood. Calling his staff officers around him, he gave orders to fall back all along the line about two hundred yards, to a new and much stronger position. His skirmishers covered the movement, which revealed to the British the smallness of the Fenian array, and encouraged them accordingly. It was a moment of great anxiety for the Irish leader, who well knew the depressing effect of a retrograde movement on even the bravest troops. His men, however, acted splendidly. With wild cheers, the Canadians dashed out of the grove, driving O'Neill's skirmishers before them. These in retreating broke to the right and left and took post behind their main body, leaving the Irish front clear, and from it blazed a stunning volley, which checked the Canadian onrush. O'Neill, on horseback, followed by his mounted aides, came out of a thin clump of trees, which commanded a view of the field, and, waving his hat, shouted: "Forward, men! Charge!" His order was vigorously obeyed, and the officer commanding the British, mistaking the Fenian leader and his staff for troopers, cried out: "Form square to resist cavalry!" As this movement could not be promptly executed while the troops were in the confusion incident to a charge, the order was unfortunate for the Canadians, who, up to this time, had borne themselves most gallantly. The Fenians caught them in the act of formation, and, charging them home, threw the whole mass into inextricable confusion. Colonel Booker, the senior officer, and long the commander of the crack militia regiment known as the Queen's Own Rifles of Toronto, is reputed to have set the example of hasty flight. Some of the younger officers made brave efforts to rally their men, but the Fenians were not to be stopped that day, and, before their impetuosity, the Canadians finally gave way and tumbled down the road in panic rout. Hundreds escaped through the fields, and a large proportion threw away their rifles, knapsacks, overcoats, and other impedimenta, in order to facilitate their escape.

CHAPTER VIII

Colonel O'Neill's Further Operations—He Retreats from the Interior and Recaptures Fort Erie, after a Sharp Fight—Not Being Reinforced, he Recrosses the Niagara River

THE end of the preceding chapter left the Canadian troops flying before the victorious Fenians at Ridgeway. O'Neill pursued the fugitives for about a mile, when, learning that the second, and more formidable, British column, under Brigadier Peacock, was advancing rapidly against him from Chippewa, he stopped the pursuit and countermarched toward Fort Erie, where he hoped to be strongly reinforced. Instead, however, on arriving at that village, he found it occupied by the Welland Canal Battery and the Dunville Naval Brigade, who had with them a small steamer, commanded by a lieutenant of the Royal Navy. A brisk fight ensued. The Canadians barricaded themselves in the houses and fired from the windows, wounding a Fenian officer and some of the rank and file. O'Neill ordered his men to collect firewood and smoke the British out of the houses. This ruse de guerre succeeded, and the village was speedily retaken by the Fenians. Some of the Canadians escaped on the steamer, but Captain King, of the Welland Battery, together with forty-five men of his own command, Lieutenant McDonald, of the British Navy, and Lieutenant Nemo, of the Royal Artillery, were made prisoners. O'Neill then took possession of the old fort, which he placed in some posture of defence, and calmly awaited further developments. He sent couriers to Buffalo to explain the situation and to hurry up reinforcements. Brigadier Peacock could not be very far distant, and another battle might be expected that evening. "If not supported," he said to the messengers, "I must recross the river, in order to save my command. Failing in that, I will make this old fort a slaughter-pen, for I will never surrender." Fortunately for him, the intricacy of his position was already well known in Buffalo, and arrangements were under way to enable him to retreat. Brigadier Peacock, who had with him the 16th and 47th British line regiments, several volunteer and militia detachments, and two fine batteries of the Royal Artillery, arrived in the vicinity of Fort Erie after nightfall on Saturday, June 2, but, not knowing how O'Neill was situated, deferred active measures until morning. Against such an overwhelming force as his, it would have been stark madness in O'Neill to oppose his feeble band. At midnight he was made aware that a big scow, drawn by a powerful tug, had arrived from Buffalo on the Canadian bank of the Niagara, near Waterloo. It was sufficient for the accommodation of all his command. The British bugles were sounding in the woods in the neighborhood of the fort early in the morning of Sunday, June 3, when O'Neill and his soldiers moved noiselessly out of it. At about 3 o'clock he and his men were on board the scow, and in midstream, when the armed tugboat, *Harrison,* acting as a river patrol for the United States revenue cutter *Michigan,* fired a shot across their bows and called upon all of them to surrender to the American government. This they did without delay. The scow was headed toward a point of land on the American side, where the Fenian troops were held as prisoners for several days, under a burning sun, and deprived of all decent accommodation. The officers, although they desired to share the privations of their men, were taken on board the *Michigan* and also kept under guard. Otherwise they were treated with consideration, although some of them complained that a stand of colors, captured from the Canadian troops, had been taken from them by Lieutenant Morris, who commanded the tug *Harrison,* and returned to the Canadian authorities. Lieutenant Morris was, by birth, an Englishman. The Fenian rank and file were paroled on June 7. On the same day, the officers were arraigned in the United States District Court charged with breaking the neutrality laws. They gave bail for their appearance at Canandaigua on the 19th, but nothing ever came of the case, and, after the excitement had run its course, the public seemed to forget all about it.

The Brito-Canadian force, which engaged the Fenians at Ridgeway, consisted of the Queen's Own Rifles, the 10th Royals, the Caledonian Rifles, who wore a Highland uniform; the 13th Rifle Battalion, of Hamilton, and the 10th Canadian Hussars, who were trained as sharpshooters—forming in all a body of about 1,600 men.

The losses at the two affairs of Ridgeway and Fort Erie, as nearly as can be ascertained, were, on the Canadian side, one officer killed, two wounded, and three captured; twelve rank and file killed, ninety-five wounded, and fifty-seven made prisoners. In addition, they lost a stand of colors. All the British prisoners were released by O'Neill on parole before he recrossed the river. The Irish loss was one officer killed, one wounded, and one captured; eleven rank and file killed, twenty-five wounded, and nine — mainly stragglers—captured. Among the prisoners made by the Canadians was Father MacMahon, a humane clergyman who devoted himself to the spiritual and physical needs of the wounded on the firing line. He was, nevertheless, held, tried, convicted, and imprisoned with his luckless companions, who, like himself, were detained for long years in harsh captivity. While we admit that it was only natural in the Canadians to feel incensed against their invaders, whose motives did not appeal to them in any sense, they should have remembered that the Fenians, during their brief occupation of British territory, had acted both honorably and humanely. They had paroled nearly one hundred Canadian prisoners, including three officers, and had offered them no indignity while they had them in their power. Therefore, Canada showed bad taste in visiting vengeance on the Fenian captives, and this was particularly so in the case of the Rev. Father MacMahon, who was, in the strictest sense, a non-combatant.

The United States proclamation of neutrality followed fast on the heels of O'Neill's evacuation of Canada, and the further operations of the Fenian army were barred, although partial attempts were made by General Spear—an American in the Fenian service—and some other officers, on the Canadian border, facing the eastern New York and Vermont boundaries. By the 5th of June, some 40,000 Fenian soldiers, from both North and South, were en route to the frontier. They crowded in the American border cities from Erie to St. Albans, but deported themselves with decorum. They were rationed by committees of benevolent ladies, whom they treated with reverential respect. Not a single act of violence, or even disorder, is on record against the Fenian soldiery during their residence in those towns. The inhabitants, who were led to think the intruders a rude set of men, bent on mischief, were agreeably surprised. Much of the good-will displayed toward the martial visitors was due to the popular feeling against English misconduct, in which Canada participated, during America's internal troubles. On this account, principally, the contemplated Fenian conquest of our northern neighbor was not looked upon with disapproving eyes by the American masses of that generation. On the contrary, the American people in general showed their unmistakable sympathy with the Fenian soldiery whenever and wherever they appeared. General Meade, the victor of Gettysburg, an officer of immediate Irish origin, was placed in command on the frontier by President Johnson. On his recommendation, the American government paid for the transportation of the disbanded Fenians to their homes, or to any point in the United States they wished to go to. It has been stated, on what seems to be good authority, that 39,000 men were provided for in this way by the government—a very wise solution of the difficulty.

This repulse practically broke the backbone of the Fenian movement, militant in America, although O'Neill made another attempt, with disastrous results, on the Vermont line, in May, 1870. His failure was complete, as he was arrested by the United States marshal, while in the very act of invasion, and was otherwise humiliated. Skirmishes occurred at Pigeon Hill, and Trout River, just across the Vermont and New York lines, which resulted in a Fenian repulse, as only a handful of men engaged the British and Canadians at those points. After other attempts in the direction of Manitoba and the Northwest Territory, which were absolutely futile, O'Neill finally settled down to the business of founding Irish-American colonies, and had a measurable amount of success. The thriving settlement of O'Neill City, in Nebraska, is named after him. He died of a pulmonary complaint in Omaha early in 1878, and a monument, erected by some of his admiring countrymen, marks his place of sepulture in that city. His main foible was vanity, which developed with extraordinary rapidity after the affair of Ridgeway. Of him it may be said, as Napoleon remarked on the character of Ney at St. Helena: "He was the bravest of men; there all his faculties terminated." As the infirmities of the great marshal's temper ruined the cause of the Emperor, so did O'Neill's puerile folly destroy the last hope of the Fenian movement in America.

Not much remains to be written of the other Fenian

chiefs concerned in the Canadian invasion. Colonel Roberts suffered a short term of imprisonment in New York, and upon his liberation devoted himself mainly to his private business, although, under protest, he served one term as president of the reorganized Fenian Brotherhood, in 1867-68. He was succeeded by O'Neill, with the unfortunate result already stated. The colonel, on retiring from the Fenian presidency, took some interest in American politics, and was appointed Minister to Chili during President Cleveland's first term in office. He died in New York City a few years ago, poor and almost forgotten. General Sweeney, after a period of probation, was restored to his majority in the regular army, and some years later, having attained promotion, and reached the age limit, was retired as brigadier-general. He passed from earthly scenes a little earlier than his friend and ally, Colonel Roberts. Both these noted Irishmen were honest, patriotic, and, in a measure, practical, but they lacked the quality of discretion. Acting under the orders of abler men, they would have done creditable service, but left to their own judgment, they drifted hopelessly, and were morally overwhelmed by the ever-multiplying difficulties and heartburnings that confronted them. It is one thing to start a revolutionary movement, and quite another to control it when started. Had General Philip Sheridan, or General Thomas A. Smythe, been commander-in-chief of the Fenian army, in May and June, 1866, all the towns of Canada, including historic Quebec, which was not, then, in a formidable condition of defence, would have fallen before the sudden onrush of an overwhelming body of veterans. We doubt that America would have allowed the Fenians, in the event of their success, to use Canada as "a base of operations" against Great Britain—the avowed intention of Roberts and Sweeney having been to issue letters of marque to privateers pledged to prey on British commerce. It is quite probable that the United States government would have intervened and compromised the matter by absorbing both Canada and the Fenians, on the ground that the former needed a more powerful protector, and that the invaders had a bad title to their conquest. England might have drawn the sword to maintain the Canadian connection, but, at the time, it would have made no difference, as we had fully 2,000,000 disbanded soldiers, counting both sections of the Republic, to draw on if needed. America was never so formidable, in a military sense, as during the ten years which followed the surrender at Appomattox.

The Fenian movement against Canada had the effect of changing "a loose confederation" into a solidified Dominion, now burdened by an enormous debt. It also scared England into agreeing to the formation of the "High Joint" Commission, which formulated the Treaty of Washington. This treaty led to the abrogation of the British assumption, "Once a subject, always a subject"—a chief cause of the War of 1812, and also led to the establishment of the Geneva Board of Arbitration, which, by a vote of four to one, awarded the United States $15,500,000 "direct damages" on account of the *Alabama* depredations on our commerce.

CHAPTER IX

How the Fenian Leaders in Ireland Fared—Long Terms of Imprisonment Awarded Them—Abortive "Risings" in Munster and Leinster —Treason of "General" Massey—The Tallaght Fiasco

MEANWHILE matters went badly with the arrested Fenian leaders in Ireland. Thomas Clarke Luby, John O'Leary, and Charles J. Kickham, who were the triumvirs of Fenianism in that country, were tried by packed juries, found guilty, of course, and sentenced to twenty years' penal servitude each. O'Donovan Rossa, who dismissed his counsel and made an able defence of himself, was sentenced for life, on account of his previous connection with the Phœnix Society, and, also, because he was the most intractable of all the "rebels" placed in the dock. His after treatment in British prisons was a disgrace to the English people, and the indignities to which the prisoner was subjected would have driven weaker men insane.

Several military prisoners, including John Boyle O'Reilly, Color-Sergeant McCarthy, Corporal Chambers, and Gunner Flood, were tried by court-martial. They had all worn the English uniform, but they had also taken the Fenian obligation. Atrocious informers swore positively against them. Some were sentenced to be shot and others to be flogged. The death sentences were finally commuted, but the floggings were duly inflicted. Nearly all of these prisoners were transported to the antipodes, whence they daringly escaped, with Irish-American, and other American, assistance. The men most instrumental in their rescue were

James Reynolds, of New Haven, Conn.; Captain Anthony, a New England skipper of the same city; John J. Breslin, the same who had engineered the escape of Stephens from Richmond Bridewell, then resident in New York; Thomas Desmond, of San Francisco, and other daring spirits. Reynolds mortgaged his house to furnish the money; Captain Anthony, who had no Irish blood in his veins, risked his ship in the cause; and Breslin, Desmond, and the rest furnished the crew who carried the plan into effect.

The minor Fenian chiefs were also speedily tried, convicted, and sentenced to various terms of imprisonment, which some of them did not survive. James Stephens transferred his residence from France to the United States, where he speedily identified himself with "the O'Mahony wing" of Fenianism, and sagely denounced Roberts's Canadian attempt, which he said had ruined the cause; 1867, he now declared, would surely be "the year of action." As this rash statement was made at a great Irish-American demonstration, held in Jones's Wood, New York City, the English profited by the information, and immediately "stood on guard" in Ireland and elsewhere. Mr. Stephens, at this same meeting, further announced that he would go to Ireland and take charge of the operations there in person. For some unexplained reason he did not fulfil his promise, and he thus lost prestige among his people at home and abroad.

The leaders who were still at large in Ireland lost all hope of effective aid from America and came to the desperate resolution of attempting an unaided revolution, chiefly, we suppose, to save the military honor of the Irish nation, which, they conceived, would be compromised if no effort to meet the English army in the field was made.

All chance of a successful uprising had already passed away.

The 12th of February, 1867, was fixed upon as the day of general "rising," but conditions became such that a countermand order was sent out the day preceding. This failed to reach the Cahirciveen, County Kerry, "Circle," which marched out toward Killarney, according to original orders. Failing to meet with expected supports, the leader became alarmed and gave the word to his men to disperse, which they did without loss of time. But their march had been observed by the police patrol, who immediately gave the alarm. The local aristocrats, with their wives and families and household goods, sought refuge in a Killarney hotel, which they fortified, after the manner of the besieged legations in Pekin. But the alarm, which begot numerous ludicrous incidents, speedily subsided, and "the gentry" returned to their abodes.

About the same time, the Fenians in England had planned the capture of Chester Castle, in which was stored a large quantity of arms and ammunition. The plan would, no doubt, have succeeded, as it was well devised, but for the treason of Corrigan, or Corydon, who had already, in secret, done the English government some service, but still retained his membership in the Fenian order. He informed the chief constable of Liverpool of the bold project, and that official promptly notified London and Chester. Before twenty-four hours had elapsed, and just in time to anticipate the Fenian attempt, the Grenadier Guards arrived in Chester, from the metropolis, and occupied the castle, where the guards had already been doubled. Hundreds of the brotherhood, who had arrived quietly in small squads, were secretly assembled in Chester when the Household Regiment, which was soon followed by other battalions, arrived. They at once recognized that they had been betrayed, and the leaders ordered them to disperse and decamp without delay. Some who landed in Ireland were arrested. Most of the others escaped. The government became profoundly alarmed, the more so as the professional informers, in order to enhance their own importance, made the authorities think the danger much greater than it actually was. Arrangements had been made by the Fenian chiefs in Birkenhead and Liverpool, in case the attempt on Chester Castle had succeeded, to ship a large number of the Order, armed with the guns obtained from the arsenal, to Ireland, there to begin the long-deferred insurrection. It was a gallant plan, but, looking at it from this distance of time, and remembering that every important Irish port was guarded by English men-of-war, and every point of the coast-line by vigilant guards, it is difficult to conceive how it could have succeeded.

The conduct of Fenian military affairs in part of Munster had been committed to an Irish-American, who styled himself Brigadier-General Massey, but about whose army career little or nothing seemed to be known, beyond the fact that, judging by his technical knowledge of the profession, he had served somewhere. He was reputed to be the natural son of a Limerick landlord, and was said to have served in his early youth in the Irish constabulary—the most unpopular representatives of British rule in Ireland. The "Brigadier's" force was to rendezvous, when the signal would be given, at Limerick Junction, a railroad centre and a strategical point "in the heart of the most disaffected district in Ireland—Tipperary, Cork, and Limerick." Massey received his orders on the evening of March 4, at his quarters in Cork, and at once boarded a train bound for "the Junction." He had hardly taken his seat when he was pounced upon and made prisoner by four stalwart detectives, fully armed. The sight of British soldiers crowding the station platform further demoralized the unmanly "Brigadier," who swooned upon the spot. The detectives then knew they had a man who would be valuable in the witness-box, and so, within a few weeks, the disgraceful spectacle of a "general" swearing against the officers he had himself appointed came to pass. Most writers are agreed, however, that Massey's treason did not spring from mercenary motives, but was the result of moral and physical cowardice. Think of the military fortunes of a brave and confiding people being placed in the control of such a debased creature! The "excuse" he gave was that only four men, beside himself, knew of the Limerick Junction plan. Therefore, some one of his confederates must have been the traitor! In this he was correct. It was the wretch Corydon, who would seem to have been taken into every scheme with implicit confidence. And all this time he was jingling English gold in his greedy pockets. It is noticeable that, throughout Irish history, the men most eager to be in possession of every secret, and most active in attendance on private meetings where they could learn all that was projected, without fear of detection as to design, have frequently been the most dangerous traitors to the national cause. However, Massey was conveyed to Dublin, and immured in one of the cells under the Castle—"those catacombs of living death where the wretch who is buried a man, lies, till his heart has time to fester and dissolve, and is then dug up a witness."

The capture of Massey, whose treason was not apparent

until some time after the event, came like a thunderclap on the Fenians of North Munster, who had begun their march to "the Junction" on the night of the 4th. Their scouts, early on the morning of the 5th, beheld, from many vantage points, the contemplated rendezvous occupied by a powerful British force of all arms. All the bands halted and soon learned the fate of the adventurer who was to have commanded them. Utterly disheartened, most of the men scattered and made for home as best they could. There occurred, however, a fierce fight between the Fenians and police at Kilmallock, County Limerick, in which many lives were lost. The police barrack would have been captured but for the unexpected arrival of another strong body of constabulary, who took the Irish force in the rear and compelled it to abandon the town, after a most stubborn resistance. At a place called Ballyhooley, in Tipperary, a skirmish occurred between the Fenians, commanded by Colonel Thomas Francis Burke, formerly in the Confederate army, and a numerous force of British regulars. The latter speedily outflanked their untrained and badly armed opponents, and retreat became imperative. Colonel Burke, who was disabled by an old wound, fell from his horse and was, with a few others, captured.

In Dublin, where the notorious butcher of the Sepoys, Sir Hugh Rose, afterward Lord Strathnairn, commanded, there was great excitement. Several thousand young patriots marched out of the capital toward a place called Tallaght, about five miles to the southward. General Rose had his troops in position before them, and, when the vanguard reached Tallaght, it was met by a volley from the soldiers, which scattered it with a loss of two men killed and many wounded. Those who followed, warned by the firing and by some of the panic-stricken fugitives, proceeded no further. They turned back to Dublin, and were arrested by dozens as they crossed the bridges of the Grand Canal, where guards were stationed to capture them.

All of the Irish who marched for Tallaght did not return without burning powder. One party compelled the police at Stepaside to surrender their barrack, and subsequently captured the constabulary stationed at Kilcullen. No harm or insult was offered to the prisoners in either case. Finding that the insurrection around Dublin was practically over, after the Tallaght fiasco, the Fenians released their captives, some of whom afterward swore against their generous conquerors and sent them into penal servitude.

The chief point of Irish revolt centred around the city of Cork, where an Irish-American known as "Captain Mackey," but whose real name was William M. Lomasney, commanded. This young man had served for a period in the Union army and was a born guerilla leader. His immediate district was the best organized in all Ireland, and its resistance continued longest. There were fierce engagements between the insurgents and the troops at Castlemartyr, Middleton, and Ballyknockane. The police barrack at the latter place was captured by Mackey's force, and he soon afterward surprised a martello tower and coastguard station, the garrisons surrendering after spirited fighting. After many daring adventures, including the taking of arms from government stores in Cork, this gallant leader was finally tracked to his hiding-place, overpowered, and made a prisoner. Some months afterward, he was tried for treason, and received a twenty years' sentence, the judge, the Right Hon. Thomas O'Hagan, shedding tears as he pronounced the young hero's doom.

Another gallant figure·of the period was a young man of good social position named Peter O'Neill Crowley. His courage boiled in the face of danger, and, with only two comrades, he dared a whole battalion of English regulars in Kilclooney wood, near Mitchelstown, County Cork, until he fell mortally wounded, cheering for Ireland with his latest breath. His companions, McClure and Kelly, were captured and spent many weary years in British prisons.

At the time of the Fenian "rising," the elements fought for England, as they did in the days of the Spanish Armada and the Bantry Bay expedition. A storm began in the afternoon of March 6th and lasted for twelve days, burying the usually verdant island in the snows of an arctic winter. The cold, too, became intense, so that the insurgents, who were without tents, or a commissariat of any kind, could not keep the field, except in a few places. The British troops, who were divided into flying columns, also suffered severely, many men and horses having been badly frozen while engaged in scouting expeditions. Neither side gained much glory in the Fenian campaign of 1867.

CHAPTER X

The Daring and Romantic Voyage of the *Erin's Hope*—Singular Impotency of the British Fleet—Fate of the Officers and Crew of the Little Vessel

THE year 1867 was not fated to pass into history without witnessing other gallant manifestations of undying devotion to a baffled cause. In April, a bold band of Irish-Americans, mostly ex-soldiers, managed to slip out of New York Harbor, on a small steamer, as if on an excursion, and boarded a brigantine called the *Jacknell,* which lay off Sandy Hook, ostensibly bound for Cuba. It carried 5,000 stand of

arms, three field-pieces, and 250,000 rounds of cartridges, together with other warlike appliances. These were sent on
board the *Jacknell* packed in piano cases, wine barrels, and
other harmless-looking receptacles. All told, the party consisted of about fifty members. The leaders were General
James E. Kerrigan, Colonel John Warren, Lieutenant-
Colonel Nagle, Major S. R. Tresilian, Captain Kavanagh,
Lieutenant Augustine E. Costello — all seasoned soldiers,
tried and true. The little vessel speedily lifted anchor and
stood out to sea, steering, apparently, for the West Indies.
During the night, her course was changed and she was
headed for Ireland, the expectation of her occupants being
that they would find the Irish people still in arms for their
liberty. Head winds prevailed during a part of the voyage,
so that the progress of the ship eastward was rather slow.
In the red dawn of the morning of Easter Sunday, April
29, the Irish national flag of green and gold, with the
"Harp Without the Crown" in the centre, was raised at the
peak and the *Jacknell* changed her name to the more fitting,
if delusive, one of *Erin's Hope*. On May 19, the distant
headlands of Connaught were first sighted by the fearless
voyagers, and next day they sailed into the harbor of Sligo.
The revolutionists expected their arrival, and sent an agent
on board in a small boat to notify them that all was lost.
The government's coastguards also sighted them, and immediately gave the alarm to the naval patrols by telegraph,
with the result that several British gunboats were soon
steaming out to sea to solve the riddle of the strange "sail's"
appearance in the bay. The schooner, or brigantine, as the
English sailors described her, did not wait to be overhauled,
but sailed away as fast as a full spread of canvas could
carry her. She managed to baffle the cruisers, and beat up

and down the western and southwestern coasts for several days without misadventure. In the first week of June, the voyagers were abreast of Helvick Head, near the port of Dungarvan, County Waterford. The report of the quartermaster showed that the cruise of nearly nine weeks had about exhausted the provisions. There were not enough left for a return voyage if all remained on board, and yet nothing practical could be gained by landing. To remain longer on the Irish coast was certain to result in the capture of the vessel, with all that she carried. At a council of war, it was determined that to allow the ship to be lost would be bad policy, so it was decided that thirty officers and men should land and the remainder take the *Erin's Hope*—now hopeless—back to New York. In order to accomplish the landing, the party "borrowed" two fishing boats, whose crews' curiosity brought them within range. These boats landed the persons selected, and were then restored to their astonished owners.

The English government had concentrated a large land force near Dungarvan, and promptly seized the entire party when they landed. Among the latter was one vile traitor, named Daniel J. Buckley; and this villain was used as a witness against his former comrades. His evidence sent Colonel John Warren into penal servitude for fifteen, and Captain Augustine E. Costello for twelve, years. The others, after a period of detention under suspension of the Habeas Corpus Act, were let go. We may here note that, as both Warren and Costello, although born in Ireland, were naturalized Americans, the question of judicial jurisdiction was raised. As aliens, under the old law, since repealed, they were entitled to be tried by a mixed jury of aliens and British subjects. The court refused this privilege, and our State Department was appealed to in behalf of both prisoners. Then came other cases of like nature, including that of O'Meagher Condon, a born American, implicated in the Manchester Rescue. Our government made vigorous representations to the British executive, and the controversy led to voluminous correspondence. Eventually, the Treaty of Washington disposed of the matter, and the English Parliament passed an act in accordance with its provisions, enabling British subjects to change their allegiance, but, thenceforth, aliens who offended against the laws on British soil were to be subjected to the same process of trial as if they were natives.

The officers and men who had remained on the brigantine brought her back in safety to New York, having managed to elude the boasted vigilance of the British Navy. Colonel Kerrigan, although deeply chagrined by disappointment, survived the voyage thirty years. Colonel Warren and Captain Costello, after enduring all the rigors of penal imprisonment for several years, were finally released and returned to America. Warren, who had fought in all the bloody battles of the Army of the Potomac, without serious injury, was killed in 1898 by the fall of a chimney tile during a slight storm in Boston. This reminds us of the story of the sailor who had sailed around the globe in safety, participating in many combats, and yet was drowned in a little pond near the house in which he was born. Another parallel is the fate of the famous French general of cavalry, Le Tort, who, having participated in every battle of the Republic and Empire, from Fleurus to Leipsic, and from Leipsic to Charleroi, was shot by a Prussian rifleman, three days before Waterloo, in a field in which he had herded cows when a boy.

Col. T. F. Burke, captured in Tipperary, in March, was tried later on, and against him appeared as witnesses "Brigadier" Massey and the still more infamous Corydon. He made a superb speech from the dock, in which he scored the informers with a power equal to that of the great Curran himself. Alluding to his aged mother, he said that, like the Spartan matron, she sent him forth to battle for liberty, with the noble injunction to return with his shield, as a token of victory, or on his shield, as a sign of his glorious death. Fate had decreed that he was not to die on the field of battle, but he was ready to die on the scaffold for Ireland. His chivalrous eloquence touched all who heard it—even the stern judge who sentenced him to death for high treason. This extreme sentence was afterward commuted by the crown to life imprisonment, and, in the end, the gallant prisoner shared in the amnesty which followed the final wreck of the once formidable Fenian movement. Many other Irishmen, and Irish-Americans—notably General William Halpin and Captain John McCafferty—suffered for their patriotism in British penal institutions. The list of victims was the longest since the uprising of 1798.

CHAPTER XI

The Fenian Movement in England—Active Patriotism of the Irish
People Settled in that Country—The Famous "Manchester
Rescue" and what Led to It

EMIGRATION from Ireland to Great Britain during the Famine period, and for many years thereafter, had swelled the Irish population in the latter country to, perhaps, three millions of souls, including, of course, Irish children born on British soil. Most of the elder generation had left their native country in as poor a condition as English rule could place them in, and, at the outset, were viewed with much disfavor by the working classes of England, with whose labor they were compelled to compete. Among this class of emigrants, as well as their better-off fellow exiles, the fires of Fenianism still smouldered, and needed but little exertion to fan them into a fierce flame. They were all bitter in their very natural resentment toward a government which had tortured their native land with a series of savage coercion laws, and reduced her to an abject provincial condition. Many of the English Chartists sympathized with them, but the masses of the British people, high and low, rich and poor, sided with their rulers. Ordinarily, the Irish and they got along well enough together, and many sincere friendships had sprung up between the two races, but, in the Fenian period, particularly since the abortive attempt on Chester Castle, all the old race hatred, except in a few instances, returned in full force. An event was now to occur which made the residence of any patriotic Irishman in Great Britain, for a time, distinctly hazardous. On the 11th of September, 1867, the Manchester police arrested two suspects, who gave the names of Williams and White. They were about to be committed to Bridewell, under the Vagrant Law, when a detective, who suspected they were Fenians, asked that they be held for a week, pending investigation. The magistrate granted the request. Within twelve hours the mystery was penetrated by the police. Williams and White were proven to be Colonel Thomas J. Kelly and Captain John Deasy, the active heads of the Fenian order in Great Britain and Ireland. The mishap to their chiefs greatly exasperated the Manchester Fenians, and, after due consultation, they decided on a bold, and even desperate, measure, considering all the circumstances—the forcible rescue of their leaders from the clutches of the police, no matter what the cost. The two prisoners were formally arraigned before, and duly committed to jail by, the magistrate on Wednesday, September 18. Warnings of an attempted rescue, sent from Dublin Castle, doubtless on the information of some traitor, were unheeded by the authorities in the main. They knew, however, that the Irish in Manchester were numerous, and, therefore, apt to make some kind of a hostile demonstration. The captives were placed in a prison van with several ordinary prisoners, some of them depraved men and women. Colonel Kelly and his companion were handcuffed and locked in separate compartments of the conveyance, while a dozen policemen, instead of the regular complement of three, were detached as an escort. Five of the officers sat on the front seat of the commodious vehicle, two occupied the rear step, four followed in a hack, and the sergeant of the party, Brett, sat inside, with the keys in his possession. At a point leading out of Manchester to Salford jail, two miles distant, on the Hyde Road, a railroad viaduct crosses the highway, which was there bordered by straggling houses and brick walls of no great height. Here a young man sprang into the middle of the causeway, pointed a pistol at the driver and called on him to halt. Instead, the driver lashed up his animals, and attempted to run past the aggressor. Immediately a dozen men, all armed with revolvers, leaped over the low walls, and fired at the horses. One of the beasts fell, and the van came to a full stop. Ten of the policemen leaped into the street and ran for dear life—a most cowardly desertion of their comrades and trust. One of those who had followed in the cab showed pluck, but was speedily overpowered. The door of the van was found locked, and, through some unfortunate oversight, no tools were at hand to break it open. In this emergency, Sergeant Brett, who stuck to his post like a brave man, was called upon to deliver up the keys, or else open the door, but he stubbornly refused. Some one then suggested to shoot through the key-hole of the lock, and, as the runaway police had now summoned a crowd to their aid, the danger to the rescuers became imminent. The shot was fired and the lock broken, but Sergeant Brett, who had been watching the operations through the key aperture, was shot through the brain and fell dead among the prisoners. The women yelled in terror, and one of them passed out the keys, which were the principal cause of the accidental tragedy. With them, the Fenians opened the van and its compartments and rescued their chiefs, whom they embraced with fervor. Allen, who afterward suffered for his zeal, exclaimed to Kelly: "I told you, Colonel, that I'd die before I parted with you"—prophetic of the poor fellow's sad destiny. The English mob had now gathered in overwhelming numbers, and attacked the rescuers with every missile within their reach. All of the latter could have escaped, but exposed themselves so as to save their leaders. As it was, several were overtaken, brutally beaten, and placed under arrest. The English, whose pride was piqued by an act of such daring, performed by Irishmen in the heart of one of their chief cities, were doubly incensed at the escape of Kelly and Deasy, who were never retaken, and reached America in safety. They pretended to think that the killing of Brett was a deliberate murder, and their press still further inflamed the national anger by appealing to race hatred. In moments of excitement, the English are excessively ferocious, and often blindly unjust and cruel, particularly against an enemy who has not much power of retaliation. In seasons of tranquillity, they are, perhaps, as reasonable as other races, except where the state, or rather the crown, comes into conflict with the subject. The English majority is always certain to be with the former, especially if the culprits happen to be Irishmen.

CHAPTER XII

"Trial" of the Manchester Fenian Prisoners—Five Sentenced to Death —Allen, Larkin, and O'Brien Hanged—The Clerkenwell Explosion—Michael Barrett Tried and Executed for the Act

THE Manchester rescue inflamed the worst passions of the English people, and the newspapers called for swift and summary punishment of the offenders—not for justice. Five of the men arrested were arraigned on charge of having wilfully murdered Sergeant Brett. These were Captain Edward O'Meagher Condon—an American citizen, born in the State of Ohio; William Philip Allen, Captain Michael O'Brien, who had served in the Union army; Thomas Maguire, an ex-marine of the English navy, and Michael Larkin, a humble artisan of Manchester, who had a large and dependent family. The English prisoners who were in the van were, with the stampeded policemen, whose vindictiveness was aroused by the ridicule heaped upon them for their cowardice, their chief accusers. The judge who presided was notoriously prejudiced, and the jury which passed on the case carefully packed. A verdict of guilty was returned against all five, on one indictment, sustained by the same evidence. They were duly sentenced to death by hanging, and the day of execution was set for November

23. All the condemned bore themselves firmly. Before sentence was passed, in reply to the usual question, each of them made a speech to the court. All denied the killing of Brett, with or without intention. Allen said: "I don't say this for mercy. I want no mercy—I'll have no mercy. I'll die, as many thousands have died, for the sake of their beloved land or in defence of it."

Maguire declared his conviction absurd, as he had served the Queen of England faithfully as a marine, and was still loyal to the British crown. He had no affiliation whatever with the Fenian Order.

Captain Condon said, in part: "We have been found guilty, and, as a matter of course, we accept our death. We are not afraid to die. At least, I am not."

At this point the other prisoners cried out: "Nor I."

Condon then remarked: "I only trust that those who are to be tried after us will have a fair trial, and that our blood will satisfy the craving which I understand exists. You will soon send us before God, and I am perfectly prepared to go. I have nothing to regret or retract. I can only say: 'God save Ireland!'"

The others echoed the prayer, which rang solemnly through the densely crowded court-room. "God save Ireland" has, since that hour, been the watchword of the national party.

Notwithstanding the popular passion for the strangling of the Irish prisoners, many liberal-minded Englishmen did not approve of the methods adopted at their trial, and the members of the press who attended all the sessions of the court came to the conclusion that the ex-marine, Maguire, at least, was innocent and strongly petitioned the Home Office for his pardon, which was finally granted. And yet, this man was condemned on the same worthless evidence that convicted his fellow-prisoners! This circumstance is what particularly imbittered the Irish heart in regard to the Manchester tragedy. Condon, owing to strenuous exertions in the United States House of Representatives, which influenced the State Department to interfere in his case, was reprieved, "pending further consideration." The remaining three, notwithstanding the earnest efforts of many humane Englishmen of all classes, who believed that a terrible mistake had been made by the witnesses for the crown, were notified that they must die on the day appointed. As the trials had taken place in the end of October, less than a month lay between the destined victims and their ghastly doom—rendered even more ghastly by the post-mortem vengeance of their enraged and relentless enemies.

Allen, Larkin, and O'Brien, attended by the sheriff, jailers, and clergymen, marched out of Salford prison, and reached the scaffold, situated above the main entrance, by a stairway leading from the jail yard, on the gloomy morning of November 23, 1867. All were resigned to their harrowing fate, but O'Brien, who had served in the Union army, showed unsurpassed firmness. He stepped, almost blithely, through the doorway to the appointed platform of death, pausing for a moment on the way to kiss, and embrace, as nearly as he could with his pinioned hands, his fellow victims. The English officials were much impressed by this touching scene, but they proceeded, nevertheless, systematically to consummate the sacrifice. All night long the prisoners might have heard the savage howls of the Manchester mob, composed of the very lowest rabble of the city, clamoring for their blood. Even as they stood upon the trap, with the fatal noose around their necks, they could hear the ribald taunts of that ignorant and ferocious multitude. In front of the scaffold, and flanking its approaches, bristled the bayonets of British battalions, row upon row. A temporary barricade had been erected, in anticipation of an attempt at rescue, and upon its summits rested the rifle-barrels of a Highland regiment, primed and loaded for the possible work of slaughter. Not a friend of Ireland was within the vision-range of the doomed men, as they took their last view of earthly scenes. Within a few minutes the black caps were drawn down over their faces, and the light of this world was shut out from them forever. The hangman drew the bolt, the trap fell with a clang, and three more names were added to the long, long bead-roll of Ireland's martyrology. No friends received their cold remains. When life was pronounced extinct, the victims were cut down, and the bodies placed in rude coffins, filled with quicklime! These were deposited in a deep trench, carefully filled with clay and covered with sods, on an even surface, so that their place of burial in the prison square could not be identified in after times. Such was the consummation of England's vengeance—the vengeance that should have belonged to a Pagan rather than a Christian nation. Some humane English people expressed their disgust at the whole savage business, but, as usual, their protests had no effect on the opinions of the vast mass of their countrymen. Neither rope nor quicklime could annihilate the spirits of the martyrs, or eradicate their memory from the fervid Irish heart. On every succeeding anniversary of that fatal event, "the noble-hearted three" have been honorably commemorated in every land where Irishmen, or their descendants, dwell.

England was again thrown into a panic of rage and fear on December 13, 1867, when a barrel, filled with gunpowder, was exploded against the outer wall of Clerkenwell prison, London, by persons who hoped to rescue Colonel R. O'S. Burke, who was there imprisoned on account of his part in the Fenian movement. The colonel was believed to be taking the usual hour of exercise at the time of the explosion. Had he been, he would have been blown to atoms. Sixty yards of the wall were destroyed, and, unfortunately, some tenement houses, occupied by working people of all races, were blown down on the side opposite the jail. Twelve persons were killed on the spot and about a hundred and twenty wounded. Colonel Burke was in his cell when the crash came, which startled jailers and prisoners alike. The authors of the explosion were not men of experience or intelligence, and had no idea of the damage an exploded barrel of gunpowder could do in a crowded neighborhood. They certainly had no design to kill or injure anybody—the sole motive of the act being the release of the Fenian prisoner. Active steps were at once taken by the government to secure the arrest of the conspirators, and several Irishmen, of the laboring class, were taken into custody. One man, named Michael Barrett, was convicted, on somewhat doubtful evidence, and suffered the penalty of death. He met his doom with heroic courage, refusing to utter a word that might lead to the detection of others. Barrett was the last man executed for connection with the Fenian outbreaks in England.

CHAPTER XIII

Effect of Fenian Violence in England on the Policy of English Statesmen—Agitation for the Disestablishment of the State
Church begun in Ireland

THE startling deeds committed by the Fenians in England, although fiercely condemned by the British press
and people, and by that anti-national Irish minority who
are always against their own country, had the immediate
effect of making English statesmen look much more earnestly into Irish grievances than had been their custom since
the days of O'Connell.   As usual, they pitched upon a minor
grievance for reform, ignoring the national demand for
self-government, and the crying evil of the landlord and
tenant system.   The Protestant Established Church had existed in Ireland, chiefly as "a badge of conquest," maintained by taxation of Catholics as well as Protestants, in
one form or another, almost since the time of the alleged
Reformation.   Its maintenance and perpetuation formed
one of the leading provisions of the Treaty of Union (1800),
the Fifth Article of which provided "that the churches of
England and Ireland, as now by law established, be united
into one Protestant Episcopal Church, to be called 'the
United Church of England and Ireland,' and the doctrine,
worship, discipline, and government of the said United
Church shall be and shall remain in full force forever,
as the same are now by law established for the Church of
England, and the continuance and preservation of the said
United Church, as the established Church of England and
Ireland, shall be deemed and taken to be an essential and

fundamental part of the Union." Eminent lawyers held, and with truth, that the abrogation of this vital article of the treaty would have the effect of vitiating the whole instrument. It was a clear violation of a fundamental provision to even seek its abrogation, the Conservative newspapers argued. England, however, has not been famous for observing treaties when they failed to suit her purpose. What seemed to her advantageous at the time of the Union, did not so appear to her political vision eight-and-sixty years thereafter. As a matter of fact, the Irish Catholic masses, who, since the abolition of the tithes, had been paying the same tribute to the landlords, for the benefit of the Protestant rectors, in the shape of increased rents, did not much disturb themselves about "the Establishment," and, in general, lived on very neighborly terms with the Protestant pastors and people in the three provinces which had, and still have, an overwhelming Catholic majority. In Ulster, where the creeds more nearly approached equality, the disturbances were frequent, chiefly for political and partisan reasons. Where the parson happened to be an active proselytizer, and pestered the peasants about their creed, he became an object of contempt and derision. His "converts," usually changed in their religious views by the pressure of animal wants, cheaply supplied, were called "soupers," and were popularly regarded as "moral lepers." The parson who attended to the ordinary duties of his calling, and who treated the people courteously, was always received by them with respect and often with cordiality. His dependants mingled on friendly terms with their Catholic neighbors, and at games, festivities, or fairs and markets, they were rarely interfered with, unless they became, in their cups, aggressive. Even then they received more consideration than did quarrelsome Catholics, because the fact of their being in the minority appealed to the native chivalry of the Irish people. The aristocratic and mercantile Catholics felt the Established Church humiliation much more keenly than did their humbler and poorer co-religionists, although, in general, the Irish Catholic aristocrats and merchant princes were quite as anti-national as Irish Protestants of similar standing. Quite naturally, the Catholic hierarchy, also, demanded the abolition of "the Establishment," although they were fully aware that the government grant for the Catholic ecclesiastical college of Maynooth would be discontinued, together with the Presbyterian Regium Donum, on the passage of the proposed disendowment act. This influential body, anterior to 1864-65, seemed to care much more for securing Catholic educational measures than for Church disestablishment. Cardinal Cullen and a few bishops had been under a political cloud since the breaking up of the Tenant Right organization—sacrificed, in a great measure, for Catholic appointments under the crown more than a dozen years previously. In addition, the hostile attitude of these prelates toward the Fenian movement had alienated the devotion of many ardent young Catholics to the Church, because the Order was, in the main, made up of the best and bravest among the Catholic youth of Ireland. Protestants also belonged to the Brotherhood, but the number was not large. Church opposition to the Irish revolutionary idea is not an attractive subject to dwell upon, but the truth of history compels the statement that Cardinal Cullen's refusal, in November, 1861, to allow the remains of the patriot-exile, Terence Bellew MacManus, to lie in state in the Dublin pro-cathedral; his stringent command to his clergy not to admit members of the Fenian organization to the sacraments; his unfriendly pastorals, and his general antagonism to the national cause, made him exceedingly unpopular in Ireland during the whole of the Fenian epoch. This unpopularity was shared by his immediate successor, Cardinal MacCabe, and also by the Right Rev. Bishop Moriarty, of Kerry, who, in one of his official utterances to his priests, declared that "hell was not hot enough, nor eternity long enough," to punish the members of the Irish Revolutionary (Fenian) Brotherhood. Language of that kind might be applied with impunity to an unlettered and awe-stricken peasantry, but the rank and file, as well as the leaders, of the Fenian body were neither ignorant nor timid, and well knew the difference between Bishop Moriarty's spiritual and political jurisdiction.

The rest of the Catholic hierarchy, although averse to any revolutionary effort whatever, refrained from making themselves obnoxious in their opposition to Fenianism, but in many other dioceses, as well as those of Dublin and Kerry, Catholic Fenians often experienced much difficulty in living up to the requirements of their faith as regarded receiving the sacraments. The police and soldiers of Catholic faith, who had, practically, taken an oath to hold their country subject to an alien power, found no such difficulty in the confessional or at the communion railing. These unwise discriminations had the effect of producing bitterness, and, finally, indifference, in the minds of many young men. Some of these fell away from the Church of their fathers and never re-entered the fold. Nothing better illustrated the unwisdom of mixing religion with politics. The Irish clergy, whether hierarchs or priests, owed nothing to England but just resentment for centuries of abuse and insult continued beyond the middle of the nineteenth century.

Many among the rank and file of the priesthood took that view of the situation, and, unless commanded by their spiritual superiors to be severe, put no difficulty in the way of Fenians who approached the confessional. Such priests became very popular, and patriotic penitents, from far and near, flocked to be "heard" by them on the appointed days of penance.

Even in the United States, the Fenians were discriminated against in many dioceses, including that of Chicago. A distinguished Irish-American Catholic of that city, who belonged to the Order, was refused absolution by an Irish parish priest. This was on a Christmas eve. He immediately proceeded to the Jesuit church and sought out the famous Father Damen, who was a Belgian. The Father confessor recognized the penitent as he knelt at the confessional, and, knowing that he belonged to another parish, asked why he had come to him. The penitent explained. "What is the real purpose of Fenianism?" inquired Father Damen. "To drive the English out of Ireland," replied the penitent. "Oh, if that's all," remarked the reverend Father, "I'd like to be a Fenian myself." He heard the confession and granted absolution. Thereafter, Father Damen's Irish constituency was largely increased.

The agitation for disestablishment began primarily in Ireland in 1864-65—the chief lay leaders being William J. O'Neill Daunt, a landed proprietor of the County Cork, distinguished as a political writer and a novelist, and Sir John Gray, M.P., editor of the Dublin "Freeman's Journal," at that time, and still, Ireland's greatest daily. Sir John was in religion a Protestant, had been an ardent Repealer, and was one of those imprisoned with O'Connell in 1844. The Fenians and the Orangemen, from very opposite motives, contrived, for some years, to keep the agitation in check. The Fenians despised agitation of any kind, believing that force alone could effect their object, while the Orangemen were scandalized at the idea of having removed from the public ken the mightiest monument of "Protestant Ascendency" in Ireland. It was not until England itself had been startled "from the centre to the sea" by Fenian attacks that practical steps were taken to carry out the policy of disendowment.

CHAPTER XIV

Revolt Against Insulting Corporation Oaths in Dublin—Progress of the Fight for Disestablishment—Gladstone's Bill Carried by a Large Majority

THE Catholic prelates and influential laymen already named, together with Sir John Gray and several liberal-minded men of all creeds represented in the island, had been in negotiation with Messrs. Gladstone, Bright, Fortescue, and other leaders of the English Liberal party, in regard to the proposed Disestablishment Act, for several years prior to the practical beginning of the agitation, but no favorable opportunity to advance the cause, and unite the entire Liberal party on the issue, was found until the late Hon. A. M. Sullivan, who had been elected a member of the Dublin City Corporation (Council), imitated the example set by O'Connell in 1829, and refused to take an obnoxious qualification oath of fealty to the Established Church, not required from Protestant members. This incident made quite a noise at the time, but public excitement was further aggravated when a Conservative member of the Corporation challenged a vote of thanks to the outgoing

Lord Mayor, Ald. McSweeney, who had presided at a meeting of the National Association—a body pledged to Disestablishment—on the ground that the retiring official, a Catholic, had been false to his oath in regard to the Church
establishment.   Quite a scene occurred, and the vote of
thanks was carried amid tumult.   The Catholic and Liberal
Protestant members united in demanding the repeal of the
"obnoxious oaths."   Other Irish municipalities followed the
example of Dublin, and a delegation of great influence was
sent to London to impress upon the British Parliament the
gravity of the issue.   The Catholic Oaths bill was introduced by the Liberals, but the Tories were in power and the
measure moved along slowly.   Twice the bill was passed
by the Commons, and twice the Lords rejected it.   The
Tory leaders felt that its passage would mean the capturing
of the outworks of the Established Church, and although
some of them, notably Benjamin Disraeli, acknowledged
the absurdity of the oaths, policy compelled them to fight
against their abolition.   The English Liberation Society,
composed of the most progressive element in England, took
up the cry against the obnoxious oaths, and, soon afterward, against the Establishment itself.   All of Great Britain became stirred up over the question.   Englishmen reasoned it out that the Fenians had not acted from choice, but
necessity, and that Irish grievances, long deemed imagin-
ary, were decidedly serious.   In March, 1868, John Francis
Maguire, one of the ablest of the Irish delegation in the
Commons, moved that the House constitute itself a committee of the whole to consider the state of Ireland, which,
he said, between conspiracy and attempted revolution on
the part of the Fenians, and the suspension of all constitutional right on the part of the government, was an eyesore

to the civilized world. Four days of passionate debate followed. Mr. Gladstone outdid himself in eloquence. His great opponent, Disraeli, who felt he was swimming against the current, also displayed his astonishing power as a debater.

Gladstone, who had held back from absolutely declaring himself, although everybody knew his sentiments, for the purpose, as some of his friends expressed it, of allowing British public opinion on the subject of Disestablishment to ripen, came out openly for the measure on this occasion, saying the time had arrived when the Established Church of Ireland must be disendowed. This was on March 16, and, on his announcing that he would, in person, present the issue practically in the House of Commons, all resolutions and amendments bearing on the subject were withdrawn. The resolutions of Disestablishment were introduced by Mr. Gladstone on March 23, and the debate opened formally a week later. On the motion to go into committee on the resolutions, the ministers, who opposed their consideration, were beaten by a vote of 331 to 270. In committee of the whole, the debate lasted for eleven nights or more, and, on May 1, 1868, the first resolution, by a vote of 330 to 265, was carried.

On May 5, Mr. Disraeli announced in the Commons that the ministers had tendered their resignations, but were requested by Queen Victoria to retain their portfolios until certain important public business was disposed of, when there would be a dissolution of Parliament. The second and third of Mr. Gladstone's resolutions were adopted on May 7 by the committee of the whole. The "Suspensory bill" was introduced by the Liberal leader on May 13. Its object was to prevent the creation of new "livings," or other interests, while Parliamentary proceedings in regard to Disestablishment were still pending. This bill was ordered read on May 22, by a vote of 312 to 258, and was subsequently carried formally in the Commons by about the same vote. The measure went to the Lords on June 18, and, on June 25, they rejected it by a vote of 192 to 97.

Parliament was prorogued on the last day of July, 1868, and was dissolved by royal edict on November 11 of that year. The general election that followed dissolution was fought out at the polls with great vehemence. The Ulster Orangemen, as usual, signalized themselves by violent words, if not actions. Their chaplain, the Rev. Mr. Flanagan, in a public speech, in which he appealed to all the old partisan and religious prejudices of his hearers, nearly approached the revolutionary boundary line, and declared that "the men of Ulster had ere then kicked a crown into the Boyne." The reverend gentleman was much laughed at by all but his own fanatical followers, because every one knew that it was an Orange "bluff," with nothing more than "wind and religion" behind it. The Liberal orators, however, made good use of Mr. Flanagan's mock heroics on the English hustings, because the average Englishman bitterly resents any "insult to the crown." Were Mr. Flanagan in earnest, he would, no doubt, have found many sympathizers even among those who desired the overthrow of the Established Church in Ireland.

Many leading Irish Protestants, not members of the Orange order, worked hard for Disestablishment, because they believed it to be a bone of contention between them and their Catholic and Dissenting fellow-countrymen. "The Church," they said, "that can not stand on its own merit should not stand at all."

The general election resulted in so overwhelmingly a defeat for the Tories that Premier Disraeli surrendered his seals of office on December 2. The queen sent for Mr. Gladstone and asked him to form a cabinet. The Liberal leader soon completed his task and the new cabinet was organized, and installed, on December 9. According to custom, the members of the ministry went again before the people for re-election, and all were returned. Parliament adjourned to February 16, 1869. Mr. Gladstone introduced his bill for the Disestablishment of the Irish Church on March 1, and the debate on the second reading of the measure began on the 18th of that month. It lasted five nights, and the Liberals and their Irish allies carried the second reading by a vote of 368 to 250—an extraordinary majority. The bill passed to a third reading on May 31, by a vote of 361 to 247. Notwithstanding the well-known hostility of a large majority of the House of Lords to the bill, that body dreaded a popular storm, and, after some hesitation, finally acquiesced. It was signed by Victoria on July 26, 1869. This, to all practical intent, ended "Protestant ascendency" in Ireland.

CHAPTER XV

Beginning of the Home Rule Movement—Parnell, Biggar, and Davitt Appear upon Scene—"Obstruction" in the Commons—Davitt Starts the Land League—Parnell's Rise, Progress, and Fall

A "HOME RULE" association had been started by John Martin, the returned political exile, in Ireland as far back as 1863, but it made very little progress during the Fenian period, as Parliamentary agitation had not yet recovered from the shock given it by the recreancy of the Keogh and

Sadlier "Brass Band" in 1852. In November, 1873, however, the Home Government Association convened a conference of leading Irishmen in the Rotunda, Dublin, which was largely attended. The sessions lasted for four days, and the gathering was presided over by William Shaw, M.P., a Protestant Home Ruler, and a leading citizen of Cork, and out of the proceedings, which were characterized by dignity and harmony, "The Irish Home Rule League" came into being. This organization set itself immediately to work to increase the Home Rule membership in the House of Commons. By attending practically to registration, it was thought that more than seventy men, pledged to Irish autonomy, could be returned at the next general election. Mr. Gladstone suddenly dissolved Parliament, in January, 1874, and the Home Rule League was taken at a disadvantage. In addition to the Home Rule issue, which then, as now, was the leading question in Irish national politics, there were included in the platform an amendment of the first Gladstone Land Act—a very imperfect measure, passed soon after the Church Disestablishment—a Catholic University for Ireland, and complete amnesty for the Fenians convicted and in prison or in penal settlements. The recognized leaders of this new movement were the illustrious lawyer, Isaac Butt, Sir John Gray, William Shaw, John Martin, and Mitchel-Henry, not one of whom was a Catholic, but all of whom were devoted to Home Rule. There was a deep policy in selecting so many Protestants to be the leaders, as in 1782, 1798, and 1848, of a country overwhelmingly Catholic. Several constituencies, in which the Catholic vote stood as 20 to 1, elected Protestant members of Parliament.

Gladstone was badly beaten in the general election of

1874, and Benjamin Disraeli again came into power. The Irish Home Rulers won sixty seats; yet the Tory majority was too great to give them the balance of power, but they formed themselves into a distinct and independent party in the English Parliament.

Charles Stewart Parnell, descended from the famous County Wicklow family of that name, who had been ever true to Ireland, stood for the County Dublin against a Colonel Taylor in the late election and was defeated. At that time he was very diffident; had an almost offensive English accent, and was a most tiresome speaker. These defects he afterward remedied, and he was particularly vouched for by "Honest John Martin," who was trusted by the Irish people as few other men were. The record of the Parnells in the Old Irish Parliament was splendid, and the young man's grandfather had been dubbed "The Incorruptible." He also enjoyed the advantage of being the son of an American mother, who was the daughter of the gallant Commodore Stewart, known throughout the American navy as "Old Ironsides" in the War of 1812.

This young candidate for Parliamentary honors was born in 1846, and was called Charles Stewart Parnell, after his maternal grandfather. He was tall, slender, and handsome, but rather cold in manner, at first—not a good qualification when dealing with so "hearty" a people as the Irish, who like dignity, but not too much distance.

In 1875, the true-hearted John Martin died, and young Parnell became a candidate for the vacancy in Meath occasioned by the old patriot's death. A cadet of the Catholic family of Fingall, whose head was the earl of that name, was put up against him, but Parnell was triumphantly elected as a radical Home Ruler.

Mr. Butt was still the recognized leader of the Home Rule party, but his methods were slow and overcautious, and many of his Parliamentary associates were chronic place-hunters of the "Brass Band" order. Parnell was very much disgusted at this condition of things. He was terribly in earnest, and despised place-hunting and timidity. His most energetic ally in the House, from the first, was Joseph Gillas Biggar, a retired merchant of Belfast, a Presbyterian patriot and a hater of all shams, whether British or Irish. He, too, felt dissatisfied with the slow leadership of Mr. Butt, and also with the Parliamentary methods of the House of Commons. Mr. Biggar was the member for Cavan, and, although verging on sixty, was active and aggressive. He set the example of tiring out the House by endless speeches on some Irish question. The more he tired it, the more he enjoyed its distress, and very soon he became a potent terror to the cold and formal British members. On one occasion, he spoke against time for many hours, totally indifferent to the furious shouts and savage howls of the impatient House, which was hungry for its dinner.

Parnell and Biggar made a strong "Obstruction" team in the Commons. The former was cold and cutting as steel, but Biggar was often coarse, and even insulting, in manner and expression to his opponents. He detested the English, and they returned his detestation with compound interest.

Gradually the bolder spirits among the Irish members joined the two "Obstructionists." Poor old Mr. Butt and his conservative friends protested in vain. The aggressive element gained the ascendency and kept it. Biggar, on one occasion, espied the Prince of Wales and his suite in the gallery of the House, and informed the Speaker that he "observed strangers." The Prince and his friends were turned out of the gallery. Disraeli and Lord Hartington protested against "such conduct," but produced no effect on the offender—"Joe" Biggar was immovable. He replied to personal taunts hurled at him with aggravating grimaces.

When Mr. Parnell joined with Mr. Biggar in the policy of "Obstruction," the Irish Home Rule delegation in the Commons were looked upon by the British members with indifference, if not contempt. Within a few years, the two earnest men, and their allies, taking advantage of the antiquated rules of the House, which they knew to the letter, made Ireland dreaded by her foes, and finally compelled the British Parliament to change its rules, in order to escape defeat and ridicule.

In addition to "Obstruction," the Parnell element supported every measure of reform introduced in the House, whether British or Irish, and strongly opposed flogging in the army and navy. This mode of punishment was finally abolished in the army, at least. They opposed, also, the annexation of the Transvaal, and other "land grabs" then attempted by the government. Mr. Butt gradually became a mere cipher, and the young, dauntless leader was recognized as "the coming man." The Home Rule Confederation of Great Britain elected Parnell President in place of Mr. Butt, in 1877, and two years later he became the undoubted leader of the Home Rule cause in both Great Britain and Ireland. Isaac Butt, a true patriot and a gifted orator, died on May 5, 1879, sincerely regretted by both friends and opponents. He had few, if any, personal enemies. William Shaw succeeded him, as nominal leader, for a period, but, in the end, Parnell's parliamentary prestige triumphed over all his rivals. In 1880, he and John Dillon, M.P., made a tour of the United States, when famine threatened Ireland, and they did much also to advance the cause of Home Rule among all classes of the American people. They received high consideration in Washington while Congress was in session. The House took a recess in their honor, and they were also received with respect by the President and Senators. Fully three-fourths of the Legislatures of the different States passed resolutions of sympathy with the Home Rule cause, and never, at any time, was the Irish question so popular in America. James Gordon Bennett, of the New York "Herald," gave $100,000 to the Irish Famine Fund, and the Canadian Parliament voted a similar sum for the same purpose. Several hundred thousand dollars were raised from other sources also, as a result of the Parnell-Dillon tour.

Sharing equally with Mr. Parnell the glory of advancing outside of Parliament what the young chief did within it, Michael Davitt, the leader of the Irish democracy, has won an imposing position in Anglo-Irish history. He was born in Mayo in 1846, and his father, with the entire family, was evicted from his farm during the Famine epoch. His early life was spent in England. When old enough he was employed in a factory, where he lost an arm; but he found other means of livelihood, and managed to secure an education which equipped his powerful mind for the rough battle with the world. Always an intense Irishman, he was identified with the Fenian movement in England, and afterward took an active interest in the Home Rule and Land Reform cause. From the great meeting which he organized in Irishtown, in his native county, in the fall of 1879, dates the foundation of the famous Irish National Land League, which still survives in principle, although under another name; and through which all the ameliorative land acts, including Gladstone's Act, amended by the Healy Tenant Right clause, the Land Courts Acts, the Ashbourne Act, et cetera, have been wrung from England. He enlisted Parnell actively in the cause of land reform after his return from America, and the two leaders and their lieutenants soon established branches of the Land League in every part of Ireland and Great Britain. In vain did the government pass drastic coercion acts to restrain it. In vain were "concessions" promised. In vain were Parnell and Davitt appealed to to be "moderate" in their demands—the League spread "like wildfire" in 1880 and 1881; and, in the latter year, while W. E. Forster, surnamed "Buckshot," was Irish Secretary and Earl Spencer Lord Lieutenant, under Gladstone, all the prominent leaders, including the two chiefs, were in prison; but other men took their places and the good work went on unchecked. Many Irish women, too, who formed Ladies' Land Leagues, were imprisoned at this time. From Kilmainham Jail, in November, 1881, the "No Rent Manifesto" was issued by the imprisoned leaders, and the Gladstone government stood face to face with "passive resistance." For a time Forster carried out his policy of wholesale arrest and imprisonment, but, at last, Gladstone, who had exhausted what he called "the resources of civilization," grew tired of the struggle. Forster was recalled in May, 1882; the Irish leaders and their lieutenants were set at liberty, and Lord Frederick Cavendish, son of the Duke of Devonshire, and a friend of Ireland, was sent over, with "a message of peace," as Chief Secretary, in Forster's place. A secret band of rather irresponsible men, who called themselves "The Invincibles," had determined to kill

Forster and Under Secretary Burke—a most unpopular official. "Buckshot" escaped to England, and when Lord Cavendish arrived in Dublin, he proceeded straight to Dublin Castle, unfortunately fell in with Burke, and together they proceeded on foot to visit Earl Spencer, at the viceregal lodge in the Phœnix Park. When near the lodge, they were overtaken by men in a jaunting car, and both were knifed to death—Cavendish, who attempted to defend Burke with his umbrella, being absolutely unknown to the assailants. This hapless tragedy occurred on Saturday, May 6, 1882, and filled both Ireland and Great Britain with horror. Ireland promptly repudiated the crime, through her chosen representatives, but, nevertheless, she was relegated to bondage for a long period. The "Invincibles" were betrayed by their organizer and leader, Alderman James Carey—a detestable traitor and poltroon, who swore away the lives of several of his dupes in order to save his own worthless life. With the execution of the convicted "Invincibles," the Irish part of the great tragedy was consummated, but Carey was pursued to Africa, whither he fled for safety, by Patrick O'Donnell, called "the avenger," who shot him as he was about to land at Port Elizabeth. O'Donnell was captured and sent to England, where he was tried, convicted, and hanged. He claimed American citizenship, and the State Department did what it could to avert his doom, but the British cabinet, of which Gladstone was chief, was inexorable, and O'Donnell died as became a true Irishman, with a smile on his face and a prayer on his lips.

A dastardly attempt was subsequently made by the London "Times," aided by "Dick" Pigott, proprietor of a Dublin newspaper, to connect Parnell with the Phœnix Park assassinations. Forged letters were printed in the "Times," which were good imitations of the handwriting of the Irish leader. Although Mr. Parnell himself took little or no notice of the slanders, Frank Hugh O'Donnell, then M.P. for Dungarvan, County Waterford, brought an action against "John Walter and another," proprietors of the "Times," for the articles entitled "Parnellism and Crime," which he claimed libeled himself among others. When the trial occurred, the defendants were acquitted. Soon afterward the British Parliament passed "an act to constitute a Special Commission, to inquire into the charges and allegations made against certain members of Parliament, and other persons, by the defendants in the recent trial of O'Donnell *vs.* Walter and another." The "Times," assisted as was generally believed by government secret agents, searched the world around for witnesses against Parnell and the other persons accused. This process developed on the witness-stand "Major" Le Caron, alias John Beach, an English spy, who represented himself to the American Irish as a Frenchman, and had risen high enough in their confidence to be appointed a "military organizer" under John O'Neill, with whom he had served in the Union army. He made a good companion picture for Pigott, the informer and forger.

The Special Commission was duly appointed with Sir James Hannen, a famous English judge, as president, and Sir J. C. Day and Sir A. L. Smith, also leading jurists, as associates. The proceedings were long and tedious—the sessions lasting almost continuously from October 22, 1888, to November 22, 1889.

Sir Richard Webster, Q.C., M.P., attorney-general for England; Sir Henry James, Q.C., M.P., and other able lawyers, appeared for the "Times." Mr. Parnell was represented by Sir Charles Russell, Q.C., M.P. (afterward Lord Russell of Killowen), and by Mr. H. H. Asquith, M.P.; most of the other Irish members included in the charges were defended by Mr. R. T. Reid, Q.C., M.P.; Mr. F. Lockwood, Q.C., M.P.; Mr. Arthur O'Connor, M.P.; Mr. Lionel Hart, Mr. Arthur Russell, and Mr. Timothy Harrington, M.P., of the Irish Bar; Messrs. T. M. Healy, M.P., and Joseph G. Biggar, M.P., undertook their own defence, and so also did Mr. Michael Davitt, who made a most able and notable speech, which occupied a full week in delivery, and produced a profound impression on the members of the Commission, the counsel, and the public at large. It was a magnificent defence of the Irish Land League, and a logical, convincing exposition of the justice of the Irish cause. At the conclusion of his effort, Sir James Hannen, a very "crabbed" judge, complimented Mr. Davitt by saying: "Your expression of regret for want of trained skill was certainly not necessary. You have put your arguments before us with great force and ability, and we are obliged to you for having given us the assistance which has been withheld from us by others."

The result of the trial before the Commission was the exculpation of Mr. Parnell and his associates. When the Irish leader again took his seat in the House of Commons, he was greeted with tumultuous cheers from the whole assembly, including even the rabid Tories. With characteristic sang-froid, he took no notice whatever of the plaudits of the British members, but bowed three times profoundly to his own followers on the Irish benches.

Parnell was greatly aided in his vindication by the Hon. Patrick Egan, former treasurer of the Irish National League in Ireland, and afterward United States Minister to Chili, who, by documents in his possession which were conveyed to Parnell by the Rev. Maurice J. Dorney, of Chicago, proved Pigott's forgeries. The infamous forger fled to Spain and, in despair, committed suicide at Madrid.

The extension of the franchise and redistribution of Parliamentary divisions under the Gladstone régime enabled Ireland to send to Parliament 83 Home Rulers out of a total delegation of 103 members. With such a force at his back, Parnell applied himself to the great task of winning Home Rule for Ireland. The Land Act had been again amended, and nothing further could be done in that direction, for a time, at least. Many Scotch, Welsh, and even English members sympathized with the Home Rule cause, but three years elapsed, after the Phœnix Park tragedy, before the question became a vital one in Anglo-Irish politics. Yet, there were signs of a coming crisis as early as 1883. The Irish National League was established, to take the place of the Land League, in Ireland, Great Britain, and America. In the United States, the Irish had held a great convention (organized by John F. Finerty) at Chicago, in November and December, 1881, at which some Irish members of Parliament —notably T. P. O'Connor and T. M. Healy—were present. The call for the convention was signed by them, and by Patrick Ford, editor of the "Irish World"; Patrick A. Collins, president of the New England Land League, and John Boyle O'Reilly, editor of the Boston "Pilot." The convention sustained the "No Rent Manifesto" which was issued by the imprisoned Irish chiefs, from Kilmainham Jail, about that time, and began a subscription for the Home Rule Fund which finally swelled to more than $500,000.

In 1883, a second great convention was held at Philadelphia, at which delegates from Ireland, not members of Parliament, however, were also present. Alexander Sullivan, of Chicago, was elected president of the American branch of the Irish National League, which was there organized, and the formation of branches and the raising of funds proceeded thereafter with great vigor. Ireland began to feel, at last, that the Irish in America stood faithfully behind her.

At length, in the fall of 1885, Parnell lost patience with Gladstone, who still procrastinated, and, by a temporary coalition with the Tories, forced him out of office, by a hostile vote on a government measure in the House of Commons, where the Irish members then held the balance of power. Parliament was dissolved immediately, and in the general election which soon followed Gladstone was badly beaten, and the Tories, led by the Marquis of Salisbury, who was asked to form a cabinet, came back to office. They coquetted, for a while, with Home Rule, but Parnell speedily became convinced of their insincerity, and having, meanwhile, sounded some of the Liberal leaders on the question, resolved to turn Salisbury out of office. This was easily effected under the circumstances; and, on a government measure, which the Tories were anxious to have passed, the Irish leader combined with the Whigs, or Liberals, to ensure its defeat. Again the Tories were hurled from power, and again Great Britain and Ireland were appealed to on the issue of Home Rule. The general election resulted in the triumph of Parnell. Gladstone came back to office an avowed Home Ruler, and recalled the fact that he had always said he would consider the question when a majority of the Irish members, on behalf of Ireland, demanded self-government. In fact, to use his own language,

Home Rule had "come within the domain of practical politics."

The Home Rule bill, which proposed to place Ireland in the same relation to Great Britain, with only trivial exceptions, as Canada, Australia, or New Zealand, was introduced by Gladstone in the House of Commons, in April, 1886. He made a superb speech on that occasion, and the debate lasted for many days and nights. When the crisis came, Joseph Chamberlain, who had a feud with his leader over office, and the Marquis of Hartington, brother of the murdered Lord Frederick Cavendish, together with George J. Goschen, another leading Liberal, and several other Whigs, "ratted," ostensibly because the bill excluded Irish members from the London Parliament, but in reality because they were hostile to any measure of Home Rule whatever. The result was the defeat of the measure by a majority of over 30 votes, on the motion for its final passage by the House of Commons. About two-thirds of the Scotch, five-sixths of the Welsh, and a third of the English members voted with the Irish Home Rulers for the adoption of the bill.

Both Parnell and Gladstone were bitterly disappointed by the result. Home Rule did not reach a vote in that House again during the short after career of the ill-fated Irish chief, but, in 1893, when Lord Rosebery was in office, a modified measure of Home Rule was passed by the Commons and overwhelmingly defeated by the Lords. It is a tradition, however, of British politics that any bill which once passes "the lower House" is bound to win in the end.

Home Rule and Greater Land Reform were again coming rapidly to the front in Parliament when, in the autumn of 1891, Charles Stewart Parnell became involved in a social scandal that would not have much injured an English politician, but which ruined his career and resulted in his sudden death. Ireland was immediately rent by faction. Parnell made desperate efforts to regain his ascendency, but failed. He was treated harshly by the people he had served so well, but, in justice to them, it must be observed that their moral sensibilities were shocked by his mistake, and they were very angry with their former idol. Many faithful friends stood by him to the last, and, when he died and was buried in Glasnevin, the cortege that followed his relics to the grave was only exceeded in numbers by that which had escorted the body of O'Connell to the same historical cemetery nearly fifty years before.

Educated, like his martial predecessor in Irish leadership, Hugh O'Neill, among the English, Parnell knew every phase of their character — their strong as well as their weak points. Englishmen, in general, hate opposition of any kind, whether exercised against themselves or the policy of their country; and nobody better knew how to throw the ordinarily phlegmatic "Anglo-Saxons" into a boiling, ungovernable rage than Parnell. He delighted in seeing them angry, making exhibitions of themselves; for this descendant of a Cromwellian swordsman hated them with more than Celtic hatred. His hate was cold and persistent, because he had often been exasperated by the taunts of his English class-mates when a student at their colleges. He had a fearless heart, an arm strong like steel, and he never failed to avenge Ireland by striking from the shoulder when some insolent English youth reflected, in his presence, upon her or her people. A distinguished member of the Irish party some years ago told the author an anecdote of Parnell which deserves to live forever in the memory of his countrymen. After one of the stormy debates in the House of Commons, usually provoked by either Parnell or Biggar, the younger Tories were more than ordinarily violent. Some among them advanced almost to the striking point as they confronted the Irish members. Parnell stood proudly before them, his arms folded, his dark eyes flashing defiance. Suddenly, he turned toward the relator of the story, and hissed out between his set teeth: "D—n it!—why can't we turn in and fight these cads?"

Ireland will yet place a monument above his last resting place around which the clouds will linger, to remind her of the Chief who, when she was striving blindly in the mists of defeat, bade the sun shine forth and led her from obscurity to fame, from nonentity to a place in the respect of the nations. Faults he had, it is true, but they were not the faults of a bad heart or an evil mind. He erred, like David, and, like the Hebrew king, his glory shall outlive his error. Whatever may be Ireland's future fate, from her lips shall be uttered "the song of sorrow," and the sweetest tones of her deathless harp will be tuned for him who, born in the ranks of her hereditary foes, took his place by her side, and, rewelding her broken shield, taught England once again that

> "Right is more than might,
> And Justice more than mail."

For nearly ten years after the great leader's death, the Irish, both at home and abroad, were a prey of faction and consequent political impotency. At last those unselfish patriots, temporarily divided on the Parnell issue—William O'Brien, John Dillon, and John E. Redmond—came together and buried the hatchet of discord. Mr. Redmond, the late chieftain's most faithful lieutenant, through sunshine and storm, was elected chairman of the Irish Parliamentary party, and Ireland again presented a solid front of 83 members in the House of Commons. Even when this body was not entirely united, they stood together for every measure of Irish reform, including the County Councils bill, which did away with the usurpation of the nonrepresentative grand juries, and gave local Home Rule to all of the Irish municipalities.

It also redounds to their honor that, when reunited under Redmond, they stood out nobly in the Commons against the Anglo-Boer War, and voted against every measure of supply that could aid England in her attack on the liberty of the Dutch republics. Michael Davitt resigned his seat in Parliament rather than be held even indirectly responsible for that outrage on decency and humanity.

In the final fight for a new Land Reform bill, the United Irish League showed all the grit of its predecessors, braved the brutality of the armed police, and, in fact, acted as bravely as the members of the old Land League did in Mayo and Clare. Many members of Parliament, including Patrick A. McHugh, of Sligo, and William Redmond, suffered imprisonment—Mr. McHugh repeatedly—in the bold assertion of their principles.

The aged Queen Victoria died toward the end of January, 1901, while the Boer War was still raging. She had made a final visit to Ireland, which she had not seen since 1861, shortly before, in the ill-disguised hope of obtaining Irish recruits for her humiliated army. In order to flatter her Irish subjects, a regiment of Irish guards was started, with Marshal Lord Roberts as honorary colonel; but the

Irish people had not forgotten the "Famine Queen," and her mission proved to be a dismal failure. Besides, the Irish nation fully sustained the action of their leaders in Parliament on the Anglo-Boer question.

The Prince of Wales, then in his sixtieth year, succeeded his mother immediately, under the title of Edward VII. This monarch is a shrewd man of the world, naturally urbane in manner and very tactful. He is wise enough to deport himself toward all his subjects in a genial and friendly way. In short, there is a good deal of his remote ancestors, the Stuarts, in his mental make-up, and he has hardly any of the harsh and disagreeable characteristics of the Guelphs and Wettins, from whom he is immediately descended. King Edward and his queen consort, Alexandra, visited Ireland during the summer of 1903, and were courteously treated by all with whom they came in contact; but there was no popular enthusiasm. The policy of the Irish leaders is opposed to offering insults to royal visitors in Ireland, even when they are obnoxious, and the people faithfully obey their chiefs.

The greatest measure of reform wrung from England by Irish effort in later years must be credited to the United Irish League, of which John Redmond, William O'Brien, John Dillon, Michael Davitt, and Thomas P. O'Connor are the acknowledged leaders. The Land Purchase bill, after a long and bitter struggle with the Irish people, in which "the Castle government" was worsted, was introduced in the House of Commons by "Irish" Secretary Wyndham in the beginning of 1903, and, after passing through the routine stages in both Houses of Parliament, was signed by Edward VII on August 14 of that year. It went into effect in the following November. This bill is the most radical agrarian measure ever passed by the British legislature. While it needs many important amendments, particularly in regard to the rights of the laborers on farms and elsewhere, it irrevocably establishes the principle of popular ownership of the land, as opposed to the feudal system, which virtually obtained in Ireland until recent times; and it, furthermore, assures, in great measure, the future happiness and prosperity of the Irish people of all classes and callings.

At the opening of the British Parliament last February, John Redmond again brought the Irish Home Rule question to the front in the House of Commons, in a speech of great ability, which asserted the right of Ireland to rule herself, and demanded back the Parliament of which she had been shamefully robbed by Great Britain in 1800.

And so, the cause of Irish self-government is still, as from the first, the chief question at issue between Great Britain and Ireland, and can never be settled satisfactorily until "the predominant partner" yields the point to the smaller country, and an Irish Parliament, truly representative of all interests in the island, resumes its long interrupted sessions in the Capitol of Ireland on College Green. Nor would even this settlement bind future generations of Irishmen, who might aspire to separate political existence. In the words of Parnell, "No man, or set of men, can place a boundary to the progress of a nation."

"How sorrowful the useless powers that glorious island yields—
Her countless havens desolate, her waste of barren fields,
The all unused mechanic might her rushing streams afford,
The buried treasures of her mines, her sea's unvalued hoard!
But, oh, there is one piteous waste whence all the rest have grown,
One worst neglect, the mind of man left desert and unsown.
Send KNOWLEDGE forth to scatter wide and deep to cast its seeds,
The nurse of energy and hope, of manly thoughts and deeds.
Let it go forth: right soon will spring those forces in its train
That vanquish Nature's stubborn strength, that rifle earth and main—
Itself a nobler harvest far than Autumn tints with gold,
A higher wealth, a nobler gain than wave and mine enfold;
Let it go forth unstained and freed from Pride's unholy leaven
With fearless forehead raised to Man, but humbly bent to Heaven.

"Deep let it sink in Irish hearts the story of their isle,
And waken thoughts of tenderest love and burning wrath the while;
And press upon them, one by one, the fruits of English sway,
And blend the wrongs of bygone times with this their fight to-day!
And show their fathers' constancy, by truest instinct led,
To loathe and battle with the power that on their substance fed;
And let it place beside their own the world's vast page, to tell
That never lived the nation yet could rule another well!
Thus, thus their cause shall gather strength; no feeling vague or
    blind,
But stamped by passion on the heart, by reason on the mind.
Let it go forth—a mightier foe to England's power than all
The rifles of America—the armaments of Gaul!
It SHALL go forth, and woe to them that bar or thwart its way;
'Tis God's own light—all heavenly bright—we care not who says
    nay!"

LORD EDWARD FITZGERALD

Francis Magan, an organizer of the United Irishmen, is charged by Mr. Fitzpatrick in his "Sham Squire" with having betrayed Lord Edward for a "reward" of £1,000, procured from the Castle government by Francis Higgins, proprietor of the "Freeman's Journal." This view is supported by other historians of the period. Nelson, or Neilson, who dined with Lord Edward and Murphy the day the former was arrested at Murphy's house, was long suspected of treachery, but appears to have been found innocent on reference to secret state papers. Magan is identified by the initial of his name, furnished by Higgins, when claiming the reward, and by documents which showed that he had correspondence with Under Secretary Cooke and other Castle officials.

ROBERT EMMET

The "nameless grave" of the young patriot martyr of 1803 was long supposed to be in St. Michan's churchyard, Dublin, or else in old Glasnevin Cemetery, but recent researches of his grand-nephew, Dr. Thomas Addis Emmet, of New York, have failed to discover the remains of the hero in either place. It is quite probable that the exact place of sepulture will never be discovered.